CHILDREN AFFECTED BY ARMED CONFLICT

CHILDREN AFFECTED
BY ARMED CONFLICT

THEORY, METHOD, AND PRACTICE

Edited by Myriam Denov and Bree Akesson

COLUMBIA UNIVERSITY PRESS   NEW YORK

COLUMBIA UNIVERSITY PRESS
Publishers Since 1893
New York   Chichester, West Sussex

cup.columbia.edu

Library of Congress Cataloging-in-Publication Data
Names: Denov, Myriam S., editor. | Akesson, Bree, editor.
Title: Children affected by armed conflict : theory, method, and practice /
    edited by Myriam Denov and Bree Akesson.
Description: New York : Columbia University Press, [2017] | Includes
    bibliographical references and index.
Identifiers: LCCN 2017002247 | ISBN 9780231174725 (cloth : alk. paper) | ISBN
    9780231174732 (pbk. : alk. paper) | ISBN 9780231539678 (e-book)
Subjects: LCSH: Children and war—Research—Methodology. | Child
    welfare—Research—Methodology. | Children—Research—Methodology.
Classification: LCC HQ784.W3 C525 2017 | DDC 303.6/6083—dc23
LC record available at https://lccn.loc.gov/2017002247

Columbia University Press books are printed on permanent
    and durable acid-free paper.

Printed in the United States of America

Cover design: Chang Jae Lee
Cover image: Jerome Sessini / Magnum Photos

Pour LMSB . . . avec amour.

—*MD*

CONTENTS

ACKNOWLEDGMENTS

OUR MOST PROFOUND GRATITUDE goes to the children whose lives and experiences are featured in the chapters of this edited collection. We thank them for opening their homes and hearts to researchers like us so we can learn more about their lives in order to work together to prevent and counter the damaging effects of war. We also thank the contributors to this book for their time, commitment, and dedication to this project. We are grateful to them for shining a light on the lived realities of war-affected children from across the globe and for their ongoing efforts to instigate change both conceptually and on the ground, through both theory and practice.

We would also like to thank everyone who helped support this project from its early development through the final stages of production, providing us with vital intellectual and practical help along the way. We are immensely grateful to research assistant Nicole Sawin whose work and commitment to this book were invaluable and unwavering. Nicole meticulously supported us since the beginning and "worked her magic" to keep us on track. We are also grateful to Dena Badawi, Neil Bilotta, Melissa Fellin, and Kalen Orme for their gracious and effective support and assistance. We would like to extend a special thanks to the staff at Columbia University Press—especially Jennifer Perillo, senior executive editor, and Stephen Wesley, associate editor—for providing us with continual guidance and supporting our vision for the book. We are also grateful to the anonymous reviewers who provided critical feedback that improved the manuscript.

We would also like to thank the Social Sciences and Humanities Research Council of Canada, the Pierre Elliott Trudeau Foundation, the Fonds de Recherche du Québec–Société et Culture, as well as the Offices of Research Services at McGill University and at Wilfrid Laurier University, for their support and financial and technical assistance, which gave us the opportunity to explore the important intersections of children and armed conflict in our research and writing.

And finally we extend heartfelt thanks to our families for their patience, kindness, and support during the planning and writing of this book.

CHILDREN AFFECTED BY ARMED CONFLICT

INTRODUCTION

Approaches to Studying Children Affected by Armed Conflict: Reflections on Theory, Method, and Practice

Myriam Denov and Bree Akesson

TODAY'S GLOBAL CONFLICTS POSE a serious global threat to the well-being of children. More than 230 million children live in 33 conflict-affected countries (UNICEF, 2014), and an estimated 13.5 million children have been internally displaced as a result of war (United Nations, 2010a). According to the United Nations High Commissioner for Refugees (UNHCR, 2015), children comprise 52% of the 59.5 million individuals forcibly displaced by war worldwide. In 2014, there were 40 recorded armed conflicts—defined as one or more states contributing troops to one or both warring sides (Pettersson & Wallensteen, 2015). At the time of writing, the places experiencing the worst humanitarian emergencies as a result of war and political violence include Syria, the Democratic Republic of the Congo, Iraq, South Sudan, Afghanistan, Yemen, the Lake Chad basin, and Libya, while other conflicts, such as in Turkey and Burundi, continue to worsen (Guéhenno, 2016).

This increase in armed conflict and political violence has resulted in exceptionally high levels of human suffering. As one example, the protracted conflict in Syria is considered to be the worst humanitarian crisis since World War II, with unprecedented numbers of civilians killed and displaced (Tobia, 2015). Recent conflicts have left millions of children killed, injured, orphaned, or separated from their families; sexually violated; and/or recruited into armed groups (UNICEF, 2012). The homes and communities that children rely on as a source of physical and social protection have often been destroyed, compromising children's well-being (Akesson, 2014a; Akesson, Basso, & Denov, 2016). Some children fall victim to a general onslaught against civilians; others die as part of a calculated genocide. Severe societal turbulence, the collapse of states, and religious and ethnic conflict, alongside persistent forms of structural violence—poverty, hunger, social exclusion, and discrimination—continue to underlie children's involvement in armed violence as victims, participants, and/or witnesses.

Given the importance of this threat and the increasing global concern, there has been a flurry during the last two decades of international research and advocacy for children affected by war. These efforts have focused on three vital areas: conceptual and theoretical debates, methodological questions and concerns, and strategies of appropriate intervention for children, whether during or in the aftermath of armed conflict. Through a "stepping back" process and reflecting on and discerning trends within this large body of theoretical, methodological, and practice work—both its accomplishments and shortcomings—several key elements emerge that deserve further attention.

THEORY

Within the realm of the conceptual, a notable trend has been a research and practice focus on trauma and victimization. Although it is important to acknowledge that children living in or displaced from war zones may witness or directly experience severe and unimaginable violence and upheaval that can have long-term psychosocial impacts (APA, 2010), a great deal of academic literature has focused primarily on children's maladaptive and antisocial behavior in the aftermath of war, as well as on negative physical and mental health outcomes (Barber & Schluterman, 2009; Derluyn & Broekaert, 2008; Huemer et al., 2011; Lambert & Alhassoon, 2015). Drawing from a romanticized Western conception of "childhood" and its association with vulnerability and the need for protection, much of the theoretical literature has tended to construct war-affected children as traumatized, dependent, helpless, and objects of assistance, rather than as agents of their own welfare (Denov, 2010; Honwana & de Boeck, 2005).

This focus on negative outcomes has tended to follow a Western, deficits-based medical model, which reflects a reliance on negative psychopathology, such as posttraumatic stress disorder (PTSD). While providing important insights into the psychosocial well-being of children facing adversity, this scholarship may inadvertently reinforce popular discourses of these children as inherently troubled, victimized, and perpetually "at risk." Furthermore, these children may be conceptualized as not only *threatened* but also *threatening* and in need of humanitarian intervention because they are perceived to be prone to engaging in violence (Marshall, 2014). Wartime victimization and participation in violence invariably characterize the experiences of many war-affected children and must be acknowledged. However, failing to explore children's capacity to overcome adversity provides a skewed picture of their reality.

In response to trauma-based conceptualizations, an increasing focus on resilience among war-affected children has emerged in the literature, highlighting children's capacities and their ability to "bounce back," "beat the odds," and "cope well" despite experiences of profound adversity and individual, familial, and structural stressors (Fernando & Ferrari, 2013; Tol, Song, & Jordans, 2013). Ungar (2008, p. 225) defines resilience as follows:

> In the context of exposure to significant adversity, whether psychological, environmental, or both, resilience is both the capacity of individuals to navigate their way to health-sustaining resources, including opportunities to experience feelings of well-being, and a condition of the individual's family, community and culture to provide these health resources and experiences in culturally meaningful ways.

Many have suggested that severe adversity can lead to "posttraumatic growth" or "posttraumatic resilience," terms that describe trauma survivors with a positive posttraumatic mental health outcome (Klasen et al., 2010). This focus on resilience has continued to gain momentum in the field through its promotion as a concept, theoretical approach, and means of intervention and practice among war-affected populations, both during and after armed conflict (Fernando & Ferrari, 2013; Kostelny & Wessells, 2013; Robinson, 2013; Werner, 2012). This emerging literature has indeed provided a valuable and nuanced understanding of children's realities and experiences, capturing and promoting their unique ability to contribute to their own development, safety, and well-being. However, just as there may be a danger to overemphasizing traumatic experiences and vulnerability of war-affected children, researchers and practitioners may risk *overemphasizing resilience* in children, assuming that all will or have the capacity to bounce back.

When examining the realities of war-affected children via the conceptual lenses of trauma or resilience, it is clear that both have provided important contributions to scholarship and practice. However, there is the danger of creating and promoting *conceptual binaries* and dichotomies whereby war-affected children are conceptualized, understood, and presented within mutually exclusive camps as either profoundly affected by traumatic events, on the one hand, or "resilient" and able to overcome adversity, on the other. Efforts to bridge this divide have been few and far between. Our own work with war-affected children and youth living in Sierra Leone, northern Uganda, Rwanda, Colombia, Palestine, and Canada has, more often than not, highlighted the ways in which war-affected children's lives are characterized by both challenging and traumatic experiences, alongside powerful and inspiring stories of survival and the capacity to overcome adversity (Akesson, 2014a; Denov, 2010; Denov & Blanchet-Cohen, 2016; Denov & Bryan, 2012; Denov & Buccitelli, 2013; Denov & Lakor, 2017; Denov & Marchand, 2014; Denov & Ricard-Guay, 2013; Fraser, Denov, Rousseau, & Daxhelet, 2014). These realities are not mutually exclusive, but instead appear to occur within the "messy" gray areas that characterize children's lives and are often overlooked when relying on conceptual binaries. Moreover, understandings of both trauma and resilience must reflect the unique sociocultural realities in which children live. Western-based understandings of these concepts may miss the mark and be at odds with local understandings and idioms of suffering, distress, and well-being. Theoretical innovations that capture the complexity of children's experiences—recognizing both capacity *and* adversity, trauma *and* resilience—within unique sociocultural contexts are thus essential.

METHOD

Given the myriad ethical issues involved in conducting research with war-affected children, as well as the need to gain a rich and complex understanding of children's lives, it is vitally important to use suitable and effective methodologies. As in the theoretical constructions noted earlier, methodological approaches have tended to view children in largely passive ways as merely "objects of research" or as "vulnerable" and "incompetent" (Clark, 2010; Denov, 2015). Such realities and research approaches have given rise to important discussions about children's involvement, capacities, and ethics within research, particularly concerning informed consent (Akesson et al., 2014), power differentials when conducting research with children (Denov, 2010), the interpretation of children's narratives and drawings (Akesson, 2015), the dissemination of research data on marginalized children (Jessee, 2011), navigating child participants' expectations (Denov, Doucet, & Kamara, 2012), the researcher's social and political location (Essers, 2009), and gendered realities and the marginalization of war-affected girls in research and policy (Coulter, 2009; Denov & Ricard-Guay, 2013). This continued questioning of children's role and realities within the context of research and the consideration of ethical dilemmas and their implications have led to a recent push to promote research methods that seek to engage children as active citizens and in which young voices are at the center, rather than the periphery, of empirical research. These research strategies include the use of visual, arts-based, and place-based methods and the increased promotion and use of participatory approaches more generally. However, as important as these methodological developments have been, they are in no way a panacea, particularly in resolving ethical dilemmas. For example, Ayala (2009) suggests that inviting individuals to actively participate in change through participatory approaches can evoke both feelings of empowerment and vulnerability, especially when research participants are compelled to challenge complex social and political dynamics. Furthermore, Cooke and Kothari (2001) question the power dynamics inherent in participatory research approaches and, in fact, refer to participatory approaches as unjust and illegitimate exercises of power, verging on the tyrannical. These criticisms highlight the multiple ethical issues that such approaches may raise, particularly around power and positionality. Therefore, further methodological explorations and innovations are vitally needed in research with children affected by war.

PRACTICE

In the realms of practice and intervention, the profound and multifaceted impact of armed conflict has led researchers and practitioners alike to develop and fine-tune psychosocial interventions to support girls and boys both during and after armed conflict. Interventions can occur at multiple levels (micro, meso, macro) and within various systems, including education, health, and justice, to name but a few. However, given the unique and complex experiences, contexts, and needs of war-affected children, service providers and practitioners have often struggled to effectively support them—whether in their country of origin or after their resettlement to a new context (Denov & Blanchet-Cohen, 2014). Moreover, as noted above, the needs of war-affected children and youth are highly contextual and depend largely on their pre- and postwar status, as well as on factors such as gender, age, race, ethnicity, socio-economic status, mobility needs, armed group affiliation, postwar living situation (internally displaced, refugee, urban, rural, etc.), and whether they are living with family members or are unaccompanied. How best to respond to the psychosocial needs of war-affected children and families is still the subject of considerable debate. Western mental health approaches, which have tended to focus on risk factors, psychopathology, and psychotherapy, may inappropriately pathologize war-affected children, can be insensitive to culture, can systematically sideline social and cultural dimensions of suffering, and may, in some cases, exacerbate stress and traumatic symptoms (Bracken, 1998; Summerfield, 1999). Some researchers and practitioners argue that psychosocial support and services are best provided to war-affected populations through holistic, culturally grounded, family-based, and community-based approaches (Kostelny, 2006). Families and local communities can contribute a rich array of cultural resources—including traditions, elders and community leaders, and community processes and tools, such as rituals and ceremonies—to the provision of psychosocial assistance (Kostelny, 2006). Because these resources reflect community values, beliefs, and cultural traditions, they give voice to community members and thus are likely to be sustainable and provide meaning. And yet, most internationally led initiatives—often grounded in a more Western approach—have tended to dominate the scholarly, policy, and practice discussions and literature on postwar recovery (De Jong & Kleber, 2007; Gupta & Zimmer, 2008; Hirsch, 2001); with few exceptions (Coulter, 2005; Kaindaneh & Rigby, 2010; Stark, 2006), less attention has been paid to local forms of postconflict interventions. Moreover, interventions have tended to be designed and implemented without considering or consulting directly with war-affected children about their perceived needs. As several chapters in this volume highlight (Akello, chapter 10; Kostelny et al., chapter 7; Veale et al., chapter 9), failing to consult with the very population affected by policy and practice may lead to interventions that miss the mark with regard to their overall and long-term impact and efficacy.

These areas of inquiry—whether theory, method, and/or practice—deserve greater attention and enhanced discussion and analysis. Therefore, this collection brings together research from top scholars and practitioners in the field whose theoretical, methodological, and practice work pushes the boundaries of empirical and practical knowledge and understandings of the lives of war-affected children around the globe. As such, this edited volume has the following three aims:

1. Explore emerging theoretical and conceptual understandings and approaches to the study of children affected by armed conflict
2. Examine innovative research methodologies that seek to both empower and actively engage children affected by armed conflict in the research process
3. Critically consider strategies of intervention that validate the perspectives and participation of children themselves

To address these aims, the chapters in this volume are guided by an emphasis on the everyday realities and perspectives of children affected by armed conflict.

POLICY

A final crosscutting element that is essential to consider when exploring children's realities is policy making, which every chapter in this volume addresses in its conclusions. Many scholars are concerned with the effects of armed conflict on children, but there is still disagreement about how to frame the questions, problems, and solutions (Shalhoub-Kevorkian, 2009). Although exploratory research adds to our knowledge base—and, indeed, we cannot *solve* a problem until we *define* the problem and its scope—it is important to ensure that research has the potential to enact change at a broader systemic level. This is also ethically significant because research participants often engage in studies with the hope that their stories will—in some way—contribute to or be a catalyst for change in policy and practice. Several chapters in this volume contribute to the policy debate by virtue of their focus and by asking vital policy-oriented questions. For example, in her study of Swati children in chapter 1, Chaudry asks, "How can policy makers at all levels work with the strengths of these remarkable children to facilitate better futures for *all* of them?" Similarly, in their study of war-affected girls in three African countries, Veale and colleagues (chapter 9) focus on how interventions can foreground the relational element of "reintegration" in a way that makes war-affected girls *central* to the process, rather than engaging with "community" as an external, separate "add-on" activity such as in "sensitization" activities. Akello (chapter 10) highlights the way in which health policies in northern Uganda are at odds with the perceived and expressed needs of war-affected children.

In addition to posing vital policy-oriented questions, the authors in this volume also provide recommendations for policy makers and planners. A commonality among the contributors is their advocacy for more open communication between citizens and government officials and, ultimately, a change in approach. Indeed, traditional policy making in education, health, justice, and social services is often done in a top-down fashion, in which policy is created from "above" (government) and experienced from "below" (citizens). This approach rarely includes the perspectives of those directly experiencing policies (Blanchet-Cohen & Cook, 2012). In particular, children are rarely consulted in policy-making processes, even though they are well placed to evaluate policies in their role as service users (UNICEF, 2009). As multiple chapters in this volume suggest, children and families affected by war and violence should not be viewed as mere policy "beneficiaries," but as having "valid insights into their well-being, valid solutions to their problems, and a valid role in implementing those solutions" (Boyden & Mann, 2005, p. 19). As Hilker and Fraser (2009, p. 43) argue, "It is critical that youth are involved in programme design, implementation and evaluation. Young people often have a clear understanding of their own situation and needs and how these relate to the needs of others."

THE VOICES OF CHILDREN ACROSS CONTEXTS: CHALLENGING BINARIES, BRIDGING DIVIDES

The chapters in this volume have several elements in common. The first is an emphasis on children's voices, which transcend geographic, social, cultural, gender, and age boundaries. Children's lives and circumstances have frequently been defined and articulated by adults, rendering children's voices and perspectives as peripheral and/or marginal. As Downe (2001, p. 165) observes,

> Despite the undeniable visibility of children in . . . academic and popular representations of despair, rarely are the experiences, thoughts, actions and opinions of the children explored analytically in a way that gives voice to these marginalized social actors or that elucidates what it means to be a child under such conditions. In effect, the children are seen, but not heard.

Over the last two decades, there has been an increased acknowledgment of the importance of integrating children and young people's own views and experiences into research (Ireland & Holloway, 2007; Morrow, 2008). In parallel, critical discussions about the theorization of childhood and its implications for research with young people have developed in the disciplines of sociology, anthropology, and geography (Ireland & Holloway, 2007; Meloni, Vanthuyne, & Rousseau, 2015; Morrow, 2008). Within the realm of the "new childhood studies," children and adolescents are now viewed as social agents able to influence their immediate contexts. Moreover, children are said to possess valid knowledge and perceptions of their environment, and their voices must be considered and articulated within research (Morrow, 2008).

Within the realm of children affected by armed conflict, the inclusion of children's voices in research and practice has grown slowly. In their 2004 book *Children and Youth on the Front Line,* Boyden and de Berry advocated for "shifting the paradigm," highlighting the need to incorporate children's direct experiences of war and "to illuminate how children in different cultures perceive suffering, misfortune, healing and recovery and the formation of their political and ideological commitments" (p. xvii). Yet Boyden and de Berry's important call to action within theory, method, and practice has yet to be fully realized.

In response, this collection seeks to highlight the uniqueness of children's voices and to hear and understand them within the broader socioecological and cultural context. Drawing from empirical studies from 11 conflict-affected countries—Burma, Colombia, Liberia, Pakistan, Palestine, Sierra Leone, Somalia, Sri Lanka, South Sudan, Thailand, and Uganda—across 5 continents, this book aims to provide a "journey" across cultures and contexts to hear the diversity of children's perspectives and realities during armed conflict and in its aftermath, highlighting the similarities, differences, and strategies for intervention.

Much of the literature on the topic of children affected by armed conflict has historically portrayed the problem as a uniquely male phenomenon or has failed to consider its unique gendered realities. While more attention is being paid to the "gendered" dimensions of war, it has taken decades of silence and exclusion for the experiences and realities of girls and women to be included in war-related research, scholarship, and practice. Acknowledging the importance of a gendered lens to understanding the realities and complexities of armed conflict, several chapters in this collection are dedicated solely to the realities of girls in the conflict-affected contexts of Colombia, Liberia, Sierra Leone, and northern Uganda.

Children can be an important source of knowledge about their own lives and communities. Yet at the same time, their experiences are constantly shaped and influenced by those around them. Children's voices and experiences cannot be understood from an ecological perspective without including parents, siblings, extended family members, caregivers, teachers, community leaders, and other members of their social environment who have day-to-day contact with them and influence their well-being. Therefore, we include research that relies on a socioecological approach and involves multiple actors and players in children's socioecological context. For example, Akesson and Denov (chapter 6), Kostelny et al. (chapter 7), Hettitantri and Hadley (chapter 2), Stewart (chapter 13), and Veale et al. (chapter 9) draw attention to children's perspectives and voices, but also include and make linkages to the perspectives of families, teachers, and community members in order to better understand children's experiences in the context of armed conflict and its aftermath. Their research underscores the importance of listening not only to children's voices but also to those who are inexorably tied to children's lives.

Alongside the inclusion of children's voices, a second core element of this volume is an attempt to bridge divides. As noted earlier, challenging the binaries and dichotomies of "trauma" versus "resilience," the chapters in this volume attempt to shed light on the complexities and blurriness of children's lives—simultaneously addressing adversity and capacity (Akello, chapter 10; Chaudry, chapter 1; Lenz, chapter 5; Pepper, chapter 3), as well as analyzing children as both victims and/or participants in armed conflict (Ospina-Alvarado et al., chapter 4; Podder, chapter 8).

Bridging divides is also relevant to our conceptualization of theory, method, and practice. Although these realms in relation to children affected by war are each vital in and of themselves, it is important to recognize that they overlap and intersect—one cannot be understood or contextualized without the other. Nevertheless, for organizational purposes, this volume is divided into sections on theory, method, and practice. However, no single chapter corresponds unilaterally to one of the three sections. For example, several chapters are included in the methods section because of their distinctive methodological approaches, including participatory and socioecological methods (see Akesson and Denov, chapter 6; Veale et al., chapter 9). Yet these same chapters are also well suited and important to theoretical discussions because of their unique conceptual approaches. Ultimately, theory, method, and practice are present in every chapter, highlighting these elements' interconnected and crosscutting nature.

Disciplinary divisions have long characterized theory, method, and practice in the realm of children affected by armed conflict. Researchers and practitioners have often worked in disciplinary "silos," missing important opportunities to collaborate and share knowledge and lessons learned. The former UN Special Advisor to the Secretary-General on War-Affected Children, Olara Ottunu (2000, p. 21) noted, "There is [a] need to collate and bring together existing research on the impact of armed conflict on children . . . [collaboration] will allow researchers to identify additional gaps, and assist in avoiding duplication of work already done." Moreover, there is an ongoing global initiative, promoted by the United Nations, emphasizing the importance of bridging disciplines to ensure the healthy development and protection of children, particularly those facing global adversity (UNICEF, 2008). The authors in this collection are working in multiple fields: anthropology, community development, education, gender studies, health science, human ecology, international affairs, medicine, peace and conflict studies, political science, psychology, public health, social work, and sociology. We also have contributors from diverse regions and contexts from the Global South, including Colombia, Iraq, Pakistan, Sri Lanka, and Uganda. Moreover, contributors include not only scholars and researchers (both emerging and established) but also practitioners who are working directly in the field with children affected by armed conflict, thereby further bridging the division between theory and practice. Our selection of authors provides a diversity of discipline and approach while simultaneously following the UN recommendations to bring people together and create synergy. Drawing from multiple disciplinary perspectives and the work of both academics and practitioners, as well as integrating theory, method, and practice, enables the complexity of children's experiences to be better understood and solutions to be developed at the intersection of disciplines, where multiple bodies of knowledge meet.

SOME NOTES ON TERMINOLOGY

A vital element in any discussion of children affected by armed conflict is the importance of language and terminology, particularly the definitions and use of the terms "child," "children," and "armed conflict," and the implications of using such terminology.

"Child" and "childhood" are contested concepts and social constructions that vary in form and content across cultures and social groups and are defined by localized understandings and values (Denov, 2010). Though convenient for research, it is important to note the problematic nature of categorizing "children" by age. Defining childhood based solely on age not only reflects a bias toward Western notions of childhood that are rooted in biomedical theory (Kemper, 2005) but also may overlook other salient cultural, social, economic, gendered, class, and other status determinants that extend well beyond the notion of age. Furthermore, armed conflict challenges preconceived notions of childhood, with children taking on positions of adults, such as caregiving or assuming an active combat role (Denov, 2010). To complicate matters further, constructed and formalized definitions of "child," "youth," "adolescent," or "young people" differ between international organizations and, in some cases, overlap. Whereas the UN Convention on the Rights of the Child considers a child to be anyone under the age of 18, the UN's World Program of Action for Youth identifies "youth" as 15–24 years old (United Nations, 2010b). Moreover, the World Health Organization and UNICEF differentiate between "adolescents" (15–19 years old), "youth" (15–24 years old), and "young people" (10–24 years old; World Bank, 2007). Ultimately, defining who is a child is "a process of negotiations between individuals, family members, peer groups and the wider community in the context of life events and rites of passage" (Mawson, 2004, p. 226). In this book, we rely on the definition of a child set out in the United Nations (UN) Convention on the Rights of the Child: "every human being below 18 years" (art. 1). However, in doing so we are highly aware of its intrinsic limitations.

Similar sociopolitical, legal, and semantic challenges arise in relation to the term "armed conflict." To better reflect the reality of contemporary armed violence, we use this term, which Wallensteen and Sollenberg (2001) define as "a contested incompatibility which concerns government and/or territory where the use of armed force between two parties, of which at least one is the government of a state, results in at least 25 battle-related deaths" (p. 643). Nevertheless, we acknowledge that this definition has limitations. It includes the phrase, "armed force between two parties," implying an equality between the two sides (often interstate) who are fighting for territorial control on a distinctive battlefield. Yet, armed conflict is rarely so simple. Today's contemporary armed conflicts are characterized by low-intensity confrontations, state violence against civilians, violent extremism, proxy wars, ethnic/racial segregation, and multiple armed groups, which may or may not include a government armed force—to name a few of their complexities. Furthermore, as the following chapters show, armed conflict is often compounded by existing factors such as poverty, family violence, and harmful cultural practices, which may also have an impact on the lives of children.

Drawing on the voices of children, the chapters in this collection, while diverse in their focus and content, collectively demonstrate the ways in which children affected by armed conflict live at the intersection of trauma and resilience, vulnerability and agency. They demonstrate that, in the face of the profound adversities that are intrinsic to war and violence, children draw on their individual and collective creativity and innovation, as well as that of their families and communities, to traverse high-risk surroundings (Denov & Buccitelli, 2013). It is these examples of agency and innovation that should help guide the development and improvement of future practices and policies that affect children living in such challenging settings.

References

Akesson, B. (2014a). *Contradictions in place: Everyday geographies of Palestinian children and families living under occupation* (Unpublished doctoral dissertation). McGill University, Montreal.

Akesson, B. (2014b). "We may go, but this is my home": Experiences of domicide and resistance for Palestinian children and families. *Journal of Internal Displacement, 4*(2), 8–22.

Akesson, B. (2015). Using mapmaking to study the personal geographies of young children affected by political violence. In N. Worth, I. Hardill, & S. Lucas (Eds.), *Researching the lifecourse: Critical reflections from the social sciences* (pp. 123–141). Bristol, UK: Policy Press.

Akesson, B., Basso, A., & Denov, M. (2016). The right to home: Domicide as a violation of child and family rights in the context of political violence. *Children & Society, 30*(5), 369–383.

Akesson, B., D'Amico, M., Denov, M., Khan, F., Linds, W., & Mitchell, C. (2014). Stepping back as researchers: How are we addressing ethics in arts-based approaches to working with war-affected children in school and community settings. *Educational Research for Social Change, 3*(1), 74–88.

American Psychological Association (APA). (2010). *Resilience and recovery after war: Refugee children and families in the United States.* Washington, DC: Author.

Ayala, J. (2009). Split scenes, converging visions: The ethical terrains where PAR and borderlands scholarship meet. *Urban Review, 41*(1), 66–84.

Barber, B. K., & Schluterman, J. M. (2009). An overview of the empirical literature on adolescents and political violence. In B. K. Barber (Ed.), *Adolescents and war: How youth deal with political violence* (pp. 35–61). Oxford: Oxford University Press.

Blanchet-Cohen, N., & Cook, P. (2012). The transformative power of youth grants: Sparks and ripples of change affecting marginalised youth and their communities. *Children & Society.* Advance online publication.

Boyden, J., & De Berry, J. (2004). *Children and youth on the front line: Ethnography, armed conflict, and displacement.* New York: Berghahn Books.

Boyden, J., & Mann, G. (2005). Children's risk, resilience and coping in extreme situations. In M. Ungar, *Handbook for working with children and youth* (pp. 3–25). London: Sage.

Bracken, P. (1998). Hidden agendas: Deconstructing post-traumatic stress disorder. In P. Bracken & C. Petty (Eds.), *Rethinking the trauma of war* (pp. 38–59). London: Free Association Books.

Clark, A. (2010). Young children as protagonists and the role of participatory, visual methods in engaging multiple perspectives. *American Journal of Community Psychology, 6*(1–2), 115–123.

Cooke, B., & Kothari, U. (2001). *Participation: The new tyranny?* London: Zed Books.

Coulter, C. (2005). Reflections from the field: A girl's initiation ceremony in northern Sierra Leone. *Anthropological Quarterly, 78*(2), 431–441.

Coulter, C. (2009). *Bush wives and girl soldiers.* Ithaca, NY: Cornell University Press.

De Jong, K., & Kleber, R. J. (2007). Emergency conflict-related psychosocial interventions in Sierra Leone and Uganda: Lessons from Médecins sans Frontières. *Journal of Health Psychology, 12*(3), 485–497.

Denov, M. (2010). *Child soldiers: Sierra Leone's Revolutionary United Front.* Cambridge: Cambridge University Press.

Denov, M. (2015). Children born of wartime rape: The intergenerational complexities of sexual violence and abuse. *Ethics, Medicine and Public Health, 11*(1), 61–68.

Denov, M., & Blanchet-Cohen, N. (2014). The rights and realities of war-affected refugee children and youth in Quebec: Making children's rights meaningful. *Canadian Journal of Children's Rights, 1*(1), 18–43.

Denov, M., & Blanchet-Cohen, N. (2016). Trajectories of violence and survival: Turnings and adaptations in the lives of two war-affected youth living in Canada. *Peace & Conflict: Journal of Peace Psychology, 22*(3), 198–207.

Denov, M., & Bryan, C. (2014). Social navigation and resettlement: Separated children in the context of Canada. *Refuge: Canada's Periodical on Refugees, 30*(1), 25–34.

Denov, M., & Buccitelli, A. (2013). Navigating crisis and chronicity in the everyday: Former child soldiers in urban Sierra Leone. *Stability: International Journal of Security & Development, 2*(3), 1–18.

Denov, M., Doucet, D., & Kamara, A. (2012). Engaging war-affected youth through photography: Photovoice with former child soldiers in Sierra Leone. *Intervention: International Journal of Mental Health, Psychosocial Work & Counselling in Areas of Armed Conflict, 10*(2), 117–133.

Denov, M., & Lakor, A.A. (2017). When war is better than peace: The postconflict realities of children born in Lord's Resistance Army captivity. *Child Abuse and Neglect, 65:* 255–265.

Denov, M., & Marchand, I. (2014). "One cannot take away the stain": Rejection and stigma among former child soldiers in Colombia. *Peace and Conflict: Journal of Peace Psychology*, 20(3), 227–240.

Denov, M., & Ricard-Guay, A. (2013). Girl soldiers: Towards a gendered understanding of wartime recruitment, participation and demobilization. *Gender and Development*, 21(3), 473–488.

Derluyn, I., & Broekaert, E. (2008). Unaccompanied refugee children and adolescents: The glaring contrast between a legal and a psychological perspective. *International Journal of Law & Psychiatry*, 31(4), 319–330.

Doucet, D., & Denov, M. (2012). The power of sweet words: Local forms of intervention with war-affected women in rural post-conflict Sierra Leone. *International Social Work*, 55(5), 612–628.

Downe, P. J. (2001). Playing with names: How children create identities of self in anthropological research. *Anthropologica*, 43(2), 165–177.

Essers, C. (2009). Reflections on the narrative approach: Dilemmas of power, emotions and social location while constructing life-stories. *Organization*, 16(2), 163–181.

Fernando, C., & Ferrari, M. (Eds.). (2013). *Handbook of resilience in children of war*. New York: Springer.

Fraser, S., Denov, M., Rousseau, C., & Daxhelet, M.-L. (2015) From seeking truths to seeking stories: The contribution of social sciences in the exploration of the reality of former child soldiers. *International Journal of Migration and Border Studies*, 1(3), 303–320.

Guéhenno, J.- M. (2016). *10 conflicts to watch in 2016*. Brussels: International Crisis Group. Retrieved from www.crisisgroup.org/en/regions/op-eds/2016/guehenno-10-conflicts-to-watch-in-2016.aspx.

Gupta, L., & Zimmer, C. (2008). Psychosocial intervention with war-affected children in Sierra Leone. *British Journal of Psychiatry*, 192(3), 212–216.

Hilker, L. M., & Fraser, E. (2009). *Youth exclusion, violence, conflict and fragile states* (Report Prepared for the DFID's Equity and Rights Team). London: Department for International Development.

Hirsch, J. (2001). *Sierra Leone: Diamonds and the struggle for democracy*. London: Lynne Rienner.

Honwana, A., & de Boeck, F. (2005). *Makers and breakers: Children and youth in postcolonial Africa*. Trenton, NJ: Africa World Press.

Huemer, J., Karnik, N., Voelkl-Kernstock, S., Granditsch, E., Plattner, B., Friedrich, M., & Steiner, H. (2011). Psychopathology in African unaccompanied refugee minors in Austria. *Child Psychiatry & Human Development*, 42(3), 307–319.

Ireland, L., & Holloway, I. (2007). Qualitative health research with children. *Children & Society*, 10(2), 155–164.

Jessee, E. (2011). The limits of oral history: Ethics and methodology amid highly politicized research settings. *Oral History Review*, 38(2), 287–307.

Kaindaneh, S. E., & Rigby, A. (2010). Promoting co-existence through sacred places in Sierra Leone. *Peace Review*, 22(3), 244–249.

Kemper, Y. 2005. *Youth in war to peace transitions*. Berlin: Berghof Research Center for Constructive Conflict Management.

Klasen, F., Oettingen, G., Daniels, J., Post, M., Hoyer, C., & Adam, H. (2010). Post-traumatic resilience in former Ugandan child soldiers. *Child Development*, 81(4), 1096–1113.

Kostelny, K. (2006). A culture-based, integrative approach. In A. Strang & M. G. Wessells (Eds.), *A world turned upside down: Social ecological approaches to children in war zones* (pp. 19–38). Bloomfield, CT: Kumarian Press.

Kostelny, K., & Wessells, M. (2013). Child friendly spaces: Promoting children's resiliency amidst war. In C. Fernando & M. Ferrari (Eds.), *Handbook on resilience in children of war* (pp. 119–129). New York: Springer.

Lambert, J. E., & Alhassoon, O. M. (2015). Trauma-focused therapy for refugees: Meta-analytic findings. *Journal of Counseling Psychology*, 62(1), 28–38.

Marshall, D. J. (2014). Save (us from) the children: Trauma, Palestinian childhood, and the production of governable subjects. *Children's Geographies*, 12(3), 281–296.

Mawson, A. (2004). Children, impunity and justice: Some dilemmas from northern Uganda. In J. Boyden & J. de Berry (Eds.), *Children and youth on the front line: Ethnography, armed conflict and displacement* (pp. 130–142). New York: Berghahn Books.

Meloni, F., Vanthuyne, K., & Rousseau, C. (2015). Towards a relational ethics: Rethinking ethics, agency, and dependency in research with children and youth. *Anthropological Theory*, 15(1), 106–123.

Morrow, V. (2008). Ethical dilemmas in research with children and young people about their social environments. *Children's Geographies*, 6(1), 49–61.

Ottunu, O. A. (2000). *The impact of armed conflict on children: Filling knowledge gaps*. New York: United Nations.

Pettersson, T., & Wallensteen, P. (2015). Armed conflicts, 1946–2014. *Journal of Peace Research*, 52(4), 536–550.

Robinson, J. A. (2013). No place like home: Resilience among adolescent refugees resettled in Australia. In C. Fernando & M. Ferrari (Eds.), *Handbook on resilience in children of war* (pp. 193–210). New York: Springer.

Shalhoub-Kevorkian, N. (2009). *Militarization and Violence against Women in Conflict Zones: A Palestinian Case-study*. Cambridge: Cambridge University Press.

Stark, L. (2006). Cleansing the wounds of war: An examination of traditional healing, psychosocial health and reintegration in Sierra Leone. *Intervention*, 4(3), 206–218.

Summerfield, D. (1999). A critique of seven assumptions behind psychological trauma programs in war-affected areas. *Social Science & Medicine, 48*(10), 1449–1462.

Tobia, P. J. (2015, July 29). The worst humanitarian crisis since World War II. *PBS Newshour.* Retrieved from www.pbs.org/newshour/updates/worst-humanitarian -crisis-since-world-war-ii/.

Tol, W. A., Song, S., & Jordans, M. J. (2013). Annual research review: Resilience and mental health in children and adolescents living in areas of armed conflict—A systematic review of findings in low- and middle-income countries. *Journal of Child Psychology and Psychiatry, 54*(4), 445–460.

Ungar, M. (2008). Resilience across cultures. *British Journal of Social Work, 38*(2), 218–235.

UNHCR. (2015). *World at war: Forced displacement in 2014.* New York: Author.

UNICEF. (2008). *UNICEF child protection strategy.* New York: United Nations Economic and Social Council.

UNICEF. (2009). *Machel study 10-year strategic review: Children and conflict in a changing world.* New York: Author.

UNICEF. (2012). *State of the world's children.* New York: Author.

UNICEF. (2014). *Children and emergencies in 2014: Facts & figures.* New York: Author. Retrieved from www.unicef.org/media/files/UNICEF_Children_and _Emergencies_2014_fact_sheet.pdf.

United Nations. (2010a). *The rights and guarantees of internally displaced children in armed conflict.* New York: UN Office of the Special Representative of the Secretary-General for Children and Armed Conflict.

United Nations. (2010b). *World programme of action for youth.* New York: UN Economic and Social Affairs.

Wallensteen, P., & Sollenberg, M. (2001). Armed conflict, 1989–2000. *Journal of Peace Research, 38*(5), 629–644.

Werner, W. (2012). Children and war: Risk, resilience, and recovery. *Development and Psychopathology, 24,* 553–558.

World Bank. (2007). *Sierra Leone: Youth and employment.* Environmentally and Socially Sustainable Development Unit, West Africa.

PART ONE

UNDERSTANDING THE REALITIES OF CHILDREN IN ARMED CONFLICT

Theoretical and Conceptual Considerations

THIS FIRST SECTION of the book aims both to capture the multifaceted realities of children affected by armed conflict and contribute to conceptual and theoretical considerations. The chapters in this section critically interrogate the concepts of resilience, social exclusion, connectedness and belonging, agency, and social construction and their implications for war-affected children in Burma, Colombia, Pakistan and Sri Lanka.

In chapter 1, "'Raising the Dead' and Cultivating Resilience: Postcolonial Theory and Children's Narratives from Swat, Pakistan," Lubna Chaudhry explores the realities of children's experiences by reflecting on their constructions of trauma, violence, and resilience in the context of the armed conflict in Swat Valley, Pakistan. In her analysis, Chaudhry engages with postcolonial theories of trauma and mourning to argue that children are social actors whose narratives of trauma—by their very articulation—become assertions of agency and even manifestations of resilience. These narratives demonstrate how children negotiate the violence around them, as well as the ways in which gender, class, ethnicity, and geographical positioning influence individual and collective identities.

In chapter 2, "Young Children's Experiences of Connectedness and Belonging in Postconflict Sri Lanka: A Socioecological Approach," Nanditha Hettitantri and Fay Hadley consider young children's experiences of connectedness to their social ecology in a postconflict Sri Lankan village. Through an analysis of the accounts of two young children, Hettitantri and Hadley demonstrate the ways in which these children experience connectedness to their social ecology and develop a sense of personal and community belonging. These factors, the authors argue, contribute to young children's resilience in a post-conflict setting and hence should be further developed and supported through service provision. Hettitantri and Hadley illustrate that listening to the voices of very young children (3- and 4-year-old children) can be fruitful in understanding their lives and that agency does not discriminate according to age.

In chapter 3, "Contending with Violence and Discrimination: Using a Social Exclusion Lens to Understand the Realities of Burmese Muslim Refugee Children in Thailand," Mollie Pepper explores the experiences of marginalization and social exclusion among Burmese Muslim children living in refugee camps in Thailand. Challenging the notion that refugee camps are inherently spaces of safety, this chapter demonstrates the ways in which children are deeply affected by discrimination and violence within refugee camps, showing that, in fact, refugee camps can be sites of social exclusion. At the same time, children's limited access to resources and services within these sites shapes their unique coping mechanisms and may foster survival strategies for themselves and their families. Pepper ultimately highlights how children navigate multiple vulnerabilities and work to actively mitigate them.

In chapter 4, "A Social Constructionist Approach to Understanding the Experiences of Girls Affected by Armed Conflict in Colombia," Maria Camila Ospina-Alvarado, Sara Victoria Alvarado, Jaime Alberto Carmona, and Hector Fabio Ospina present an alternative approach to child development that does not view children affected by armed conflict as mere victims. Drawing on a social constructionist approach and relying on the narratives of Colombian girls affected by armed conflict, the study proposes a shift from deficit-based and individualized views of children to perspectives that are collective in approach and that emphasize the role of boys and girls and their socializing agents in peace building, democracy, and reconciliation.

Chapter 5 addresses the realities of former girl soldiers in postwar northern Uganda. In "Armed with Resilience: Tapping into the Experiences and Survival Skills of Formerly Abducted Girl Child Soldiers in Northern Uganda," Jessica Lenz argues that reintegration programs tend to ignore the resilient qualities that children gain from their experiences in armed groups and instead draw on approaches that assume that children are traumatized victims. Lenz demonstrates that, even though they experienced brutality and violence, the girls within the Lord's Resistance Army (LRA) nonetheless gained multiple skills, including nursing, teaching, cartography, and team-building and negotiating skills. Lenz argues that current reintegration programs may weaken a girl's resilience by (1) failing to build on her existing strengths; (2) explicitly or implicitly encouraging her to conform to generalized programs, rather than recognizing her unique potential; (3) encouraging her to forget the past; and (4) promoting traditional gender roles. By challenging existing models of reintegration, Lenz suggests the need not only to broaden theoretical understandings of girls as resilient but also to challenge assumptions surrounding the experiences of girls formerly associated with armed groups.

The theories and concepts that are drawn on in these chapters offer explanatory frameworks and ways of seeing that can help us make sense of the complexity of children's lives, behavior, and experiences. Moreover, these theories and concepts can act like a blueprint to guide practice, providing a relatively clear direction and structure for practice, intervention, and action. Although theories and concepts are based on particular worldviews and assumptions, the changing nature of knowledge development requires that they change as new information influences the way we understand things or disproves ideas altogether. The chapters in this section offer theoretical and conceptual explanations that should be seen as fluid, changing, and shifting as new knowledge emerges.

1

"RAISING THE DEAD" AND CULTIVATING RESILIENCE
Postcolonial Theory and Children's Narratives from Swat, Pakistan

Lubna N. Chaudhry

FOR DECADES MOST ACADEMIC LITERATURE on war-affected children was motivated by a biomedical paradigm (Boyden & de Berry, 2004b); it generally cast children as one-dimensional victims. More recently there have been moves to embrace the psychosocial aspects of children's lives and experiences in conflict situations (e.g., Boyden & de Berry, 2004a; Lloyd & Penn, 2010; Shakya, 2011; Williams & Drury, 2011). This burgeoning body of research, while still concerned with children's trauma, underscores the importance of also looking at their resilience—on how children cope in situations of chronic and acute violence—and of putting children's voices at the center of analysis. This focus on resilience and children's own representations of their experiences facilitates an understanding of their creative responses to violence (Nordstrom, 1997) and helps locate sites of strategic interventions to augment their mental and social resources in conflict situations by building on existing strengths and spaces (Williams & Drury, 2011).

The objective of this chapter is to explore children's constructions of trauma, violence, and resilience in the context of the beautiful Swat Valley in Pakistan, where three entities—the Pakistani Taliban, civilians supporting or resisting the Taliban, and the Pakistani military—were involved in armed conflict. Memories of the past and commentaries of the present are interwoven in narratives collected from 30 children aged 10–15 (half of them girls), just as personal experiences remain imbricated with collective identities in these accounts. Written in the vein of the new sociology of childhood (see, for example, Christensen & Prout, 2005), this chapter posits Swati children as social actors and reflexive subjects, as *human beings* who actively negotiate the words and spaces around them to make meaning and take action.

From 2006 onward, the lives of these children have unfolded in a complex sociopolitical scenario in which violence, both direct and physical (e.g., brutality against people and the destruction of property by the Taliban and Pakistani military) and indirect and structural (e.g., the sanctions against "Western" education by the Taliban and the inability of the state to effectively facilitate the evacuation of families before the invasion in 2009), contributed to the intense suffering of Swati communities.[1] Children's accounts at times blur the distinction between conflict-generated violence and everyday "peace-time crimes" (Scheper-Hughes & Bourgois, 2004, p. 19)—forms of violence, mostly structural, generated by oppressive social hierarchies that pre-date the conflict with the Taliban. These forms of violence persist into the so-called postconflict phase, with the addition of new forms related to the militarization of the region. State-sanctioned discourses center on celebrating the victory of the Pakistani military, which restored Swat to its tranquil mountain resort status (Khattak, 2014). However, children's narratives undercut both descriptions of the idyllic pre-Taliban society and a triumphalist telling of the encounter with the Taliban. The articulation of trauma itself becomes an assertion of agency, ostensibly even a manifestation of resilience, as children insist on speaking their truths.

Although socioecological approaches to children in war-torn societies that emphasize the need to examine experiences within families, schools, and communities (see, for example, Akesson & Denov, chapter 6; Boothby, Strang, & Wessells, 2006) do inform my analysis, the use of postcolonial theories of trauma and mourning adds another layer to my reading/listening of children's narratives. The Swati children I interviewed clearly positioned themselves as historical and political subjects. A postcolonial lens allows for an examination of how larger sociohistorical forces affected the everyday realities of the research participants.

Postcoloniality often does not represent a condition of celebration; around the world, including in Pakistan, nation-building or national security enterprises continue to be characterized by the state's violence against its own citizens (Chaudhry, 2014). Postcolonial scholars (for example, Durrant, 2004; Holland, 2000) write of how memories of past violence project into the future, making the experiences of the present plight indistinguishable from historical trauma. This body of literature points to the nonlinear, recursive, and incomplete nature of grief, of the "ceaseless labor of remembrance" that "allows one to live in memory of both the dead and all those whose living human presence continues to be disavowed by the present world order" (Durrant, 2004, p. 1). From such a perspective, interviews became spaces to "raise the dead," to permit the children "to speak about the unspoken"—that which has "slipped between the cracks of language" (Holland, 2000, pp. 3–5). "Raising the dead becomes a figurative enterprise, as well as an intellectual and therefore concrete endeavor. The task [is] . . . not only uncovering silences but transforming inarticulate places into conversational territories" (Holland, 2000, pp. 2–3).

In this chapter, I am especially concerned with the diversity of children's experiences and perspectives. Gender is a salient category of differentiation and works with other axes of difference, such as ethnicity, socioeconomic status, and geographical location in Swat, to constrain and enable children's agency in circumstances marked by extreme violence (see James, 2009, for my conception of agency). Children's agency, or its lack thereof, becomes an indicator of resilience (Williams & Drury, 2011). This chapter addresses children's capacity to negotiate the multiple forms of violence impinging on their lives and they ways in which they choose to respond, even if those choices are not always comprehensible to those who do not participate in their life-worlds.

Agency, as Lange and Mierendorff (2009) point out, can be reproductive or resistant, with the latter form having the potential to transform the generational order. In the case of Swati children, agency could also take both forms: Reproducing the generational order as envisaged by one set of adults might be regarded as resistant agency by another set. In addition, resistant agency can be enacted in relation to systems, such as the state apparatus. Integrating a postcolonial orientation into a socioecological framework makes it possible to note this form of agency. From such a perspective, the expression of resilience takes place along a continuum, with survival representing one pole and resistant agency the other one.

The next section provides a brief history of the Swat conflict. It is followed by a description of the research methodology and a discussion of the findings. The concluding section pulls together the different strands of analysis shared in the chapter and presents implications for policy and further research.

CONTEXT

The Swat Valley, located in northwestern Pakistan, is part of the "tribal belt" governed by the province, Khyber Pakhtunkhwa, which other Pakistanis generally regard as comprising "backwards, uncivilized peoples" (Chaudhry, 2013). The Swat State was annexed to Pakistan in 1969. Before that, it was relatively independent, even though until 1947 the British regularly interfered in its internal matters and determined its relationship to other states in the region

(Rome, 2008). Yusufzai Pathans (commonly known as Pashtuns), who came from Afghanistan in the sixteenth century and occupied Swat, are the majority population and represent the most powerful segment of Swat society, owning most of the land (Chaudhry, 2013). Other communities, referred to generally as the artisan communities, are in the minority both numerically and in power relations (Chaudhry, 2013). Swati children grow up with a strong sense of their identity because their social milieu places such an emphasis on the differences between Pashtun and non-Pashtun, landowners and artisans.

The Tehrik-i-Taliban Pakistan, or the Pakistani Taliban, began to establish themselves as a socioreligious movement in Swat in 2003, using religious education to disseminate their views (Akhtar, 2010). Indeed, many parents sent their children to the *madrassahs* (schools for religious education). The Taliban benefited from Swat's particular history with Islam: The Pashtuns were strongly influenced by Muslim religious leaders both during colonial times and during the period of Swat's independent, pre-Pakistan status (Rome, 2008). In addition, the Taliban stoked the discontent that many Swatis felt with Pakistan's rule over Swat (Akhtar, 2010). Furthermore, the local leader for the Taliban in Swat, Fazlullah, was a charismatic Yusufzai Pathan who managed to establish the foundations for the Taliban rule through his connections with his own clan and an appeal to the sense of disenfranchisement faced by non-Pashtuns in Swat (Akhtar, 2010). Some of the more powerful Khans—Pashtun "influentials"—were indeed the first targets of Taliban attacks in Swat, and many who felt disenfranchised by the Khans' authority did join in the violence (Chaudhry, 2015b). Many children were inducted into the Taliban fold as combatants.

From 2007 to 2009, the Taliban regime ruled in Swat, although some factions in Swat continued to resist their authority (Chaudhry, 2013). As the Pakistani Taliban began to take control of Swati institutions, challenging the writ of the state and setting up parallel structures to govern the area, the violence they deployed intensified (Zalman, 2009). Most girls' schools and colleges were destroyed, although many boys' schools and colleges were bombed as well (Chaudhry, 2015b). Women were prohibited from entering public spaces, policemen and civil employees were systematically killed, and dissenters were hanged or slaughtered and their bodies displayed in public venues (Akhtar, 2010). Children were witnesses to all these atrocities.

The Pakistani military was stationed in Swat in 2007 (Zalman, 2009). At first it operated by equipping civilians with arms, thereby creating militias among Swati communities and using them as their surrogates to fight the Taliban (Chaudhry, 2015a). After engaging in a few skirmishes with the Taliban, however, the military took on a more active role and, through a series of battles, dislodged the Taliban in 2009 (Zalman, 2009). Even then, the top-ranking Taliban mostly managed to escape, with the security forces either apprehending or killing their lower class allies (Rome, 2013). According to Fleischner (2011), as of 2011, 2,500 alleged terrorist suspects were still being detained by the military. The Pakistan army continues to maintain its visible presence in Swat, a presence that is opposed by some Swatis, but seen as necessary by others (Khattak, 2014).

METHODS

I identified potential research participants with the help of research assistants,[2] whom I hired locally in Swat. Using a convenience approach to sampling, these assistants helped me recruit 10 (5 girls and 5 boys, aged 10–15) research participants from each of three areas in Swat where the conflict had been the most intense: Kabal, an area that blends the suburban with the rural; Matta, a chiefly rural site with some remote and far-flung villages; and Char Baagh, a small town. Of the 30 children I interviewed, 6 (3 boys and 3 girls) came from affluent Pashtun families, 5 (2 boys and 3 girls) from middle-income Pashtun families, 8 (4 boys and 4 girls) from working-class and relatively poor Pashtun families, 3 (1 boy and 2 girls) from middle-income artisan families, and 8 (4 boys and 4 girls) from poor artisan families. I also interviewed family members and neighbors of the 30 research participants, thereby contextualizing the children's narratives in larger community processes. For each child, I conducted a focus group interview that included parents (if they were available), extended family, and at least two residents of the neighborhood; each group consisted of seven to eight participants. In these interviews, the participants were asked to share briefly their accounts of the armed conflict and the impact it had on children. These interviews lasted about an hour. The children moved in and out of these groups, but they were mostly quiet during these interviews.

In accordance with scholarship that advocates a child-centered methodological approach (Clark, 2011; Lange & Mierendorff, 2009), children's words are at the heart of the discussion in this chapter. Both parental permission and children's assent were secured before data collection. Before the interview, a short questionnaire was administered to gather information from children and their parents about ethnicity, parents' educational level and vocations, household income, expenditure, and assets. The interviews with the children were conducted in an oral history mode, whereby research participants were encouraged to narrate their life story with minimal probing on my part. After the children finished their oral histories I asked them questions raised by the narratives. These interviews, which took place in the children's homes, lasted from 90 minutes to 2 hours. The children were given a choice of language— Pashto (their first language) or Urdu (the national language)—to use in their interview. Most children spoke in a mixture of the two languages. The research assistants acted as interpreters (Urdu is my first language, but my knowledge of Pashto is rudimentary). Although I told the research participants that they could have a family member present during the interview, most children preferred to be alone with the researchers.

Data were collected between December 2009 and December 2012. Although the long time span between the first and the last interviews could have resulted in differences in memory, I found that the children's narratives from 2012 were as detailed and graphic as the ones collected in 2009–2010. For the analysis, I employed a grounded theory approach: Categories of analysis were generated by the data, and emergent themes informed subsequent data collection. Following Charmaz (2011), I used a constructivist version of grounded theory in which the emphasis was on how the research participants gave meanings to their thoughts and actions, even as connections were made to arrive at a higher level of abstraction.

FINDINGS AND DISCUSSION

NARRATING TRAUMA AND "RAISING THE DEAD"

Most children, like 10-year-old Masoom Khan,[3] spoke of the fear around them as they grew up, a fear that cut across class, ethnicity, and gender:

> As far back as I can remember, I remember my parents being frightened about going outside our house. They would talk in whispers and then go all quiet when one of us children went near them. But then sometimes when my uncles and aunts would come they would all talk more loudly. They would still look very afraid, but we heard them talking about the Taliban, about whether to join them or not. My mother's brother wanted my father and other uncles to join. He

called them "cowards." One day he came to my school and asked me and my older brother to go with him. I was in third grade at that time. He took us to Mingora on his motorbike. He took us to a place where there was a huge crowd. And then holding our hands he pushed toward the front of the crowd. I thought I saw an animal hanging in the intersection with blood dripping all over it. I looked at my brother who was staring at the intersection. Then my uncle jerked my hand and said, 'Look at that man. He was not a good Muslim. So, he was punished.' That's when I saw the arms and legs and the face. I wanted to scream but no sound would come out. Later when I tried to tell my friends at school, they asked me, "Was it a beheading?", 'Was it a hanging?", "Was it a slaughtering?" I could not remember. All I remember was my fear and revulsion. My mother got very angry with my uncle, but I could tell she was also afraid of him. My brother told me it was because he had joined the Taliban.

All the boys and two of the girls from Kabal had witnessed a corpse hanging in the intersection in Mingora, Swat's biggest city (Kabal lies adjacent to Mingora). However, the majority of children talked about hearing of these corpses and having nightmares in which they saw themselves or others being slaughtered or beheaded.

For one child, Faizan, a 14-year-old boy from a poor artisan family in Char Baagh, the encounter with violent death was not just visual:

He made me hold the knife. I dropped it. He picked it up and pushed my hand on top of it and then pushed the knife, my hand, on the person's neck and started to slaughter him. Blood came out. I wrestled myself free and ran, but they chased me and brought me back, and they pushed me on top of the dying man. I was only 13 at that time. I continued to work with the Taliban, but then they gave me a gun to carry, just like that to scare people. When the army came they were all killed, other boys like me, but I did not die. I was in a room full of dead boys for God knows how long, and then I managed to go home. My father had not left town with the others because he was waiting for me. He did not take me to see a doctor because he was afraid someone would point me out as someone who worked for the Taliban. My arm and leg do not work properly since then.

Faizan's family had put him to work for the Taliban both because they believed in the Taliban's claim that it was fighting for the poor and because they needed the money the Taliban offered. In Char Baagh, it was also safer for parents to offer their own child instead of waiting for him or her to be kidnapped or coerced into joining the Taliban.

Although the danger faced by boys came from the Taliban's need for recruits, women and girls felt particularly threatened by the Taliban after the injunction banning women from appearing in public spaces. Shahana, an 11-year-old girl from a relatively poor Pashtun family living in a rather remote village in Matta, shared her mother's story:

> My mother is a Lady Health Worker.[4] She goes from home to home to help people. The Taliban sent her a death threat. But she still continued her work. One day an old man even ran after her calling her bad names and almost hitting her with a stick. Then the Taliban sent a message to my mother saying they will kidnap her children. That was the first time I saw my mother look terrified. She stopped doing her rounds. She did call her superiors in Saidu Sharif (Swat's capital city) but they also advised her to protect her family. I guess my mother felt completely alone. Our father died when we were little, and our uncles give us very little from the lands, so my mother got the LHW training to bring in some money. My mother still helped people if they came to our house, but she stopped us from going to school even before the school was blown up.

Most of the girls reported that the feelings of insecurity engendered during the Taliban times have persisted into the present. These feelings were especially strong in relation to school attendance. The Taliban broadcast their hatred of girls' education over the radio and also sent messages to individual girls and young women, threatening them with dire measures if they continued to attend school. Several girls' schools were then bombed.

Five of the children from affluent Pashtun backgrounds left the Swat Valley to go to school in Peshawar or Islamabad in 2007 when the Taliban killings peaked, and they only came back in 2009 when the region was declared safe by the military. Most of the children, however, lived through the Taliban's reign of terror. As Shabnam, an 11-year-old child from a middle-income artisan family put it, "We did not have the means to support a migration of our entire family." Thirteen-year-old Aftab, from a middle-class Pashtun household from Kabal, recalled that when he was nine years old, on the verge of leaving Swat after borrowing money from relatives, he saw his father, a policeman, shot and killed:

> The Taliban took responsibility for his murder. My father was in the hospital for forty days. How I prayed for his life! But God did not listen to me. When he

died, I cried and I cried. It's been three years but I still cry. He had such a warm personality. I used to wait for him to come home. When he came home it was as if the world was brighter. He was so generous. When we were borrowing money to leave town no one said "No" to us, because he had never said "No" to anyone. He was so brave. He knew it was dangerous, but he continued to do his duty. He was going to stay on in Swat after sending us off. The government gave him no protection. The government gave none of the policeman any protection. That day he came back from duty, and he and I stepped out for some fruit. I only realized something happened when he fell to the ground. His eyes were open, but he did not talk.

Aftab "raised the dead" as he relived the moment of terror. He spoke about the death of his father to share his love and admiration for the man, but he also seized the opportunity to highlight the general insecurity that permeated the lives of Swatis during those times. The postcolonial state could not protect its citizens. Nageena, a 14-year-old girl from a poor Pashtun family in Matta, also "raised the dead" to bemoan the lawlessness in Swat:

> Where was the government? Where was the Pakistani government when those Taliban jumped over the walls in our neighborhood and killed two people, two poor men, two poor men with children. They were just peons in a government office and they were brutally killed. Someone called the number of the army for help but they said, "We don't have our orders." So who could protect us? There was blood on our floors. There was so much blood. No one came. I kept on asking when the police would come, but someone said the policemen in Matta had mostly been killed. The rest had run away or were too afraid to get out of their houses. The Taliban could do anything, could kill anyone, could fill all of Matta, all of Swat with blood, and no one would stop them. We were just not in Pakistan anymore.

Other children were also vocal in expressing their resentment against the Pakistani state. Another girl, 15-year-old Najma, from a poor artisan family in Char Baagh, spoke eloquently about the losses incurred during the 2009 evacuation of Swat:

> We only found out we had to leave one hour before the shelling started. It was a strange sight. Everybody in our neighborhood holding bundles and children, and pushing and pulling at the older people, dragging them along. I really felt like laughing, but then got scared. I was losing my mind. We were

barely out of town when the mortar started to hit the ground. A couple of
people were killed and then we had to carry the injured. They had promised
buses, but we saw none. So we just walked and walked till we crossed over the
border of Swat. On the way one little boy just died, and two old women fell
down and did not get up. They were quietly left by the side of the road. Their
families said that they would go back from them. But I think they just lied.
Just like the Pakistani government lied about the buses. How could anyone
allow such suffering? If it happened in Lahore and Karachi, even in Peshawar,
it would be such big news. But this was just Swat and there were just poor
Swatis.

Najma thus "raised the dead" to speak of continuing governmental neglect of
the postcolonial state.

Research participants from different class, ethnic, and geographical backgrounds also spoke of state collusion with the Taliban in Swat. Fourteen-year-
old Ali Khan, from an upper-class Pashtun family in Kabal, put it this way:

Where did the Taliban get their weapons? Their FM channel equipment?
Their headquarters were not in any cave. They had this large space right there
in the heart of Kabal. Why did the government not take any action against then
while Swatis were being killed and persecuted? They created the situation.
They just want more War on Terror money, and they sacrificed Swat and Swatis
to get it. Now people think of us Swatis as terrorists. The neighboring province
would not even take us in as refugees. We have been blacklisted, and it's the
government's fault.

The majority of the children narrated their trauma as a "psychosocial" phenomenon that infused their everyday social being as postcolonial subjects, rather
than as an experience that was merely psychological (Lykes, 1993, p. 155). Rehan,
a poor 15-year-old Pashtun boy from Matta, said,

It's the poor that hurt the most. The poor went hungry before the Taliban. The
Taliban harassed everyone, but it's the poor that did not recover. The Taliban's
poor companions were the one that got caught. It's the poor that suffered the
most during the evacuation. We had no cars. And in the bombing when our
houses got damaged we barely got any compensation, because our houses
were too little, too cheap. And now the military checks us the most at their
checkposts. They disrespect us through their words, but they also use physical

violence sometimes. I haven't heard someone who owns a car has ever been beaten up. It just goes on and on, this targeting of the poor. I know now my life is just going to be like this. No one is there to protect me or other poor people.

"Raising the dead" thus involved sharing the sense of "totalizing violence" (de Mel, 2002, p. 99), painting a picture of intense, continual trauma that characterized their existence in a postcolonial nation-state. The interviews became sites for mourning individual loss as well as collective disenfranchisement as Swatis or as the poor in so-called independent Pakistan. Children's testimonies highlighted the suffering that is a consequence of postcolonial relations of power.

NEGOTIATING MULTIPLE FORMS OF VIOLENCE AND THE CULTIVATION OF RESILIENCE

Children's narratives present an unremitting sense of horror and loss. However, the children also shared how they negotiated the violence around them. The Taliban recruited children as spies in the villages of Kabal. Aasiya, a girl of 15 from a poor Pashtun family, managed to fool the Taliban into thinking she was a spy for them and continued to enjoy the rewards of such a designation for a while:

> The Taliban gave many of us children mobile phones with cameras and tape recorders. They would give us candy and chips if we brought them news of people they were spying upon. I was little at that time. Like seven maybe. But I was clever. I did not tell the Taliban anything bad about anyone, but still got candy and rewards from them. Other girls had to be confined in their homes when they were 10 or 11. I was almost 13 before the Taliban made me stay at home. I was their favorite spy.

Aasiya's agency in this regard did not really interrupt the status quo, so it is hard to see it as resistance; still it is definitely an example of resilience—the capacity to create conditions under which one can continue to survive and cope (Nordstrom, 1997).

For Irfan Ali, a poor artisan boy of 15, also from Kabal, working for the Taliban meant rebelling against both the powerful Pashtun landlords and state systems:

My mother was always working to feed us, but we were still hungry. How can you study on an empty stomach? My father sent all he earned in Saudi Arabia to his parents. They gave us nothing. The Khans just made us work and also gave us almost nothing. For everybody it was okay if we just died. I convinced my older brother and my mother that we should listen to the promises of justice that Fazlullah was making. My brother learned to drive a Jeep for them and was paid handsomely. I did little errands and sometimes carried a gun. The Pakistani government has done nothing for us. I really believed that the Taliban would establish a government in Swat that would benefit the poor, give us justice. So, yes, I supported them.

Irfan's agency in choosing to work for the Taliban could be seen as resistant agency because he was striving for a new, just order. His resilience could be partly attributed to his strong relationship with his mother. It was her acute realization of the structural violence framing their life that fostered this awareness in Irfan and led him to support the armed conflict. During the 2009 military operation, Irfan's brother was apprehended by the military. When we interviewed him in 2012 he was still in custody—the family had not seen him for three years. Irfan saw this lack of due process as another form of structural violence and was working with his mother to learn how to navigate the system. He had managed to contact the regional Human Rights Commission, Pakistan (HRCP) chapter, which was helping him fight his brother's case.

Another boy, Jamal Khan, who was 14 when we interviewed him and was from a middle-class family in Matta, managed to take a stand against his entire immediate and extended family. In early 2009, some army men came to his village and asked Jamal's uncle, who was a prominent Pashtun landlord in the area, to lead an armed battle against some Taliban sympathizers who lived in the same village. Despite his young age, Jamal was vociferous in his opposition to the plan. No one listened to him, and the battle against the Taliban-supporting neighbors ensued; however, Jamal refused to participate, as he recounted:

I wouldn't even load their guns. I somehow knew it was wrong of us to fight our neighbors. And you know what, I was right. The battle only deepened the rift. But something good did come out of my stand. When we came back home after the 2009 evacuation some Khans from the neighboring villages tried to negotiate peace for my family and those we fought. They actually only trusted me. They knew of my stand. The peace between us and our neighbors is still not solid, but because of me the boys in the village sit together now.

Although stories told by the other children about their agency were not as dramatic as the examples presented in this section, all the research participants talked about the everyday nature of their survival strategies. Every child spoke of his or her deep reliance on family and friends throughout the Taliban period and into the reconstruction phase. In the absence of the provision of any counseling, such relationships were crucial in building resilience. When schools were closed, the children were particularly bereft; the girls spoke about their attempts to continue going to school despite Taliban threats and having to face the consequences of doing so. For example, one girl who tried to go to school in Char Baagh was chased home by men brandishing guns. After the schools were closed, many of the children would get together in each other's houses to co-analyze the situation they were in and lament Swat's future; to seek each other out, the older girls had to either jump from roof to roof, which was only possible in the villages in Kabal, or wait until dark. Those children who remained isolated during those days, mostly because their homes were far away from friends, spoke of finding little or no relief from their traumatic existence. Children living in Matta, where houses were very spread out, were particularly isolated.

When Swatis were evacuated in 2009, Swati children who found refuge with families in other parts of Khyber Pakhtunkhwa fared better than those who were herded into makeshift camps. Fourteen-year-old Nageena said,

Many people had relatives and they went to them. Strangers opened their house to us, and took care of us like they had known us all their lives. I was very sad to be away from home, sad about everything that happened, but the kindness was like a balm on my heart. They had tears in their eyes when we left for Swat.

Children who stayed in the refugee camps were more bitter about the government, and some of them had internalized a negative self-image as Swati. In the words of Shahrukh, a poor artisan boy of 12 from Char Baagh,

I don't blame the other provinces for not taking us. We don't know how to live anymore. We fight with each other in our homes, and we quarreled with each other in the camps. I was so disgusted. We could not keep anything clean. We would try to snatch morsels of food. We have no self-respect anymore.

Children who had lived in the camps also exhibited weaker "psychosocial resilience" than those who had been housed with other families, relatives or otherwise (Williams & Drury, 2011, p. 74). Those who had stayed with families readjusted to life in postconflict Swat more smoothly than those living in the camps. Fortunately, most Pashtun children were able to live with relatives when they were displaced, because their extended family members were spread around Pakistan. Although it is not the goal of this research to general-ize the results, given that I am drawing from interviews with only 30 children, the 10 children in my sample who did not resume schooling once they were back home had all lived in the camps. Nine of them were from poor back-grounds, seven of them were from artisan families, and six were girls.

Readjustment in life in Swat after the defeat of the Taliban has meant accommodating to the presence of the Pakistan Army, which remains as a peace-keeping force. Reports of excessive violence by soldiers in postconflict Swat abounded, and all the children complained of unnecessarily lengthy scrutiny by the military men at checkposts. Two of the boys, both Pashtun (one from Kabal and one from Matta), were part of the military's neighborhood watch program. Pashtun boys, regardless of their backgrounds, seemed more defiant in their interactions with the Pakistan military than were boys from artisan families and girls in general. Hassan, a poor 13-year-old boy from a Pashtun family, narrated the following incident:

> I was on watch that night, but I fell asleep in the fields. A military man came and woke me up rudely. He tried to hit me, but I pushed him away and started screaming. Soon my cousins were there. The military man was rude to them too, telling them that I was evading my responsibility. My cousin used his mobile to call a Pashtun kinsman who had some clout in the region. The guy came and dealt with the military man who then went away.

Other Pashtun boys spoke of lodging protests against checkpost workers if they were disrespectful in any way. "My mother has taught me to ask for their supe-riors if they are not respectful," said Mohsin, a boy of 13 from a rich Pashtun family. Whereas the girls felt that they were merely invisible to the military men, who very rarely talked to them, the artisan boys reported that they were afraid of the army men and tried to avoid eye contact with them. Akhter, a middle-class 12-year-old boy from an artisan family, said, "My whole day gets spoiled if I have to deal with an army man. They take away my dignity."

The Pashtun boys' resilience in the face of intrusive military behavior can of course be attributed to their membership in the dominant ethnic group in the area. However, it also seems to be a consequence of a particular form of masculinity that their identity as a Pashtun bestowed on them. When military men were disrespectful or brutish, the Pashtun boys felt they had response options: They could call a superior officer or enlist the help of a clan member. In contrast, the artisan boys just felt debased, helpless, and traumatized. This was a powerful example of postcolonial relations of power serving the elite and silencing the marginalized even further.

Most children ended their narratives by regaling their efforts to rebuild their lives in Swat after the armed conflict, even as they struggled with traumatic memories. The visible presence of the military disallows a sense of normalcy, and the government's inadequate reconstruction efforts have meant low levels of economic activity in the region. The artisan families especially spoke of their suffering with regard to the economy; the conflict interrupted their trade of shawls and other handicrafts, and the government has done nothing to restore it. Children were mostly dismissive of nongovernmental organizations' efforts to build resilience within communities. For example, the notion of "safe spaces" created by UNICEF in postconflict Swat generated a good deal of hilarity. Yet they were appreciative of the fact that schools had been built and reopened in an efficient manner. For the poor children, especially those who had discontinued their education, resilience became about learning to adapt to the roles circumscribed by their families—which generally entailed contributing to the family's income in some way.

CONCLUSION

This chapter has shared how Swati children constructed their experiences of trauma, violence, and resilience during the course of their oral histories and in response to my follow-up questions. Children presented themselves as thoughtful meaning-makers who responded to tremendous oppression and violence through a complex interplay of resourcefulness and compromise. Most prominently, they cast themselves as survivors willing to share their truths, risky and otherwise. In other words, because the Taliban were no longer a danger, the children "raised the dead" in the face of a dominant postcolonial culture of silence that emphasized relegating everything to the past and just moving on (Khattak, 2014). A postcolonial theoretical lens allowed for the articulation of children's negotiation of life in the midst of death, even as it provided opportunities to analyze multiply embedded cultures of violence that have become entrenched and flare up during certain critical periods.

Children's telling of their stories could thus be seen as resistant acts of agency, even as those stories revealed further acts of agency and resistance during the Taliban period and into the reconstruction phase. For practitioners and policy makers, such stories highlight the value of making children's voices central to strategies of intervention in contexts of violence, not just in Pakistan but also around the globe where children's lives unfold in cultures of violence.

Viewed from such a theoretical perspective, the children situated themselves within historical and political processes, and my analysis highlights the significance of gender, ethnic, and class hierarchies in the playing out of these historical and political subjectivities in the arena of the postcolonial nation-state. Most of the children perceived the terror in Swat as aimed against Swatis and saw the neglect, or perhaps even collusion, by the government as a crime against Swatis in general. However, for the poor children and girls, the terror and neglect were felt most acutely at particular intersections of gender, class, and ethnicity. According to some of the poor children from non-landlord backgrounds, the unjust treatment of their communities predated the Taliban and continued to be a hallmark of the present. The girls spoke of their persistent insecurity when venturing out, especially when going to school.

Children were vocal about how interactions with family and community contributed to strengthening their agency and resilience during and after the conflict. Mothers were especially key in determining choices and cultivating resilience. Children who stayed with extended family members or friends during their displacement from Swat fared better than those living in refugee camps. Furthermore, children who were able to connect with other children when the Taliban closed their schools seemed to have coped better than those who were more isolated. The findings thus support an ecological reading of children's lives in times of conflict. Again for policy makers and practitioners such findings have important implications for how refugees are harbored and placed during crisis situations around the world. Camps need to mirror the everyday life situations of children. They need to be places where children spend time with each other and have positive interactions with those not negatively affected by crises.

During my interactions with them, many research participants asked me if other people would hear their stories. It seemed very important to them that I would carry their stories over the boundaries of Swat and Pakistan, so that those far away could listen to what happened to them. They were appreciative of the few reconstruction workers who listened to Swatis as they decided how Swat was to be rebuilt after the conflict, just as they were quite angry at those who did not listen and did not care what priorities Swatis had as they reestablished themselves in their homes and communities.

The question that I would like to leave my readers with is this: How can policy makers at all levels work with the strengths of these remarkable children to facilitate better futures for *all* of them? Empowering Swati communities entails not only providing culture-specific counseling services and augmenting institutional services at the regional level but also involves developing governance structures whereby people construct healthy relationships with the state and its apparatus, including the military. One simple step could be the consistent availability of government and military officials for purposes of consultation and even just reporting of complaints. Although I agree with Ward (2013) that articulating and analyzing traumas in postcolonial contexts are of value, Swati children's narratives underscore the fact that systemic change is needed before the dead can be readily put to rest. The federal and provincial governments need to ensure that Swatis have a voice at every level and that their voices are heard and manifested in policies that affect their everyday lives. This holds true for contexts of violence around the world: those at the center of the conflict need to sit at negotiation tables and in arenas where strategies for rebuilding are conceived, and as this chapter advocates, these participants should include children from different class and gender backgrounds.

The findings of the study presented here also indicate the need for extensive research with children in the different sub-regions affected by conflict. We can derive implications for other contexts from this study, but as an ethnographer I am acutely aware of the need for in-depth contextual analyses. Further research should consider perspectives that take into account the postcolonial reality of insecurity, neglect, and state collusion with the multilayered violence circumscribing children's lives. How do other children "raise the dead" in their constructions of the conflict? How does this "raising of the dead" suggest spaces for policy intervention? What familial, community, and sociopolitical mechanisms and processes can be strengthened to cultivate further resilience in the face of adversity? Participant observation of children in these different contexts could provide insights into the long-term relationships that help shape resilience, thereby suggesting measures that can be taken to balance the social ecologies framing children's worlds.

Notes

1. The literature on structural violence uses the concept to draw "our attention to unequal life chances, usually caused by great inequality, injustice, discrimination, and exclusion, and needlessly limiting people's physical, social, and psychological well-being" (Uvin, 1998, p. 105).
2. The research assistants helped recruit participants, took notes, and acted as interpreters. In 2009–2010 I had one research assistant, a man. In the summer of 2010 I had two research assistants, a man and a woman. In 2012 there were two female and two male research assistants.
3. Fictitious names have been used to retain the research participants' anonymity.
4. Lady Health Workers (LHW) are community-based health workers who have a minimum of 8 years of schooling and receive 15 months of training. Their primary tasks are to provide family planning counseling services, health education, and treatment for minor illnesses, mainly in peoples' homes. They also facilitate antenatal care and skilled attendance at birth. More recently, their repertoire has been expanded to include polio immunization campaigns, treatment for tuberculosis, malaria control, and emergency relief activities.

References

Akhtar, A. S. (2010). Islam as ideology of tradition and change: The "new jihad" in Swat, Northern Pakistan. *Comparative Studies of South Asia, Africa, and the Middle East, 30*(3), 595–609.

Boothby, N., Strang, A., & Wessells, M. (Eds.). (2006). *A world turned upside down: Social ecological approaches to children in war zones.* Bloomfield, CT: Kumarian Press.

Boyden, J., & de Berry, J. (Eds.). (2004a). *Children and youth on the frontline: Ethnography, armed conflict, and displacement.* New York: Berghahn Books.

Boyden, J., & de Berry, J. (2004b). Introduction. In J. Boyden & J. de Berry (Eds.), *Children and youth on the frontline: Ethnography, armed conflict, and displacement* (pp. xi–xxvii). New York: Berghahn Books.

Charmaz, K. (2011). Grounded theory methods in social justice research. In N. K. Denzin & Y. S. Lincoln (Eds.), *The Sage handbook of qualitative research* (pp. 359–380). Los Angeles: Sage.

Chaudhry, L. N. (2013). Researching the War on Terror in Swat Valley, Pakistan: Grapplings with the impact on communities and transnational knowledge production. *Journal of Social Issues, 69*(4), 713–733.

Chaudhry, L. N. (2014). Mohajir women survivors in postcolonial Karachi: On grief. *South Asian History and Culture, 5*(3), 349–364.

Chaudhry, L. N. (2015a). Maternal pedagogies in Swat Valley, Pakistan: Mothers' perspectives on faith, jihad, and peace. In T. Takseva & A. Sgoutas (Eds.), *Mothers under fire: Mothering in conflict areas* (pp. 98–116). Bradford, Canada: Demeter Press.

Chaudhry, L. N. (2015b). Women in post-conflict Swat: Notes on agency, resistance, and survival. In H. Ahmad-Ghosh (Ed.), *Walking the tightrope: Asian Muslim women and their lived realities* (pp.83–102). Albany: State University of New York Press.

Christensen, P., & Prout, A. (2005). Anthropological and sociological perspectives on the study of children. In S. Greene & D. Hogan (Eds.), *Researching children's experiences: Methods and approaches* (pp. 42–60). London: Sage.

Clark, C. D. (2011). *In a younger voice: Doing child-centered qualitative research.* Oxford: Oxford University Press.

de Mel, N. (2002). Fractured narratives: Notes on women in conflict in Sri Lanka and Pakistan. *Development, 45*(1), 99–104.

Durrant, S. (2004). *Postcolonial narrative and the work of mourning: J. M. Coetzee, Wilson Harris, and Toni Morrison.* Albany: State University of New York Press.

Fleischner, J. (2011). *Governance and militancy in Pakistan's Swat Valley.* Retrieved from http://csis.org/publication/governance-and-militancy-pakistans-swat-valley.

Holland, S. P. (2000). *Raising the dead: Readings of death and (black) subjectivity.* Durham, NC: Duke University Press.

James, A. (2009). Agency. In J. Qvortrup, W. Corsaro, & M. Honig (Eds.), *The Palgrave handbook of childhood studies* (pp. 34–45). London: Palgrave Macmillan.

Khattak, S. (2014, April). *Between the Taliban and the military: Women, security, and militarization In Pakistan's Swat Valley.* Paper presented at Rutgers University, New Brunswick, NJ.

Lange, A., & Mierendorff, J. (2009). Methods and methodology in childhood research. In J. Qvortrup, W. Corsaro, & M. Honig (Eds.), *The Palgrave handbook of childhood studies* (pp. 78–96). London: Palgrave Macmillan.

Lloyd, E., & Penn, H. (2010). Working with children who are victims of armed conflict. *Contemporary Issues in Early Childhood, 11*(3), 278–287.

Lykes, M.B. (1993). Children in the storm: Psychosocial trauma in Latin America. In M. Agosin (Ed.), *Surviving beyond fear: Women, children, and human rights in Latin America* (pp. 152–161). Buffalo, NY: White Pine Press.

Nordstrom, C. (1997). *A different kind of war story.* Philadelphia: University of Pennsylvania Press.

Rome, S. (2008). *Swat State (1915–1969).* Oxford: Oxford University Press.

Rome, S. (2013). The Swat crisis. In B. D. Hopkins & M. Marsden (Eds.), *Beyond Swat: History, society, and economy along the Afghanistan-Pakistan frontier* (pp. 149–162). New York: Columbia University Press.

Scheper-Hughes, N., & Bourgois, P. (2004). Introduction: Making sense of violence. In N. Scheper-Hughes & P. Bourgois (Eds.), *Violence in war and peace: An anthology* (pp. 1–32). Malden, MA: Blackwell.

Shakya, A. (2011). Experiences of children in armed conflict in Nepal. *Children and Youth Services Review, 33*(4), 557–563.

Uvin, P. (1998). *Aiding violence: The development of enterprise in Rwanda.* West Hartford, CT: Kumarian Press.

Ward, A. (2013). Understanding postcolonial traumas. *Journal of Theoretical and Philosophical Psychology, 33*(3), 170–184.

Williams, R., & Drury, J. (2011). Personal and collective psychosocial resilience: Implications for children, young people and their families involved in war and disaster. In D. T. Cook & J. Wall (Eds.), *Children and armed conflict: Cross-disciplinary investigations* (pp. 57–75). London: Palgrave Macmillan.

Zalman, A. (2009). Terrorism timeline: Pakistan and the global war on terror. Retrieved from http://terrorism.about.com/od/globalwaronterror/tp/Pakistan.

2

YOUNG CHILDREN'S EXPERIENCES OF CONNECTEDNESS AND BELONGING IN POSTCONFLICT SRI LANKA
A Socioecological Approach

Nanditha Hettitantri and Fay Hadley

THIS CHAPTER EXPLORES YOUNG CHILDREN'S experiences of connectedness and sense of belonging to both their social and physical environment (socioecology) in a developing resettlement village in Sri Lanka. Connectedness refers to the secure connections to "people and place" that support a sense of belonging and attachment to those people and spaces (Robinson & Truscott, 2014, p. 7). In postconflict contexts, connectedness and a sense of belonging contribute to feelings of inclusion, acceptance, coping, and resilience. They also facilitate the development of social networks and returning to a sense of normalcy (Hobfoll et al., 2007). Using a socioecological approach, this chapter examines young children's experiences of connectedness and sense of belonging. It assesses how socioecological factors, including social structures and relationships, affect the children and their families. Drawing on the voices of two child participants in a larger study, the chapter argues that young children's experiences of connectedness to people and places in a postconflict context are related to a sense of belonging to family, school, village, and community. We propose that the factors that support young children's connectedness to their socioecology—for example, appropriate affection, care, and protection from the family and social networks; provision of support and educational services; and participation in play activities—can promote a powerful and important sense of belonging in young children.

The chapter begins with a discussion of the conceptual framework that guided the analysis; in particular, notions of connectedness, belonging, and the socioecological model. It then describes the armed conflict and the situation of postconflict Sri Lanka, thereby providing the context for the analysis. The study and its methodology are then introduced, followed by the study findings in the form of two children's case studies. Finally, we discuss the children's experiences in terms of their connectedness to family, school, neighborhood, and community, as well as the implications for conducting research with young children.

CONCEPTUAL FRAMEWORK: CONNECTEDNESS AND A SENSE OF BELONGING

Connectedness is a spatial and social concept, built on a sense of a positive, emotional relationship between the individual, place, and other people. Robinson and Truscott (2014) explain connectedness as being a sense of relationship to both place and people. They argue that both the number and quality of connections support a sense of belonging to the symbolic spaces that feel familiar, comfortable, and secure and to which a person feels emotionally attached (p. 7). A sense of belonging is important to a person's emotional and psychological well-being. Other scholars have also equated connectedness with a sense of belonging (Bronfenbrenner, 1979; Lerner, 1991) and a sense of community (Zeldin & Topitzes, 2002). Antonsich (2010, p. 645), who analyzed scholarship that discussed a sense of belonging, argues that the concept needs to be defined within the two dimensions of "place belongingness" and the "politics of belonging":

> Belonging as a personal, intimate feeling of being "at home" in a place (place-belonging) and belonging as a discursive resource which constructs, claims, justifies, or resists forms of socio-spatial inclusion/exclusion (politics of belonging).

Sumsion and Wong (2011, p. 232) define a sense of belonging as a construction of *multilayered dimensions and axes*. These dimensions—social, spatial, cultural, and emotional—are the multiple ways through which one experiences a sense of belonging, and they hold vital information regarding how a sense of belonging is nurtured, lived, and influenced by the context. Woodhead and Brooker (2008) argue that fundamental to all definitions of a sense of belonging are the connections a person (or a child) makes to the social and physical environment; these connections include the relationships established with people and places and the beliefs and practices that are a part of that place.

Members of communities affected by armed conflict and disasters frequently suffer the breakdown or loss of connectedness to both place and people. Yet, in postconflict contexts, connectedness and a sense of belonging can play a particularly important role in developing sustainable and healthy societies. The empirical literature on psychosocial interventions for people affected by disasters and armed conflict, which is of particular interest to our study, defines connectedness as the social support and sustained attachments to loved ones and social groups that foster a sense of acceptance, respect, and self and collective efficacy among affected communities (Hobfoll et al., 2007, p. 296). Hobfoll and colleagues (2007) argue that connectedness supports the development of social networks, boosts the necessary skills and capacity of the people in their recovery, and encourages positive adaptation to these situations.

Several studies conducted in areas affected by conflict and violence discuss children's connectedness to place and people that leads to a sense of belonging. Some examples are research with refugee children in Australia (McFarlane, Kaplan, & Lawrence, 2011), Palestinian refugee children in Jordan (Hart, 2004), children in segregated communities in Ireland (Kytta, 2004), and young children (those younger than 8 years old) in the occupied Palestinian territories (Akesson, 2012) and in postconflict Belfast (Connolly & Healy, 2004). These studies report that the connections and relationships between the person and environment (both social and physical) were important for the development of a sense of belonging, which is fundamental for children's well-being in conflict-affected contexts. There is consensus among researchers that promoting connectedness should be a key element of interventions for trauma-affected communities (Hobfoll et al., 2007).

THE SOCIOECOLOGICAL MODEL

The socioecological model suggests that child development occurs within the context of interacting socially organized subsystems or nested structures (Betancourt & Khan, 2008; Bronfenbrenner, 1994). These ecological structures (for example, micro-, meso-, and macro-systems) are interconnected by being situated each inside the other. The micro-system is the structure closest to a child—for example, the child's family and school—whereas the macro- system encompasses the broader policies, beliefs, values, and culture in a given society. Increased attention has been given recently to the validity and suitability of a socioecological approach to the study of children in conflict and postconflict contexts, because this approach can capture children's experiences within the multiple layers of their lives (Betancourt & Khan, 2008;

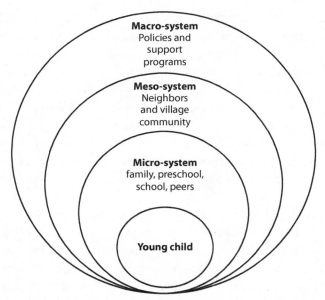

FIGURE 2.1 The socioecology of a young child (adapted from Bronfenbrenner, 1994).

Wessells & Monteiro, 2008). The case studies reported in this chapter used a socioecological approach to analyze young children's experiences of connectedness in postconflict Sri Lanka (see Figure 2.1).

BACKGROUND: SRI LANKA AND THE ARMED CONFLICT

Sri Lanka is an island in the Indian Ocean with a heterogeneous population of approximately 20 million people. Its ethnic makeup, as recorded in a 2012 demographic study, is Singhalese (74.9%), Sri Lankan Tamils (11.2%), Indian Tamils (4.2%), Muslim Moors (9.2%), and others (0.5%: European descendants and Sri Lankan *Veddas,* or indigenous peoples) (Economic and Social Statistics of Sri Lanka, 2013). The Singhalese are predominantly Buddhists, whereas the Tamils are predominantly Hindus. Catholicism, Christianity, and Islam are also practiced in the country. The two local languages (Singhalese and Tamil) and English are the official languages. Being a democratic socialist republic, the government of Sri Lanka functions as a welfare state providing free education, health care, and a number of other government-subsidized services; as a result, the social development indicators are positive, such as literacy rates of

91% for adults and low infant mortality rates of 9.9 per 1,000 live births (Department of Census and Statistics, 2008).

Despite its positive social indicators, Sri Lanka has experienced societal turmoil, which has been exacerbated by an armed conflict that lasted for 26 years (1983–2009). The conflict was between the government of Sri Lanka (GoSL) and the armed groups from the Tamil community (in the northern and eastern parts of the country)—later dominated by the Liberation of Tamil Tigers of Elam (LTTE)—which fought for "a separate, autonomous Tamil state within Sri Lanka" (Neumann & Fahmy, 2012, p. 171). Since the end of the war, Sri Lanka has been functioning as a rebuilding postconflict state.

POSTCONFLICT SRI LANKA

The armed conflict affected members of the Sri Lankan population in different ways (Samarasinghe, 2015). Children and families, for example, lost their loved ones (either combatants or civilians who were exposed to civil war, bombing, landmines, and targeted and untargeted attacks in villages and public places) or incurred injuries that resulted in permanent disabilities. In addition, thousands of people—primarily Tamils, Singhalese, and Muslims in the northern and eastern parts of the country—were internally displaced for periods ranging from 2 years to nearly 3 decades (Saparamadu & Lall, 2014). Some left the country altogether (De Votta, 2004, 2010).

In postconflict Sri Lanka, the Ministry of Resettlement has managed and coordinated the resettlement of displaced communities, supporting their efforts to rebuild their lives in previously conflict-affected traditional villages (Saparamadu & Lall, 2014). This chapter uses the GoSL's definition of resettlement as referring to the "return, resettlement, and relocation" of all types of internally displaced people (IDPs) from temporary settlements to permanent settlements (as cited in Saparamadu & Lall, 2014, p. 8). In the armed conflict, the traditional villages that had provided a protective environment were destroyed, resulting in a breakdown of communities (Somasundaram, 2004, 2007). Although evidence indicates that the majority of the recovery and rebuilding efforts have been successful, in some postconflict settings, suicide, domestic violence, family breakdown, child abuse, and antisocial behaviors have been reported, suggesting the persistence of negative impacts after conclusion of the armed conflict (Somasundaram & Sivayokan, 2013).

YOUNG CHILDREN IN POSTCONFLICT SRI LANKA

There are few studies of young children (under 8 years of age) in postconflict Sri Lanka. Research addressing older children, although still limited, has found that the 26-year armed conflict disrupted their lives through the loss of caregivers and family members and the breakdown of traditional villages and protective socioecological systems. Furthermore, according to some studies, during the armed conflict many children exhibited signs of developing symptoms of posttraumatic stress disorder (PTSD), whereas others showed signs of poor adaptation to adverse experiences (Catani et al., 2010; Chase et al., 1999). In addition, children living in conflict-affected areas experienced an increase in domestic violence (Catani, Schauer, & Neuner, 2008). However, on a more positive note, one study in postconflict Sri Lanka found that the provision of care from parents or parental figures, education, social welfare services, and social networks helped children develop coping abilities and resilience (Fernando & Ferrari, 2011).

THE STUDY

The two case studies reported in this chapter are drawn from a larger study that investigated the multiple realities of young children's experiences and perspectives of well-being in a rebuilding, postconflict context and how caregivers, community leaders, and government and nongovernment service providers perceived these phenomena.

The methodological framework of the study was designed to support young children's right to participate and to be heard as articulated by the United Nations Convention of the Rights of Children (United Nations, 1989). Because we considered young children to be competent social actors and the most knowledgeable of their life experiences (Mayall, 2002; Prout & James, 1997), the key research participants were 16 young children aged between 3 and 7 years. Twelve children (Tamil) were from families who had permanently resettled and lived in the postconflict village under study for at least 2 years, and four children (Singhalese) were from transient families who were in the process of permanently resettling in that village. Young children's caregivers (N=53), village community leaders (N=5), and the government and nongovernment service providers (N=13) were also part of the study. Data collection was conducted in Sri Lanka between January and February 2014.

RESEARCH CONTEXT: THE VILLAGE OF "MALGAMA"

The field study was conducted in a village (assigned the pseudonym "Malgama") in the Eastern Province of Sri Lanka. It has a land area of about 40 square kilometers. In the surrounding area are paddy fields, cultivated lands, and some uncleared forests. Although geographically isolated, the study village is connected by paved roads to other towns, the nearest of which is about 20 kilometers away.

Before the war, Malgama had been home to Tamil, Singhalese, and a few Muslim families who lived as small community groups in geographically segregated areas within the village. When the conflict escalated, beginning in 1983, all the families left the village, leaving the entire geographical area under control of the LTTE until the end of the war in the Eastern Province in 2007. After Malgama was rebuilt in late 2008, families began to return and resettle there. The Grama Niladhari (the GoSL-appointed village administrative officer) for Malgama reported that, by the end of 2012, 180 families were registered as residents in the village; of these, the majority (Tamils) were permanently resettled in Malgama, whereas about 20% of the families (Singhalese) were transient, continuing to live in temporary settlements and cultivating their lands in Malgama.

Both the Tamils and Singhalese have been challenged by the resettlement process, which required their adjustment to a new social and physical environment. Half of the families resettled in Malgama identified themselves as the traditional owners of the village. However, because of the lengthy displacement, most of the families who returned were second-generation residents— the children of former inhabitants—and were relatively young, with small children and few close relatives still residing in Malgama. During their displacement, most returnees had lived in more urban settings either in the government or nongovernment organization (NGO) supported resettlement camps for IDPs or with their friends and relatives.

Although adapting to this new social and physical context and rural life was challenging, adult participants in the study reported that numerous support services were available in Malgama to facilitate their adjustment. In the areas where the families permanently resettled, the infrastructure—roads, electricity, telecommunication, community buildings, health center, a public school and preschool, places of worship, a building for milk collection, a reservoir, and an electric fence for protection from wild elephants—had been rebuilt. Government agencies and NGOs provided support for children and community development and welfare services. For example, they supported the formation and development of community groups, such as the Samurdhi Society (for the distribution of government welfare and subsidies to low-income families), a mothers' group, a village development society, a child protection committee, and a children's group.

In addition, traditional livelihoods of cultivation and fishing had been restored. During the period of displacement, many men and some women had worked as paid employees of development projects in urban areas; some were still working in those positions. Although at the time of the study the majority of the families were still living in temporary houses, some were close to moving into their permanent brick houses, which had been built with funding from the GoSL and international and local NGOs. Despite these resettlement and rebuilding services, village life in Malgama was still shaped by the long-lasting effects of the conflict. According to the service providers who participated in the study, resettled families in Malgama experienced social problems such as poverty, alcoholism, domestic violence, family breakdown (sometimes due to migration for work, in particular females' foreign employment), and divisiveness between the ethnic communities. Many adolescents were dropping out of school.

YOUNG CHILDREN IN MALGAMA

The young children in Malgama had been the beneficiaries of various post-conflict Early Childhood Care and Development (ECCD) policies and interventions that were aimed at establishing child-friendly villages for young children (ECCD Model Village Project, 2009). The newly built preschool in Malgama is staffed by a trained preschool teacher and has a safe and appropriate facility, furniture, teaching and learning materials, and a playground. The mothers' group promotes caregivers' involvement in this preschool. The public school in the village also is a safe and adequate facility, with a playground, desks and chairs, a small library, electricity, two computers, a place to prepare food for children, clean drinking water, and sanitation. It is staffed by a GoSL-appointed school principal and trained teachers and benefits from the effort of a supportive group of parents and NGOs. Since their resettlement, the children, their families, and the overall community in Malgama have received an array of GoSL free services, such as health care (vaccinations, monthly clinics, doctors' visits, and midwifery services), ECCD programs (ECCD officer, ECCD model village project, ECCD awareness and community mobilization), and protection (a Children's and Women's Police Desk at the nearest police station, child rights promotion officer, and child care and probationary services officer), as well as NGOs' services such as nutrition programs and children's mothers' groups.

METHODOLOGY: A MOSAIC APPROACH

Young children's experiences were explored through the mosaic approach (Clark & Moss, 2001). The mosaic approach draws on the theories of children as competent social actors and is guided by the understanding that children share their views using different ways that are unique to themselves (Clark & Statham, 2005). It uses varied data collection methods—traditional methods of interviews and observations, participatory methods of focus group discussions, participant-led tours, and visual methods of drawings and photographs—from diverse informants of children and adults in a participatory manner to develop a picture or mosaic pattern, based on participants' meaning-making processes (Clark, 2011). The mosaic approach also integrates the views of the adults (including the researchers) on the issues under investigation without denigrating or overlooking children's perspectives. Thus, it creates a detailed picture of the child's world—a mosaic—by integrating children's and adults' data.

The mosaic approach was initiated and widely used in Western contexts in early childhood centers to capture young children's perceived experiences (Clark & Moss, 2001). Previous research, however, has found that various methods integrated in the mosaic approach have also been useful and effective in disadvantaged contexts, suggesting that this approach is suitable for research with young children even in conflict-ravaged contexts. For example, the visual methods of drawing, ethnographic methods of interviews and narratives, and participatory methods of focus group discussions and participant led-tours, which are widely used in the participatory rural appraisal method (Chambers, 1994), were found to be useful in gathering authentic views of children in various conflict-affected contexts (e.g., Akesson, 2012; Boyden, 2004; Hart, Galappatti, Boyden, & Armstrong, 2007).

In our study using the mosaic approach, the data collection methods with children consisted of child drawings, photography, interviews, child-led tours, and analysis of the children's group discussion, which focused on children's lived experiences in their social and physical environments in Malgama. Data on the adults were gathered in structured interviews, focus group discussions, adult-led tours in the village (i.e., "transect-walks") with caregivers, and interviews with the service providers and community leaders. These methods were used to obtain adults' views about the experiences of young children in relation to the rebuilding postconflict social and physical environment. Researcher observations and field notes were collected, and child case studies were also constructed (Yin, 2009) to further understand the diverse experiences of young children. Two of these case studies form the basis of this chapter's analysis and discussion.

We conducted a pilot study in mid-2013 with four young children and their caregivers in a recently developed village in a disadvantaged area in postconflict Sri Lanka; this pilot study confirmed that the data collection methods, including children's drawings, child-led tours and photography, and children's interviews, were effective ways to collect data from young children in the Sri Lankan context. In the full study all interviews, focus group discussions, children's descriptions of their drawings and photographs, and tour commentaries were recorded and translated into English and prepared as MS Word documents. The caregivers' responses during structured interviews were quantitatively analyzed using MS Excel, and we developed a coding system using qualitative data analysis software (NVivo Version 10) to identify emerging themes from the qualitative data (Braun & Clarke, 2006). Each author coded the data separately to ensure the accuracy and to validate the coding and analysis. Key themes that emerged from the data analysis included connectedness within the family (in the form of care and support within the family), social connectedness (in the form of social networks beyond the family), and strengths and gaps in the protection and provision of children's rights.

RECRUITMENT AND ETHICAL CONSIDERATIONS

The Macquarie University Human Research Ethics Committee for Human Sciences and Humanities and the Ministry of Child Development and Women's Affairs in Sri Lanka approved the study. The field study was conducted by the first author, who is from Sri Lanka and had experience in conducting research with disaster- and conflict-affected communities in many sites in the country. By adhering to the Sri Lankan research protocols, the first author minimized any potential or perceived risks both to the researcher and the participants. For example, both the authorities and community members were well informed of the study, and courtesy visits were made to the GoSL's Divisional Secretariat and the Grama Niladhari (village administrative officer) before coming to Malgama.

Using the preschool and the school as entry points to the community and with the services of a village volunteer, the researcher communicated with all caregivers of children younger than 8 years in Malgama and managed the recruitment process to mitigate any potential coercion for participation. Information about the research and invitations for participation were shared verbally and in print in local languages in meetings organized for all caregivers of children younger than 8 years. Invitations to participate in the study were extended to both community groups—families who were permanently resettled (Tamil) and transient (Singhalese) families—to ensure a diverse sample. Information about the study and individual invitations to participate were also given to service providers and community leaders.

The voluntary nature of the participation was emphasized with all potential participants. We obtained informed consent for participation verbally to allow the participants to freely express their views without fear of any perceived consequences. To address the issues of unequal power relationships between children, adults, and adult researchers (Punch, 2002), the caregivers were asked to talk about the study, its aims, and the nature of the participation with their children before obtaining an agreement to participate from them. After the caregivers provided consent for their child's participation and for their own participation, the researcher spoke with each potential child participant and also obtained his or her verbal assent. We ensured the confidentiality and privacy of the participants by using pseudonyms for the participants and removing all identifiable information from the data.

LIMITATIONS OF THE STUDY

The study was not without its limitations. Postconflict contexts are diverse, and this was a small study conducted in one postconflict community in Sri Lanka. Therefore, findings from this study may not be generalizable to the wider population in postconflict contexts. It would be important to conduct further research in other postconflict settings in Sri Lanka and other parts of the world to ascertain the generalizability of both the methodology and findings. In addition, the first author, sometimes with the support of a translator, conducted all interviews, translations, and transcriptions. Because of her lack of training as a translator, the meaning of some local phrases, monosyllabic answers, or words may not have been fully captured. Furthermore, in terms of the findings presented in this chapter, a limitation is the lack of a child case study of a transient (Singhalese) family.

FINDINGS

To illustrate the key theme of *connectedness* to the social ecology of children in postconflict Sri Lanka, this chapter presents child case studies of Thilu, a boy, and Shani, a girl, both from the permanently resettled Tamil community. These two cases illustrate the connections of these children with their families, the formal education institution (school), the neighborhood, and the overall village and community. They were chosen to illustrate both a girl's and a boy's experiences, as well as the diversity and complexity of the young children's experiences: Shani is an informally adopted child from a separated family, and Thilu lived with his biological parents in a stable family.

THILU

Five-year-old Thilu had resettled in Malgama with his family (mother, father, and two elder sisters) 4 years before the study was conducted. He had attended the preschool in Malgama and had started primary school recently. He participated in the research activities of child drawings, child photos, narratives and interviews, a child-led tour around his school, and the group discussion with the Children's Group. To describe his experiences, Thilu mostly spoke in very short phrases or gave monosyllabic answers, yet he confidently used gestures, symbols, and visuals such as photographs and drawings during interviews and child-led tours. His mother was involved in the individual interviews and the caregivers' focus group discussions.

Thilu's family had aspirations for their three children to be well educated. His parents sent their two daughters to the secondary school in the nearby town where they had formerly lived in a temporary resettlement camp. Thilu seemed to receive appropriate care and protection as indicated by his interviews, which described numerous ways his mother and father looked after him. His mother was the main caregiving figure in all aspects of his life. Thilu approached her when he needed material things or psychosocial support, such as when he was scared of cobras or when he felt happy and wanted to share his emotions, suggesting that he had developed a strong connectedness and attachment to his mother. Thilu's drawings and explanations suggested that his father also played an important role in his life.

However, the family members with whom Thilu had fewer interactions were excluded from his drawings, illustrating different levels of connectedness to family members. He mentioned his two sisters, but he did not include them in his first drawing of the family. As he explained, he did not have much interaction with them because they were attending a school in the nearby town and were away from home for long periods of time each day. At home he either played by himself or with two children in the neighborhood or was with his mother.

Thilu's family allowed him to be involved in both everyday and special activities. He talked about going to the well for bathing and fetching water with his mother. Thilu also mentioned worshiping God before going to school and to the nearest town with his mother. He was allowed to attend the children's group (with children aged 4–14 years in Malgama), which was facilitated by an NGO in the village.

Thilu stated that he liked school. In the child-led tour, he took photographs of the school buildings, the playground, and the small library room. He proudly showed off the different places in his school:

Nanditha: Where do you like to be most?
Thilu: In school
Nanditha: Can you tell me why?
Thilu: [I can] learn, write.
Nanditha: What do you do while you are in the school?
Thilu: Playing. Learning.

Thilu's experiences of connectedness extended beyond the family and the school to the wider community in the village. His participation in community activities through the children's group connected him to the wider village community. This group met during the afternoons, and its members shared their toys, played, sang, and socialized together. The children were encouraged to discuss topics that they thought were important. For example, they talked about the value of education, hygiene practices, nutritional food, and more complex topics of adults' disputes over resources and aid. During the meetings, Thilu also participated in singing (Singhalese and Tamil songs) and took pride in demonstrating his ability in singing songs in the "other" (Singhalese) language (researcher observation).

SHANI

Five-year-old Shani's family had resettled in Malgama approximately 4 years before the study was conducted. Like Thilu, she had attended preschool and was now attending the primary school in Malgama. She preferred to participate in the research through interviews and drawings. Her primary caregiver was involved in interviews at her residence.

Shani is an informally adopted child, living with her father's sister (whom she referred to her as her "Malgama *Amma*" [Malgama mother]) and other extended family members, including her uncle and grandfather. Shani explained that her biological mother had gone abroad for work and her father lived in Colombo. She talked about her *chitthi* (stepmother) who lived with her father. Shani's case presents some of the societal issues that emerged in postconflict developing villages and affect children's lives. Family breakdown and migration for work emerged as key elements of Shani's experiences within her family.

Yet Shani's experiences also revealed a predictability and sense of "normalcy" in her life. For example, she mentioned that she played with her pots and sand, read books, and attended school often. Furthermore, she participated in both everyday activities and any special activities in which her family was involved. She talked about going to the well and fetching water in a small bucket with her Malgama mother. When prompted by her Malgama mother, Shani said she swept the house, a dwelling that was their temporary home. She explained that when her uncle attended to the family's goats she fed plants to the small kids and also carried them around and played with them. She mentioned going to *Kovil* (Hindu temple) and attending a wedding ceremony with her family.

Shani's descriptions of her experiences suggested that, despite being an informally adopted child, she received consistent affection and care from her Malgama mother and had a strong connection to her. Shani's account also suggested that she was in the middle of a circle of care by her extended family members to whom she felt connected:

> Malgama Amma boils water, prepares hot water and bathes me
> [Malgama] Amma prepares green salads, boils manioc and gives to eat
> Uncle carried me and walked to school. Uncle bought biscuits. Malgama Appa [grandfather] also buys and gives me (biscuits). I got this for Christmas from Jenny aunty—brought this too [showing her pencil case and the water bottle].

Shani conveyed the ways her extended family were connected to her and indicated that they played an important part in her life by providing for her material needs (her aunty giving her school supplies); by providing care (her grandfather looking after her while her Malgama mother was away, another aunty taking her to the doctor); and by her uncle playing a parental role (taking her to school, protecting her, and involving her in daily activities).

For Shani, the neighbors were temporary caregivers and protectors and thus were important people in her life as well. She mentioned that her aunt (who is both her relative and a neighbor), who lived next door, would take her to see the doctor and would intervene when her Malgama mother and uncle had disputes. Shani also mentioned another group of neighbors from her "old place." She recalled the girls whom she used to play with and with whom she was invited to stay and study. In addition, Shani mentioned her previous preschool and showed interest in the school she was attending now, highlighting a connectedness to both places.

Shani also discussed a person she met on one of her visits "who was speaking Singhalese." She said she ate *bath* (a Singhalese term for cooked rice) and took pride in further explaining that *bath* is the word for cooked rice in Singhalese. These accounts suggest that Shani was not only aware of Singhalese (language and people) as "different" in her community but was also making a place for herself in a new environment.

DISCUSSION

Connectedness, which supported a sense of belonging, emerged as an important theme in both Shani and Thilu's experiences in resettling within Malgama. This connectedness to place and people was revealed in their experiences within their family, school, neighborhood, and community.

CONNECTEDNESS TO FAMILY

Both Thilu and Shani showed connectedness to their primary caregiver (the mother or mothering figure) and family, regardless of biological ties. Their primary caregiver met their developmental and welfare needs by providing material goods, protection, food, love and care, and opportunities for education, play, and participation. Connectedness to the household and the family was evident from their experiences of receiving care and protection from the other members in the family. Thilu and Shani drew or named their mother or other members of the family (either from their nuclear family or extended family) when asked which people they liked to be with.

CONNECTEDNESS TO SCHOOL

Thilu and Shani showed connectedness to their school in diverse ways. Both drew and mentioned the school that they were attending as one of the places where they liked to be. Thilu linked school to his future aspirations (to becoming a teacher), and Shani mentioned that she would continue to go to school when she is grown up. School also helped them develop friendships and was a place where they could play and be with people whom they liked; for example, their teachers and peers.

CONNECTEDNESS TO THE NEIGHBORHOOD AND COMMUNITY

Thilu and Shani showed connectedness with the neighborhood and community in Malgama in varied ways. Thilu saw his neighbors as playmates and as a supportive group with whom he could travel to school. In Shani's case, her closest neighbors were also her relatives. She perceived them as protectors; for example, they looked after her when her Malgama mother was away, and another family invited her to stay with them, play, and study with the older girls in that family. In addition, Shani's connectedness to the neighborhood was demonstrated through her sense of place and understanding of her environment. For example, she could explain where her previous home was in Malgama (which was much closer to the main road) and where she lived with her adopted family now. Furthermore, she was well aware of the environmental issue of wild elephants and how the animals affected their cultivation. She was also aware of how the adults took care of their livestock. These findings suggest that feelings of connectedness to the neighborhood and acceptance by the people around them were established in these young children's lives within a short period of their resettlement in Malgama.

CONNECTEDNESS LEADING TO A SENSE OF BELONGING

Both Thilu and Shani reported predictable and routine daily experiences, suggesting that they experienced perceived "normalcy." The children's accounts included waking up in the morning, having tea, bathing or washing, going to school, returning home, having some food, playing or having a nap, and studying and sleeping after eating. When asked to share an important incident that had happened recently, Shani mentioned visiting the nearby town with her aunt, which also showed her connectedness to other members in her extended family. The children also reported conditions that made life difficult—the presence of wild elephants and venomous snakes (environmental threats), for example. The researcher observed as well the temporary housing and limited infrastructure, such as unpaved roads, limited electricity, and running water, which had the potential to disrupt or create problems in daily life.

Despite these issues, children's experiences suggested that their connections to people and place (such as family, school, and neighborhood) contributed to their developing and strengthening connectedness and a sense of belonging and safety in a developing postconflict context. Neither child showed signs of extreme fear of environmental threats, for example. Both were confident that adults would protect them from those threats: Shani explained that the elephants came at night when children were asleep and the adults chased them away, and her uncle killed any snakes near their home. Thilu's interviews showed that he sought protection from his mother.

Thilu and Shani's experiences suggest that young children's right to development was recognized and being supported through the GoSL, NGOs, caregivers, and community, which provided opportunities for education, play, and participation. These children seemed to be experiencing a range of supports—a school with trained teachers and suitable facilities, free health and medical care, a child protection committee, a children's group program, and an ECCD model village project—that helped them feel valued in their community and supported at home. Thilu's active participation in the children's group activities made him feel part of the wider community. Both children mentioned studying/learning as one activity they would also do at home. They also mentioned playing in various places: at home, school, and in the neighborhood or with other children in the village. Play with their friends seemed to be a vital experience for these children; it was an important avenue for building peer relationships and thus a sense of connection in and out of school hours.

The ways that Thilu and Shani experienced connectedness to their social ecology in this study provide insight into the elements that supported a sense of belonging in young children in this postconflict village in Sri Lanka. These young children felt connected to their primary caregivers and the family: They felt included, accepted, and recognized with appropriate protection, affection, and care. This circle of care and support, although limited in numbers, seemed to develop through the friendships, social networks, and relationships that Shani and Thilu had with the children and adults in their neighborhood and community.

IMPLICATIONS FOR RESEARCHING YOUNG CHILDREN

Listening to children regarding matters that affect them is increasingly seen as important (Clark, 2005; Moss, Clark, & Kjorholt, 2005). However, research that shares the voices of young children in postconflict contexts is limited. This chapter has presented the voices of two disadvantaged young children from one postconflict context. The use of several data collection methods in the mosaic approach enabled young children to participate and contribute in ways that felt comfortable to them, suggesting that if the appropriate tools are used and flexibility is ensured, even young children from disaster- and conflict-affected contexts can meaningfully participate in research.

The findings of the current study strengthen already established claims of the importance of connectedness and a sense of belonging in children's lives, especially in disaster- and conflict-affected contexts. Young children's experiences of affection and care from a primary caregiver (or a parental figure) have been widely discussed ways of strengthening connectedness and well-being among young children in conflict-affected contexts (Feldman & Vengrober, 2011; Massad et al., 2009). Earlier research has found that the threats and stressors from societal and environmental risks can be mitigated among children when connectedness is promoted through community acceptance and perceptions of social support in postdisaster/conflict contexts (Betancourt, McBain, Newnham, & Brennan, 2013).

This study also provides new perspective of the lives of young children. The children's perceptions of those who are not in their own community as "others" (MacNaughton, 2001)—those who are not like them and thus less connected—suggested that young children, even with very limited opportunity for exposure to the outside world, are aware of the societal differences in their postconflict context. For example, Shani and Thilu, both of whom spoke Tamil, mentioned "Singhalese words," "Singhalese songs," and a "Singhalese person." Nevertheless, these children's remarks did not suggest feelings of discrimination or exclusion, but rather indicated an understanding of difference.

Several key policy and practice implications can be drawn from the voices of these two young children from a developing postconflict context in Sri Lanka. Young children may have particular ways to contribute to creating a favorable community in postconflict Sri Lanka that may be overlooked if their voices are not heard. This study showed that children were well supported by adult caregivers (despite economic, social, and infrastructural gaps in Malgama), who ensured they were well looked after and provided with education, health and protection, and opportunities for developing connectedness within and beyond their immediate families. Policy makers and those who are actively involved in the processes of postconflict resettlement should support the resettlement of families with young children by providing housing, employment, and other infrastructure that are essential for children's caregivers to feel safe, supported, and provided for. The families, with these supports, can then ensure the care, protection, and development of their young children, strengthening connectedness within families.

Most importantly, connectedness, if extended toward unknown "others" (in this case Singhalese community members), could contribute to building acceptance and respect for diversity. Positive connectedness appears vital for developing a sense of belonging and rebuilding peaceful and sustainable societies. Therefore, another important implication for policy and practice is that it is important to equally recognize the needs and rights of all affected young children (regardless of gender, family status, language, or resettlement status), their families, and communities and to extend equitable support and services in the return, resettlement, and rebuilding process to ensure that the whole community feels a sense of belonging. In the current context, we recommend the provision of language education (for example, in Singhalese and English) and of opportunities for young children to be positively exposed to other language and cultural groups. Furthermore, strengthening already established social networks at the village and provincial levels may sustain connectedness and a sense of belonging first among the families and diverse community groups and second among children in developing postconflict contexts.

CONCLUSIONS

This study used a socioecological lens to identify the ways young children experienced connectedness and a sense of belonging in families, educational institutions, neighborhoods, and communities in a postconflict context. The factors that supported young children's connectedness to their social ecology— appropriate affection, care, and protection from the family and social networks and provision of support and services for education, play, and participation— promoted connectedness and a sense of belonging in postconflict Sri Lanka. The young children's experiences presented in this chapter suggest that policy and practice should aim to promote positive connectedness because the feeling of being connected to family and communities may positively affect children's well-being.

Protection of the rights of all children and families who live in postconflict contexts should be the aim of all those who work in policy and practice roles. The ECCD policy in Sri Lanka calls for equal access to quality health, nutrition, and psychosocial stimulation for every child (Children's Secretariat, Ministry of Child Development and Women's Affairs Sri Lanka, 2004). It urges all responsible parties within the child's socioecological framework—caregivers, community members, services providers, and policy makers—to protect all children's equal right to develop connectedness and a sense of belonging within the family, community, and wider society. Thus, this chapter argues that all young children's right to access to care, protection, education, quality services, and participation needs to be heard, recognized, and equally respected. This is one of the keys to laying the foundation for sustainable and healthy communities in postconflict Sri Lanka, as well as in other postconflict societies.

References

Akesson, B. (2012). The concept and meaning of place for young children affected by political violence in the occupied Palestinian territories. *Spaces and Flows*, 2(2), 245–256.

Antonsich, M. (2010). Searching for a sense of belonging—An analytical framework. *Geography Compass*, 4(6), 644–659.

Betancourt, T. S., & Khan, K. T. (2008). The mental health of children affected by armed conflict: Protective processes and pathways to resilience. *International Review of Psychiatry*, 20(3), 317–328.

Betancourt, T. S., McBain, R., Newnham, E. A., & Brennan, R. T. (2013). Trajectories of internalizing problems in war-affected Sierra Leonean youth: Examining conflict and postconflict factors. *Child Development*, 84(2), 455–470.

Boyden, J. (2004). Anthropology under fire: Ethics, researchers and children in war. In J. Boyden & J. de Berry (Eds.), *Children and youth on the front line: Ethnography, armed conflict and displacement* (pp. 237–258). New York: Berghahn Books.

Braun, V., & Clarke, V. (2006). Using thematic analysis in psychology. *Qualitative Research in Psychology*, 3(2), 77–101.

Bronfenbrenner, U. (1979). *The ecology of human development: Experiments by nature and design*. Cambridge, MA: Harvard University Press.

Bronfenbrenner, U. (1994). Ecological models of human development. *International encyclopedia of education* (2nd ed., Vol. 3, pp. 37–43). London: Routledge.

Catani, C., Gewirtz, A. H., Wieling, E., Schauer, E., Elbert, T., & Neuner, F. (2010). Tsunami, war, and cumulative risk in the lives of Sri Lankan school children. *Child Development*, 81(4), 1176–1191.

Catani, C., Schauer, E., & Neuner, F. (2008). Beyond individual war trauma: Domestic violence against children in Afghanistan and Sri Lanka. *Journal of Marital and Family Therapy*, 34(2), 165–176.

Chambers, R. (1994). Participatory rural appraisal (PRA): Analysis of experience. *World Development*, 22(9), 1253–1268.

Chase, R., Doney, A., Sivayogan, S., Ariyaratne, V., Satkunanayagam, P., & Swaminathan, A. (1999). Mental health initiatives as peace initiatives in Sri Lankan schoolchildren affected by armed conflict. *Medicine, Conflict and Survival*, 15(4), 379–390.

Children's Secretariat, Ministry of Child Development and Women's Affairs. (2004). *Early childhood care and development policy [ECCD policy] in Sri Lanka*. Battaramulla, Sri Lanka: Author.

Clark, A. (2005). Ways of seeing: Using the mosaic approach to listen to young children's perspectives. In A. Clark, A. T. Kjorholt, & P. Moss (Eds.), *Beyond listening: Children's perspectives on early childhood services* (pp. 29–50). Bristol, UK: Policy Press.

Clark, A. (2011). Breaking methodological boundaries? Exploring visual, participatory methods with adults and young children. *European Early Childhood Education Research Journal*, 19(3), 321–330.

Clark, A., & Moss, P. (2001). *Listening to young children: The mosaic approach*. London: National Children's Bureau for the Joseph Rowntree Foundation.

Clark, A., & Statham, J. (2005). Listening to young children: Experts in their own lives. *Adoption & Fostering*, 29(1), 45–56.

Connolly, P., & Healy, J. (2004). *Children and the conflict in Northern Ireland: The experiences and perspectives of 3-11 year olds*. Retrieved from www.ofmdfmni.gov .uk/equalityresearch/childrenandconflict.pdf.

Department of Census and Statistics. (2008). *MDG indicators of Sri Lanka: A mid term review—2008*. Colombo, Sri Lanka: Author.

De Votta, N. (2004). *Blowback: Linguistic nationalism, institutional decay, and ethnic conflict in Sri Lanka*. Stanford, CA: Stanford University Press.

De Votta, N. (2010). From civil war to soft authoritarianism: Sri Lanka in comparative perspective. *Global Change, Peace & Security*, 22(3), 331–343. doi:10.1080/1478115 8.2010.510268.

Economic and Social Statistics of Sri Lanka (2013). Retrieved from www.cbsl.gov.lk /pics_n_docs/10_pub/_docs/statistics/other/econ_&_ss_2013_e.pdf.

Feldman, R., & Vengrober, A. (2011). Post-traumatic stress disorder in infants and young children exposed to war-related trauma. *Journal of the American Academy of Child & Adolescent Psychiatry*, 50(7), 645–658. doi:10.1016/j.jaac.2011. 03.001.

Fernando, C., & Ferrari, M. (2011). Spirituality and resilience in children of war in Sri Lanka. *Journal of Spirituality in Mental Health*, 13, 1–26.

Ganguly, R. (2004). Sri Lanka's ethnic conflict: At a crossroad between peace and war. *Third World Quarterly, 25*(5), 903–918.

Hart, J. (2004). Beyond struggle and aid: Children's identities in a Palestinian refugee camp in Jordan. In J. Boyden & J. de Berry (Eds.), *Children and youth on the frontline: Ethnography, armed conflict and displacement* (Vol. 14, pp. 167–186). New York: Berghahn Books.

Hart, J., Galappatti, A., Boyden, J., & Armstrong, M. (2007). Participatory tools for evaluating psychosocial work with children in areas of armed conflict: A pilot in eastern Sri Lanka. *Intervention, 5*(1), 41–60.

Hobfoll, S. E., Watson, P., Bell, C. C., Bryant, R. A., Brymer, M. J., Friedman, M. J., . . . Ursano, R. J. (2007). Five essential elements of immediate and mid-term mass trauma intervention: Empirical evidence. *Psychiatry, 70*(4), 283–315.

Kytta, M. (2004). The extent of children's independent mobility and the number of actualized affordances as criteria for child-friendly environments. *Journal of Environmental Psychology, 24*(2), 179–198.

Lerner, R. (1991). Changing organism-context relations as the basic process of development: A developmental contextual perspective. *Developmental Psychology, 27*(1), 27–32.

MacNaughton, G. (2001). Beyond "othering": Rethinking approaches to teaching young Anglo-Australian children about indigenous Australians. *Contemporary Issues in Early Childhood, 2*(1), 83–93.

Massad, S., Nieto, F. J., Palta, M., Smith, M., Clark, R., & Thabet, A. (2009). Mental health of children in Palestinian kindergartens: Resilience and vulnerability. *Child and Adolescent Mental Health, 14*(2), 89–96. doi:10.1111/j.1475-3588.2009.00528.x.

Mayall, B. (2002). *Towards a sociology for childhood: Thinking from children's lives.* Buckingham, UK: Open University Press.

McFarlane, C., Kaplan, I., & Lawrence, J. (2011). Psychosocial indicators of well-being for resettled refugee children and youth: Conceptual and developmental directions. *Child Indicators Research, 4*(4), 647–677.

Moss, P., Clark, A., & Kjorholt, A. T. (2005). Introduction. In A. Clark, A. T. Kjorholt, & P. Moss (Eds.), *Beyond listening: Children's perspectives on early childhood services* (pp. 1–16). Bristol, UK: Policy Press.

Neumann, R., & Fahmy, S. (2012). Analyzing the spell of war: A war/peace framing analysis of the 2009 visual coverage of the Sri Lankan civil war in western newswires. *Mass Communication and Society, 15*(2), 169–200.

Prout, A., & James, A. (1997). A new paradigm for the sociology of childhood? Provenance, promise and problems. In A. James & A. Prout (Eds.), *Constructing and reconstructing childhood: Contemporary issues in the sociological study of childhood* (pp. 7–33). London: Falmer Press.

Punch, S. (2002). Research with children: The same or different from research with adults? *Childhood, 9*(3), 321–341.

Robinson, S., & Truscott, J. (2014). *Belonging and connection of school students with disability.* Lismore, Australia: Centre for Children and Young People, Southern Cross University. Retrieved from www.cda.org.au/belonging-and-connection.

Samarasinghe, G. (2015). Psychosocial programming in post-war Sri Lanka. In B. Hamber & E. Gallagher (Eds.), *Psychosocial perspectives on peacebuilding* (pp. 117–145). Basel: Springer.

Saparamadu, C., & Lall, A. (2014). *Resettlement of conflict-induced IDPs in Northern Sri Lanka: Political economy of state policy and practice* (Working Paper 10). Retrieved from www.securelivelihoods.org/resources.

Somasundaram, D. (2004). Short and long-term effects on the victims of terror in Sri Lanka. *Journal of Aggression, Maltreatment & Trauma, 9*(1–2), 215–228. doi:10.1300/J146v09n01_26.

Somasundaram, D. (2007). Collective trauma in northern Sri Lanka: A qualitative psychosocial-ecological study. *International Journal of Mental Health Systems, 1*(5), 5–5. doi:10.1186/1752-4458-1-5.

Somasundaram, D., & Sivayokan, S. (2013). Rebuilding community resilience in a post-war context: Developing insight and recommendations—A qualitative study in northern Sri Lanka. *International Journal of Mental Health Systems, 7*(1), 1–25.

Sumsion, J., & Wong, S. (2011). Interrogating "a sense of belonging" in a sense of belonging, being and becoming: The early years learning framework for Australia. *Contemporary Issues in Early Childhood, 12*(1), 28–45.

United Nations. (1989). *United Nations Convention on the Rights of Children (UNCRC).* Retrieved from www.ohchr.org/EN/ProfessionalInterest/Pages/CRC.aspx.

Wessells, M., & Monteiro, C. (2008). Supporting young children in conflict and post-conflict situations: Child protection and psycho-social well-being in Angola. In M. Garcia, A. R. Pence, & J. L. Evans (Eds.), *Africa's future, Africa's challenge: Early childhood care and development in sub-Saharan Africa* (pp. 217–330). Washington, DC: World Bank.

Woodhead, M., & Brooker, L. (2008). A sense of belonging. In *Early childhood matters: Enhancing a sense of belonging in the early years* (Vol. 111, pp. 3–6). The Hague, Netherlands: Bernard van Leer Foundation.

Yin, R. K. (2009). *Case study research: Design and methods* (4th ed.). Thousand Oaks, CA: Sage.

Zeldin, S., & Topitzes, D. (2002). Neighborhood experiences, community connection, and positive beliefs about adolescents among urban adults and youth. *Journal of Community Psychology, 30*(6), 647–669.

3

CONTENDING WITH VIOLENCE AND DISCRIMINATION

Using a Social Exclusion Lens to Understand the Realities of Burmese Muslim Refugee Children in Thailand

Mollie Pepper

CHILDREN FACE ARMED CONFLICT IN ways that both reflect and differ markedly from the experiences of adults. Based on qualitative research conducted with Burmese Muslim refugees living in Thailand, this chapter examines the ways in which children are uniquely vulnerable within the refugee context and how gender, age, and ethnicity intersect to affect the circumstances and coping mechanisms of children in circumstances of armed conflict. This work builds on scholarship that argues that children are not distinct from adults in terms of their developmental capacities, as is often assumed, but rather have differential access to knowledge and power (Boyden, 2013; Boyden & James, 2014). Aligned with these perspectives, I argue that children's unique coping mechanisms are shaped by their experience of intensified challenges and limited access to resources and services. This work positions children as a distinct group capable of responding to their experiences and proposes that the recognition of children's agency is essential to understanding the needs of children affected by armed conflict.

This chapter presents the experiences of marginalization and social exclusion of Muslim children from Burma[1] living as refugees in Thailand. Children arriving in refugee camps in Thailand have already experienced violence and marginalization in Burma; they seek refuge in Thailand only to find that victimization and marginalization continue. Although refugee camps are typically thought of as spaces of safety for displaced people, conflict, violence, and discrimination can migrate along with populations and can further arise from relations with citizens of the countries to which they migrate. These sources of discrimination often make camps locations of social exclusion.

Children are not immune to exclusion and marginalization, but rather have specific experiences that result from larger trends of inequality and violence

(Korbin, 2003). However, as scholars have argued, children are not only uniquely vulnerable but also uniquely agentic (Boyden & Mann, 2005): They engage with circumstances of vulnerability and precariousness in ways that mitigate the challenges they face and contribute to survival strategies for themselves and their families (Crivello & Boyden, 2014).

Using qualitative data collected in a refugee camp and border town in Thailand, this chapter illustrates some of the conditions of marginalization and vulnerability that Muslim children face as members of the Muslim refugee community. Through the accounts of parents and migrant and refugee youth, it is possible to see both the ways that children's experiences are fundamentally tied to the larger context and how they take active roles in responding to their circumstances. Rather than focusing solely on children's vulnerabilities and denied capabilities, the chapter highlights examples of the ways they responded to conditions of exclusion and hardship by engaging in action and rational decision making.

The chapter opens with a discussion of social exclusion as a framework for considering the experiences of Burmese Muslim children living as refugees in Thailand—particularly as members of the Muslim minority in camps that are majority ethnic Karen. After a discussion of methods and limitations of the research, I turn to the data to illustrate the dynamics at work in the lives of children. The chapter brings together the perspectives of parents and youth while offering a broader discussion of the experiences of Muslim children as members of a group that is socially excluded from a variety of angles, including schools, livelihoods, and gender. Throughout, and in line with this edited collection's goal to challenge binaries, I highlight the capacities of children alongside their realities of vulnerability.

CONTEXT

FORCED MIGRATION FROM BURMA

Burma is located in Southeast Asia bordered by Thailand, Laos, China, India, and Bangladesh. It is a remarkably diverse country: The Burmese government recognizes 8 major ethnic groups that are divided into 135 distinct subgroups (Fink, 2009). Within this diverse country, however, the ethnic Burman majority makes up approximately two-thirds of the population and dominates the country's military and political system. Ethnic nationalist groups have struggled for autonomy and recognition by the government since the end of the colonial period. These struggles for recognition are widely recognized as a significant part of the country's nearly 70-year-long civil conflict, which has encompassed armed conflict, enforced conscription, and ethnic cleansing by the Burmese military (Callahan, 2005). Human rights violations and a repressive military government have resulted in widespread international sanctions against Burma, which have exacerbated the effects of the government's isolationist policies. The result is a highly repressive military regime that has severely limited economic and human development and facilitated protracted conflict between the state armed forces and nonstate armed groups.

Burma's protracted civil conflict has resulted in multiple waves of out-migration to neighboring countries, with Thailand receiving the largest numbers of migrants. Since the 1980s, refugee camps and associated humanitarian aid organizations have populated the Thailand side of the Thailand-Burma border. However, most of those originally from Burma and now living in Thailand do so as undocumented migrants without refugee status or humanitarian support. In addition, the vast majority of migrants and refugees from Burma living in Thailand have directly experienced violence and deprivation as a result of the conflict. Forced displacement, armed violence, raids on villages, and chronic resource deprivation are some of the many stressors and traumas experienced by those who have left Burma for Thailand. Children are not insulated from these situations and experience displacement, violence, and fear alongside adults. By the time children arrive in a refugee camp in Thailand, they have already been exposed to trauma and marginalization.

Currently, Burma is in a state of political transition and is making an effort to ending its prolonged civil conflict. In an unanticipated shift beginning in 2012, the government of Burma began moving toward "disciplined democracy," a process bringing significant changes for the people of Burma and marked by cautious optimism on the part of the country's citizens (Huang, 2013). As part of this process of democratization, the military has initiated ceasefire negotiations with several of the ethnic nonstate armed groups, which could indicate that it may become safe for refugees and other displaced persons to return to Burma.

SOCIAL EXCLUSION IN THAILAND

Thailand is not a signatory to the 1951 Convention Relating to the Status of Refugees or the 1967 Protocol Relating to the Status of Refugees and is thus not obligated to provide the rights outlined in these documents. The last refugee registration process in the refugee camps in Thailand was conducted by the United Nations High Commission for Refugees (UNHCR) in 2005, and there has been no formal registration or legal recognition of new refugees since then. The Thailand Burma Border Consortium (TBBC), the organization responsible for providing rations to the residents of the camps on the border, has been permitted to adjust its feeding numbers and ration allocation to include verified residents of the camp. However, the verification process can be quite slow, and newer refugees have reported waiting several months and up to 2 years in one case for partial rations. Both in and outside of the camps, a great number of people from Burma live in Thailand as forced migrants with precarious legal statuses and limited recognition (Saltsman, 2009).

The effects of this policy climate on children are multiple. The problems of legal recognition result in precarity for children and their families, who risk deportation without formal recognition as refugees. Further, unaccompanied children or children who are under the care of families other than their birth families have a harder time achieving legal recognition, especially when they lack birth certificates. Food security challenges that come from residing in a refugee camp with few economic opportunities while not receiving rations mean that children are often malnourished. Because aid delivery in camp takes place through the family unit, food insecurity is exacerbated for children who are unaccompanied or are not under the official guardianship of those who care for them. In practical terms, this means that an accompanied Muslim child cannot independently enter a camp and receive rations; it is only through the Muslim school, which is supported by the Muslim community, that he or she is able to receive food and clothing.

CONTINUING EXCLUSION: MUSLIM IN A KAREN REFUGEE CAMP

Muslims experience severe discrimination and violence within Burma, and their marginalized status in Burma serves as important background to contextualizing the Muslim Burmese experience in Thailand. Conditions of persecution and oppression have come to the forefront in media coverage, notably by the BBC (2012) and the *New York Times* (Ritu, 2012), as well as in the reports of human rights groups such as Human Rights Watch (2013) and Amnesty International (2012). It is essential to note that the Muslim population in Burma experiences repression and violence not only from the state but also from other ethnicities within Burma. Much of the media coverage that addresses violence against Muslims in Burma focuses on the Rohingya. Although this specific group of Muslims has experienced extreme violence and marginalization in Burma, non-Rohingya Muslims are the majority of Muslims living in Thailand and the states bordering Thailand. Violence committed against non-Rohingya Muslims has specifically been documented in Karen state, the origin of the majority of camp residents (Fink, 2009; Human Rights Watch, 2002; Mathiesen, 2014). Although it is difficult to say to what degree this discrimination carries over into the refugee context, there is a reality of marginalization and ethnic violence in the refugee camps, whether it is created or re-created there.

The majority of the camp population is ethnically Karen and religiously Christian, and Burmese Muslims experience exclusion within the displaced population as a minority ethnic and religious group. Exclusion is evident in the low levels of Muslim participation in camp leadership and as staff in camp-based programing and organizations, as well as in the lack of integration into the Karen majority community (TBBC, 2010). Karen domination persists despite significant demographic changes in the refugee camps along the Thailand-Burma border. For example, although the Muslim population made up approximately 13% of the total population in the camp where this research was conducted (TBBC, 2011), as of 2010 no Muslim had been elected as a camp committee member (Karen Refugee Committee, 2010).

SOCIAL EXCLUSION

Framing social inequality as dynamic, relational, and multidimensional, social exclusion theory offers a useful approach to conceptualize the ways that this population of Muslim children is made vulnerable. The case of Burmese Muslim refugees in Thailand provides an example of a community that experiences social exclusion on multiple levels: They are excluded in their country of origin, as displaced persons in Thailand, and as Muslims, a minority ethnic and religious group within the refugee community.

At its most fundamental level, social exclusion can be thought of as an alternative to or as synonymous with marginalization. In this case, the application of social exclusion theory is instructive because it provides a framework that presents the marginalization of the Muslim refugee population in Thailand as occurring in complex and layered ways. Social exclusion occurs at multiple levels and in both active and passive forms, a consequence of which is the denial of capabilities to access full human rights (Sen, 2000). Exclusion can take place through processes by which a group is administratively excluded by a state (Beland, 2007); processes of active exclusion of one group by another in which those who are excluded are at the mercy of the more privileged (Jordan, 1996); and processes of exclusion from fully participating in social life (Barnes et al., 2002; Room, 1995). A framework of social exclusion as arising from multiple locations allows for nuanced thinking in a context where marginalization is rooted in several factors, including national origin, ethnicity, age, and gender. In this case, social exclusion is predicated on multiple factors, including identity as foreign nationals, ethnic minority status within the migrant population, and religion. Age and gender further influence the ways that social exclusion is experienced. For children of the minority Muslim community in the refugee camps in Thailand, exclusion arises from their religious and ethnic identities and precarious legal status, and it manifests in particular ways because of their age—in the context of education, livelihoods, and other aspects of refugee life.

Earlier scholarship has argued that children are sensitive to social exclusion and are capable of recognizing it, which has serious implications for their psychosocial development (Abrams & Christian, 2007; Abrams & Killen, 2014; Bar-Tal, 1996; Eisenberger, Lieberman, & Williams, 2003). In addition, social exclusion has lasting effects on children who are excluded from fundamental human rights not only in material ways but also by creating cycles of stress (Killen, Rutland, & Ruck, 2001). Much research has focused on the reduced capabilities of children in the context of social exclusion, but work that characterizes children as actors who take an active approach to dealing with exclusion is lacking (Biggeri, Ballet, & Comim, 2011). This chapter seeks to address this gap by illustrating both the social exclusion of Burmese Muslim children and the ways they actively engage to manage it. Acknowledging the reality that children experience social exclusion in ways similar to adults, but with additional challenges and limitations, this chapter seeks to bring attention to how these children experience social exclusion and, just as importantly, how they respond.

METHODS

This study presented in this chapter was based on qualitative data collected during two different periods of fieldwork in Thailand. The first was conducted in 2011 in the Muslim community of a Burmese refugee camp in Thailand.

The original purpose of this research was to learn about the ways that social exclusion of minority Muslims manifested as gendered in economic life. Consequently, this research was primarily conducted with adults, including many parents, guardians, teachers, and other caregivers. However, in the process of analysis, a great deal of information about children emerged, and it became clear that children have experiences that differ from those of adults. To learn more about those differences, a second period of fieldwork focused on migrant and refugee youth from Burma living in Thailand was planned. It took place in an urban area in Thailand near the border with Burma in 2015 and focused on the narratives of youth from Burma who were living in Thailand. These narratives included descriptions of their experiences as children living as refugees in Thailand, and it is this aspect of their accounts that is presented in this chapter, which also presents interviews with parents and guardians.

The research design for the fieldwork conducted in 2011 was developed in collaboration with an international aid organization based in the United States and working in the camp. The organization is well established and respected and has been running programming in refugee camps in Thailand for nearly 30 years, focusing its efforts on protection and legal services. The Institutional Review Board at my home institution and the aid organization with which I collaborated approved the research. It was also approved by camp leadership before access to the camp population was granted. In 2015, the research was developed independently, not in partnership with any organization, and Tufts University's Institutional Review Board approved the research.

In 2011, 42 qualitative interviews were conducted in one of the largest refugee camps for Burmese refugees in Thailand, which is located in a rural area of Thailand near the border with Burma. The camp is administered by UNHCR and a variety of international aid organizations that share responsibility for infrastructure, resource provision, and camp management. The Thai military guards the camp and also participates in its management. Programs in the camp provide health care, education, vocational training, and protection services to residents. Children are typically in school until the age of 12 or 13, with limited options for continuing education. An orphanage in the camp is run by a community-based women's organization, and a youth organization has representatives on the camp leadership committee. Several organizations, including Right to Play, World Education, and the Border Consortium, provide child-centered programming.

The camp has a Karen ethnic majority, with resident minorities of other ethnic groups from Burma, including the Mon, Shan, and Karenni. The

TABLE 3.1 Research Participants (2011)

CHARACTERISTIC	VALUE
Participants	42
Age range (years)	18–67
Mean age (years)	37
Gender	
Female	26
Male	16
Occupation	
School staff	3
Shopkeepers	7
Camp leadership	2
Day laborers	30
Parents	33

inclusion criteria limited participation to individuals who self-identified as Muslim, and every respondent identified him- or herself as Muslim both in terms of ethnicity and religion. Interview participants reflected a broad cross-section of the Muslim community and included shop owners, parents, school staff, camp leadership, and members of women's community-based organizations. Participants were recruited using convenience sampling from the Muslim residential sections of the refugee camp. Table 3.1 presents information about the research participants in the 2011 fieldwork.

In 2015, 53 qualitative interviews were conducted with migrant and refugee youth from Burma living in Thailand in an urban area near the border. A large number of people from Burma do not live in the refugee camps and instead seek education, work, and other opportunities in the cities and villages surrounding the refugee camps. In this urban area, several organizations and initiatives provide services to these refugees. Interviewees were recruited as a purposive sample through visits to migrant youth organizations and schools. Access was granted by school and organization leaders, participation was voluntary, and informed consent was obtained in all cases. Interviews were recorded with the informed consent of participants. The interviews were then transcribed and the translation checked by a different translator. The corrected and transcribed interviews were then entered into a qualitative data analysis software

TABLE 3.2 Research Participants (2015)

CHARACTERISTIC	VALUE
Muslim participants	7
Age range (years)	18–26
Mean age (years)	22
Gender	
Female	5
Male	2
Occupation	
Student	6
Teacher in training	1

program, where they were systematically coded by theme for analysis. Confidentiality was strictly maintained, and names and locations were excluded or altered to ensure anonymity.

In this period of fieldwork, the inclusion criteria did not limit the sample to Muslims. However, seven Muslim youth were interviewed for the study, and their voices are emphasized in this chapter. Table 3.2 presents demographic information about these seven Muslim young people.

LIMITATIONS OF THE RESEARCH

The first round of field research was conducted in a refugee camp in Thailand and focused exclusively on the Muslim community. The second period of fieldwork was informed by the first and was conducted outside of the refugee camps with migrant youth. There was a significant time gap between the two rounds, which may have implications for both data collection and the findings presented here. Circumstances, opportunities, and constraints for participants may have changed, and other factors cannot be controlled for within the context of this analysis. To mitigate this problem, findings were discussed with community members to ensure that they continued to be relevant.

To protect participants, identifying information was not collected and participants were guaranteed confidentiality, which made follow-up interviews impossible. To mitigate this disadvantage in the process of data analysis, I corroborated the validity of the findings by confirming that information was obtained from a minimum of three sources. This process was facilitated by qualitative data management software. Data interpretations and findings were also checked with members of the community.

I conducted interviews in collaboration with interpreters, who were vetted by local aid organizations with which I was affiliated. They were thoroughly briefed on the purposes of the research, their role as translator, and the confidentiality and ethical issues involved in the research, after which they signed confidentiality agreements. Translation services were necessary because of the linguistic diversity of people from Burma.

Given language barriers, the majority of these interviews would have been impossible without assistance, but there were both benefits and disadvantages to the use of translators. Translators from the same ethnic background and with more familiarity with the local context were able to generate a sense of ease with participants that I, as a white foreign researcher, would have been unable to create myself. Further, I ascribe to Fadiman's (1997) view of interpreters as powerful "cultural brokers" who are able not only to offer translation but also to explain nuance and context. However, there are several disadvantages to using interpreters. First, there is always the risk that the translation will not be accurate or will be colored by the translator's biases and expectations. Second, the use of translators may raise questions concerning confidentiality, thereby reducing the comfort level of the participant. To some extent, I was able to check translations using my own language knowledge, and interpreters were carefully selected and trained to minimize these risks. In addition, I shared the major findings with participants who wished to be contacted and with others from and familiar with the area to check the plausibility and accuracy of analysis.

FINDINGS

The data indicate that exclusion among Burmese Muslim refugee children in Thailand manifests in a variety of ways. Muslims are still not proportionately included in leadership and political processes in camp, and they are hired at lower rates for jobs with relief organizations. In addition, their exclusion results in the Muslim population feeling that they do not have access to resources. When asked about NGO-provided health services offered in camp, one young Muslim woman revealed that she could go to the shops and buy medicine, but she could not go to the NGO-run camp health center, explaining, "I am

Muslim; that is a Karen hospital, I think I have no chance there." Muslim children experience these circumstances of exclusion based on their ethnic and religious identity, while contending with the challenges of greater food insecurity, discrimination, vulnerability to violence, and their precarious legal and community status.

Marginalization is not limited to exclusion from representation and resources in camp; it also manifests in violence, which can be directed at children. Two violent incidents occurred in camp during the course of the research: the stoning of a mosque and the burning of a Muslim-owned shop. Visiting the family that owned the burned shop, we sat in the part of their storefront that had been reconstructed and contained the goods that had been salvaged. With the smell of wet ashes around us, the father of this family explained that they were sad, but not surprised: "It happens all the time here. We never know. Sometimes it is at the mosque, sometimes it is stealing; sometimes we are beaten in the street." Whether this experience is exceptional or the norm, particular to the Muslim population or not, Muslim identity may serve as an added risk factor for young people in camp.

Children were widely reported as targeted for violence around camp related to their ethnic and religious identity. Harassment around camp was reported as a problem for girls who sold small items throughout the camp and for those who walked to school. One mother responded to the question of whether her children attend school by saying,

> We come from Burma, so we are already afraid. When we came, I don't want to send my daughter to school because it is not close to the house and the youth in the camp make a problem for my daughter. They see her skin is Muslim and her dress is Muslim and they make a problem.

Two incidents of boys being physically assaulted in the streets were reported during the course of this fieldwork. Both attacks were committed against Muslim adolescents as they were walking home from Friday prayers at the mosque. The assailants were groups of young men from other sections of camp, who uttered ethnic slurs during the attacks, calling one of the boys a "black pig." "Black" is sometimes used to refer to Muslims because their skin tends to be darker than that of ethnic Karen or Burmese, and this slur is interpreted as an attack on ethnic identity.

In another reported incident, students at the Muslim school were harassed by Karen youths for carrying handouts of text from the Q'uran. The youth threatened the Muslim students, specifically targeting them for speaking Burmese rather than Karen and for carrying a religious text other than the Christian Bible. One of the harassed boys said,

> They said that this was not a Burmese camp, this is a place for Karen and if we are not for them then we are their enemies. They warned us that the only way to speak in camp is to speak Karen, and the only religion is Christianity.

In this case, Muslim youth were explicitly attacked for displaying an identity other than Karen through language and religious affiliation; the incident made clear that Karen is the only acceptable language and cultural expression permitted.

When asked how they cope with violence and harassment in camp, youth cited strategies of restricting their movement to familiar parts of camp and avoiding speaking Burmese and languages other than Karen outside of the house. Parents also mentioned these strategies used by their children. When asked how she managed harassment in camp, one mother turned to her teenage son who was cooking lunch in the back of the house and asked him to tell me which way he went to school. He replied that he first went to the neighbor's house to meet up with other Muslim children who would be walking to school so that they could go together. Furthermore, he explained that they chose their route to avoid problem areas:

> We go around the hill that way, so that we don't walk through the festival grounds. It is too open there and sometimes maybe it causes a problem to be seen there. It is the Karen part of camp. Better for us to stay in the Muslim camp on our way to school.

Children manage their risks and vulnerability by traveling in groups through parts of camp they perceive as hostile or by avoiding them as much as possible by selecting alternative routes. Although these strategies do not eliminate experiences of harassment and violence, they reflect active engagement on the part of children to mitigate risks.

SCHOOLS AS SITES OF EXCLUSION

The impact of the exclusion of the Muslim community on children might be most evident in the context of camp schools. This finding is consistent with scholarship that has found that access to education depends on various factors: exclusion based on individual characteristics such as gender, ethnicity, and language; and refugee governance and policies at multiple levels (Dryden-Peterson, 2011). Refugee camps house schools to educate children from the refugee population in keeping with UNHCR's stated goal to "ensure the right to education for all people of concern to UNHCR by achieving universal primary education . . . with special focus on girls, urban, and protracted situations" (UNHCR, 2009, p. 4). The majority of schools in refugee camps in Thailand are affiliated with NGOs and run through the Karen Camp Committee.

Karen is the default language in schools, which results in the exclusion of non-Karen-speaking children from the camp educational system in higher grades where the language barrier becomes increasingly challenging. One mother explained,

> When my daughters were small, it was ok. They could understand enough. But we don't talk like Karen people at home, so now they are older and they cannot understand at school. For this reason, we cannot send.

Her explanation was echoed by three of the interviewed youth who had spent time in camp schools. One said,

> When I was small, it was ok because it wasn't difficult. When I was older I could not understand the teacher and could not do the lessons because Karen language is not my language.

In response to Karen-language schooling in the camp, the Muslim community has established a Muslim school that uses Burmese as the primary language and that provides religious education in addition to the standard curriculum. This school was supported by the Muslim community through donations and provided education for children of the community. In accordance with Islamic custom of providing sex-segregated schooling, girls ended up being excluded from the school because there was insufficient space to create separate learning areas. Although many people, including the headmaster of the Muslim school, expressed the idea that there should be a school established for the education of Muslim girls, no such institution existed.

School-related costs pose a real burden to families, because livelihood strategies are already restricted and income-generating activities are extremely limited. For Muslim children in particular, if there is little anticipated benefit from education because of the primary use of the Karen language in the classrooms, it is difficult to justify the costs of school attendance, along with the loss of income from children's reduced participation in family economic strategies. Several families mentioned that their children were not in school because they needed to work to help support the family. The purchase of school-appropriate clothing and shoes is an additional cost to families. Families reported that they pay weekly for their children to attend school: In one camp families were paying 10 THB ($0.31 USD) per week for each child to attend school. To put this fee in context, the households that participated in this research reported incomes ranging from 0–3000 THB per month, with most making 200–1,000 THB ($6.17–$30.85 USD) each month. Tuition for one child costs approximately 40 THB per month, plus the additional expenses of school supplies, clothing, and snacks. These expenses constituted a significant financial barrier. Eighteen of the 44 households with children reported that they were unable to afford school costs. One respondent explained,

> Even though we get support from others, but there is nothing for education, so we have money problems. . . . So if we don't have money, that is a big problem for our children to be educated. . . . The rich can send, but the poor cannot.

Stratification within the camp community is thus reflected in the schools where language, cultural, and economic barriers faced by the Muslim community constitute obstacles to participation for their children.

In addition to receiving an education, children who participate in the camp school system are at a significant advantage. The Thailand Burma Border Consortium (TBBC), which provides rations to the camps along the border, manages a nursery school feeding program that provides more than 8,000 children in the nine camps with lunch (TBBC, 2011). School also serves as a form of child care, which allows parents more flexibility in their daily schedules to earn money and pursue their own skill development or education in camp-based programs. Education, too, provides the foundational skills needed for employment later in life and to pursue education opportunities beyond those available in camp.

GIRLS

Gender is another important site of exclusion within the Muslim community. One of the most glaring challenges facing young girls in camp is obtaining access to education. In addition to the challenges for Muslim children discussed earlier, and the global pattern of reduced access to education for girls (Dryden-Peterson, 2011), there are particular barriers for Muslim girls. This exclusion is a larger problem than it may initially appear, with repercussions that extend beyond access to education. Education in and of itself is, of course, important, but children who attend schools gain additional benefits, including meals, a sense of community, and, for some children, housing and guardianship. Excluding girls from schools thus deprives them of access not only to education but also to resources that enhance their well-being.

Within the Muslim community, girls are excluded from school on the basis of their gender. One respondent, a mother of three girls, said,

> When you are educated, you know your culture and girls can improve their lives and language skills and literacy so they can do anything. There is already opportunity for boys, but not for girls.

When pressed on the issue of the inclusion of girls, the Muslim school headmaster exclaimed in an exasperated tone, "We know that to educate girls is very important. We know Aung San Suu Kyi, but at this time we cannot provide for them and the boys must be cared for."[2] Despite the acknowledgment that girls can benefit from education and that there are problems that accompany their exclusion from schooling, there is a clear tendency to favor education for boys.

Unable to seek education, with limited work opportunities, and being still quite young, girls are left with no clear role in their homes or communities. This results in a characterization of them as "trouble." One camp leadership official referred to them as "bad girls," expressing the opinion that their lack of a structured role in the community left them idle and prone to misbehaving. However, girls are not so much a source of trouble as they are at risk for being targets of violence. An assessment conducted by the International Rescue Committee (IRC) in collaboration with community-based organizations found that forced and early marriage is a significant issue for adolescent girls who are not in school; the report named these other risks as well: "sexual exploitation, trafficking, rape by family members and men outside the family, and rape sanctioned by parents" (2011, p. 47).

Though found to be prevalent in earlier research conducted in the community that focused on gender-based and sexual violence, parent-sanctioned rape was mentioned by only one participant in this research, a mother of three small children, who told the story of a neighbor's family:

> The mother and father have a lot of debt. Maybe he gambles a little or some drinking. But then they have no money and they have to find the money. So they say, "Ok, you can come to our daughter" and the man comes and rapes her so her mother and father do not have to pay anymore. Sometimes then the girl must marry the man, but sometimes he already has a wife or does not want her. Then she is shamed and cannot marry in our culture.

The actual frequency of parent-sanctioned rape in camp or the Muslim community is unknown. However, this report and the camp-based assessment from the IRC identify it as a problem for female adolescents that is deeply entwined with larger issues of social exclusion, lack of livelihood opportunities, and the vulnerability of girls.

Although counterintuitive, participants cited early marriage as a way that youth exercise agency when other opportunities of schooling and work are not available. Young people often elope, and this action—though often conflated with forced marriage and considered by aid organizations to be a serious obstacle to the protection of women and girls—should be assessed separately. Because marriage allows young people to step into a different role in the community, eloping is a way that young people attempt to cope with their circumstances. It, however, comes with drawbacks and limitations. One respondent explained,

> They elope! They have no education and no money and cannot look after themselves but they decide to marry because there is nothing else to do. But then, the family still has to take care of them.

Early marriage and elopement are attempts by youth in camp, albeit possibly failed ones, to actively ensure their survival under extremely challenging circumstances.

LIVELIHOODS

Earlier research has connected social exclusion to livelihood limitations in refugee communities, and this is certainly the case for Muslims from Burma living as refugees in Thailand (De Haan & Zoomers, 2005; Dick, 2002). Livelihood strategies reflect the Muslims' exclusion from camp-based employment and the need to earn money in the absence of sufficient rations (Jacobsen, 2005). Children contribute to their families' livelihood strategies as active participants in a variety of income-generation activities (Panter-Brick & Smith, 2000). These activities are as diverse as managing family livestock, working as vendors for family household businesses, and creating their own value-added products, such as rolled betel nuts or homemade snacks, for sale throughout camp.

Many people leave camp during the day to engage in various income-generating activities and return at night. Every household interviewed in the course of fieldwork reported that at least one of its members leaves camp without official permission to fish, forage, or work as day laborers. Often, these adults take children with them. One mother reported, "Everyone who is in good health can go to find the [bamboo] shoots, children after maybe 10 years old, and women too." The goods they collect are used for both household consumption and for sale within the camp.

Adults also regularly leave camp to engage in wage labor for days or weeks at a time (Jacobsen, 2005). Every household interviewed reported that at least one member leaves camp every month to seek work. Sometimes, when the adults in a household exit the camp for work, they leave children alone to manage for themselves for extended periods, without guardianship. Children left temporarily without adult supervision had various ways of managing their situations. Often, older children took over care of the younger ones and managed to maintain the household until their guardians returned, cooking meals and maintaining livestock or small vending operations on their own. Other methods of coping included begging, reaching out to extended family members for help while their parents were gone, or temporarily entering the Muslim school's boarding system. This final option, however, is limited to boys because girls do not yet have a place within the Muslim religious school. Thus children participate actively in the livelihood strategies of their households and manage their own needs independently when necessary.

UNACCOMPANIED CHILDREN

A large number of youths interviewed for this project reported coming to Thailand from Burma as unaccompanied children. The two reasons cited for their migration were the inability of their parents to financially support them and the greater educational opportunities afforded to migrant children in Thailand. Sometimes, they were sent with other family members or were sent to stay with family who had already migrated to Thailand. The majority of youth respondents, however, traveled without a guardian and entered the migrant schools or refugee camp boarding houses independently. The youngest was 9 years old when he left his family to come to Thailand: "My parents . . . couldn't take care of me. I have seven brothers and sisters, there was no school in my village; I knew that if I wanted anything for myself I had to leave." On arrival, he entered a migrant boarding school where he received basic support and education. The youths who chose to leave their homes and families and travel to Thailand to receive an education showed a remarkable degree of independence.

Three of the seven Muslim youths who participated in these interviews traveled independently to Thailand without parents or guardians. They each enrolled in a Muslim school in town or in a refugee camp, with none spending more than a few weeks in a non-Muslim school or boarding house. One explained his choice to move on to the Muslim school in camp after first arriving in a boarding school in Thailand as follows:

> That place was not for me. I was not to go to pray, I did not have good food (halal) to eat, and they treated me badly. I knew that I could stay and try to not be Muslim, and I knew they would treat me wrongly, or I could go to the Muslims in camp. So I went to camp.

Of the risks that children from Burma face, living as an unaccompanied minor poses the most dangerous ones. They experience marginalization unless they are able to gain access to the few places where their Muslim identity does not impede their opportunity to receive basic support and education.

CONCLUSIONS

This chapter emerged from my observation of the precocity of children and the initiative they take in their own lives to manage conditions of violence, food insecurity, and disadvantage within the camp community. It presents children's experiences of social exclusion and marginalization based on their ethnicity, age, gender, and refugee (non)status. The children living in the refugee camps arrive there already having experienced victimization and trauma in Burma; they seek safety in Thailand's refugee camps only to find that they become ongoing sites of marginalization and violence. In this context of on-going and multiple sites of exclusion and vulnerability, the chapter illustrates the ways in which children actively attempt to mitigate both their vulnerability and the challenges posed by exclusion.

Engaging the lens of social exclusion facilitates examination of individual experiences in relation to larger structural-social dynamics in a nuanced way, thereby enabling an understanding of multiple layers of exclusion. For this analysis, using the lens of social exclusion allows for exploration of the ways that age, race, gender, religion, displacement and other vectors of difference and oppression can lead to marginalization on the group level, which results in experiences of victimization and violence for individuals and informs the coping mechanisms that emerge in response.

To sufficiently address the unique needs of conflict-affected children in any context, the particularities of their experiences must be taken into account. Children are subject to the conditions of vulnerability and violence that come with conflict and discrimination, and they experience unique consequences as a function of their age and other identities. As noted by Chaudhry (see chapter 1), treating children solely as victims or serving them only through the family unit is insufficient. It is essential that children be understood as having agency and as capable of decision making and active participation in their own lives, their families, and their communities. However, this recognition must also take into account context-specific power differentials that limit the extent to which they are able to exercise agency and to mitigate their risks and vulnerabilities. It is also necessary to note that agentic action on the part of children is often part of an effort to survive.

Policy makers and practitioners, then, should recognize children's strategies and limitations and work to support them in their efforts to navigate their lives. Age is an important and underrecognized vector of oppression. Children and youth require particular attention and consideration in the development of aid delivery to ensure that they are not further marginalized by the systems and structures that are intended to protect and serve them. Recognizing children as actors who are able to make choices, assess risks, and take action is key to effective programming for children and for families. It is essential to treat children as individuals who are both part of and apart from families and to acknowledge that effective aid distribution and programming in humanitarian settings should not exclusively take the family as its target unit.

More research on children in situations of displacement as members of disadvantaged minority groups is needed. Minority status within displaced populations is already an understudied aspect of displacement, but as this chapter demonstrates, it is of particular importance for children and youth. Awareness of the age, racial, ethnic, gender, and other dimensions of exclusion and discrimination within spaces such as refugee camps is essential to sensitive intervention and policy making. Though such spaces are typically thought of as sites of safety and refuge, they can become spaces of continuing marginalization and victimization.

Future research should seek to better understand how various programmatic approaches work to mitigate the effects of social exclusion for children living as refugees. In particular, education, health, and ration distribution should be examined to determine what works and what does not for meeting the needs of children who are not members of the dominant group and of children who may not be consistently attached to a family unit. Considering children as active agents shifts the way that programming might be developed to effectively protect them both as members of families and as individuals. Recognition of children's capacity to mitigate challenging situations allows those working with displaced groups to consider how families and communities can leverage their skills and initiative. Finally, there continues to be a lack of understanding of the long-term outcomes for children who grow up in contexts of social exclusion and displacement. Better understanding of the long-term implications of such conditions in childhood will be informative for practice and policy.

Notes

1. "Muslim" is not typically used as a descriptor of ethnicity. Although Muslims from Burma have a variety of origins, in the context of the Thailand-Burma border area it is appropriate to consider Muslims as a group; that is because individuals tend to self-identify as ethnically Muslim and are recognized by the camp community as a distinct ethnic group, and it is standard practice on the border to consider the Muslim population as an ethnic group. Although this is not without its problematic aspects, it is the model I have adopted. Participants in this research referred to their country of origin as Burma. "Burmese" should be understood as referring to all people from Burma, regardless of ethnic identity.

2. Aung San Suu Kyi is the key democratic opposition leader in Burma. After more than 15 years under house arrest following her landslide electoral victory in 1990, she was elected to parliament in 2012. She was educated at Oxford and as a result is often held up as an example of progressive attitudes toward women in Burma.

References

Abrams, D., & Christian, J. N. (2007). A relational analysis of social exclusion. In D. Abrams, J. N. Christian, & D. Gordon (Eds.), *Multidisciplinary handbook of social exclusion research* (pp. 211–232). Chichester, UK: Wiley-Blackwell.

Abrams, D., & Killen, M. (2014). Social exclusion of children: Developmental origins of prejudice. *Journal of Social Issues, 70*(1), 1–11.

Amnesty International. (2012). *Myanmar: Abuses against Muslims erode human rights progress*. New York: Author.

Barnes, M., Heady, C., Middleton, S., Millar, J., Papadopoulos, F., Room, G., & Tsakloglou, P. (2002). *Poverty and social exclusion in Europe*. London: Edward Elgar.

Bar-Tal, D. (1996). Development of social categories and stereotypes in early childhood: The case of "the Arab" concept formation, stereotype and attitudes by Jewish children in Israel. *International Journal of Intercultural Relations, 20*(3), 341–370.

Béland, D. (2007). The social exclusion discourse: Ideas and policy change. *Policy & Politics, 35*(1), 123–139.

Biggeri, M., Ballet, J., & Comim, F. (2011). *Children and the capability approach*. New York: Palgrave Macmillan.

Boyden, J. (2013). "We're not going to suffer like this in the mud": Educational aspirations, social mobility and independent child migration among populations living in poverty. *Compare: A Journal of Comparative and International Education, 43*(5), 580–600.

Boyden, J., & James, Z. (2014). Schooling, childhood poverty and international development: Choices and challenges in a longitudinal study. *Oxford Review of Education, 40*(1), 10–29.

Boyden, J., & Mann, G. (2005). Children's risk, resilience, and coping in extreme situations. In M. Ungar (Ed.), *Handbook for working with children and youth: Pathways to resilience across cultures and contexts* (pp. 3–27). Thousand Oaks, CA: Sage.

British Broadcasting Corporation (BBC). (2012, July 20). *Muslims in Burma's Rakhine state abused*. London: BBC World News.

Callahan, M. (2005). *Making enemies: War and state building in Burma*. Ithaca, NY: Cornell University Press.

Crivello, G., & Boyden, J. (2014). On childhood and risk: An exploration of children's everyday experiences in rural Peru. *Children & Society, 28*(5), 380–391.

De Haan, L., & Zoomers, A. (2005). Exploring the frontier of livelihoods research. *Development & Change, 36*(1), 27–47.

Dick, S. (2002). *Liberians in Ghana: Living without humanitarian assistance* (New Issues in Refugee Research 57, pp. 28–29). Geneva: United Nations High Commission for Refugees (UNHCR).

Dryden-Peterson, S. (2011). *Refugee education: A global review.* Geneva: UNHCR Policy Development and Evaluation Service.

Eisenberger, N. I., Lieberman, M. D., & Williams, K. D. (2003). Does rejection hurt? An fMRI study of social exclusion. *Science, 302*(5643), 290–292. doi:10.1126/science.1089134.

Fadiman, A. (1997). *The spirit catches you and you fall down: A Hmong child, her American doctors, and the collision of two cultures.* New York: Noonday Press.

Fink, C. (2009). *Living silence in Burma: Surviving under military rule* (2nd ed.). New York: Zed Books.

Huang, R. L. (2013). Re-thinking Myanmar's political regime: Military rule in Myanmar and implications for current reforms. *Contemporary Politics, 19*(3), 247–261.

Human Rights Watch. (2002). *Crackdown on Burmese Muslims* (Briefing Paper). New York: Author.

Human Rights Watch. (2013). *"All you can do is pray": Crimes against humanity and ethnic cleansing of Rohingya Muslims in Burma's Arakan state.* New York: Author.

International Rescue Committee. (2011). *Gender-based violence prevalence, causes, solutions in refugee camps in Thailand.* New York: Author.

Jacobsen, K. (2005). *The economic life of refugees.* Bloomfield, CT: Kumarian Press.

Jordan, B. (1996). *A theory of poverty and social exclusion.* New York: Wiley.

Karen Refugee Committee. (2010, February). *Karen refugee committee newsletter and monthly report.* Thailand: Author.

Killen, M., Rutland, A., & Ruck, M. D. (2011). Promoting equity, tolerance, and justice in childhood. *SRCD Social Policy Report, 25*(4), 1–25.

Korbin, J. (2003). Children, childhood, and violence. *Annual Review of Anthropology, 32*, 431–446.

Mathiesen, D. S. (2014). *What Burma's census missed* (Human Rights Watch Dispatches). New York: Human Rights Watch.

Panter-Brick, C., & Smith, M. (2000). *Abandoned children.* Cambridge: Cambridge University Press.

Ritu, M. S. (2012, July 12). Ethnic cleansing in Myanmar. *New York Times.*

Room, G. (1995). *Beyond the threshold: The measurement and analysis of social exclusion.* Bristol, UK: Policy Press.

Saltsman, A. P. (2009). *Contested rights: Subjugation and struggle among Burmese forced migrants in exile* (Unpublished master's thesis). Boston College, Boston.

Sen, A. K. (2000). *Social exclusion: Concept, application, and scrutiny* (Report No. 1). Manila: Office of Environment and Social Development, Asian Development Bank.

Thailand Burma Border Consortium (TBBC). (2010). *Three sides to every story: A profile of Muslim communities in the refugee camps on the Thailand Burma border.* Mae Sot: Author.

Thailand Burma Border Consortium (TBBC). (2011). *Population figures.* Retrieved from www.tbbc.org

United Nations High Commissioner for Refugees. (2009). *Education strategy: 2010–2012.* Geneva: Author.

4

A SOCIAL CONSTRUCTIONIST APPROACH TO UNDERSTANDING THE EXPERIENCES OF GIRLS AFFECTED BY ARMED CONFLICT IN COLOMBIA

Maria Camila Ospina-Alvarado, Sara Victoria Alvarado,
Jaime Alberto Carmona, and Hector Fabio Ospina

IN 2014, A UNICEF REPORT indicated that more than 300,000 boys and girls had been recruited as soldiers for official and unofficial armed groups throughout the world (UNHCR, 2014). In Colombia, the number of child soldiers increased from 14,000 in 2002 (Coalición española para acabar con la utilización de niños soldado, 2004) to 18,000 in 2012 (Springer, 2012). It thus ranks alongside Sierra Leone and the Democratic Republic of the Congo as having the largest number of boys and girls recruited as soldiers (Carmona, Moreno, & Tobón, 2012). In this chapter, we use the UNICEF (1997) definition of a child soldier as "any person under 18 years of age who is part of any kind of regular or irregular armed force or armed group in any capacity, including but not limited to cooks, porters, messengers, and anyone accompanying such groups, other than family members." This definition is valid in the Colombian context because Colombian law defines children as those under the age of 18.

Children in the armed conflict in Colombia have been deeply affected by the moral degradation, despair, and state of anomie that have set in as a consequence of the presence of Colombian armed groups. In many cases, children are forced to fight in the ranks of the nonstate armed groups. Others are enslaved or forced to work to obtain illegal sources of income. Springer (2012, p. 129) claims that in Colombia "no less than 100,000 are linked to sectors of the illegal economy directly controlled by illegal armed groups and criminal organizations."

Official statistics reveal the extent of the harms done to children. Since 1985, more than 5 million children have been displaced in Colombia, "of which 40% are minors" (UNICEF, 2013, p. 9). A government agency found that more than 2.5 million children—16% of those younger than 18—have been injured by landmines, lost one or both of their parents due to the conflict, or had a family member who became seriously injured or went missing (DANE, 2014). In 2015, the Colombian family welfare institute (Instituto Colombiano de Bienestar Familiar, ICBF) reported that between 1999 and January 2015, it had served 5,708 former child soldiers from guerrilla, paramilitary, and criminal groups (*Verdad Abierta* 2015). These figures, however, are likely to underreport the numbers of affected children.

In this chapter, we adopt a social constructionist approach (Gergen, 2007, 2009) to examine the experiences of female children who have lived in contexts of armed conflict in Colombia and have engaged in combat. Among children linked to illegal armed groups in Colombia in the second decade of the present century, one third—between four and five thousand children—were girls (Carmona, 2013; Coalición Contra la Vinculación de Niños, Niñas y Jóvenes al Conflicto Armado en Colombia, 2015; Springer, 2012). In early 2016, even as the Colombian government was negotiating peace with the FARC guerrilla group (Fuerzas Armadas Revolucionarias de Colombia)—the oldest and largest guerrilla group in the country—the problem of girls linked to illegal armed groups persisted.

In this chapter, we present research findings that reveal powerful examples of these girls' capacity for agency. Girls that have this capacity are not limited to reproducing the violence that they have endured, nor are they resigned to remaining in the position of passive victims. Instead, their actions, connections, and decisions influence and shape their immediate contexts—their own and those of their closest relational agents, whether parents or extended family members (Boyden, 2003; Boyden & de Berry, 2004; Boyden & Mann, 2005). Colombian girls' actions, reactions, and interactions—during and after their involvement in armed conflict—are shaped by a *process of social construction* (Gergen, 2007, 2009). Moreover, their actions cannot be understood through linear causality under a determinist schema of psychological and family factors or within a traditional framework of child and human development. Rather, these girls' responses must be understood as processes of interaction in which they are social actors who are not only affected by the social realities in which they live but who also interpret and transform it. In this chapter we focus on the actions of the girls that contrast with military ideals and the objectives of war and instead favor life, care for themselves and others, and peace building in their relational contexts.

We begin with a brief history of the Colombian war to help frame the discussion and then examine the elements of social constructionism relevant to our analysis. We next analyze the narratives of girls who have been involved in the armed conflict to illustrate their capacity for agency and their roles as social actors who carry out acts of peace in spite of the context of armed conflict in which they live.

GLOBAL ARMED CONFLICT

War is a historical phenomenon and, as such, changes across time. To understand the effects of the Colombian armed conflict on children, it is important to first examine the history of global armed conflict in the 20th and early 21st centuries. According to some researchers (Kaldor, 2001; Pardo, 2004; UNICEF, 2009), there were three distinct periods of conflict in the time period. In the first half of the 20th century, the majority of wars were fought between states and allied states. World War I and II are paradigmatic of this period. At the same time, in Latin America there were also peasant revolts and socialist revolutions, characterized by anticolonial struggles. During the second period—from the 1950s until the 1980s—the majority of wars were civil wars characterized by violence between state security forces and rebels; these conflicts were inspired by political projects with strong ideological bases. Though characterized as civil wars, these wars were affected by global forces, having been preceded by colonialist actions and influenced by proxy. Paradigmatic of this period were the guerrilla wars that occurred in almost all of Latin America. The third period, which began in the 1980s and has continued until the present day, is characterized by what Kaldor (2001) refers to as "new wars" or "postmodern wars." These wars tend to not be contained within the borders of one country, but include broad geographical regions. Furthermore, they do not generally concern only movements against the state, but may involve a larger number of actors. Another related and important characteristic of new or postmodern wars is an increasing tendency toward terrorist actions in which the victims are not adversaries of an opposing army, but rather innocent civilians, including children. This characteristic is especially apparent in the Colombian armed conflict.

According to Kaldor (2001), another shared feature of these new wars is that they begin, grow, and die out around legal or illegal sources of natural wealth. Pardo (2004) offers the following examples: oil in Iraq and Libya, diamonds in

Sierra Leone, opium in Afghanistan, and psychoactive substances and precious metals in Colombia. In some instances, most of the wealth generated by these disputed resources is consumed in the war itself. Furthermore, there is variation in the way the actors involved are linked to each other, such as in proxy wars. Wars can extend indefinitely, mutating into new armed conflicts and occurring alongside a more or less normal functioning state. At times, the illegal movements that spring up within these wars are allied with the state; for example, groups of mercenaries receive remuneration to carry out illegal operations for which state forces are not authorized but that they support, such as murders and disappearances of civil actors who sympathize with insurgent groups. In other conflicts, ideological and ethical elements tend to weaken or disappear among groups that fight against the state. Many new combatants, especially the very youngest, do not know the context in which the war began and show little interest for the political instruction imparted by the armed groups. One of the principal characteristics of the new wars is an increasing tendency to recruit children as soldiers; this strategy is facilitated by new technologies that make weapons lighter and easier to handle (UNICEF, 2009).

The prolonged Colombian armed conflict began around 1964 and emerged from a longstanding conflict against the state (violence between state forces and rebel movements). Because of the factors mentioned here, especially the prevalence of drug trafficking in the regions where it is being fought, the Colombian armed conflict has gradually evolved to share many characteristics of the so-called new wars.

THE HISTORY OF THE COLOMBIAN ARMED CONFLICT

For more than 50 years, Colombians have been living with war. It began in the early 1960s as a guerrilla movement inspired by a socialist project, and over the following decades, various guerrilla organizations emerged that shared the same political aim, but with different nuances and operating independently. Of those, only two continue to operate: Las Fuerzas Armadas Revolucionarias de Colombia (FARC) and the Ejército de Liberación Nacional (ELN), which is almost as old as FARC, but is smaller. The objectives, methods, and dynamics of both these guerrilla movements are fundamentally similar. In the 1980s, other armed actors appeared in the form of ultra-right-wing death squads known as paramilitaries or self-defense organizations and financed by drug traffickers, cattle ranchers, and industrial interests. These armed bands waged war against the guerrillas and their collaborators and sympathizers; they also assassinated and forcibly caused the disappearance of union members, student activists, and defenders of human rights. The paramilitary groups began to function as armies in various regions of the country, carrying out criminal actions similar to those of the guerrilla groups, such as extortion, kidnappings, forced displacement, and massacres, sometimes with the veiled support of state security forces.

The Colombian government signed an agreement under which these paramilitary groups were to submit to justice. After their supposed demobilization, the paramilitary groups mutated into what the Colombian government has named "criminal bands" (BACRIM), which share their predecessors' characteristics, objectives, and modes of financing and operating and benefit from the complicity of state security organizations (Duncan, 2015).

As peace negotiations with the FARC guerrilla group continue at the time of writing, the actors in the Colombian armed conflict can be placed into three broad groups: the left-wing guerrillas, FARC and ELN; illegal extreme right-wing armed groups that take on different names in each region ("El Clan del Golfo" in Antioquia, "La Cordillera" in the coffee-growing region, and "Aguilas Negras" in the east of the country, for example); and Colombian state security forces comprising the army, air force, navy, and police. Sometimes the extreme right-wing groups act with the complicity of members of the state security forces, and on other occasions they act independently.

The goal of the study presented in this chapter, based on the tenets of social constructionism (Gergen, 2007, 2009), was to identify alternative perspectives on the effects of the Colombian armed conflict on children, particularly their individual and relational potential and the peace-building actions that they have already taken, are taking, or will be able to take.

A SOCIAL CONSTRUCTIONIST APPROACH

This study employs the framework of social constructionism (Alvarado et al., 2012; Gergen, 2007, 2009; Ospina-Alvarado, 2013a, 2013b, 2015; Ospina-Alvarado, Alvarado, & Ospina, 2014; Ospina-Alvarado, Carmona-Parra, & Alvarado-Salgado, 2014; Valencia, Ramírez, Fajardo, & Ospina-Alvarado, 2015) as an alternative perspective on the development of children affected by the armed conflict in Colombia. Child development is no longer viewed as a process marked by clear stages in accordance with the life cycle

(Rosas & Sebastián, 2001). Instead, from a social constructionist perspective, it is a social and relational process that involves children's ongoing subjective involvement in processes of transformation and interaction (Alvarado et al., 2012). This framework dissolves the barrier between children's internal worlds and the external world in which they develop. In reflecting on this approach, Gergen (2009) argues that subjects construct meaning about what is *real* and *good* in the world in the conversations in which they participate. With this relational construction of what is real and good, boys and girls in the context of armed conflict build their own meanings and ways of positioning themselves to cope in the world; that is, they construct themselves as subjects within the relationships in which they participate.

Statements of hope, memory, intentions, attitudes, emotions, thoughts, and desires create mental events and simultaneously construct people's identities, subjectivities (Gergen, 2009), and their multiple egos (Gergen, 2006). It is therefore not possible to discuss the social construction of children in the context of armed conflict without referring to the ways in which these statements are presented in the lives of these boys and girls, their families, and communities and in the relationships that develop between them.

The capacities and resources that have allowed boys and girls and those in their socioecological context to move forward are based on the concepts of agency (Sen, 2000) and resilience (Campo, Granados, Muñoz, Rodríguez, & Trujillo, 2012). In general, these capacities are often overlooked in mainstream approaches to understanding children in contexts of armed conflict (Alvarado et. al., 2012; Ospina-Alvarado, 2013a, 2013b, 2015; Ospina-Alvarado, Alvarado, & Ospina 2014; Ospina-Alvarado, Carmona-Parra, & Alvarado-Salgado, 2014; Valencia et al., 2015). These traditional approaches have tended to view children as either passive victims of conflict or as aggressors (Alvarado et al., 2012). Moreover, children's voices are typically silenced and excluded, particularly those of girls. For example, in chapter 5, using the narratives of former girl soldiers in northern Uganda, Lenz argues that current reintegration efforts often ignore resilient qualities that girls gain during their involvement in armed groups and thus may in fact weaken resilience.

According to a social constructionist approach, statements or *worlds of meaning* (Gergen, 2012) are constructed in relationships. Gergen (2007) suggests that the ability to transform worlds of meaning and maintain what is relevant in them requires participation in relationships. In the context of armed conflict, military recruitment and the risk of being killed as a perceived enemy collaborator can lead to the breakdown of ties and relationships, as people from the same territory or even from the same family become allies or collabo-rators of groups in confrontation. This leads to mistrust among members of a community, who may become enemies in spite of sharing a common path in life. However, such situations also facilitate new ways of connecting, joint action, and experiences of solidarity, because they create new ties among people who become connected with one or another of the groups or who live in simi-lar situations. New kinds of collective identity are created; for example, after forced displacement, community members from the same territories may help each other move ahead and obtain work in the cities in which they have re-settled. Although most research with girls associated with armed groups has emphasized breakdowns in ties and relationships, armed conflict can also work to strengthen new modes of relating that may influence the postconflict context. For children and their families affected by armed conflict, it is funda-mentally important to build new relationships and to protect and reestablish existing ones in a way that also constructs new meanings and actions (Al-varado et al., 2012).

As girls establish new relationships in the aftermath of their involvement in armed groups, it is possible that alternative statements begin to emerge, from which they construct their own meanings through their agency and peace-building potential. From a social constructionist view, it is vitally important that social research focus on these alternative narratives, as they demonstrate young people's capacity to be active political subjects in peace building, rather than as mere victims of the conflict. Moreover, Gergen (2009) suggests that, through relationships, it is possible to contribute to the transformation of meanings and consequently of practices. In this way, social constructionism highlights the ways in which children and those key players who surround them, such as family, teachers, and community members (whom social con-structionists refer to as relational agents) can be transformed through relation-ships (Ospina-Alvarado, Alvarado, & Fajardo, 2016, p. 272). Here, new meanings and alternative actions can be brought about, replacing individualized and deficit-based views.

In new communities formed in the aftermath of forced displacement, there are opportunities for boys and girls to participate with others and to construct new meanings and statements proposing their interest in living a future differ-ent from the violent past. In this way, agency and resilience, although they are not concepts originating in a social constructionist perspective, have defini-tions and uses in the social sciences that are consistent with social construc-tionist approaches and practices, such as the importance placed on human and relational potentials in peace building. In this study, agency and resilience allow us to focus on resources and to foster actions in the present, with roots in the past, that favor the emergence of future possibilities, all of these being nodal ideas from social constructionism.

Our position is also aligned with White and Epston's (1993) claim that a single story or event does not cover a person's entire experience, even though in dominant stories about the lives of children and families affected by war, it appears that few other experiences, outside of their experiences as participants in war, are presented to contradict the dominant story (Defensoría del Pueblo, 2002, 2006; Ila, Martínez, Arias, Núñez, & Caicedo, 2009; Montoya, 2008; ONU, 2010; Romero & Castañeda, 2009; Torrado, Camargo, Pineda, & Bejarano, 2009; Valencia et. al., 2015; Watchlist on Children and Armed Conflict, 2004). Thus, although the stories and statements about the lives of children affected by war are principally marked by the normalization and routinization of violence (Alvarado et al., 2012), it is possible to identify realities that contradict the story of violence as the only postwar narrative.

The present research, using the generative, appreciative, and relational approach of social construction, centers on the views of girls as key agents in peace building. It focuses on their creative potential and their abilities to transform reality through combined actions with others and to critically evaluate and become responsible for their own actions at individual and collective levels.

METHODS

The study on which this chapter is based had three phases: the initial phase or pilot study, a second phase of fieldwork, and a third phase analyzing information. In this chapter we focus on results relating to a subsample of girls and young women.

OVERVIEW OF THE PILOT STUDY

Research methods used in the pilot study methodology included testimony, in-depth interviews, participant observations, creative workshops, and the analysis of narratives. The initial phase of the fieldwork tested the instruments in three institutions: (1) an educational institution in Manizales (Institución Educativa la Asunción), (2) a school in Antioquia (Colegio Creadores del Futuro), and (3) a community in Bogotá (Benposta Nación de Muchachos). The work was carried out with a total number of 23 boys, 26 girls, 2 fathers, 9 mothers, 2 siblings, 1 grandmother, and 41 educational staff members. Although all three sites were located in zones of armed conflict, only six participants had directly been affected by the war. Here, eight educational staff also participated.

Pilot fieldwork was also carried out in a kindergarten in Bogotá (Jardín Infantil de la Secretaría de Educación de Bogotá, Casita de los Rincones, San Cristóbal Sur). Four workshops were held with each of the following groups: teachers (N=10), and children (4 girls and 6 boys) and parents (N=6).

The methodological design of the full study was adjusted based on the pilot study and subsequently revised and validated by a committee of experts. Its workshops, interviews, and focus groups were implemented in seven institutions.

OVERVIEW OF THE FULL STUDY

METHODOLOGICAL DESIGN The research used a hermeneutic approach that was simultaneously critical and participatory (Alvarado, Gómez, Ospina-Alvarado, & Ospina, 2014; Ospina-Alvarado et al., 2016). It sought to reveal the meanings and significance of the social reality in times of armed conflict to generate frameworks of interpretation that clarify the narratives of children, and to generate political processes of transformation. This study aimed to ensure an understanding of the flow of experiences that shape the political experience of agents and their statements regarding peace (Alvarado et al., 2012). To achieve this, the study had a narrative focus.

SELECTION OF ACADEMIC INSTITUTIONS AND RECRUITMENT OF PARTICIPANTS The fieldwork was carried out in several educational institutions in three regions: Ejo Cafetero, Antioquia, and Bogotá. To reflect our research goals, we chose educational institutions that already enrolled children and families affected by war and were already carrying out work on peace building, which our intervention aimed to affect. The educational institutions and teachers were provided with an overview of the project. Participants included 151 children between the ages of 8 and 12, 26 female teachers, 11 male teachers, 88 mothers, 12 fathers, and 7 brothers and 4 grandmothers of the children. In addition, the sample included 20 young women between the ages of 12 and 18, who had been demobilized from armed groups and had already participated in a study carried out by one of the co-authors. The participants were living in the cities of Bogotá, Medellín, Manizales, and Armenia. These cities were chosen because the study was part of a broader research program carried out in these regions of Colombia. Two universities (Universidad de Manizales and Universidad Pedagógica Nacional) and a center for research and development (Centro Internacional de Educación y Desarrollo Humano [CINDE]) provided support for the study, which also received support and financing from the Colombian state entity responsible for science and technology (Colciencias).

The most significant issues affecting the participating children and families were: the recruitment of children by armed groups; the death, disappearance, mutilation, and injury of relatives; forced displacement; the looting of land; family disintegration; anomie; uncertainty; and different forms of destruction of the social fabric. In the Eje Cafetero and Antioquia regions, the girls, boys, and their families were victims of the armed conflict, having suffered displacement. In Bogotá, the majority (68%) of families stated that the children were very young when displacement occurred and so did not experience it directly. The remaining families stated that their children had experienced the conflict directly.

FORMAT OF WORKSHOPS AND TOOLS USED TO GATHER DATA Data collection was carried out within the educational institutions and in participants' homes. In all cases, informed consent and assent of the individuals participating in the research were obtained, as well as the informed consent and approval of the parents and teachers of the child participants. The data were collected by social and human sciences professionals, primarily psychologists and educators, with the support of undergraduate, master's, and doctorate students. The facilitators were trained based on the themes of the study: the history and realities of the armed conflict, the construction of subjectivities and identities, and peace building. In addition, practical training was provided through the piloting process. The workshop facilitators were, at all times, concerned with the well-being of participants and ensured that all necessary precautions were taken to avoid situations that could revictimize or cause any form of discomfort for the children. For example, they oriented questions and activities toward peace-building potentials and learning, rather than victimization and description of events in the context of armed conflict.

Although the focus of the study was on hearing the children's voices—taking a social constructionist approach and understanding that these voices are constructed relationally and socially—to understand the children's experiences, it was also important to hear the voices of their significant relational agents. Therefore, information was collected from 45 educational workshops with parents. There were also 15 focus groups with teachers: 6 in Eje Cafetero, 4 in Antioquia, and 5 in Bogotá. In addition, 50 workshops were conducted with boys and girls, and interviews were carried out with some of the children and their families.

All the instruments—workshops with boys and girls, educational workshops with families, focus groups with teachers, and semi-structured interviews with children and families—had the same focus: the armed conflict, social construction of subjectivities and identities, and peace building; however, they approached the same themes in different ways. The workshops with children used creative tools such as play and art. Educational workshops with families involved storytelling, the connections between families, educational processes, and artistic expression. The focus groups with educational staff began with some basic questions to explore their narratives about the armed conflict, its effects on children and families, and peace-building processes in the educational environment. Lastly, semi-structured interviews were carried out, in some cases individually and in others collectively.

OVERVIEW OF SUBSAMPLE In total, 299 individuals, of whom 79 were girls, participated in the research. This chapter focuses on that subsample of girls whose families or, in some cases, themselves were living in a context of armed conflict. This chapter also discusses another group of 20 young women, formerly associated with illegal armed groups, who had returned to civilian life and had participated in another study completed by one of the researchers. In general, these 99 girls and young women had moved from areas where violence related to the armed conflict was present to other territories only to find there, in many cases, that circles of violence and exclusion were reproduced. These contexts involving violence were marked by a patriarchal pattern of power inequality in which the girls and young women often had to do housework and take care of younger siblings. Yet, through their life narratives these girls and young women have managed to break cycles that reproduce violence and to position themselves actively as peace builders in contexts such as the family, school, and community.

DATA ANALYSIS Information was analyzed with a focus on the categorical analysis of narratives (Creswell, 2007) using the Atlas.ti software. This analysis generated the following categories: (1) contexts and experiences with regard to armed conflict, (2) the social construction of subjectivities and identities, and (3) peace-building processes. In the next section, we highlight narrative accounts that show girls' critical capacities and demonstrate resistance in the face of various armed actors.

FINDINGS AND DISCUSSION

Our exploration of Colombian girls' lives in the aftermath of their participation in armed conflict revealed their narratives about contexts and experiences related to the armed conflict, which, as social constructionism claims (Gergen, 2009, 2012), maintain a deficits-based approach that is based on Western frameworks. Thus, some of their narratives address the banality and normality of violence in community cultural practices:

> I feel badly because people should not kill, but the truth is that some people go looking for it. (girl, age 9, 2014)

> Children [from areas of armed conflict] are very used to saying, when grown up, "I am going to be the police," "I am going to be part of the armed forces to kill all of those that are attacking." So their mentality is that they want to be the person who defends the family, who defends the people around them. (teacher, 2014)

This study focused on the capacities of Colombian children for agency and the reconstruction of their life goals, as well as their potential for peace building. We gave priority to the testimonies of girls formerly associated with armed groups, because they represent a more invisible population in the published literature on this topic. As might be found in contexts where armed groups have military control, the agency of the girl participants took the form of distrust, suspicion, criticism, and resistance. These girls also showed attitudes of subtle or open defiance. For example, in private conversation with trusted companions, they began to doubt what the commanders had told them during instruction, made jokes about the ideals of the group, or openly expressed their objections and refusal to obey orders. An example can be seen in the narrative of a girl who paid little attention to discussions about the political principles of the armed group in which she participated: "The political talks bored me a lot. I would start talking, or would prefer they sent me on guard duty" (girl, age 17, 2009). The girls recruited into the ranks of armed groups expressed their ability to create distance from their commanders and the military values of the group by mocking the ideals of the group among themselves and dissuading other country girls from joining. Thus, the girls contributed, in ways that distanced them from victimization, to the *social construction of subjectivities and identities.*

Therefore, as indicated by social constructionism (Gergen, 2012; Ospina-Alvarado, Carmona-Parra, & Alvarado-Salgado, 2014) and narrative approaches (Ospina-Alvarado, 2015; White & Epston, 1993), one single and exclusive story—that of the banality and culture of violence—does not cover the whole of the lives of the children, who expressed gestures of solidarity and compassion beyond military values and an ability to devise and carry out plans of escape and collaboration, including preventing the involvement of other children. In their involvement in programs that return girls to civil life, the children's agency and their potential for peace building are reflected in their ability to reconstruct their own identity, in their construction of affective bonds with other children who were linked to enemy groups, and in the open and celebratory attitude with which they assume their new role as free citizens. As this teacher commented in relation to conflict-affected girls:

> While, among the girls I have seen, they maintain a rather critical stance. They're, like, more aware of what happens in society, because they have moved ahead through their critical view of the world. I believe that is the difference I have been able to see. (teacher, 2014)

The girls' construction of identity as active citizens, a process highlighted in social constructionism (Ospina-Alvarado, Alvarado, & Ospina, 2014; Ospina-Alvarado, Carmona-Parra, & Alvarado-Salgado, 2014) and political socialization (Alvarado et al., 2012), is also shown in the narrative of one of the girls when she spoke of the armed groups:

> I told them [her parents] that I promised them that I was not going to start with the bad guys, that I was going to make a great effort to have a career, that I did not want to become that way. . . . . I want to get a career before having children. I want to provide for my parents, I want to have an apartment. (girl, age 11, 2014)

In the following quote, a girl remembers the moment she began to reject the guerrilla groups who had taken one of her family members. Her account reflects the bonds of solidarity and compassion, which the girls described as fundamental elements for peace building:

> The guerrillas made people attend the meeting. My cousin said no, that he did not want to be involved in problems with anyone, that he was not going to go, that if the Army arrived and found him there, that he did not want to have problems with anyone, and they tied him up, they told him that they were going to kill him. From that point forward, something grew inside me, like something against the guerrillas. (girl, age 17, 2009)

The girls demonstrated other forms of resistance to military life and values. When some were involved with the illegal armed groups, they constructed meaning from experiences not connected with military matters, using values related to love, the protection of life, and solidarity with others. The social construction (Gergen, 2012; Ospina-Alvarado, Alvarado, & Ospina, 2014) and narrative approaches (Ospina-Alvarado, 2015; White & Epston, 1993) posit that such values enable the construction of alternative narratives of peace that are closely related to the actions that come into play in relationships:

> Over there [in the jungle], I did mostly nursing, which involved helping civilians a lot, those who were sick. I would go and apply medicines, prescribing medicines to regular civilians and the militias. I felt great, being a nurse over there because I felt useful . . . and to know that you put your hand on someone and that someone heals, that is pride to me. (girl, age 16, 2009)

What stands out in this story is that this girl, after she was recruited, preferred to devote herself within the group to serving the community and not to the tasks of war. In this way, she rewrites her life story, narrating about herself and relating to others not as a girl warrior, but as a healer. She and many other girls also developed life skills as a part of her participation in the armed groups, earning the support and loyalty of communities and challenging the dominant narrative of them as victims or perpetrators.

It is striking to find, among the girls' expressions of self-reflection and self-criticism, critical thinking that counters and challenges the exaltation of militarism. When acted on, critical thinking begins to favor the emergence of peace-building processes:

> I was on watch at midnight. . . . I began to think, and I said, "My God, what I am doing here killing people who maybe are here . . . like I am, without doing

anything, or rather, innocent. They fight like that for nothing, so we kill each other, and I think [thought], since when did I have so many enemies?" (girl, age 17, 2009)

An example of critical thinking that the girls put into action was opposing the orders of their commanders as a means of preventing other girls with whom they had previous relationships with from experiencing the same fate:

One girl told me that she had a desire to leave [her family and join the armed group] because she was very bored at home. . . . Right then, I told her, "Do not go," and to my little sister, I also said, "Don't go." We advised her a lot [not to join the armed group]. (girl, age 15, 2009)

The girl recalls how she did exactly the opposite of what she was asked to do—to encourage other girls to join the armed group—because of the great importance she placed on her relationship with her companion and her younger sister, which superseded orders received from her commanders. This shows the great transformative potential present in relationships, as set out in social constructionism (Gergen, 2012).

In deciding to escape from armed groups and to risk their own lives, girl participants showed a political subjectivity and the ability to critically evaluate their situation and guide their own actions. In this way, worlds of meaning and critical thinking were closely related to action (Alvarado et al., 2012; Gergen, 2012):

I was bored, and I had asked to leave to go to home from everything, and they did not let me, and I said to them, "One of these days, I will go away from here," and indeed, when I went home, I surrendered. (girl, age 15, 2009)

The role that Gergen (2009) attributes to language not only in the construction but also principally in the reconstruction of the person—what we call the construction of political subjectivities for peace—was evident in the girls' narratives. The importance of language, and of the way in which the girls name themselves and are named by others as political subjects, was demonstrated through the nonlineal nature of their experiences and the possibility of transformation that emerged from relocation to another community. Girls spoke of reverting to their former civilian identities after demobilization, forsaking their militarized names (in Colombia it was common practice for boys and girls to receive a different name on joining the ranks of an armed group). On demobilizing, one girl decided to change her *nom de guerre* back to her own given name, with significant implications for her life and relationships:

> Again, with the same name, I was the same as before. Again I felt [like] the same woman that [I] was in civilian life. Normal. The anger, hatred, and all that left me. I felt the same as before. (girl, age 17, 2009)

One of the most powerful examples of girls' ability to foster reconciliation and peace in the aftermath of violence and to reconstruct both individual and collective identities occurred in interactions among children who were formerly associated with opposing armed groups. These interactions illustrate the transforming potential of relationships (Gergen, 2012):

> The relationship was difficult because there were the *paracos* [paramilitaries]. I had a problem with a girl *paraca*. It was difficult, but in the end we were perfect friends, we became friends. (girl, age 17, 2009)

> I argued with one of the boys because he defended the paramilitaries, and I defended the guerrillas. He said that the guerrillas were thieves, and I told him, "Boy, I was in a guerrilla group and never witnessed a robbery by the guerrilla. . . . It is the paramilitaries who are truly thieves." And, afterwards, [it was] normal. We got along. We didn't argue any more. We said, "We are no longer [part of] any of that, so it goes." (girl, age 16, 2009)

Perhaps the most radical demonstration of the authenticity of the girls' new identity and manner of being in the world and also of their possibilities for constituting themselves as political subjects was their ability to have intimate relationships and plan families with ex-combatants from opposing groups. These are alternative stories in which the girls construct their political identities through love and through those favorable to peace building:

> I went out with a *paraco*. He was so beautiful! I told him [as a joke] "Hey, don't you think it's weird that you're going out with a guerrilla girl, because you were fighting us, and we were fighting you?" And he said, "No, it's normal. It's that here, as civilians, we live in peace." And I said to him [continues joking], "I'm not going to make peace with you," when I was his girlfriend. There, it was

normal that ex-guerrillas got together with *paracos*. Normal! Weren't we civilians by then? (girl, age 15, 2009)

The natural manner in which the girl jokes with her partner in this quote demonstrates the clarity with which she internalized their new roles in civilian life. She had given new meaning to her self-image, her image of another person, and their symbolic universe. They were no longer enemy combatants. They could be a couple and laugh at the past.

The following narrative shows the change in those who come from opposing armed groups, from calling themselves enemies to establishing relational practices:

> When I arrived and found out that there were *paracos* there. Umm . . . oh, no! Look, I felt everything. . . . It made me want to return, to turn tail [run and go back to the armed group] and say no, . . . but as days passed, and I kept going there, I did not talk with any of them, and he [refers to her partner who accompanied her to the interview, a youth formerly associated with the paramilitary groups], as he was such a bad one. . . . Oh, Lord! He would look at you and want to kill with a look. . . . Do you hear! (girl, age 18, 2009)

In this quote, we can see how children and young people, when they first enter programs designed to facilitate their return to civilian life, see individuals from the other groups in terms of the roles they had as enemies in the interactions during the war. However, they soon take a reading of the new roles they play in this different context of interaction and in their participation in relationships (Gergen, 2012). They give new meaning to and reconstruct their identities and become disposed to constructing new links, new meanings, and new realities with those who, only days earlier, had been their enemies.

We found that some girls who were linked to armed groups and were involved more deeply in actions of war were also more decisively empowered on their return to civilian life. They tended to collaborate more enthusiastically with others, a further demonstration of their capacity for agency, self-transformation, peacemaking, and reconciliation. This finding reflects the resilience shown by these girls, revealing that there is not a linear connection between the experience of armed conflict and the continuation of a life dominated by violence. Indeed, it is possible for agency and potential to emerge, despite negative experiences related to armed conflict.

CONCLUSIONS

Contrary to evolutionary approaches and approaches to child development based on maturation, such as those of Piaget, Kohlberg, or Freud (Alvarado et al., 2012), our study underscores that child development is not a linear process of stages that a child experiences in a passive way or that invariably occur beyond the scope of children's agency. Rather, it is a process in which social contexts, such as war and armed conflict, and the child's capacity for agency become factors, with varying results. Some children express understandings of reality, positions, and decisions that would be overlooked by a deficit-based reading of girls as minors or victims. This chapter describes children's subjective repositioning, development of attitudes, criticisms, and resistance to the militaristic values of the armed groups. Building on the work of Gergen (2012), Alvarado et al. (2012), and Ospina-Alvarado and colleagues (Ospina-Alvarado, Alvarado, & Ospina 2014; Ospina-Alvarado, Carmona-Parra, & Alvarado-Salgado, 2014), this research opens new horizons of meaning that enable the transformation of relational practices.

This study challenges the idea that girls who are socialized in contexts of violence are invariably condemned to reproduce, as active aggressors, what they experienced as victims. Our study findings instead reaffirm the ability of girls and their relational agents, who—after experiencing contexts of violence and circumstances in which everything would seem to favor the expression of violent tendencies—make statements, take positions, and perform actions that are clearly in opposition to war and in favor of peace. In some cases, they put their own lives at risk. This conclusion aligns with the social constructionist approach (Gergen, 2012; Ospina-Alvarado, Alvarado, & Ospina 2014; Ospina-Alvarado, Carmona-Parra, & Alvarado-Salgado, 2014) and narrative approaches (Ospina-Alvarado, 2015; White & Epston, 1993) in which the commitment to transformation, or in the case of the present study to peace building, implies an appreciative perspective on the subjects, their potentials, and their agency that takes into account the creative role of dialogical and relational practices. We conclude from our research that, even in contexts of war, in which there exist conditions for children to develop attitudes and ways of relating in keeping with the conflict, children can develop attitudes, links, and meanings in accord with peace building and reconciliation because of their capacity for agency and their interactions with others.

Relationships play a fundamental role in transforming narratives and actions, as seen in the radical changes in relations, actions, positions, and decisions on the return to civilian life of children previously recruited by illegal armed groups. The fundamental role of relationships in processes of peace building coheres with the relational potential for social transformation proposed by social constructionism (Gergen, 2012).

The most important conclusion of this study is that even the girls most affected by armed conflict, including those who were deeply involved in violent armed actions, show the potential to transform into active agents in the reconstruction of their own subjectivity and their life goals. They become social actors in processes of peace building and reconciliation with other children who have also suffered the horrors of armed conflict.

Our research therefore contributes to educational research practices on socialization in which girls participate, taking into account the influence of changes in meanings and relationships in the educational context. In that context, it is important to prioritize visions of children coming from the armed conflict from the viewpoint of their capacity and not their victimization. The girls whose voices are included in this chapter displayed resistance to militarized and belligerent culture and actively positioned themselves in peace-building efforts through their ways not only of signifying themselves but also of acting and relating.

This study also contributes to the macro-level approach derived from public policies in a setting such as Colombia. First, it emphasizes the importance of constructing strategies that strengthen the potential for peace building among children coming from contexts of armed conflict and that do not subject them to revictimization. Second, it sees strengthening of children's relationships as a means to build peace in a process in which families, communities, and educational contexts are prioritized and the reconstruction of social fabric is broadened. Third, restoring rights should be prioritized over repressive policies in processes of resocializing children who have been involved in illegal armed groups. Relating to demobilized children through their potentials, learning, capacity for agency, the reconstruction of the social fabric and relational ties in which they participate, and the restitution of their rights not only facilitates their development but also transforms their meanings and actions regarding themselves, others, and the world and, through that, the contexts in which they construct their realities with others.

Thus, in both the Latin American and international contexts, this research encourages practices and policies with and for girls in the context of violence and armed conflict that recognize and enhance their learning, strengths, and potentials and allow them, together with relational agents in their socio-ecological context, to contribute to processes of peace building.

References

Alvarado, S. V., Gómez, A., Ospina-Alvarado, M. C., & Ospina, H. F. (2014). La hermenéutica ontológica política o hermenéutica performativa: Una propuesta epistémica y metodológica. *Revista Nómadas, 40*, 207–220.

Alvarado, S. V., Ospina, H. F., Quintero, M., Luna, M. T., Ospina-Alvarado, M. C., & Patiño, J. A. (2012). *Las escuelas como territorios de paz: Construcción social del niño y la niña como sujetos políticos en contextos de conflicto armado*. Buenos Aires: Clacso.

Boyden, J. (2003). Children under fire: Challenging assumptions about children's resilience. *Children, Youth & Environment, 13*(1), 1–29.

Boyden, J., & de Berry, J. (2004). Introduction. In J. Boyden & J. de Berry (Eds.), *Children and youth on the front line: Ethnography, armed conflict and displacement* (pp. xi–xxvii). New York: Berghahn Books.

Boyden, J., & Mann, G. (2005). Children's risk, resilience and coping in extreme situations. In M. Ungar (Ed.), *Handbook for working with children and youth: Pathways to resilience across cultures and contexts* (pp. 3–26). Thousand Oaks, CA: Sage.

Campo, R., Granados, L. F., Muñoz, L., Rodríguez, M. S., & Trujillo, S. (2012). Caracterización del avance teórico, investigativo y/o de intervención en resiliencia desde el ámbito de las universidades en Colombia. *Universitas Psychologica, 11*(2), 545–557. Bogotá: Pontificia Universidad Javeriana.

Carmona, J. (2013). *Las niñas de la Guerra en Colombia*. Manizales: Fondo Editorial Universidad Católica de Manizales.

Carmona, J., Moreno, F., & Tobón, J. (2012). *La carrera de las niñas en los grupos guerrilleros y paramilitares de Colombia: Un estudio desde el punto de vista del agente*. Medellín: Funlam.

Coalición contra la vinculación de niños, niñas y jóvenes al conflicto armado en Colombia. (2015, December). *Boletín de Monitore, 15*. Retrieved from www.coalico .org/images/stories/bonca15_rev.pdf.

Coalición española para acabar con la utilización de niños soldado. (2004, November 17). *Informe Global: Niños soldado, edición resumida*. Retrieved from www.cns.org.py/noticias/InformeGlobal.pdf.

Creswell, J. (2007). *Qualitative inquiry & research design: Choosing among five approaches*. Thousand Oaks, CA: Sage.

DANE. (2014). *Demografía y población, proyecciones de población*. Retrieved from www.dane.gov.co/index.php/poblacion-y-demografia/proyecciones-de-poblacion.

Defensoría del Pueblo. (2002). *La niñez en el conflicto armado colombiano*. Bogotá: Author. Retrieved from www.unicef.org/colombia/ conocimiento/boletn -8.htm.

Defensoría del Pueblo. (2006). *La niñez y sus derechos. Caracterización de las niñas, niños y adolescentes desvinculados de los grupos armados ilegales: Inserción social y productiva desde un enfoque de derechos humanos.* Retrieved from www .publicaciones.unicefcolombia.com/wp-content/uploads/2006/03/Boletin -defensoria.pdf.

Duncan, G. (2015). *Los señores de la guerra.* Bogotá: Debate.

Gergen, K. (2006). *El yo saturado: Dilemas de identidad en el mundo.* Barcelona: Paidós Ibérica.

Gergen, K. (2007). *Construccionismo social: Aportes para el debate y la práctica.* Bogotá: Universidad de los Andes, Celso.

Gergen, K. (2009). *Relational being.* New York: Oxford University Press.

Gergen, K. (2012). *Social construction: Orienting principles.* Retrieved from www .taosinstitute.net/theoretical-background.

Ila, P., Martínez, A., Arias, A., Núñez, P., & Caicedo, M. (2009). Conflicto armado en la primera infancia en tres territorios colombianos: Putumayo, Magdalena Medio y Arauca. In A. Mejía (Ed.), *Colombia: Huellas del conflicto en la primera infancia* (pp. 147–156). Bogotá: Número Ediciones.

Kaldor, M. (2001). *Las nuevas guerras. violencia organizada en la era global.* Barcelona: Tusquets Editores.

Montoya, A. M. (2008). Niños y jóvenes en la guerra en Colombia. Aproximación a su reclutamiento y vinculación. *Opinión jurídica, 7*(13), 37–51. Retrieved from www. udem.edu.co/NR/rdonlyres/F1740B7A-0538-474D-9870-13A0729E5205/10922 / articulo2ninosyjovenes.pdf.

ONU. (2010). *Informe del Secretario General del Consejo de Seguridad* (A-65-268-S/2011/250). Retrieved from http://daccess-dds ny.un.org/doc/UNDOC/ GEN/N11/275/36/PDF/N1127536.pdf?OpenElement.

Ospina-Alvarado, M. C. (2013a). La subjetividad de niños y niñas en el conflicto armado colombiano: Una construcción social. In S. V. Alvarado & J. Patiño (Eds.), *Jóvenes investigadores en infancia y juventud, desde una perspectiva crítica latinoamericana: Aprendizajes y resultados* (pp. 37–59). Manizales: Centro Editorial Cinde, Childwatch, Universidad de Manizales.

Ospina-Alvarado, M. C. (2013b). Política de protección la primera infancia colombiana en contexto de conflicto armado. *Colección Red de Posgrados en Ciencias Sociales, 46.* Retrieved from http://biblioteca.clacso.edu.ar/clacso/posgrados /20140120034623/OspinaAlvarado.pdf.

Ospina-Alvarado, M. C. (2015). Construcción social de las paces desde las potencias: Niños y niñas de la primera infancia y sus agentes relacionales le cierran la puerta a Don Violencio. In D. F. Schnitman (Ed.), *Diálogos para la transformación: Experiencias en terapia y otras intervenciones psicosociales en Iberoamérica,* (pp. 34–53). Chagrin Falls, OH: Taos Institute Publications, WorldShare Books.

Ospina-Alvarado, M. C., Alvarado, S. V., & Fajardo, M. A. (2016). Prácticas de transformación social e interculturalidad de niños y niñas en el contexto del conflicto armado colombiano: Un abordaje desde la hermenéutica ontológica política. In V. Di Caudo, M. C. Ospina-Alvarado, & D. Llanos (Eds.), *Interculturalidad y educación desde el sur: Contextos, experiencias y voces* (pp. 269–294). Cuenca: UPS-Giei, Clacso, Cinde.

Ospina-Alvarado, M. C., Alvarado, S. V., & Ospina, H. F. (2014). Construcción social de la infancia en contextos de conflicto armado en Colombia. In V. Llobet (Ed.), *Pensar la infancia desde América Latina. Un estado de la cuestión* (pp. 35–60). Buenos Aires: Clacso.

Ospina-Alvarado, M. C., Carmona-Parra, J. A., & Alvarado-Salgado, S. V. (2014). Niños y niñas en contexto de conflicto armado: Narrativas generativas de paz. *Revista Infancias Imágenes, 13*(1), 52–60.

Pardo, R. (2004). *La Historia de las Guerras.* Bogotá: Hombre Nuevo Editores.

Romero, T., & Castañeda, E. (2009). El conflicto armado colombiano y la primera infancia. In A. Mejía (Ed.), *Colombia: Huellas del conflicto en la primera infancia* (pp. 31–53). Bogotá: Número Ediciones.

Rosas, R., & Sebastián, C. (2001). *Piaget, Vigotski y Maturana. Constructivismo a tres voces.* Buenos Aires: Aique.

Sen, A. (2000). *Desarrollo y libertad.* Barcelona: Planeta.

Springer, N. (2012). *Como Corderos entre Lobos.* Bogotá: Springer Consulting SAS.

Subdirección Red Nacional de Información (SRNI), Unidad para la Atención y Reparación Integral a las Víctimas. (2015). *Porcentaje de niñas, niños y adolescentes víctimas de vinculación a actividades relacionadas con grupos armados.* Retrieved from http://rni.unidadvictimas.gov.co/infancia-adolescencia-y-juventud?q=v-reportes.

Torrado, M., Camargo, M., Pineda, N., & Bejarano, D. (2009). Estado del arte sobre primera infancia en el conflicto. In A. Mejía (Ed.), *Colombia: Huellas del conflicto en la primera infancia* (pp. 53–78). Bogotá: Número Ediciones.

UNHCR. (2014). *Young and innocent.* Retrieved from www.acnur.org/a-quien-ayuda/ninos/.

UNICEF. (1997). *Principios de Ciudad del Cabo sobre la prevención del reclutamiento de niños en las fuerzas armadas y desmovilización y reintegración social de los niños soldado en África.* Ciudad del Cabo: Author.

UNICEF. (2009). *Machel study 10-year strategic review: Children and conflict in a changing world.* New York: Author.

UNICEF. (2013). *Informe anual 2013.* Retrieved from www.unicef.org/spanish/sowc2013/.

Valencia, M. I., Ramírez, M. P., Fajardo, M. A., & Ospina-Alvarado, M. C. (2015). De la afectación a nuevas posibilidades: Niñas y niños en el conflicto armado. *Revista Latinoamericana de Ciencias Sociales, Niñez y Juventud, 13*(2), 1037–1050.

Verdad Abierta. (2015, February 23). *Cuántos niños hay en la guerra?* Retrieved from www.verdadabierta.com/victimas-seccion/reclutamiento-de-menores/5629 -cuantos-ninos-hay-en-la-guerra.

Watchlist on Children and Armed Conflict. (2004). *Colombia: La guerra en los niños y las niñas.* Retrieved from www.watchlist.org/reports/pdf/ colombia.report .es.pdf.

White, M., & Epston, D. (1993). *Medios narrativos para fines terapéuticos.* Barcelona: Paidós.

5

ARMED WITH RESILIENCE

Tapping into the Experiences and Survival Skills of Formerly Abducted Girl Child Soldiers in Northern Uganda

Jessica A. Lenz

We have a very powerful voice on peace. We look down on ourselves because we are told to believe that because we were abducted and missed out on our education we have no future. We are uneducated and only the educated can bring peace. We are told that we have suffered and we can't do anything. I spent years in captivity . . . people tell me I'm traumatized. I don't feel traumatized! Even the educated whom we fear have failed to bring peace. We have lived and seen both sides. I have lived with Kony, I have listened to him speak and I know his thoughts and his ways. If anyone is to bring peace it is the ones that have seen both sides. (Atimango, 18 years old, 6 years in captivity)

Within the past decade, more attention has been given to understanding the roles that girls play in armed conflict. Conventional thinking would have us believe that girls' involvement goes only as far as carrying out traditional gender roles such as cooking, cleaning, or serving men as their sexual slaves. Recent studies (Carroll, 2015; Fernando & Ferrari, 2013; McKay & Mazurana, 2004; Wessells, 2009) suggest otherwise. Explorations of the roles and responsibilities of female child soldiers across many contexts have shown that girls have served as soldiers, commanders, porters, and spies and in other roles that serve military and combat objectives (Carroll, 2015; McKay & Mazurana, 2004). For example, during the height of the conflict in northern Uganda, two-thirds of children serving in the militia-controlled forces of the Lord's Resistance Army (LRA) were girls. Although many were used as porters or forced to perform domestic duties, they also served as soldiers, undergoing military training and taking up guns and weapons. They were forced to kill and fight alongside their male counterparts as equals in the "movement" (Mazurana & McKay, 2003).

Despite recognition of the wide spectrum of experiences that females may encounter in armed conflict, this chapter argues that programs supporting former female child soldiers continue to fail to identify and analyze their unique and context-specific skills as a means to support their reintegration back into their communities and families. Though many children involved in armed conflict undergo brutal experiences, those working with both boys and girls have been far too quick to jump at the notion that all these children are traumatized and in need of rehabilitative therapy (Boyden, 2000). For the most part, reintegration programs have been based on the assumption that children are helpless victims and need assistance to recover and return to a more "normal" childhood (Boyden, 2000). This is often at the cost of children's resilience and, more specifically for girls, at the cost of new and empowered gender roles (Barth, 2002; McKay & Mazurana, 2004). Studies have shown that although conflict "can oppress girls and women, it can also expand their possibilities" (McKay & Mazurana, 2004, p. 17).

Through an in-depth study in northern Uganda, this chapter challenges the "cookie-cutter" approach to reintegration of former child soldiers that too often embraces incorrect assumptions and ignores resilient qualities within the child. Although explored through the lens of girls in northern Uganda, this study seeks to promote new approaches that support a more nuanced analysis of the skills and experiences of former female child soldiers and thereby strengthen reintegration programs across contexts. Programs that truly build on the resilient aspects of former female child soldiers will not only better support girls' reintegration but also strengthen their sense of self, confidence, and empowerment in the communities and families to which they return.

In this chapter, I first discuss the existing research on resilience in children affected by adversity and how it is applied in resilience-based programming in humanitarian action. Then, I explore how the experiences of girls within the LRA gave them numerous skills that enhanced their resilience. Finally, I examine what it looks like to build on existing skills and how to strengthen the policy and practice of reintegration programs for former child soldiers.

CONTEXT

In northern Uganda in 2003–2004 (the time of this research), the country was at the height of a brutal cross-border war that left thousands abducted and forced into service in both rebel and government military forces. Thousands of people were killed, and more than a million people fled their homes to live in internally displaced people's (IDPs) camps.

Joseph Kony, a self-proclaimed spirit medium, is the mastermind of the "movement" of the Lord's Resistance Army (LRA). Since 1987, the LRA has waged a brutal civil war since against the Ugandan government and is responsible for countless atrocities committed against the civilian population in northern Uganda and South Sudan. At the time of this writing, the fighting continues in the Democratic Republic of Congo and the Central African Republic.

The LRA is known for its ruthless killings, mutilations, and severe punishments of the children it abducts to serve in its rebel forces. By 2004, it had abducted more than 20,000 children (Human Rights Watch, 2003). These children undergo intense military training and endure brutal punishments. For example, they are often made to kill their own family members or other children. According to Human Rights Watch (2003), this harsh punishment strengthens their endurance and hardens them, preparing them for the battles they will face as they join the movement.

Despite the extreme brutality experienced within the LRA, most children survive. Over the past several decades, numerous studies have been conducted on the resilience of children around the world. They show that children who have experienced armed conflict are not only vulnerable but also embrace various qualities of resilience that help them overcome and triumph over the adversities of life (Daniel & Wassel, 2002). Many children who have experienced tragedy or witnessed life-threatening events emerge with a positive outlook on life; have a good capacity to form positive, fulfilling relationships; achieve a high level of personal success; and develop effective resources for dealing with future negative events (Gallagher, 2002). Cross-country studies on resilience analyzing children who have experienced war, lost a parent, or witnessed a significant tragedy find that 75% managed to overcome adversity and still achieve good developmental outcomes (Bernard, 2004).

Resilience is the human capacity to face, overcome, and even be strengthened by the adversities of life (Bernard, 2004; Grotberg, 1997; Rutter, 1987). Although the social, behavioral, and biological sciences each refer to resilience in a slightly different way—from articulating it as a process, an outcome, or a capacity—the "essence of resilience is a positive, adaptive response in the face of significant adversity" (Center on the Developing Child at Harvard University, 2015, p. 1).

Several studies point to certain factors that contribute to a child's resilience (Grotberg, 1997). Although there is debate about whether all these factors are universal, for the most part, most cultures have certain versions of each factor that help promote resilience in children. These include the following:

I *have* . . . meaning the child has people around whom they trust, admire, respect, and who assist when the child is sick (e.g., external support and resources, trusting relationships).

I *am* . . . meaning the child feels that others like him or her, the child believes in his or her abilities, and the child is considerate of others (e.g., self-esteem, confidence, sense of being loved, faith).

I *can* . . . meaning a child has people around them with who they can share problems, the child can solve problems on his or her own, and the child is able to identify people to go to when he or she is in need of help (e.g., interpersonal skills, positive role models, emotional support outside of home).

Although each factor is significant, no single one guarantees resilience. On an individual level, research identifies resilience as a protective process that changes constantly and is influenced by one's connectedness or sense of community or belonging in relation to specific factors that exist within one's life (Rutter, 1987).

In support of this theory, recent studies point to a growing body of evidence that demonstrates that resilience stems from supportive relationships, adaptive capacities, and positive experiences (Center on the Development of the Child at Harvard University, 2015). In particular, they note the significance of a child having at least one stable and committed relationship with a supportive adult, peer, or role model: In such relationships, the interactions between the child and the adult or supportive peer build "key capacities—such as the ability to plan, monitor, and regulate behavior and to adapt to changing circumstances— that enable children to respond to adversity and to thrive" (Center on the Developing Child at Harvard University, 2015, p. 1). Therefore, it is not simply having a supportive relationship, but the interconnectedness and capacities that grow from this relationship that predispose children to positive outcomes in the face of adversity.

The presence and strength of resilient factors are also dependent on the changing environment and social structures that revolve around the child. The dynamic nature of resilience should be understood within the broader ecological environment; that is, the family, peers, adult relationships, and the wider social environment. Studies using a socioecological framework to understand resilience show that there are a common set of factors that predispose children to positive outcomes in the face of adversity; these factors are directly linked to the strengths and capacities developed through family, peer, and community relationships (Center on the Developing Child at Harvard University, 2015). When these factors are present, they counter the negative effects caused by adversity (Masten, 2014). The quality of interpersonal relationships and the availability of networks of support foster resilient tendencies that build adaptive skills and capacities, such as mastery over life circumstances and a supportive context that affirms faith or cultural beliefs (Kasen, Wickramaratne, Gameroff, & Weissman, 2012; Masten 2014; Ungar, 2012).

RESILIENCE-BASED PROGRAMING

Reintegration programs play an important role in the healing of former girl combatants. After the conflicts in Sierra Leone, Angola, Liberia, Sri Lanka, and northern Uganda, several programs of the UN, international nongovernmental organizations (INGOs), and state civil society institutions sought to support both the rehabilitation and reintegration of child combatants. Responding to the needs of these girls brought with it unique challenges and opportunities. For example, many centers were not set up to cater to those who returned from captivity with babies and young children. Because these girls were often viewed as having been raped, services focused on the provision of physical and psychosocial support addressing this abuse, but failed to provide other needed services such as child care, parenting skills, and educational opportunities. At the same time, some girls were quite vocal about their needs, but the programs were not flexible enough to adapt to the changing needs of those returning from captivity.

Programs for former girl soldiers were designed to help them not only deal psychologically with traumatic experiences but also adjust to return to a civilian life. Rehabilitative centers were established in different contexts that provided various levels of support, including material support, medical care, reunification with members of the family, psychosocial support, education, and economic support. Some provided a physical space for a child to live in and receive counseling, as well as training opportunities that might assist them in their reintegration. For example, in Sierra Leone, Liberia, and northern Uganda, former girl combatants were trained in tailoring skills and small business skills. Boys received training in carpentry and mechanics.

Many child-focused organizations claimed that the concept of resiliency was the fundamental factor underlying their programs (Lenz, 2004). More recently, these organizations have embraced a resilience agenda writ large that not only addresses individual levels of resilience in their programming but also fosters a resilience-based approach and framework for prevention and responses to crisis. Newer resilience-based models adopt a socioecological perspective to address multiple layers within the environment that can foster resilient tendencies of communities to better respond to crisis and cope through protective mechanisms, therefore minimizing negative impacts and ensuring communities can "bounce back."

Although there is significant work around general resilience-based frameworks (Masten, 2011; Masten & Powell, 2003) and on children affected by armed conflict (Betancourt & Khan, 2008; Halevi, Djalovski, Vengrober, & Feldman, 2016; Masten & Narayan, 2012), the current study focuses on the individual level of resilience as defined by organizations in their programs to support the psychosocial recovery and empowerment of children affected by conflict. Because the initial research was carried out before the shift to a macro-level conception of resilience within the humanitarian and development community, the findings are limited to a more micro-level interpretation of resilience-based programming. However, the study does attempt to show the linkages with a wider socioecological perspective of resilience.

METHODOLOGY

The central part of the study took place in northern Uganda over six months in 2004. Subsequent observation and monitoring of the project have taken place periodically since.

SAMPLE

Although many reintegration programs had records of children passing through their centers, many girls returned directly to their communities, and therefore it was difficult to identify every former child soldier in the area. In consultation with the research team (described later) we decided to use word of mouth to spread a message across the northern region of Uganda, inviting girls who had been in captivity to participate in a two-day overnight retreat. The retreat was described as an opportunity to bring together girls who had been abducted to share their experiences on return or escape from the LRA; No services were promised except room and board during the retreat. This activity was included within the research methodology and was supported by an INGO and a partner organization providing services to former child soldiers. More than 130 girls participated in the two-day retreat. There were no official statistics to determine whether the girls were all former child soldiers; therefore, the research team relied on the participants themselves to verify the authenticity of each other's involvement within the LRA. Because of the close relationships that many of the girls had with each other within the LRA, it became apparent early on who was and who was not formerly abducted. It was from this pool of 130 girls that a sample was selected for the in-depth interviews.

Although not entirely randomized, the sampling process ensured that participants met the following criteria: (1) they were former female child soldiers with the LRA; (2) they were between the ages of 14–25 years at the time of the research, but were under 18 years while in captivity; and (3) they were held in captivity for at least one year. To represent a wide variety of experiences, the sample included both participants who returned from captivity pregnant or with a child/ren and those who returned from captivity without children, as well as participants who passed through a rehabilitation center and those who did not pass through a rehabilitation center before returning to their communities/families.

The average age of the participants in the sample was 19.2 years old at the time of the study. When abducted, participants were between 7 and 18 years old, with the average participant abducted when she was 12.5 years old. Participants were held in captivity from 1 to 12 years and 9 months, with the average number of years spent in captivity being 6 years. Participants had returned from captivity to the community between 2 to 5 years earlier, with the average being 2.3 years. Some participants returned from captivity pregnant or had up to three children while in captivity, with the average participant returning with 1.6 children conceived or born in captivity.

INCLUSION OF CO-RESEARCHERS

I initially approached six girls who went through rehabilitation centers and were living back in the community to serve as co-researchers, and join me as part of the research team. At the time of the research, they were under the age of 21, but had all been younger than 18 when abducted by the LRA. I shared with them the full scope and expectations for their involvement. They were encouraged to ask questions and raise issues. The girls were not expected to read or write, although this was an important skill that would support their engagement. Four of the six girls chose to participate as co-researchers. Their involvement was critical in formulating the appropriate research questions and interpreting the data for analysis.

The co-researchers went through a week of individualized and group training with the researcher and two of the three social workers on the research team. Social workers were involved in the research to ensure that ethical standards were met and that girls participating in the study (including the co-researchers) had access to psychosocial services if needed. The training provided an overview of the research topic, interview skills, focus group facilitation techniques, basic counseling techniques, and communication skills.

METHODS OF DATA COLLECTION

The research team used a multitiered approach to collect data: (1) the two-day overnight retreats with 130 formerly abducted girl child soldiers, (2) a series of in-depth interviews with 30 formerly abducted girl child soldiers, (3) 14 interactive workshops on peace and resilience with former girl child soldiers and girls in the community affected by the conflict, and (4) a child/youth-led peace initiative that emerged from the initial findings of the research. Following data collection, the girls involved in this study formed a community-based NGO that continues to build on the findings from the research. This organization, called Empowering Hands, is an officially registered NGO that offers peer-to-peer support for children and families affected by the conflict in northern Uganda. The organization is led and managed by the girls (now young women) who participated in this study. Monitoring and yearly engagement with the leadership of the organization continue.

Each tier of the study was designed to engage children not only as subjects of the study but also as key informants in its design, implementation, and analysis. Child participatory techniques were used as ways to include children and value their insight. These techniques included spider web mapping, role playing, art and dance accompanied by storytelling, and photography.

Although the co-researchers were instrumental in the study's design and analysis, participation of all the girls was emphasized and highly valued. We made every attempt to include every participant in decisions related to the study. Participation did not mean simply being subjects; it meant they had the right to determine *how* their testimonies would be used, *who* would have access to them, and *how* they would be represented and portrayed. For example, girls were asked about the location where interviews would take place, whether outside individuals could join discussions (this was specifically done during the peace-building initiative), and how they wanted the findings to be shared. Finally, they had a right to understand and learn from the research findings and contribute recommendations on how to best meet their own challenges. The girls' decision to co-found a community-based organization after completion of the study is testament to their ownership and involvement in its full scope.

In total, each participant engaged in a two-day overnight retreat with plenary and focus group discussions, three in-depth interviews carried out by the co-researchers, three focus group discussions on targeted themes, a two-day workshop on resilience, and a peace-building initiative that included four three-day workshops on peace building, empowerment, communication, and advocacy. The workshops were designed to build on the findings from the in-depth interviews and focus group discussions and engage the participants in a series of participatory techniques to provide further data for the study.

In addition, key informant interviews and focus groups were carried out to understand the socioecological dimensions of the participants' experience and reintegration into their communities. There were more than 30 additional interviews with family members and community leaders, randomized neighbor interviews in camps, key informant interviews with social workers and NGO staff, and focus groups with communities and schools.

Finally, a desk review and timeline of activities and historical facts were done to understand fluctuations in violence, conflict, and movement of populations affected by the war in northern Uganda and to triangulate information collected in the in-depth interviews.

DATA ANALYSIS

The research team—consisting of the co-researchers and me—completed the data analysis. Several of the social workers also participated in the analysis to provide additional insight and help articulate and fine-tune the findings. Analysis of facilitated discussion groups with different stakeholders including the girls themselves, comparison maps and charts, timelines, and detailed coding were done at interval stages throughout the six-month study. These interval stages were linked to each phase of data collection, enabling the development of additional questions and activities throughout the research process. The analysis triangulated the key factors of resilience and reviewed this interconnectedness against an ecological framework to explore how relationships have a significant bearing on overall resilience.

ETHICAL STANDARDS

Strict ethical standards were upheld throughout the study: Consent forms were used for all participants and co-researchers, participants engaged in decision making about how information was shared and used, the principle of confidentiality was upheld, and security measures were established. In some contexts where children have been recruited into armed forces, those who escaped or returned may maintain the ties they established with individuals within the armed groups. Thus there was a risk that some participants in the study would use the focus groups and/or workshops to gain information and convey sensitive details to members of the LRA, therefore jeopardizing the participants and others involved in the study. A comprehensive assessment of the environment and the participants themselves was undertaken to address security risks that could cause harm to anyone engaged in the research study and activities. In addition, the level of trust between and among participants was evaluated and individually assessed before the start of the study. This was done by engaging in discussions with key participants—in particular, the girls—about their fears, expectations, concerns, and opportunities that might arise as a result of the study. This information was analyzed and cross-checked with past patterns of risk to determine the level of harm and security risks that could occur. Findings from this risk analysis were shared with the girls to engage them in decision making about the methods used for the study. Given the high level of transparency and involvement bestowed on the girls, trust grew.

In addition to external threats, it was important to address the risks that could arise from participating in the study itself. The consent forms acknowledged that the participants would be asked sensitive issues regarding past experiences occurring both before and during their captivity within the LRA. Trained social workers participated in every interview, focus group discussion, and workshop to ensure there was emotional support if needed. If additional support was needed, social workers were aware of referral pathways that could be used.

FINDINGS

Shaped by the lifecycle of the girls while in captivity, the findings highlight the unique factors that contribute to resilience. Even though the study reviewed contributing factors before, during, and after captivity, this chapter only discusses the resilient factors that emerged while in captivity.

This study identified more than 60 roles and responsibilities that the girls were assigned and for which they were subsequently given training. Some examples are nursing, teaching, cartography, event coordination and management, accounting, public speaking, peer counseling, farming, construction, leadership roles such as commanders, and soldiers. The study also explored the various resilient factors that organically developed as the girls continued to find ways to survive. These factors included team-building skills, negotiating skills, faith, selflessness, assertiveness, social skills, effective communication skills, and initiative.

Each factor was measured against the three elements of resilience—I have, I am, I can—and assessed against the ecological context of the girls. A timeline of events that affected their resilience was also created to explore the process, adaptation, and ability of the girls to bounce back throughout the length of their captivity with the LRA. A summary of some of these factors is presented next.

TRUSTING RELATIONSHIPS ("I HAVE AND I CAN")

Most girls expressed the danger posed by finding and making friends while in captivity. Many girls said it was difficult to trust anyone because of the risk of being reported to commanders who would administer severe punishments or death. Despite the great risk posed by speaking about their issues and problems, the girls found ways to secretly interact with various people, including commanders, with whom they developed relationships. These relationships encouraged the girls and provided a form of counseling when they needed advice and support:

> I stayed under emotional torture for a while, but then I realized that I needed to share it and I began to share it with some friends and they counseled me and helped me get through the difficult times. (Havia, 17 years old, 2 years in captivity)[1]

More than 67% of the girls noted that they had one good friend while in captivity to whom they could always turn. Eighty-three percent of the girls said they knew someone in captivity—either a school friend, neighbor, or a relative—who provided them with tremendous support in knowing they were not alone. Some of the commanders also provided encouragement to the girls and reminded them about the life they would have once they escaped. The girls, however, went to great lengths to keep these relationships secret.

SENSE OF SPIRITUAL BELIEF AND FAITH ("I AM AND I CAN")

The Acholi culture of northern Uganda is rich in traditional beliefs. Religion too, specifically the Christian faith, is deeply rooted in and linked to the Acholi culture, and it played an enormous role in the "movement" of the LRA. Everyday life in the LRA was therefore filled with moments of prayer and rituals. Although the girls were never forced to pray to any specific god, they all were required to pray and perform various rituals throughout their time in captivity. These rituals could be as elaborate as a full pre-battle ceremony with dance, drama, and prayer or as simple as marking their bodies with red paint to protect their heart from oncoming bullets. Prayer was seen as a way to gain courage, find escape from death and punishment, protect oneself during battles, and seek advice, and comfort oneself through every tribulation:

> Prayer helped me when I was in captivity, especially when we were near fighting. . . . I would pray heavily and the bullet would not touch me. I developed a deeper trust in God because God was protecting me from bullets and bombs that were released by the helicopters. (Okonya, 19 years old, 6 years in captivity)

Performing rituals also played a unique and important role in the life of the girls—serving as a way to cleanse the sins they had been forced to commit in the LRA. These rituals allowed the girls to feel positive about themselves even when they were forced to commit atrocious acts of violence. These cleansing rituals therefore played an important role in the girls' psychosocial well-being while in captivity.

EMOTIONAL ENCOURAGEMENT AND A SENSE OF SELF-BELIEF ("I AM AND I CAN")

At the time of their abduction and during their first year in captivity, the girls reported that they were made to feel weak, useless, and stupid by being made the targets of insults and punishments delivered not only from commanders but also from other children and "wives" of the commanders. Many of the girls said they did not believe the insults, but merely put up with them. The longer they spent in captivity the more confident they became to report abuses. Girls noted that their level of confidence to reach out to their "husbands," other commanders, and other girls when abuses grew as they observed and came to understand others' temperaments, personal styles, and levels of trust. Their level of respect, position, and relationships contributed to minimizing the insults:

> The other soldiers used to push me as we walked, trying to make me fall down. They wanted me to be killed. They said I was weak. I persevered and fought back with my strength so that I would not fall to the ground. (Lagen, 21 years old, 2 years in captivity)

The girls also received positive comments from commanders, other "wives," and other children within the LRA. They ranged from looking beautiful, having a positive character, being strong, acting respectful, and being friendly. Girls who demonstrated good character were able to make friends easier, were given less strenuous work (e.g., bookkeeping, translation of radio transmissions, selling in the markets in Sudan), and suffered less abuse.

SENSE OF APPRECIATION/APPROVAL ("I AM")

When media stories of the LRA are full of unspeakable accounts of cruelty, it is difficult to fathom that the girls were praised or encouraged during their captivity. However, they mentioned instances when they were praised and rewarded by commanders, other children, and other "wives." Praise was given mostly for military achievement, but also for everyday duties such as cooking. A girl who excelled at a task could be given a leadership position, such as a commander, or assigned greater responsibility that came with less punishment and hardship:

> If you did well and completed the training successfully you were given a gun. Being given a gun meant you were worthy of such a responsibility and that you were strong. (Atimango, 18 years old, 6 years in captivity)

Extra food or items of clothing were also given to the girls when they performed well, and sometimes, their workload was decreased. Some girls were singled out in front of other children and commanders, recognized for their achievements, and even applauded. The girls noted that this praise gave them inner strength: "Those of us that did very well in the military training were taken aside and taught additional skills that others were not" (Maga, 23 years old, 10 years in captivity). This "award" helped stimulate their inner confidence and strength.

A SENSE OF LEADERSHIP ("I AM AND I HAVE")

Leadership positions brought more privileges and greater chances for survival. Having additional leadership responsibilities gave them more opportunities to gain increased clout with the commanders, attain more food or clothes, and be respected by other children, soldiers, and commanders. One girl explained that she was given the responsibility to carry the gun of the commander's wife. She saw this task not only as a way to protect herself if they were attacked but she also no longer had to carry the heavy loads she had been formerly been commanded to hold.

However, being given additional responsibilities or leadership roles did not always bring favorable results for the girls. Fulfilling those tasks often required girls to be stricter and fiercer (e.g., ordering the punishment or death of another child), which many of the girls did not want to be. Yet, even though attaining a leadership position meant that they sometimes had to deliver punishment, they also had more control over how severe that punishment would be. They could choose to lessen the severity of the punishment to those below them.

A SENSE OF SECURITY OR ROUTINE ("I HAVE")

Girls' lives became much more routine after reaching Sudan. Studies show that when children are faced with extreme chaos and disruptive events, such as war, the more routine their situation, the better the child will be able to cope with the negative events (Save the Children, 2001). The same is true for girl child soldiers.

Stability in Sudan meant the girls had access to a hospital and steady supply of food, thus minimizing their chances of starvation and need to rely on looting and handouts. The girls had a house to live in, schools for their children to attend, markets to visit, and a regular routine of prayer. The girls also spoke about the moments they felt happy, relaxed, and at peace and were able to laugh, smile, tell stories, dance, sing, and enjoy themselves. These experiences contributed to their levels of resilience.

Time spent in the LRA included celebrations and lively events that brought everyone together to dance, listen to music, and participate in dramas and story-telling. These celebrations were accompanied by large feasts and often followed by days of rest. The LRA celebrated 12 holidays during the year in which all children participated, including Kony's Day, Women's Day, Independence Day, and New Year's.

SENSE OF VALUE ("I AM")

Girls were valued in the LRA, and the longer they stayed in captivity, the more important they became. They were seen not only as soldiers of the "movement" but also as bearers of the "new Acholi generation." This status alone granted them more privileges—including opportunities for release. Girls were prepared for their release and return to society, given special training to develop their skills in reading, writing, accounting, and business skills.

DISCUSSION: REINTEGRATION INTO NORTHERN UGANDA

This study made no attempt to deny or minimize the brutality the girls experienced: All the children suffered greatly throughout the duration of their captivity. They all witnessed and participated in killings and beatings of their family members and friends, often by their own hands. All the children were also indoctrinated with propaganda about the "movement" of the LRA. Yet the depth and array of skills and coping mechanisms attained and used by the girls were so significant that even the girls themselves, after contributing to the analysis of the data, transformed how they defined their experience. Their ability to endure such an extreme, horrific, and demanding environment demonstrates their great coping capacity and also illustrates a great inner strength too often ignored by methods used during reintegration programs.

Although their skills differed, both the girls who conceived children while in the LRA and those who remained servants or "wives" without children developed coping mechanisms that would prove to enhance their quality of life under the extreme conditions of the LRA. Contrary to other studies on child soldiers, the more time they spent in captivity, the more resilient most girls became (Save the Children, 2001). Those taken to Sudan had increased responsibilities and opportunities, providing more means to foster resilience and cope with the abuse. Girls became less fearful of the commanders as they developed relationships with them and acquired skills that enabled them to feel more confident when speaking to commanders. Some girls even gained enough confidence to report mistreatment by commanders—a remarkable demonstration of an increase in confidence and skills when compared to the speechless state of terror that understandably gripped most girls early in their captivity.

When the girls were asked what kind of skills or responsibilities they attained while in captivity, the first response was always that they were transformed into soldiers, followed by cooking, cleaning, and digging. This study, however, uncovered numerous other roles and responsibilities, each of which contributed greatly to the girls' development of new abilities and capacity to cope with the extreme environment, enabling the process of resilience to emerge.

At the time of this research, the aims of programs for former girl soldiers in northern Uganda were to help them heal and to smooth their transition to civilian life. To those ends, they offered counseling sessions, recreational activities, educational opportunities, and skill training options. Most programs also included community outreach initiatives that attempted to sensitize the community about the girls and assist in their acceptance.

Although grounded in a resilience-based model attempting to (1) reduce a negative chain reaction following risk exposure, (2) establish and maintain a child's self-esteem and self-efficacy, and (3) open up opportunities—elements often described as necessary to foster resilience (Rutter, 1987)—these reintegration programs continue to miss a core method of enhancing resilience: *fostering that which already exists.* Their failure to do a comprehensive analysis of the girls' past experiences inherently limits their effectiveness and inevitably pushes the girls back into the mode of "helpless victim." The programs may have the best interest of the child in mind, but their rejection of the girls' past or assuming they had undergone a particular set of experiences or only had a limited set of skills that were acquired inappropriately has placed former female child soldiers into a particularly narrow group. This categorization undermines the unique potential of each girl and merely generates a "healed victim" from a crisis over which she had no control.

At the time of this research, program staff knew little about the girls' experience, skills, and strengths attained while in captivity. Rather than explore resilient qualities that already existed within the girl, the programs focused on new ways to create resilience. Though some programs offered a sense of security by providing skills training in such areas as tailoring or small business, all programs inadvertently weakened aspects of the girls' resilience by (1) failing to build on their existing strengths and treating them all the same, (2) pushing them to forget the past, and (3) molding them into traditional gender roles.

BUILDING ON EXISTING STRENGTHS AND TREATING THEM ALL THE SAME

Most reintegration programs offered few options to girls returning from captivity that might have supported their livelihood and reintegration back into the community. Fewer options meant fewer opportunities to explore their strengths in unique, individual ways. The prevailing belief within the organizations was that the skills acquired during captivity were predominantly military skills. Therefore, there was a tendency to focus on developing new skills that could provide a legitimate income and thereby assist the reintegration into civilian life by moving them from destructive behaviors or tendencies they might have learned while under the strict environment of the LRA. Although teaching new skills is not a bad thing, acquired skills are better integrated and maintained when they strengthen already existing skills rooted within.

While in captivity in the LRA the girls were assigned to numerous roles and responsibilities—from household activities to nursing roles, to military commanders, to cartographers. Yet, because they lacked the formal education necessary to build on those skills, the girls were ineligible to pursue such opportunities after they returned to their communities.

The variety of skills the girls had developed and the coping mechanisms they used while in the LRA should inform services that help them reintegrate into the community, thereby facilitating the adjustment process in the long term. For example, elements of the "military" environment could be considered when placing girls in employment. If the past years were orderly and disciplined, positions or employment that have some sort of structure in place could provide a better fit. Teaching new trades that offer an opportunity to foster team-building and collaborative skills could be more effective than training for positions in which employees work alone. Opportunities to use public speaking, communications, counseling, or teaching skills could help build on the strengths many of the girls acquired while under the LRA. Being forced to "brainwash" other children about the "movement" of the LRA taught girls how to enunciate, project their voice, perfect the art of storytelling, and use techniques of public speaking. Girls put in teaching positions or asked to be mother's helpers or peer mentors/guides learned patience, empathy, and listening skills.

Unfortunately, a missed opportunity to tap into innovative approaches resulted in the continuation of the status quo. Programs in northern Uganda continued to place all the girls at the same level, in the same position, doing the same work. They went through the assembly line and came out at the other end like everyone else. This cookie-cutter approach not only overlooked the individual potential of each girl but also did a tremendous disservice to the community at large by ignoring the girls' potential contributions.

HEALING AND EMBRACING THE PAST

> When I get sick people tell me that I am still possessed by the evil spirits of the bush. They say I am traumatized, but I don't feel like I am. I feel normal. (Havia, 17 years old, 2 years in captivity)

Rehabilitative and reintegration programs are designed to counsel and assist children to deal with some of the traumatic experiences they have endured. With good intentions, programs that attempt to erase all memories—as a way to "forget the past" and instill a sense of normalcy—insist that doing so will provide the child with more appropriate behaviors and skills that will facilitate adjustment to life in the community. Social workers interviewed for this research reported that it was important and necessary for children to forget their past so they could move on, reiterating that there were no positive aspects of their past that could be used in the present. Forgetting the past, however, denies children access to experiences that may have empowered them. It also may quiet them into tolerating their life and accepting the status quo.

Indeed, the programs did help children handle the pain they experienced—but they went too far, considering the continued resurfacing of the past in their lives as a sign of failure. Having the ability to forget the past was seen as a quality of strength, and any indication that one could not forget meant a girl was in need of additional therapy. Girls who were unable to separate their past from their present lives became convinced that they were possessed or weak. Rather than recognizing their "inappropriate behavior" as a newly gained skill or a sign of assertiveness, they felt marginalized and in need of therapy.

In northern Uganda, cultural influences play an enormous role in how rehabilitation is carried out (Okuma, 2003). Traditional cleansing ceremonies symbolically bring healing and forgiveness as well as a sense of welcome and acceptance back into the community (Stark, 2006). These ceremonies can enhance recovery and social reintegration for some children, but unless done alongside programs that allow for expression and a sense of agency, they can limit the sustainability of such healing (Green & Honwana, 1999). Without harnessing the rage and other emotions that may accompany this process, healing ceremonies alone merely silence those feelings within the child, causing them to reject the anger, sadness, and feelings of isolation or rejection and thereby missing an opportunity to channel this negative energy into something more positive.

Many children, after undergoing traditional ceremonies and feeling cleansed of the painful and negative aspects of the war, still affirm a desire to "get angry." In other words, they have a yearning for certain aspects of their past though they no longer feel they are possessed. When feelings from the past do arise, the verbal abuse received by the community may seem like a justified reaction because the child is assumed to still possesses traits of an "uncleansed" person. The child herself may start to accept such treatment and begin to believe that perhaps she is still "possessed." This reaction and community view reinforce the image of a former child soldier as a helpless, passive victim unable to contribute to improving his or her situation.

What appeared to be lacking in these programs and the girls' lives was a real opportunity to channel some of that energy and confusion into a process where they could see a value in their future as well as their past. With former girl child soldiers specifically, what may be viewed as uncharacteristic, disrespectful, or simply "bad" conduct—all of which would create the belief of being "possessed"—could actually be seen as a threat to traditional gender roles.

EMPOWERED GENDER ROLES

More than their male counterparts, female child soldiers pose a challenge to traditional society when they resist returning to old gender roles (Barth, 2002). Part of their "forgetting the past" was rejecting the new status many females acquired while in captivity. Girls in combat took on similar and equal roles to those of males (Mazurana & McKay, 2003). In northern Uganda, girls were given leadership positions and ranks in the military forces, and they fought alongside men. This changed status made adjustment difficult when the girls returned to a community that did not recognize these achievements and new, more equal roles. Females who decided to speak out against the exclusion and marginalization they received from the community were labeled unfit for society, when in actuality they had gained more assertiveness, confidence, and the belief that they had the right to express their opinions, something often denied females in their own culture.

Rather than embrace the equality the girls experienced, the reintegration programs undermined the girls' ability to act as role models or advocates for the rights of girls and women. The programs replicated a patriarchal system that prevented them from making a positive change in the status of females. Reintegration programs that attempted to "mold" the girls back into accepted female behavior seemed to chip away at the resilience innate within each one. In fact, as the findings in this study suggest, girls more often than not felt disempowered because of the reintegration programs. This feeling of disempowerment slowly broke down the coping mechanisms—which had been steadily developed in captivity and had given rise to a sense of self-determination—into a form of dependence once the girls returned to the community. If left unaddressed, this break from civil society's expectations of appropriate gender norms and behaviors has enormous implications for girls' reintegration into society (Barth, 2002).

CONCLUSIONS

In northern Uganda, girls not only served as soldiers but also held leadership positions as commanders and higher ranks within the LRA forces. These roles often gave them a tremendous amount of respect during their military service and leadership skills that they could use in civilian life (Barth, 2002; McKay & Mazurana, 2004; Veale, 2003).

The harsh and often demanding war environment exposes children to different challenges to their physical, social, cognitive, and psychological development, and reintegration programs may fail to fully grasp how these complex changes have influenced the child. Too many programs have a knee-jerk response, erasing the past and shaping the child back into a "normal" functioning child citizen who will be able to live in the community. In doing so, especially with girls, organizations reinforce "a return to traditional structures and patriarchal practices" (McKay & Mazurana, 2004, p. 17). Though it is more comfortable for the community, this process once again denies an opportunity to capitalize on what could be a positive change not only for the child but also for the community at large. Capitalizing on this opportunity could result in greater respect for girls' rights, a more diverse community, and a stronger workforce equipped with different skills.

Though reintegration programs are able to provide counseling and training in new technical skills to former child soldiers, many fail to build on existing skills that the children acquired while serving in military forces. Too often seen as negative and only detrimental to the child's new life, these skills are downplayed or, more often, never even acknowledged. Children themselves fail to identify their own strengths and dismiss these strengths as merely "military skills" or "skills of killing or survival" that they are encouraged to forget. Thus, these strengths are not seen as opportunities that can be used to enhance future possibilities. What may at first appear to be a negative attribute (e.g., the harsh military training, killing and looting of villages) may actually be the basis for a productive and important skill. As this study identified, there is an enormous opportunity to harness and productively build on existing skills and experiences, thereby promoting a sense of confidence, self-esteem, and self-determination. If programs embrace these skills, whether negative or positive, children's success rate of reintegration may be stronger and more sustainable.

Yet, merely putting in place programs that highlight past skills without the consultation and full participation of children could hinder their rehabilitative process. Just as denying their past undermines their potential, linking past skills to present programming could also be detrimental if not done via thoughtful and skilled planning and training. Attachment to a particular skill, even if valued, could serve as a negative reminder, thus hindering the healing process. Programs that are open and attentive to alternative possibilities offer a greater chance for a full, meaningful reintegration. Meaningful participation can boost child empowerment, allowing them more freedom to decide which skills they choose to hold onto and which they choose to change.

These research findings challenge service providers to take a closer look at the gender dynamics and differences among children returning from LRA captivity. They illustrate the danger in classifying the experience of all children as the same and reiterate the importance of undertaking a comprehensive analysis that explores the unique potential and coping mechanisms of children to effectively build on resilient factors while not undermining existing strengths.

Resilience is not provided alone by services that organizations offer for children (i.e., placing them in skill training programs) or by the efforts that others make on their behalf (i.e., advocating for children's right for an education). These are necessary in their own right and have a place in a child's development and attainment of his or her rights. However, reintegration programs that look to foster and build on a child's resilience must reexamine their approach and move away from the "what we do" (e.g., skills training, sports activities, life skills workshops) to strengthening the "how we do what we do" (e.g., communicating with children, supporting children's agency, understanding self-protective mechanisms). This approach will enhance how we build on existing strengths and increase the child's likelihood for continued resilience.

Four ways are recommended to increase the effectiveness of reintegration programs and thereby support the resilience innate within children:

1. The programs need to speak to and value the individual beyond the collective so they can develop systems and frameworks that enhance specific skills needed to foster resilience. This requires funding and resources dedicated to strengthening continuous analysis and fine-tuning of the programs.

2. Reintegration efforts should underscore the importance of relationships and social integration that encompass adaptive coping, sound decision making, and participation as fundamental to maximizing resilience in children. Emphasis should be placed on *how* programs are carried out and the type of methods used to strengthen resilient factors and should move away from preset activities as the solution.

3. The programs should develop new frameworks that integrate and build on existing and past coping mechanisms as a way to enhance resilience innate within children. This requires investment in social welfare systems that value and recognize the importance of social workers' development of empathy and relationship-building skills, that have improved case management systems that capture more comprehensively the experience of children affected by conflict, and that adopt practices that support children's participation across the entire system.

4. The programs should reflect a gender dimension to acknowledge and support the diversity of experiences, strengths, unique challenges, capacity, and opportunities among children affected by armed conflict. Investment in context-specific analysis and children's agency and decision-making skills can improve practice.

Today, the postwar context in northern Uganda has changed significantly. Rehabilitative centers have closed, and new community-based programs have emerged. The focus has shifted from humanitarian aid to longer term development promoting livelihoods, economic stability, peace and reconciliation, education, and gender equality. Twelve years later, there is still much learning to build on. I am planning a longitudinal study to examine how the resilience within the girls manifested over the past 15 years. This research will explore whether programs changed based on the findings from this study, how girls themselves capitalized on past skills, and whether or not there are opportunities to strengthen reintegration programs for children affected by conflict. The study will also explore the significance of the girls' agency and how it contributed to changed gender norms, decision-making skills, and overall resilience.

A significant outcome of this research project was the creation of the community-led organization, Empowering Hands, founded by 30 of the girls who participated in the study. The involvement of the girls in the design, study, and analysis of the research prompted them to take ownership of the project and build on the results of the findings (Lenz, 2004). The organization, led and managed by the young women themselves, illustrates the strength and empowerment that can be tapped into when initiatives engage, acknowledge, and give ownership to beneficiaries.

Using skills of coordination, event planning, team building, and leadership, the young women formed and managed a community-based organization that has shifted their lives from helpless, dependent victims to empowered and respected peace builders. As a testament to the potential that this approach offers, several of the girls were able to transform one skill (inspirational speaking, used formerly to brainwash other children) into a powerful tool to support peace-building efforts. Assisting other children who were affected by the conflict, these girls engage with international peace-building efforts and senior diplomatic missions and participate in local conflict resolution initiatives as they relate to internal displacement. Ten years on, their work continues, and as these young women embrace their future while seizing their role as peace builder, they are reminded that they are not only equipped with skills from their past but are also armed with resilience.

Note

1. All names used in this chapter are pseudonyms to protect the identity of the girls who participated in the study. The girls chose their own pseudonyms.

References

Barth, E. (2002). *Peace as disappointment: The reintegration of female soldiers in post-conflict societies: A comparative study from Africa.* Oslo: International Peace Research Institute.

Bernard, B. (2004). *Resilience: What we have learned.* San Francisco: WestEd.

Betancourt, T. S., & Khan, K. T. (2008). The mental health of children affected by armed conflict: Protective processes and pathways to resilience. *International Review of Psychiatry, 20*(3), 317–328.

Boyden, J. (2000). *Social healing in war-affected displaced children.* Refugees Study Center. Retrieved from http://asylumsupport.info/publications/rsc/healing.htm.

Carroll, S. (2015). Catch them young: Participation and roles of girl child soldiers in armed conflicts. In S. Shekhawat (Ed.), *Female combatants in conflict and peace: Challenging gender in violence and post-conflict reintegration* (pp. 36–52). London: Palgrave Macmillan.

Center on the Developing Child at Harvard University. (2015). *Supportive relationships and active skill building.* Cambridge, MA: Harvard University. Retrieved from http://developingchild.harvard.edu.

Daniel, B., & Wassel, S. (2002). *Adolescence: Assessing and promoting resilience in vulnerable children* 3. London: Jessica Kingsley.

Fernando, C., & Ferrari, M. (2013). *Handbook of resilience in children of war.* New York: Springer.

Gallagher, R. (2002). *Building resilience in children in the face of fear and tragedy.* New York: New York University Child Study Center.

Green, E. C., & Honwana, A. (1999). Indigenous healing of war-affected children in Africa. In *World Bank: Knowledge and Learning Center: Africa Region* (Report no. 10). Washington, DC: World Bank.

Grotberg, E. (1997). *The International Resilience Project, research and application.* Paper presented at the Annual Convention of the International Council of Psychologists, Graz, Austria.

Halevi, G., Djalovski, A., Vengrober, A., & Feldman, R. (2016). Risk and resilience trajectories in war-exposed children across the first decade of life. *Journal of Child Psychology and Psychiatry, 7*(10): 1183–1193.

Human Rights Watch. (2003). *Stolen children: Abduction and recruitment in northern Uganda* (Vol. 15, no. 7[A]). New York: Author.

Kasen, S., Wickramaratne, P., Gameroff, M. J., & Weissman, M. M. (2012). Religiosity and resilience in persons at high risk for major depression. *Psychological Medicine, 42*(3), 509–519.

Lenz, J. (2004). *Armed with resilience: A study addressing the issues of reintegration and resiliency of formerly abducted girl child soldiers in northern Uganda and their potential role as peace builders.* Oxford: Center for Development and Emergency Practice, Oxford Brookes University.

Masten, A.S. (2011). Resilience in children threatened by extreme adversity: Frameworks for research, practice, and translational synergy. *Development and Psychopathology, 23*(2), 493–506.

Masten, A. S. (2014). Global perspectives on resilience in children and youth. *Child Development*, 85(1), 6–20.

Masten, A. S., & Narayan, A. J. (2012). Child development in the context of disaster, war, and terrorism: Pathways of risk and resilience. *Annual Review of Psychology*, 63, 227–257.

Masten, A. S., & Powell, J. L. (2003). A resilience framework for research, policy, and practice. In S. S. Luthar (Ed.), *Resilience and vulnerability: Adaptation in the context of childhood adversities* (pp. 1–25). Cambridge: Cambridge University Press.

Mazurana, D., & McKay, S. (2003). *Girls in fighting forces in northern Uganda, Sierra Leone, and Mozambique: Policy and program recommendations*. Montreal: CIDA's Child Protection Research Fund.

McKay, S., & Mazurana, D. (2004). *Where are the girls? Girls in fighting forces in northern Uganda, Sierra Leone, and Mozambique: Their lives during and after war*. Montreal: International Center for Human Rights and Democratic Development.

Okuma, P. (2003). *A study on the views, perspectives, and experiences of social integration among formerly abducted girls in Gulu, northern Uganda*. Copenhagen: Save the Children Denmark.

Rutter, M. (1987). Psychological resilience and protective mechanisms. *American Journal of Orthopsychiatry*, 57(3), 316–333.

Save the Children. (2001). *Children in crisis: Care and protection of children in emergencies field guide series (education, youth, child soldiers)*. Washington, DC: Author.

Stark, L. (2006). Cleansing the wounds of war: An examination of traditional healing, psychosocial health and reintegration in Sierra Leone. *Intervention*, 4(3), 206–218.

Ungar, M. (2012). *The social ecology of resilience: A handbook of theory and practice*. New York: Springer.

Veale, A. (2003). *Violence, reconciliation and identity: The reintegration of Lord's Resistance Army child abductees in northern Uganda*. Pretoria: Institute for Security Studies.

Wessells, M. G. (2009). *Child soldiers: From violence to protection*. Cambridge, MA: Harvard University Press.

PART TWO

METHODOLOGICAL APPROACHES TO UNDERSTANDING THE REALITIES OF CHILDREN AFFECTED BY ARMED CONFLICT

CHILDREN ARE CONSTANTLY INFLUENCING and being influenced by their social and physical environments. Yet research studies of war-affected children have not fully explored this dynamic and dialectical relationship. This section highlights multiple methodological approaches to data collection and analysis, including socioecological research methods, rapid ethnography, participatory methods, as well as narrative methods and storytelling.

In chapter 6, Bree Akesson and Myriam Denov present socioecological approaches to data collection in their chapter titled "Socioecological Research Methods with Children Affected by Armed Conflict: Examples from Northern Uganda and Palestine." Drawing from examples of community consultations and intergenerational interviews in northern Uganda and collaborative family interviews in Palestine, the chapter discusses the strengths and challenges of using a socioecological approach to better understand the experiences and needs of war-affected children.

In chapter 7, "What Children and Youth Can Tell Us: A Rapid Ethnography Approach to Understanding Harms to Children in Somaliland and Puntland," Kathleen Kostelny, Ken Justus Ondoro, and Michael G. Wessells present an innovative participatory methodology of rapid ethnography. Rather than relying on expert-driven learning that is focused on deficits and affords limited inputs from children, this methodology allowed the authors to explore the children's perspectives and lived experiences in regard to child protection issues. Finding that children's views on harm diverged significantly from those frequently put forth by adults and child protection professionals, the authors argue that child protection approaches, policies, and supports need to learn from the voices of children themselves.

In chapter 8, "Surviving Disorder: Children, Violence, and War Stories," Sukanya Podder uses narrative analysis to demonstrate how the war stories of child soldiers who participated in the Liberian civil wars become "performances" for transmitting agency when coping with violence. Podder illustrates how children actively shape their power and position in postconflict settings through the telling of war stories. By presenting the narratives of two young people affected by war, she highlights how her study participants created particular types of self-image: One presented a victim narrative, whereas the other relayed a story of survival. Podder discusses the implications of the relationship between children and violence for children's agency, as well as the ways in which human rights discourses approach child protection issues in conflict settings.

In chapter 9, titled "Reweaving Relating in Social Reintegration: Participatory Action Research with War-Affected Young Mothers and Their Children in Liberia, Sierra Leone, and Northern Uganda," authors Angela Veale, Miranda Worthen, and Susan McKay present a participatory action research (PAR) methodology that sought to promote the social reintegration of young mothers and their children in Liberia, Sierra Leone, and northern Uganda. The study highlights the ability of a PAR methodology to address reintegration in a socioecological way by placing young mothers at the center of their relational networks and helping them mobilize those networks, thus creating sites of "joint action." The authors focus on how trauma is socially embedded and should be addressed as such. The PAR methodology altered the outcomes of many young mothers from a developmental trajectory of increasing vulnerability to a state of empowerment within which their actions fostered increased community acceptance and encouraged them to work together. The authors highlight the importance not only of individual agency but also of *relational* agency—actions taken by the actor in question must be supplemented and supported by further action of others in the social ecology.

The studies in this section not only illustrate the complexity of war-affected children's experiences within the contexts of Palestine, Liberia, Sierra Leone, Somalia, and northern Uganda but also show how using creative and innovative research methods can enhance our understanding of their daily lives, including their challenges and opportunities.

6

SOCIOECOLOGICAL RESEARCH METHODS WITH CHILDREN AFFECTED BY ARMED CONFLICT
Examples from Northern Uganda and Palestine

Bree Akesson and Myriam Denov

ARMED CONFLICT DAMAGES THE SOCIAL fabric that fosters healthy child development and well-being. This social fabric is made up of multiple elements such as families, schools, neighborhood communities, society, and culture that are key factors in children's lives. Although strengthening family and community-based supports is considered to be one of the most effective ways to address children's psychosocial well-being (for example, see Boothby, 1996; Wessells, 2009; Wessells & Monteiro, 2004), as noted in the chapters in this volume, much of the current body of research with children affected by armed conflict focuses on mental health issues such as posttraumatic stress disorder (PTSD) and other forms of individual symptomatology (for example, see Tol, Barbui, et al., 2011; Tol, Patel, et al., 2011). The words of Cairns and Dawes (1996, p. 129), challenging researchers to move forward on an alternate path and away from negative mental health outcomes, still resonate today nearly 20 years after they were first published:

> The field can still be said to be in its infancy. Part of the problem is that, for many years, investigators have been content to explore whether political violence has negative psychological consequences for children, but have neglected to move much beyond this broad premise.

In response, there have been calls to take a socioecological approach to working with children affected by armed conflict (Boothby, 2008; Boothby, Strang, & Wessells, 2006). Ecological approaches deemphasize the individual and instead consider the child's well-being from an individual, familial, social, cultural, and political perspective (Tol, Haroz, Hock, Kane, & Jordans, 2014). Although scholars have emphasized socioecological approaches as an overarching theoretical approach to understanding children's lives (Boothby et al., 2006; Tol, Jordans, Kohrt, Betancourt, & Komproe, 2013a), less attention has been paid to socioecological *research methods* used to study children affected by armed conflict, which is our focus.

This chapter begins with a summary of the state of research with children affected by armed conflict. After examining a socioecological theoretical approach and presenting research studies that have used such an approach, we explore its potential application to research methods with war-affected children. We present examples of research projects in northern Uganda and Palestine that have implemented socioecological approaches to research methods with war-affected children and youth, while highlighting the unique contributions and limitations of the approach to research methods more generally. We end the chapter by identifying trends in research methods with children affected by armed conflict, underscoring how such methods may lead to researchers embracing more socioecological approaches in the future.

STATE OF THE CURRENT RESEARCH ON CHILDREN AFFECTED BY ARMED CONFLICT

As noted in this volume's introduction, the theoretical literature on children affected by war, drawing from Western conceptions of childhood and its association with vulnerability and the need for protection, has tended to portray children as dependent and helpless (Denov, 2010; Honwana & de Boeck, 2005). Moreover, drawing on Western mental health approaches, trauma interventions for children affected by war have typically been based on risk factors and evidence-based cognitive behavioral activities that focus on altering cognitive distortions around trauma through one-on-one and small group interventions. Such individualized therapeutic interventions have been critiqued for overlooking the reality that children have an inherent expertise that can be built on, that their social and cultural surroundings and practices may provide protection from traumatic symptoms, and that trauma is neither static nor linear (Boyden & Mann, 2005; Denov & Blanchet-Cohen, 2014).

These critiques have been echoed in the research on children affected by armed conflict. Although much research has relied on individualized approaches, a growing body of literature is now addressing the issue of war-affected children from a socioecological perspective. In their edited collection

A World Turned Upside Down: Social Ecological Approaches to Children in War Zones, Boothby, Wessells, and Strang (2006) examine the wide-ranging experiences of children in war zones across the globe from a psychological and socioecological perspective. The authors suggest that work with children affected by armed conflict should incorporate knowledge of the multiple and interacting factors at each level of the child's socioecological system. Yet, a decade after Boothby et al.'s call for the use and implementation of socioecological approaches to children affected by armed conflict, there remains a strong emphasis on individual maladaptive conditions. In a brief review of research on children affected by armed conflict, published between January 2014 and June 2015, we found a continued focus on the psychological effects resulting from armed conflict and subsequent mental health disorders such as posttraumatic stress or other pathology, with less attention on children's relationships with families, neighborhoods, communities, and cultures/societies (for example, see Amone-P'Olak et al., 2014; Karam et al., 2014, Lai, Hadi, & Llabre, 2014; Punamäki et al., 2015). Others have found a similar focus. In examining the literature on resilience among children affected by armed conflict, Tol, Jordans, Kohrt, Betancourt, and Komproe (2013b) note that few research studies include findings that span the broad range of social and physical environments with which children engage—highlighting the importance and need to rethink not only how we conceptualize but also how we conduct research with children in these contexts.

DEFINING SOCIOECOLOGICAL APPROACHES

Countless factors affect an individual child's development and well-being. In addition to individual-level factors—such as genetics and temperament—social and physical environments continually interact with the child at different levels. In contrast to individualized approaches that often neglect important contextual realities, a socioecological approach views children as nested within multiple interlocking spheres of family, school, community, the nation-state, and higher order systems such as society and culture. Disruption or disturbance within any of these spheres, which often happens during times of armed conflict, can potentially alter the course of a child's development and overall well-being.

The core of the socioecological approach is the notion that children cannot be considered or studied in isolation from their surrounding context.

Instead, the approach recognizes that children's lives and experiences are constantly shaped and influenced by the powerful structures, communities, and individuals that encircle them, as well as the dynamic interactions and relationships between these elements. Vital "systems"—whether family, school, or peer group—are key determinants of war-affected children's developmental outcomes (Boothby et al., 2006). For example, the family, including extended family in many parts of the world, is the key micro system within which children develop and where basic protections and needs are provided. The relevance of home and family spaces in contributing to or lessening children's well-being cannot be overstated. Armed conflict has a powerful impact on family life and family structures, causing many children to become separated from their parents, lose family members, choose not to live with their family, or, in some cases, become heads of households. As such, when we refer to family, we are not assuming a "natural" or singular form of family. Rather, notions of family are fluid and are often defined by the individuals and institutions in question. Nonetheless, what is important in relation to a socioecological perspective is that, however a "family" is defined or understood, those who make up that family have a key role to play in children's lives. In addition, the socioecological approach can help contextualize how the home can serve as a site of protection in the midst of armed conflict or a space where the line between private and public is blurred when the armed conflict enters the home space (Akesson, 2014a). Likewise, schools often provide key first encounters with social institutions and are critical spheres of interaction for and between children, including peers and teachers (Akesson, 2015; Boothby et al., 2006). Children's socialization and development also occur within wider social systems that include vital community members. On a much broader macro level, children's lives are informed by historical, political, social, cultural, religious, and legal norms, practices, and institutions.

All of these systems are fundamentally affected by the onset of war and armed conflict, profoundly altering children's lives. A socioecological approach thus considers both micro- and macro-level features that shape children's lives and enables a more complex understanding of young people's relations and interactions with family, school, community, and the broader sociocultural context. Importantly, in examining these diverse systems and levels of inquiry, the socioecological approach is able to identify, explore, and elicit both the risk and protective factors within the multiple systems surrounding the child. Understanding the experiences of children affected by war from a socioecological perspective thus requires an analysis not just of children's lives during and after war but also of those of their parents, siblings, extended family members, caregivers, teachers, community leaders, and other members of their social environment who have day-to-day contact with children and influence their well-being. As Boothby (2008, p. 502) notes,

> An ecologic approach to understanding children and war thus begins with a thorough examination of the protective capacities (and deficits) of key people and systems that surround them. It should form the basis for thinking with appropriate breadth of potential influences on children's well-being . . . the goal is to identify features of both micro and macro systems that together can be seen to form a potential protective shield around children, not eliminating risks and vulnerabilities but protecting children from their full impact.

This approach is able to not only provide a more holistic understanding of the child in his or her context but also can ensure an intergenerational and multi-dimensional understanding and analysis of the impact of armed conflict on children and their families.

THE SOCIOECOLOGICAL APPROACH AS METHOD: RESEARCH EXAMPLES FROM NORTHERN UGANDA AND PALESTINE

For several decades, research on diverse areas related to children and childhood has taken a socioecological approach. In fact, a broad range of child-related research has relied on a socioecological perspective, particularly regarding HIV/AIDS (Steele, Nelson, & Cole, 2007), school bullying (Ncube, 2013), adolescent behavior problems (Beam, Gil-Rivas, Greenberger, & Chen, 2002; Scholte, 1992), substance abuse (Brenner, Bauermeister, & Zimmerman, 2011; Elkington, Bauermeister, & Zimmerman, 2011), immigrant youth and identity (Chen, Lau, Tapanya, & Cameron, 2012; Dyson, 2013), physical activity and obesity (Casey, Eime, Payne, & Harvey, 2009; Vella, Cliff, & Okely, 2014; Willows, Hanley, & Delormier, 2012), and public health (Earls & Carlson, 2001).

Most studies on war-affected children and youth that have employed a socioecological approach have used a socioecological *theoretical* approach to analyze the multiple systems that affect children (Betancourt & Khan, 2008; Garbarino, 2001; Kohrt et al., 2010; Lustig et al., 2004; Tol et al., 2013a). However, fewer studies have used a socioecological approach to frame and shape their research *methodologies*. One exception is the study by Bushin (2009), which used a "children-in-families" methodological approach by conducting interviews with *both children and their caregivers* to explore family migration decision-making and migration processes. By adopting a children-in-families approach, Bushin argues that it is possible to develop a deeper theorization of family migration decision making that reflects the involvement and experiences of children. We fully support Bushin's premise, as well as her efforts to include both child and family perspectives within the process of data collection. However, we believe that in keeping with a socioecological perspective, other elements of the socioecological system, including community and cultural perspectives, should also be part of the research methodology to provide a more holistic picture of the populations under study.

In this section we provide practical research examples illustrating how a socioecological approach can be used to frame research methods with war-affected children in northern Uganda and Palestine. Although different in context, content, and population, our research projects nonetheless integrated socioecological methods into the research design. Within both projects, war-affected children were not the *solitary* focus of data collection and analysis, but rather a key element at the heart of multiple socioecological systems.

BORN OF WAR: CHILDREN BORN IN CAPTIVITY
IN NORTHERN UGANDA

Sexual violence during armed conflict is one of the most recurring wartime human rights abuses.[1] In the last decade, it has been estimated that tens of thousands of children have been born as a result of wartime mass rape campaigns, sexual violence, and forced pregnancy. Born of war, these children are deeply affected by the social upheavals that brought about their conception (Carpenter, 2010). Research has begun to reveal that children born of wartime rape may face profound social, cultural, economic, and psychological consequences, including stigma, abandonment, violence, barriers to legal citizenship, and lack of access to formal health, education, and employment systems (van Ee & Kleber, 2013; Zraly, Rubin, & Mukamana, 2013). However, postconflict policies and services have yet to address this population of children in in-depth and comprehensive ways. In addition, noticeably absent from the literature are the voices of the children themselves, particularly in relation to their unique and long-term needs.

In the context of northern Uganda's civil war (1987–2007), the abduction, forced marriage, and impregnation of females were key military strategies of the Lord's Resistance Army (LRA). The LRA abducted an estimated 60,000 children—30% of whom were girls—using them as combatants, porters, and domestic workers and "wives" (Carlson & Mazurana, 2008; Veale, McKay, Worthen, & Wessells, 2013). Roughly 10,000 abducted girls became pregnant as a result of sexual violence, giving birth to two or more children (Akello, 2013). Although not all of these children survived LRA captivity, thousands are still living in northern Uganda (Watye Ki Gen, 2015). Funded by the Pierre Elliott Trudeau Foundation, the research project in question is concerned with the well-being of children and families affected by war, with a particular focus on children born in LRA captivity (Denov, 2015). To gain a more socioecological understanding of those children, the project has incorporated the perspectives of children, family members, and community members.

GATHERING COMMUNITY PERSPECTIVES: COMMUNITY CONSULTATIONS Before beginning the research process, the research team, which included Uganden and Canadian Researchers, organized in-depth community consultations in three districts of northern Uganda—Gulu, Pader, and Agago—representing both rural and urban contexts. The consultations sought to engage a broad range of family and community members who held vital knowledge on children born in captivity and to ensure that their perspectives were incorporated into the research design and implementation. Key stakeholders who attended the consultations included children and youth born in LRA captivity, mothers/guardians, grandparents and other extended family members of children born in captivity, schoolteachers, religious/community leaders, organizations working on transitional justice and children's rights issues, and cultural and religious institutions. To elicit their perspectives on relevant research questions, the research design, appropriate methods, and approaches to undertake during the course of the research, the team met individually with these stakeholders, as well as in small group discussions and large group meetings. The consultations, which were held with a total of 77 people—26 in Gulu, 19 in Pader, and 32 in Agago—provided vital direction, leadership, and guidance to the research team. Community members suggested key themes to examine during data collection, including (1) identity; (2) stigma, belonging, and social exclusion; (3) family structure and support;

(4) heritage and citizenship; (5) challenges and experiences in school; and (6) long-term community reintegration. They also informed the research team what issues they felt were most important in relation to each theme.

EXPLORING MULTIPLE ECOLOGICAL SYSTEMS: CHILDREN, MOTHERS, EXTENDED FAMILY, AND TEACHERS Much of the research on children born of wartime rape, and specifically on children born in LRA captivity, has been based largely on historical analysis (Mochmann, 2008; Mochmann & Lee, 2010), compilations of existing literature (van Ee & Kleber, 2013), legal frameworks (Markovic, 2007; Qin, 2003), and accounts from mothers (Akello, 2013; Zraly et al., 2013). Noticeably absent from the literature are the *perspectives and voices of the children themselves.* Children's views on the mother/father/caregiver-child relationship, experiences of community belonging and stigmatization in the postconflict context, and the meaning and implications for social identity and legal citizenship remain largely unexplored. In response, this research project directly investigated the lived realities and experiences of those born in LRA captivity in northern Uganda, thereby gaining a more comprehensive understanding of the intergenerational effects of wartime sexual violence and how they affect multiple cohorts, postconflict maternal and community well-being, children's postconflict identity, citizenship and belonging, community supports, and child protection and rights.

Life story interviews and focus groups were conducted with 20 children and youth born in LRA captivity in three districts (N=60). To supplement interviews and focus groups and to enable participants to express themselves in multiple forms, child and youth participants were invited to draw and/or map out places and individuals that hold particular importance to them within their socioecological contexts.

With the hope of attaining a more holistic understanding of the realities and experiences of children born in captivity, data were collected from key stakeholder groups. This included in-depth interviews held with mothers, grandmothers, uncles, and aunts of children born in captivity (N=48). Such accounts enabled an exploration of children's relationships with their families, areas of support, protection, and risk. The research team also interviewed teachers employed at schools attended by children born in LRA captivity. These were done in response to statements of child and youth participants, who identified teachers as playing a key role in both their protection and marginalization at school. Although the study is still ongoing, the socioecological approach has provided a unique and multifaceted lens from which to examine and understand the realities of children born in LRA captivity. In particular, by including the multiple voices and perspectives of children, mothers, extended family members, community members, and teachers at various stages of the research—from design to data collection—a more complex view of the postwar period has emerged.

CONTRADICTIONS IN PLACE: EVERYDAY GEOGRAPHIES OF PALESTINIAN FAMILIES

As a place affected by decades of violence and armed conflict, Palestine is inscribed with physical, emotional, and cultural scars. Children living in Palestine have been particularly affected by high rates of morbidity and mortality related both to the Israeli occupation and intra-Palestinian violence (e.g., child abuse, family violence, gender-based violence, and poverty) (Morris et al., 2010; Palestinian Central Bureau of Statistics, 2008). Fifty percent of children in Palestine are regularly exposed to violence in their homes, at schools, on the streets, or when traveling between these places (Defence for Children International [DCI], 2008). Palestinian childhood is also characterized by violent experiences at the hands of the Israeli army and settlers, such as arrests of family members, home demolitions, wall construction around or through their communities, and personal assaults and injuries (Arafat & Boothby, 2003; DCI, 2012; Strickland, 2014).

From 2010–2012, a research team conducted fieldwork in the West Bank and East Jerusalem to understand how and to what extent the occupation and political violence affected Palestinian children and families' relationships with place and how different kinds of places—home, school, neighborhood communities, and the nation-state—protect or do not protect children and families.

A FOCUS ON THE FAMILY USING PLACE-BASED METHODS This research was originally designed to focus on children's experiences with place in the context of violence and armed conflict. However, at the beginning of the research process, the researcher discovered that children's geographies could not be disengaged from their family systems. Therefore, the research design evolved to place a strong emphasis on the role of the family as an element of children's social ecology. All family members—both children and adults—were represented in the research process, with their narratives intertwined and told in concert to better understand how individual and family experiences can be co-constructed. The research design also included place-based methods that aimed to unpack research participants' complex relationship with place.

Collaborative family interviews were conducted with 18 families from various geographical settings—refugee camp, city, village, and encampment—yielding a total of 149 individual research participants. Research was conducted in vivo, within families' homes and communities, in order to observe their interactions with the different social (individuals, family members, neighbors) and physical (the home and neighborhood) elements of the socioecological framework. In an effort to include younger children's voices in all family interviews, at least three family members were asked to participate in the research: a young child (under the age of 9), his or her older sibling (age 9 and older), and an adult caregiver. Several generations were also represented within the family sample to better understand intergenerational experiences with place. Because of the timeline of the Israeli occupation of Palestine, inclusion by these three members provided a complete picture of the family's everyday experience living under occupation. The younger child provided data about his or her experience growing up after the end of the second *intifada* (the Arabic word for the Palestinian uprisings against Israeli occupation that occurred from 2000–2005), the older sibling added to the data by reflecting on his or her experience growing up during the violence of the second *intifada*, and the adult caregiver reflected on the whole experience of living under occupation over several decades. The inclusion of all three family members in the research sample also supported the premise that caregivers—whether parents or older siblings—influence children's experience with place. Collaborative family interviews often included members of both the immediate micro-level nuclear family (*a'ila*) and the extended meso-level larger family (*hamula*). Ultimately, the inclusion of the *hamula* enabled a complex portrait of family life.

During these interviews, family members—both children and adults—were invited to make drawings to illustrate a point or tell a story and to better elucidate how they negotiated and understood their social and physical environments. To authentically include children in the family interview without eclipsing their voices, children were encouraged to produce at least three drawings—(1) a drawing of their choice, (2) a map showing the important places in their neighborhood community, and (3) a dream place where they would like to go one day—all of which provided rich data on children's inter-actions with various socioecological systems.

The research also included a physical exploration of the macro-level neigh-borhood community. At the end of the family interview, all children were invited to participate in neighborhood walks (with parental permission), guid-ing the research team through their neighborhood and showing them the places they move within and through in their daily lives. This physical and mobile approach method is best suited to children's natural ways of commu-nicating and is far more active than the traditional interview setting. Global positioning system (GPS) technology recorded the length of the neighbor-hood walks in both distance and time, producing a visual record to corre-spond with any detailed and annotated commentary using the qualitative ap-proach. This method capitalized on the relationship between physical movement, the rhythms of walking, and the telling of stories, which facilitates the recounting of memories and traces a participant's history with his or her social and physical environment. Through this place-based method, the re-search team was able to observe children's movements in and between the home, school, neighborhood communities, and their wider socioecological environment.

Finally, the research design included 10 interviews with key informants. These interviews were conducted with local and international nongovern-mental organization (INGO) personnel and others working with children and families in Palestine, such as social workers. They explored ideas raised by other methods of data collection, identified populations or issues for further investigation, refined data collection efforts, assessed progress, and generated recommendations (Education Development Center, 2004). Ultimately, con-versations with these community members resulted in discovering new infor-mation that was not revealed through the other methods.

The use of these socioecological methods in combination generated diverse readings of children's and families' experiences with their social and physical environment and added to an understanding of the role of place in their lives. The research was able to describe the multiple places within children's socio-ecological environment, as well as how and why places are created for, and by, children. It recorded the supervised and unsupervised movement of children at the meso-level of the home and beyond to the macro level of the neighbor-hood community. Through this process, the research team noted particular kinds of place-related practices that were found to be effective in addressing inequalities that determine how place and space affect children's lives. Using place-based methods as a socioecological research tool helped the research team explore children's and families' experiences with safe and unsafe places as a means of enhancing child well-being in a context of armed conflict.

DISCUSSION: STRENGTHS AND LIMITATIONS OF SOCIOECOLOGICAL RESEARCH METHODS

STRENGTHS

The use of socioecological methods in these two studies illustrates how research can creatively and effectively explore the complexities of children's lives affected by armed conflict in ways that include the voices and perspectives not only of the children themselves but also of their surrounding families and communities.

A socioecological approach has numerous strengths. First, the inclusion of family and community perspectives is likely to yield a richer and more accurate picture of war-affected children's experiences as influenced by these multiple systems. In the northern Uganda study, the research team found differences between children's and mothers' perspectives of the postconflict period. For example, mothers often viewed the postwar period of freedom from violence and LRA oppression as a vast improvement over their lives during LRA captivity. However, because of postwar stigma and severe community marginalization resulting from being born in LRA captivity, many of their children believed that they had actually been better off during the war, when their family had been more intact and cohesive and, relatively speaking, had held greater status and power within their communities. These differing perspectives provided a more nuanced picture of the postwar period for multiple family members and systems and highlighted the role of community members in perpetuating stigma against children born in LRA captivity.

Similarly, in the Palestine study, through the use of place-based research methods reflecting a socioecological approach, analysis uncovered a richness of data that illuminated what Akesson (2014b) identifies as "contradictions in place" that arose as children navigated and negotiated space and place in the face of armed conflict. For example, some children and families described home as a beloved and safe place in the context of armed conflict, as depicted frequently in children's drawings. Yet, the meaning of home was much more complicated: Other participants described home as an unstable and unhealthy place due to poverty, violence, and the pervasive occupation (Akesson, 2014a).

Second, data emerging from multiple sources, including children, family, and community members, can help ensure that interventions are relevant and align with the unique needs of numerous actors within the socioecological system. The study in northern Uganda revealed the differing needs of mothers and their children and that developing generic programs for "families" as a whole may miss the mark in achieving long-term child and mother well-being. Similarly, by using a methodology that obtained data from the multiple systems that affect children's lives, the research conducted in Palestine revealed the importance of those systems' contributions (or harms) to the protection of children. The study also showed the need to address both individual and family-level needs, such as the material need for shelter, as well as the psychosocial need for safety, connection with others, and hope. By using a socioecological approach, interventions for children affected by armed conflict in these settings can capitalize on the ways that informal systems (e.g., families, communities, religious institutions) are already protecting children, rather than creating new programs that replicate or replace these systems. Therefore, interventions should attempt to directly engage with all members of a child's social environment so that families can help guide and shape programs for their children. Families also benefit from their involvement with program development, because they can suggest ways that the services can be integrated into their existing routines, thereby making them more successful and sustainable.

Third, socioecological research methods show the value of including adult voices when researching children's lives. There has been a movement to address adultism in research with children by encouraging child participation, with a focus on the individual child and children as the sole interpreters of their own experiences. However, some have criticized this approach for swinging too far in this direction; for example, Fielding (2007, p. 304) notes the "too sharp and too exclusive a focus on the standpoints of young people." The shift toward children's participation as a means to contest adultism has, in some cases, eclipsed and marginalized adult voices, causing children's and adults' participation to be seen as being somehow separate and incompatible (Boyden & Ennew, 1997; Wyness, 2012). When using socioecological research methods, the participation of adults and children is not an "either/or" option, as the examples from Uganda and Palestine show.

Children's role in research does not have to be—and, from a socioeco-logical perspective, we strongly argue it should *not* be—independent of their families. Children's experiences are clearly shaped by those around them. Understanding children from a socioecological perspective demands that other members of a child's socioecological system contribute to the research. As our examples illustrate, research with children should take into account the form and nature of children's relationship with adults, so it can better ad-dress the interdependent relationships they have in diverse settings. As it seeks a more balanced perspective, a strength of a socioecological approach is that it includes adults as partners, contributors, actors, and co-creators of children's and family's narratives. This inclusion relocates children's participation in research within the socioecological framework, offering the possibility of better understanding the complexity of children's lives in the context of armed conflict.

Finally, integrating socioecological research methods into research with children affected by war is a useful way to understand the role of the physical environment in their lives. For example, the Palestine study used methods that emphasized that the places where children live, play, and work matter because they can provide a sense of place in a turbulent world. Using a socioecological lens, research can find that children and families engage in diverse acts of re-sistance, participation, and negotiations within their social and physical envi-ronments. Therefore, research conducted with children should support their active role in place and space.

LIMITATIONS

Socioecological research approaches are not a panacea and raise multiple practical and ethical issues that need to be kept in mind. First, in conducting family collaborative interviews, there is a danger that because of adult-child power relations, as well as children's typically subordinate role within fami-lies, children's voices and perspectives may be rendered invisible or silenced during interviews where parents and adult family members are present. In-terviewing both children and adults together in a family interview raises an important ethical dilemma, because it has the potential to create a context of unequal power relations within the interview process. For example, at times in the Palestinian study, children's voices were obscured by the voices of their older family members. At other times, the interview seemed to devolve into chaos, as individual family members raised their voices and verbally competed with each other to convey their particular opinions. Though these scenes raised process-related difficulties (for example, with translation and transcription), they also provided a valuable opportunity for the research team to observe the family in action and the child's actual role within the family system. The silencing of children's voices can be minimized by including activities within the research design that ensure that those voices are heard in the research process. As in the Palestinian research example, the use of drawing, mapmaking, and neighborhood walks all emphasized children's participation, thereby giving children of all ages a voice in the research.

Second, including family and community perspectives in any qualitative research study is likely to add complexity to research. Not only may it require greater time to collect data involving multiple levels of the socioecological system, but also the analysis may require more layers of complexity, particularly in relation to intergenerational understandings of issues. For example, in the project in northern Uganda, many children reported that, because they were born of wartime rape, their mothers rejected and mistreated them. Many of their mothers, however, saw their relationships with their children very differently. Making sense of such differing perceptions requires a unique sensitivity in terms of data analysis and interpretation and also illustrates the intricacies of obtaining multiple perspectives on the same issue.

CONCLUSIONS: THE FUTURE OF SOCIOECOLOGICAL METHODOLOGIES WITH CHILDREN AFFECTED BY WAR

Despite some key challenges, there is clearly much value in applying the socioecological approach to both existing and future research methods, and more research using this approach is needed to understand how different elements of the system may contribute to and ameliorate the challenges facing war-affected children. Furthermore, researchers must create a culture of learning by sharing their successes and failures in implementing a socioecological research approach so they can better understand what works and what does not work within this challenging context. Based on the earlier discussion, we conclude with a brief overview of two methodological trends—participatory and visual methods—in research with children affected by war that we believe can be further refined using socioecological research methods.

PARTICIPATORY METHODS

Participatory methods, such as participatory action research (PAR) and participatory rural appraisal (PRA) techniques, have been increasingly used with children to facilitate their participation in research (Baker, 1996; Boyden & Ennew, 1997; Edwards, 1996; Johnson, 1996; Narayanasamy, Dwaraki, Tamilmani, & Ramesh, 1996; Nieuwenhuys, 1996; Sapkota & Sharma, 1996; Theis, 1996). One strength of these participatory approaches is the "integration of researchers' theoretical and methodological expertise within non-academic participants' real-world knowledge and experiences into a mutually reinforcing partnership" (Cargo & Mercer, 2008, p. 327). Such approaches are vital to research with war-affected children: They not only confront power differentials and engage children as active citizens, but also increase data quality, reliability, and validity (Veale, 2005).

We suggest, however, that participatory methods can be vastly improved by integrating a socioecological approach and engaging multiple players in a child's socioecological system. This would mean ensuring that participatory methods include not only children but also, where possible, families and communities. The inclusion of children, siblings, caregivers, and community members in the research process reinforces the understanding that the perspectives of these multiple systems are valuable to the research process. The use of participatory methods affords participants' input into the research design, process, and outcomes, and valuing participants' input can lessen the hierarchies that may result from the inclusion of multiple systems in a socioecological methodological approach. For example, in the Palestinian research described earlier, the methodology included neighborhood walks, a participatory method that gave the child participants an opportunity to contribute to the research independent of their adult family members. We believe that introducing a socioecological approach into participatory research methods can increase project impact, scope, and reach.

VISUAL AND ARTS-BASED METHODS

Growing out of the emerging field of participatory research is visual research (Thomson, 2008). Visual techniques are "an analytically charged set of methodologies which incline researchers towards the tracing of connections between things of quite different social scope and scale" (Knowles & Sweetman, 2004, p. 8). Social researchers have found visual methodologies effective in describing the multiple connections among social issues affecting children in armed conflict with more than just words. As a form of research data, visual images illuminate how small units of social analysis operate within broader social landscapes. In this way, visual strategies enable researchers to understand "how the personal is social and the social personal" (p. 7). Visual techniques have also facilitated social researchers' fascination with people and place, thereby making them ideal for socioecological research. These techniques illustrate

> the intersections between people and place, the placing of people and the people of place. In this framework people are the architects of social scenes, relationships and processes, which in turn fabricate their lives and their being in the world. (Knowles & Sweetman, 2004, p. 8)

To ascertain war-affected children's psychosocial well-being and mental health, they are encouraged to creatively express themselves through drawings and subsequent in-depth discussions (Harrison, Clarke, & Ungerer, 2007; Leitch, 2008; Veale, 2005). Moreover, as a form of knowledge production and sharing, visual images (drawings, for example) can sometimes be more accessible and powerful than academic text. Creating a drawing requires participants to reflect, contemplate, and conceptualize their responses to research inquiries. As producers of knowledge, participants are encouraged to contribute to the interpretations of their drawings, either verbally or through writing. Researchers and participants thus collaborate to analyze and make meaning from their visual work.

Visual techniques are well suited to a socioecological research design, because of their ability to assist research participants in describing and analyzing their experiences. They can make children's experiences with their social and physical environment more readily accessible by the use of image making than by a sole reliance on verbally oriented methods. Moreover, visual techniques can be employed with adults and children, obtaining unique perspectives while also promoting participant activism, engagement, and empowerment (Denov, Doucet, & Kamara, 2012; Mitchell, 2011).

Promising and interesting trends are currently enhancing research on war-affected children and youth, many of which are highlighted in this volume.

One such trend, the socioecological approach to research, emphasizes the importance of gathering data from multiple sources in the child's social environment. In contrast to the large number of studies that rely on a single source of data from a parent or teacher, future research should integrate data gathered from a variety of sources (including caregivers, teachers, community members, and especially children themselves), using methods that suit the research question and the participants. In addition, socioecological research methods are not only innovative in and of themselves but can also be merged with other methods, such as participatory approaches or arts-based approaches, to ensure a more holistic analysis of a context or population. Ultimately, as our examples from Uganda and Palestine demonstrate, socioecological research methods have the capacity to enrich our understanding of children affected by war and importantly, their surrounding social context.

Note

1. Sexual violence refers as any act of a sexual nature committed on a person under circumstances that are coercive. Sexual violence is not limited to physical invasion of the body (International Criminal Tribunal for Rwanda, 1998).

References

Akello, G. (2013). Experiences of forced mothers in northern Uganda: The legacy of war. *Intervention*, 11(2), 149–156.

Akesson, B. (2014a). Castle and cage: Meanings of home for Palestinian children and families. *Global Social Welfare*, 1(2), 81–95.

Akesson, B. (2014b). *Contradictions in place: Everyday geographies of Palestinian children and families living under occupation* (Unpublished doctoral dissertation). McGill University, Montreal.

Akesson, B. (2015). School as a place of violence and hope: Tensions of education in post-intifada Palestine. *International Journal of Educational Development*, 41, 192–199. doi:10.1016/j.ijedudev.2014.08.001.

Amone-P'Olak, K., Jones, P., Meiser-Stedman, R., Abbott, R., Ayella-Ataro, P. S., Amone, J., & Ovuga, E. (2014). War experiences, general functioning and barriers to care among former child soldiers in Northern Uganda: The WAYS study. *Journal of Public Health*, 36(4), 568–576.

Arafat, C., & Boothby, N. (2003). *A psychosocial assessment of Palestinian children*. West Bank and Gaza: U.S. Agency for International Development.

Baker, R. (1996). PRA with street children in Nepal. *PRA Notes*, 25, 56–60.

Beam, M. R., Gil-Rivas, V., Greenberger, E., & Chen, C. (2002). Adolescent problem behavior and depressed mood: Risk and protection within and across social contexts. *Journal of Youth and Adolescence, 31*(5), 343–357. doi:10.1023/A:1015676524482.

Betancourt, T. S., & Khan, K. T. (2008). The mental health of children affected by armed conflict: Protective processes and pathways to resilience. *International Review of Psychiatry, 20*(3), 317–328. doi:10.1080/09540260802090363.

Boothby, N. (1996). Mobilizing communities to meet the psychosocial needs of children in war and refugee crises. In R. J. Apfel & B. Simon (Eds.), *Minefields on their hearts: The mental health of children in war and communal violence* (pp. 149–164). New Haven, CT: Yale University Press.

Boothby, N. (2008). Political violence and development: An ecologic approach to children in war zones. *Child and Adolescent Psychiatric Clinics of North America, 17,* 497–514.

Boothby, N., Strang, A., & Wessells, M. G. (Eds.). (2006). *A world turned upside down: Social ecological approaches to children in war zones.* Bloomfield, CT: Kumarian Press.

Boyden, J., & Ennew, J. (Eds.). (1997). *Children in focus: A manual for participatory research with children.* Stockholm: Rädda Barnen.

Boyden, J., & Mann, G. (2005). Children's risk, resilience and coping in extreme situations. In M. Ungar (Ed.), *Handbook for working with children and youth: Pathways to resilience across cultures and contexts* (pp. 3–26). Thousand Oaks, CA: Sage.

Brenner, A. B., Bauermeister, J. A., & Zimmerman, M. A. (2011). Neighborhood variation in adolescent alcohol use: Examination of socioecological and social disorganization theories. *Journal of Studies on Alcohol and Drugs, 72*(4), 651–659.

Bushin, N. (2009). Researching family migration decision-making: A children-in-families approach. *Population, Space and Place, 15*(5), 429–443. doi:10.1002/psp.522

Cairns, E., & Dawes, A. (1996). Children: Ethnic and political violence—A commentary. *Child Development, 76*(1), 129–139.

Cargo, M., & Mercer, S. L. (2008). The value and challenges of participatory research: Strengthening its practice. *Annual Review of Public Health, 29,* 325–350.

Carlson, K., & Mazurana, D. (2008). *Forced marriage within the Lord's Resistance Army, Uganda.* Somerville, MA: Feinstein International Center, Tufts University.

Carpenter, C. (2010). *Forgetting children born of war: Setting the human rights agenda in Bosnia and beyond.* New York: Columbia University Press.

Casey, M. M., Eime, R. M., Payne, W. R., & Harvey, J. T. (2009). Using a socioecological approach to examine participation in sport and physical activity among rural adolescent girls. *Qualitative Health Research, 19*(7), 881–893. doi:10.1177/1049732309338198.

Chen, J., Lau, C., Tapanya, S., & Cameron, C. (2012). Identities as protective processes: Socio-ecological perspectives on youth resilience. *Journal of Youth Studies*, 15(6), 761–779. doi:10.1080/13676261.2012.677815.

Defence for Children International (DCI). (2008). *Under attack: Settler violence against Palestinian children in the Occupied Territory*. Jerusalem: DCI.

Defence for Children International (DCI). (2012). *Bound, blindfolded, and convicted: Children held in military detention*. Ramallah, Palestine: DCI–Palestine Section. Retrieved from www.dci-palestine.org/documents/bound-blindfolded-and-convicted-children-held-military-detention-2012.

Denov, M. (2010). *Child soldiers: Sierra Leone's Revolutionary United Front*. Cambridge: Cambridge University Press.

Denov, M. (2015). Children born of wartime rape: The intergenerational realities of sexual violence and abuse. *Ethics, Medicine and Public Health*, 1(1), 61–68.

Denov, M., & Blanchett-Cohen, N. (2014). The rights and realities of war-affected refugee children and youth in Quebec: Making children's rights meaningful. *Canadian Journal of Children's Rights*, 1(1), 18–43.

Denov, M., & Lakor, A. A. (2017). When war is better than peace: the post-conflict realities of children born of war time rape in northern Uganda. *Child Abuse & Neglect* 65, 255–265.

Denov, M., Doucet, D., & Kamara, A. (2012). Engaging war affected youth through photography: Photovoice with former child soldiers in Sierra Leone. *Intervention*, 10(2), 117–133. doi:10.1097/WTF.0b013e328355ed82.

Dyson, L. (2013). In the convergence of ethnicity and immigration: The status and socio-ecological predictors of the self-concept of recent Chinese immigrant school-age children in Canada. *Journal of Child and Family Studies*, 24(1), 1–11. doi:10.1007/s10826-013-9808-0.

Earls, F., & Carlson, M. (2001). The social ecology of child health and well-being. *Annual Review of Public Health*, 22(1), 143–166. doi:10.1146/annurev.publhealth.22.1.143.

Education Development Center. (2004). Key informant interviews [Online course]. Center for Substance Abuse Prevention Northeast Center for the Application of Prevention Technologies (NECAPT). Rockville, MD: SAMHSA.

Edwards, M. (1996). Institutionalising children's participation in development. *PLA Notes*, (25), 47–51.

Elkington, K. S., Bauermeister, J. A., & Zimmerman, M. A. (2011). Do parents and peers matter? A prospective socio-ecological examination of substance use and sexual risk among African American youth. *Journal of Adolescence*, 34(5), 1035–1047. doi:10.1016/j.adolescence.2010.11.004.

Fielding, M. (2007). Beyond "voice": New roles, relations and contexts in researching with young people. *Discourse: Studies in Cultural Politics of Education*, 28(3), 301–310.

Garbarino, J. (2001). An ecological perspective on the effects of violence on children. *Journal of Community Psychology, 29*(3), 361–378. doi:10.1002/jcop.1022.

Harrison, L. J., Clarke, L., & Ungerer, J. A. (2007). Children's drawings provide a new perspective on teacher-child relationship quality and school adjustment. *Early Childhood Research Quarterly, 22*(1), 55–71. doi:16/j.ecresq.2006.10.003.

Honwana, A., & de Boeck, F. (2005). *Makers and breakers: Children and youth in postcolonial Africa.* Trenton, NJ: Africa World Press.

International Criminal Tribunal for Rwanda. (1998, September 2). *The Prosecutor versus Jean-Paul Akayesu,* Case No. ICTR-96-4-T, Count 12.

Johnson, V. (1996). Starting a dialogue on children's participation. *PLA Notes,* (25), 30–37.

Karam, E. G., Fayyad, J., Karam, A. N., Melhem, N., Mneimneh, Z., Dimassi, H., & Tabet, C. C. (2014). Outcome of depression and anxiety after war: A prospective epidemiologic study of children and adolescents. *Journal of Traumatic Stress, 27*(2), 192–199.

Knowles, C., & Sweetman, P. (2004). Introduction. In C. Knowles & P. Sweetman (Eds.), *Picturing the social landscape: Visual methods and the sociological imagination* (pp. 1–17). London: Routledge.

Kohrt, B. A., Jordans, M. J. D., Tol, W. A., Perera, E., Karki, R., Koirala, S., & Upadhaya, N. (2010). Social ecology of child soldiers: Child, family, and community determinants of mental health, psychosocial well-being, and reintegration in Nepal. *Transcultural Psychiatry, 47*(5), 727–753. doi:.10.1177/1363461510381290.

Lai, B. S., Hadi, F., & Llabre, M. M. (2014). Parent and child distress after war exposure. *British Journal of Clinical Psychology, 53*(3), 333–347.

Leitch, R. (2008). Creatively researching children's narratives through images and drawings. In P. Thomson (Ed.), *Doing visual research with children and young people* (pp. 37–58). London: Routledge.

Lustig, S. L., Kia-Keating, M., Grant-Knight, W., Geltman, P., Ellis, H., Kinzie, J. D., . . . Saxe, G. N. (2004). Review of child and adolescent refugee mental health. *Journal of the American Academy of Child and Adolescent Psychiatry, 43*(1), 24–36.

Markovic, M. (2007). Vessels of reproduction: Forced pregnancy and the ICC. *Michigan State Journal of International Law, 16,* 439.

Mitchell, C. (2011). *Doing visual research.* London: Sage.

Mochmann, I. C. (2008). Children born of war. *OBETS: Revista de Ciencias Sociales, 2,* 53–61. doi:10.14198/OBETS2008.2.04.

Mochmann, I. C., & Lee, S. (2010). Menschenrechte der Kinder des Krieges: Fallstudien vergangener und gegenwärtiger Konflikte [The human rights of children born of war: Case analyses of past and present conflicts]. *Historische Sozialforschung,* 268–298.

Morris, A., Rudolf, M., Halileh, S., Odeh, J., Bowyer, J., & Waterston, T. (2010). Child health in the West Bank: Experiences from implementing a paediatric course for Palestinian doctors and nurses working in primary care. *Medical Teacher*, 32(11), e486–e491. doi:10.3109/0142159X.2010.509411.

Narayanasamy, N., Dwaraki, B. R., Tamilmani, B., & Ramesh, R. (1996). Whiter children's hour? An experimental PRA among laboring rural children. *PRA Notes*, (25), 65–69.

Ncube, N. (2013). The family system as a socio-ecological determinant of bullying among urban high school adolescents in Gweru, Zimbabwe: Implications for intervention. *Asian Social Science*, 9(17). doi:10.5539/ass.v9n17p1.

Nieuwenhuys, O. (1996). Action research with street children: A role for street educators. *PLA Notes*, 25, 52–55.

Palestinian Central Bureau of Statistics. (2008). *Population, housing and establishment census—2007.* Press conference on the preliminary findings (population, buildings, housing units, and establishments). Ramallah: Author.

Punamäki, R. L., Palosaari, E., Diab, M., Peltonen, K., & Qouta, S. R. (2015). Trajectories of posttraumatic stress symptoms (PTSS) after major war among Palestinian children: Trauma, family-and child-related predictors. *Journal of Affective Disorders*, 172, 133–140.

Qin, L. L. (2003). Situating children of genocidal rape: Towards membership in an ethnic community. *Singapore Law Review*, 23, 45.

Sapkota, P., & Sharma, J. (1996). Participatory interactions with children in Nepal. *PLA Notes*, 25, 61–64.

Scholte, E. M. (1992). Prevention and treatment of juvenile problem behavior: A proposal for a socio-ecological approach. *Journal of Abnormal Child Psychology*, 20(3), 247–262. doi:10.1007/BF00916691.

Steele, R. G., Nelson, T. D., & Cole, B. P. (2007). Psychosocial functioning of children with AIDS and HIV infection: Review of the literature from a socioecological framework. *Journal of Developmental and Behavioral Pediatrics*, 28(1), 58–69.

Strickland, P. O. (2014). *Growing up between Israeli settlements and soldiers.* Palestine: Defense for Children International Palestine.

Theis, J. (1996). Children and participatory appraisals: Experiences from Vietnam. *PLA Notes*, 25, 70–72.

Thomson, P. (2008). Children and young people: Voices in visual research. In P. Thomson (Ed.), *Doing visual research with children and young people* (pp. 1–19). London: Routledge.

Tol, W. A., Barbui, C., Galappatti, A., Silove, D., Betancourt, T. S., Souza, R., . . . van Ommeran, M. (2011). Mental health and psychosocial support in humanitarian settings: Linking practice and research. *Lancet*, 378(9802), 1581–1591.

Tol, W. A., Haroz, E. E., Hock, R. S., Kane, J. C., & Jordans, M. J. D. (2014). Eco-logical perspectives on trauma and resilience in children affected by armed conflict. In R. Pat-Horenczyk, D. Brom, & J. M. Vogel (Eds.), *Helping children cope with trauma* (pp. 193–209). East Sussex, UK: Routledge.

Tol, W. A., Jordans, M. J. D., Kohrt, B. A., Betancourt, T. S., & Komproe, I. H. (2013a). Promoting mental health and psychosocial well-being in children affected by political violence: Part I—Current evidence for an ecological resil-ience approach. In C. Fernando & M. Ferrari (Eds.), *Handbook of resilience in children of war* (pp. 11–27). New York: Springer.

Tol, W. A., Jordans, M. J. D., Kohrt, B. A., Betancourt, T. S., & Komproe, I. H. (2013b). Promoting mental health and psychosocial well-being in children affected by political violence: Part II—Expanding the evidence base. In C. Fer-nando & M. Ferrari (Eds.), *Handbook of resilience in children of war* (pp. 29–38). New York: Springer.

Tol, W. A., Patel, V., Tomlinson, M., Baingana, F., Galappatti, A., Panter-Brick, C., van Ommeren, M. (2011). Research priorities for mental health and psychosocial support in humanitarian settings. *PLoS Medicine, 8*(9), e1001096.

van Ee, E., & Kleber, R. J. (2013). Growing up under a shadow: Key issues in research on and treatment of children born of rape. *Child Abuse Review, 22*(6), 386–397. doi:10.1002/car.2270

Veale, A. (2005). Creative methodologies in participatory research with children. In S. Greene & D. Hogan (Eds.), *Researching children's experience: Approaches and methods* (pp. 253–272). London: Sage.

Veale, A., McKay, S., Worthen, M., & Wessells, M. G. (2013). Children of young mothers formerly associated with armed forces or groups in Sierra Leone, Libe-ria, and northern Uganda. In J. O'Riordan, D. Horgan, & S. Martin (Eds.), *Early childhoods in the Global South: Local and international contexts* (pp. 27–45). Oxford: Peter Lang.

Vella, S. A., Cliff, D. P., & Okely, A. D. (2014). Socio-ecological predictors of participation and dropout in organized sports during childhood. *International Journal of Behavioral Nutrition and Physical Activity, 11*(1), 62. doi:10.1186/1479-5868-11-62

Watye Ki Gen. (2015) *Documentation of children born in captivity.* Gulu, Uganda: Author.

Wessells, M. (2009). *What are we learning about protecting children? An inter-agency review of the evidence on community-based child protection mechanisms in humanitarian and development settings.* London: Save the Children.

Wessells, M. G., & Monteiro, C. (2004). Internally displaced Angolans: A child-focused, community-based intervention. In K. E. Miller & L. M. Rasco (Eds.),

The mental health of refugees: Ecological approaches to healing and adaptation (pp. 67–94). Mahwah, NJ: Erlbaum.

Willows, N. D., Hanley, A. J., & Delormier, T. (2012). A socioecological framework to understand weight-related issues in Aboriginal children in Canada. *Physiologie Appliquée, Nutrition Et Métabolisme, 37*(1), 1–13. doi:10.1139/h11-128.

Wyness, M. (2012). Children's participation and intergenerational dialogue: Bringing adults back into the analysis. *Childhood, 20*(4), 429–442.

Zraly, M., Rubin, S. E., & Mukamana, D. (2013). Motherhood and resilience among Rwandan genocide-rape survivors. *Ethos, 41*(4), 411–439.

7

WHAT CHILDREN AND YOUTH CAN TELL US

A Rapid Ethnography Approach to Understanding Harms to Children in Somaliland and Puntland

Kathleen Kostelny, Ken Justus Ondoro, and Michael G. Wessells

ANALYSES OF WAR-AFFECTED CHILDREN FOCUS mostly on the children affected by active fighting. Although it is appropriate to focus on the children who face gravest danger, all children in a war-torn country may be affected, even though many may live outside of areas of active fighting. Such children may be at risk due to the war-shattered economy, resource scarcity, insecurity, the unraveled social fabric, weakened government capacities and services, tensions between host and displaced people, and the proliferating threats to children. As Kachachi notes in chapter 12, war weakens the social environment and necessitates holistic supports for all children, not just those who survive trauma and direct attack.

An important question, however, is how we can learn deeply about the lived experiences and situation of war-affected children. Quite often, research is driven by experts, is focused on deficits, and affords relatively limited inputs from children. For example, in rapid assessments, the experts ask mostly preconceived questions about children and their situation. Although valuable, such questions may overlook children's own understandings of adversity and risk. Not uncommonly, children are treated as a homogeneous category, with little attention given to differences in gender, age, socioeconomic status, and clan. Worse yet, children may be treated as sources of data, rather than as active agents who have a relatively deep understanding of how to navigate a complex, dynamic environment.

What is needed is a more elicitive approach that facilitates learning in a systematic, contextualized manner about the lived experiences of children and their views of harms and concerns. Using a methodology of rapid ethnography focused on child protection, which had proven useful in other African contexts (Wessells, Kostelny, & Ondoro, 2014; Wessells et al., 2012), the research presented in this chapter aimed to learn about the perspective and lived experiences of young children and youth in the Somaliland and Puntland areas of Somalia.

Rapid ethnography is a condensed form of ethnography, one of the primary tools of cultural and social anthropology. As with full ethnography, researchers live in the community, establishing relatively high levels of trust and using nonjudgmental methods like participant observation and elicitive methods, such as in-depth, respondent-driven interviews, to learn about the practices, beliefs, and values of local people regarding a particular topic—in this case, child protection and well-being. Unlike other methods, rapid ethnography avoids preconceived questions in favor of learning about local categories and understandings and children's lived experiences. Taking a nonjudgmental stance and wanting to build on local views of children and their needs and well-being, it avoids use of the international language of child protection.

In this chapter we examine harms to children through their perspective. Our research aimed not only to center the voices of children but also to learn from the children themselves about the realities and implications of being out of school, having to do heavy work, engaging in substance abuse, and being subject to beatings.

CONTEXT

Somalia won independence from colonial powers in 1960 with the fall of dictator Siad Barre. Since then, the Somali people have lived in a context of contested power without a central government, enduring ongoing armed conflict, mass displacement, and chronic instability. Still, they have strong internal assets (Harper, 2012), particularly their Islamic faith and clan structures, which organize much of social life. Somalis have maintained internal order less through government law than through Islamic law (*shari'a*) and customary law (*xeer*), which defines children as people younger than 15 years of age.

Somalia has three main regions. The south-central region, which is controlled mainly by Al-Shabaab, is highly dangerous. Children in that region live in areas that lack law and order; they are exposed to continuous hostilities and crime and are victims of sexual assault (UNICEF/Somalia, 2003). A 2013 study found that Al-Shabaab was abducting children and using them as child soldiers (U.S. Department of Labor, 2013). Puntland, which is located in the northeastern region, declared itself autonomous in 1998. Its clan-based government (Accord, 2009) has been relatively stable by comparison to that of the south-central region, although most of the pirates who captured ships and took hostages throughout 2012 lived in this region and children there have been recruited into piracy (U.S. Department of Labor, 2013). Children living in Puntland experience displacement, assault, loss of their homes, and family violence (UNICEF/Somalia, 2003), and the vast majority are not in school: In 2004, only 14.3% of boys and 8.5% of girls were attending primary school (Puntland Development Research Center, 2004). In addition, children in both Puntland and Somaliland are sometimes imprisoned with adults in harsh conditions as a punishment for fighting, family disputes, or disobedience (Gerstle, 2007).

Somaliland, the northwestern region, declared its independence in 1991 and has extensive government systems, but has not been recognized internationally as an independent state. Although Somaliland enjoys relative stability, children living there are exposed to many risks: family violence, lack of education, early marriage, child labor, and gender-based violence (GBV), including female genital mutilation/cutting (FGM/C) (UNICEF/Somalia, 2003, 2012). Children with disabilities experience even higher rates of discrimination and abuse, particularly sexual abuse (CESVI & Handicap International, 2012).

THE RESEARCH STUDY

The research was part of a larger study (Columbia Group for Children in Adversity, 2013) that focused on both children and adults and addressed how people in Somalia understand childhood and child development, the main sources of harm to children, the mechanisms used by families and communities to address those harms, preventive factors in the family and community, traditional mechanisms of protection, and the linkages of community mechanisms with the national child protection system. The study presented in this chapter examined children's views of harms to children and also included the views of young people (aged 18–25) who were close to childhood and still in transition.

SITE SELECTION

To achieve diversity, UNICEF/Somalia selected three sites in Somaliland and three sites in Puntland according to criteria such as demographic diversity, feasibility of the research, high level of child protection issues, security, and the ability to add value to the government and UNICEF programming strategy. In both Somaliland and Puntland, one site was a community of farmers, one consisted of urban dwellers, and one was an internally displaced persons (IDP) camp. The Somaliland sites were an urban IDP camp in the capital, an agro-pastoralist village near the Ethiopian border, and an impoverished urban area near the coast that included recent IDPs. The Puntland sites were a large urban IDP camp, a small town of agro-pastoralists, and a rural village with nomadic people. Because of the lack of security in the south-central region, it was not possible to include that area in this research.

STUDY POPULATION AND PARTICIPANTS

Of the combined population of approximately 73,500 people in the two regions, nearly half were children aged 5–17-years. A total of 863 children aged 5–17 participated in the in-depth interviews, group discussions, and body mapping, and 188 young women and men in the transitional age of 18–25 years participated in in-depth interviews and group discussions.

RESEARCH TEAM, PREPARATION, AND OVERSIGHT

Two teams of Somali and international researchers conducted the study. The Somali researchers were recruited from research organizations in Somaliland and Puntland who met these selection criteria: prior qualitative research experience, an understanding of the local language and culture, good interpersonal skills, experience working in Somali communities, and the ability to speak English as well as Somali. The Somali researchers took part in a highly participatory, two-week training that included field practice. Field testing took place in a community in Hargeisa, the second-largest city in Somalia and the capital of Somaliland. In this Hargeisa community, the Somali researchers conducted group discussions and in-depth interviews with teenagers and young people, as well as body mapping with children. The tools were fine-tuned based on what was learned during the field testing. The international researchers—two co-principal investigators, two operational researchers who lived in Somaliland and Puntland during the data collection (checking records and mentoring) phase, and a lead trainer—oversaw the technical aspects of the research.

RESEARCH TOOLS

The research tools are described in table 7.1. To build trust and enable a depth of learning, the Somali researchers lived in or near each site for approximately three weeks. Rapport with community members was created by partnering with child protection organizations that employed respected child advocates in the communities, who accompanied the researchers on their initial visits with the community elders and stakeholders.

TABLE 7.1 Methods Used to Collect Data from Children and Young Adults

METHOD	AGE AND GENDER OF PARTICIPANTS	DESCRIPTION
Participant observation	Girls and boys, birth to 17 years	Visiting schools and homes and accompanying people to their farms, the researchers observed children in the context of family, peers, school, work, religious practice, and community life and prepared written records.
In-depth interview	Girls and boys, 13–17 years; young adult women and men, 18–25 years	Researchers conducted one-on-one, recorded interviews in the Somali language and lasting approximately one hour with a diverse group of young people. The interviews were conducted in a contextual, open-ended manner that took into account the participant's gender, situation, and social position, as well as interest and willingness to discuss particular topics. The interviews were not strictly scripted, and the researchers were trained to ask probing questions and to follow participants' interests.
Group discussion of harms	Girls and boys, 13–17 years; young adult women and men, 18–25 years	Group discussions (recorded) were conducted for approximately 90 minutes with 7–10 participants each. The participants identified the things that harm children and then ranked them, noting the three that were "most serious" or most concerning.
Body mapping	Girls and boys, 5–8 years and 9–12 years	In this method, which enabled learning from a group of approximately 10 boys or girls, a child volunteered to lie on a large sheet of paper while other children used crayons to trace an outline of his or her body. Having colored in the drawn figure and named it, the children were asked questions such as "What do the eyes see that they like?" and "What do the eyes see that they don't like?" Similar questions were asked regarding the ears, mouth, head, hands, stomach, heart, and feet. Care was taken not to probe what the children said because the intent was to avoid exploring the child's own, possibly painful experiences.

The in-depth interviews and group discussions asked open-ended questions such as "What are the things that harm children here?" and followed respondents' lines of thought about various issues facing children. The researchers then asked probing questions to learn in a deeper way about the key questions, as appropriate. The group discussions of harms to children were conducted with groups of 8–10 teenagers (13–17 years) and young adults (18–25 years) in gender-segregated groups to allow participants to speak freely. A total of 41 group sessions (24 with teenagers and 17 with young adults) were held with 347 participants (205 teenagers and 142 young adults), and 72 in-depth interviews were conducted (36 with teenagers and 36 with young adults).

To learn from young children (5–12 years), the research used body mapping because it was perceived as a fun activity/game by children, rather than interviews. This mapping activity typically lasted 45–60 minutes, and separate groups were conducted for boys and girls according to age (5–8 years and 9–12 years), with approximately 10 children in each group. A total of 658 children participated in 61 groups that met for a total of 86 sessions.

The researchers also collected observational data through participant observation. Daily, they observed children in the context of family, peers, community, school, work, and play and took detailed notes. This design made it possible to triangulate the observational and narrative data.

RESEARCH ETHICS

The research design took account of the ethical complexities and dilemmas associated with research on children (Alderson & Morrow, 2011; Allden et al., 2009; Boyden, 2004; Graham, Powell, Taylor, Anderson, & Fitzgerald, 2013). The researchers were trained in and agreed to abide by a Code of Conduct modeled on the UN Standards of Conduct (United Nations, 2013). To avoid raising expectations of material aid, the researchers told the participants they were representatives of their research organizations, rather than saying they were associated with international NGOs or UNICEF. They also avoided making promises they could not keep. So as not to cause unintended harm, the questions asked to children and adults were general in nature and did not probe their personal situation. Because of the low literacy rates, the oral culture, and the fear of written documents, informed consent was obtained verbally, with the researchers following a script that had been field tested.

DATA COLLECTION

The data were collected from January to March 2013. In most cases, the gender of the interviewer matched the gender of the participants: This was most appropriate culturally and enabled more open discussion. During each in-depth interview, the researcher took notes and recorded the interview if permission had been obtained. Soon afterward, the researcher used the notes and the recording to prepare a verbatim transcript in English. The group discussions were conducted by two researchers, with one serving as facilitator/interviewer and the other as note taker. Shortly after the group discussions ended, the two researchers reviewed the notes, filled in key points, and used the audio recording to develop the verbatim transcript. Two researchers facilitated the body mapping activities, with one researcher taking notes on what the children reported. Written records were also prepared of the daily participant observations.

To reduce suspicion and build trust, the emphasis during the first week was on group discussions and group activities. During the second week, there was greater emphasis on individual methods such as in-depth interviews. In using the different tools, the research teams sought to collect data from people who differed in socioeconomic status, as indicated by proxy indicators such as the quality of housing materials, occupation, or number of animals owned.

DATA ANALYSIS

The international researchers analyzed the data using a grounded methodology (Charmaz, 2006; Strauss & Corbin, 1990). This entailed reading and re-reading the data in a holistic manner until natural categories and consistent patterns emerged. The triangulation of data from different participants and methods was a key part of this search for consistent categories and patterns, which served as working hypotheses that were then checked by rereading and further analytic discussion among the researchers. NVivo and SPSS were also used in the analysis to discern differences by gender and age. In analyzing the group discussions, frequency analyses were used to disaggregate the top-ranked harms to children according to different gender and age subgroups.

LIMITATIONS OF THE RESEARCH

The short time frame of this research limited the depth of what was learned by comparison with the thick descriptions provided by multiyear ethnography.

In addition, the research has limited generalizability because the areas studied did not comprise a representative national sample.

FINDINGS: HARMS TO CHILDREN

As shown in table 7.2, the top-ranked harms to children varied according to context, yet commonalities were visible as well.

In all six sites, being out of school was identified as one of the most serious harms. Other highly ranked harms in multiple sites were neglect by parents (i.e., not providing food, shelter, and basic necessities or tying young children to a pole at home and leaving them alone when they went to their day jobs), hard and heavy work, substance abuse (glue sniffing, *khat* chewing, and alcohol use), and rape. Neglect was reported as a top harm in all of the communities in Somaliland and in two of the Puntland communities. Hard work was one of the top-ranked harms in two communities in Somaliland (one urban

TABLE 7.2 Top-Ranked Harms to Children in Each of the Sites

	SITE A	SITE B	SITE C
Somaliland	Out of work	Lack of water	Out of school
	Hard work	Hard work	Rape
	Glue sniffing, *khat* chewing	Lack of nutrition	Street children
	Neglect	Out of school	Neglect
	Gangs	Falling into water catchment areas	Beating
	Rape	Neglect	Glue sniffing, *khat* chewing
Puntland	Houses burnt by fire	Falling into boreholes	Hard work
	Out of school	Out of school	Out of school
	Rape	Injured while playing	Drugs and cigarettes
	Neglect	*Khat* chewing	Drowning in boreholes
	Lack of sanitation	Hard work	Early marriage
	Beating	Children fighting	Beating

and one rural) and in two rural communities in Puntland. Substance abuse was a serious problem in all sites in Somaliland and two rural sites in Puntland. Rape was a problem in the two urban areas in Somaliland and in one community in Puntland. Additional harms included beatings, children injured and killed while playing in the road, emigration (i.e., children lost and killed while trying to get to another country or being abused if they succeeded in reaching a new country), girls not sent to school, girls working in the market, girls fetching water, diseases, female circumcision, early marriage, thieves, and HIV/AIDS.

Serious harms specific to particular contexts included children drowning in boreholes and water catchment areas while fetching water in the rural areas of Somaliland and Puntland, and children burned when their houses (traditional huts made of old clothes, sticks, and cardboard) caught fire in the crowded urban IDP camp in Puntland. This last harm was suffered by children who were tied to a pole in the home while their parents were away and could not escape the fire. Other site-specific harms included children injured while playing on the road in urban areas of Somaliland, children working and living on the streets in an urban IDP camp in Somaliland, and early marriage in a rural area of Puntland. As shown in the following discussion, the narratives of children, teenagers, and young adults helped clarify the nature and sources of the most serious harms to children.

OUT-OF-SCHOOL CHILDREN

Teenagers themselves articulated the value of having an education, which they saw as necessary for learning good behavior and having a positive future:

> It is very important to have education, because it is the key to everything. If a child were educated, he would have not do all those bad things and would not face those harms. (teenage girl, group discussion, urban area, Puntland)

Participants identified poverty and food insecurity as among the main reasons why children dropped out of school. Although school was free, very poor families, including those headed by mothers, needed or preferred their children to work and earn money rather than attend school.

Because of gender discrimination, more girls than boys were reported as not going to school. Parents, who could often afford to send only one child to school, usually sent their son. Some adults viewed education for girls as a waste, because once they married, they were expected to stay home and perform all the household chores. Moreover, before they were married, performing all the daily chores—such as cooking meals, washing clothes, cleaning the house, taking care of younger siblings, and tending animals—did not leave enough time for girls to attend school:

> The community people do not send their girls to schools, they only send the boys to learn. The girls are those looking after the camels, goats and cows. . . . The parents say to the girls, "Go and cook the meal and wash the dishes!" (young man, group discussion, rural community, Somaliland)

The denial of education to girls caused significant mental distress:

> The girl says, "Let me go to the school!" But the parents say to her, "You stay at the house and mop the house for us to sit here." So the girl has a lot of worry. She tries to go to the school one day and the other days she works. So she gets demoralized and she worries a lot. (teenage boy, group discussion, urban area, Somaliland)

In addition, girls who did not go to school were more likely to be raped or to have an "illegal pregnancy" (pregnancy out of wedlock). The latter presented additional harms such as the pregnant girl being stigmatized and chased away from her community, the girl "throwing away the child" (infanticide), or committing suicide:

> The number of girls who go to school are very small, so those girls who do not get a chance to learn are not happy. . . . They are at risk to be pregnant. . . . So when she becomes pregnant without father she may kill herself. (teenage girl, in-depth interview, urban IDP camp, Somaliland)

In some cases, girls who had been denied education ran away to a town where they might obtain education in a madrassa (Muslim religious school).

Numerous factors in addition to poverty and discrimination caused children to not attend school. Nomadic children often missed years of education and, when given the opportunity to go back to school, refused because they did not want to sit alongside much younger children. A minority of children reportedly dropped out of school because they were beaten or verbally abused by their teachers. In addition, some children refused to go to school and preferred to play or to earn money, even when parents could pay their school fees. These children were often stigmatized, ridiculed, and even beaten by community members because they were viewed as exhibiting bad behavior.

Regardless of what caused children to leave school, being out of school created vulnerability to a variety of risks such as living on the streets, joining gangs, and sniffing glue:

> When he leaves school, the child will face many obstacles. When the child reaches the age of 15 he will join a strong gang. And when he hurts a person, he is arrested by the police instead of getting advice. Even sometimes the other people beat him when he tries to take the mobile phones from them. (teenage boy, group discussion, urban IDP camp, Somaliland)

> Those who didn't get to school cross the border and become street children in the nearby towns of Ethiopia. You can see children who did not reach 15 years of age sitting under the shadow of the beer shops selling by the ladies. (young man, group discussion, rural community, Somaliland)

KHAT CHEWING, GLUE SNIFFING, AND ALCOHOL ABUSE

Teenage boys sniffed glue, drank alcohol, and chewed *khat* (the leaves and buds of a shrub grown in the horn of Africa that has narcotic properties when chewed). Engaging in these activities has been a social custom of men for thousands of years in the region:

> The child starts bad things like *khat* and sniffing glue because the child sleeps outside and tries to survive his life. (teenage boy, group discussion, urban IDP camp, Somaliland)

> Children are addicted to drugs like *khat*. That is the main issue. The bad friends encourage them to take *khat*—this is increasing. (teenage boy, group discussion, rural community, Puntland)

Glue sniffing, which was the primary method of substance abuse in the urban IDP camp in Somaliland, occurred mostly among boys, although girls sometimes sniffed glue. Glue sniffing was common among children living on the street, particularly those who had no father or who had run away from home because of beatings. It was also associated with children in urban areas who had to work at a young age instead of going to school and were exposed to peers using glue. However, some children who lived at home also sniffed glue, particularly when the mother worked outside the home and could not monitor her children. Such children—mostly boys—often went with other boys to sniff glue instead of going to school. In the body mapping activities, young children aged 5–12 years reported that children did not like to see or taste *khat*, alcohol, glue, or other drugs.

NEGLECT

Participants attributed neglect within the family to economic hardships, death of a parent, parental fighting and spouse beating that led mothers to flee their homes, and men's widespread use of *khat*. Moreover, when a father announced that his marriage was dissolved and left his family, children were at risk of being neglected. Neglected children were seen as at risk of dropping out of school because they had to work, often at dangerous jobs where they were beaten by employers, customers, and gangs. Such children were also then at risk of joining gangs for protection, sniffing glue, and using *khat* and alcohol:

> Children are neglected. It happens every day in this community. We have seen today couples who were fighting and the man says to her, "What are you doing here? Why didn't you go?" And the women are vulnerable. So if the men try to beat her, she runs away and the children get neglected. And all that is caused by the circumstances because the people are poor. (young woman, group discussion, urban IDP camp, Somaliland)

RAPE

Rape was a widespread problem for girls and also, to a lesser extent, for boys. Rape by community members reportedly occurred frequently as girls walked home at night after work or fetched water. Girls who worked as servants in people's houses were sometimes raped. Because most of the community's households did not have latrines, girls were also raped when they went to the bush during the night to urinate. In addition, boys sometimes tricked the girls into going on a picnic and then raped them. Rape by multiple boys or men also occurred: Participants reported that, when one boy or man assaulted a girl, he typically called others to join in the rape:

It occurs every and each night in this community. If one man calls a girl from their house, after she came he immediately calls other boys . . . they will use her as they want. (young man, in-depth interview, urban IDP camp, Somaliland)

The lack of latrines in IDP camps was a significant enabler of rape:

Rape normally comes because of lack of latrines. When the girls go out for either a short call [urination] or a long call [defecation], men wait for them outside and rape them. (teenage girl, in-depth interview, urban area, Puntland)

Teenagers spoke of the psychosocial impact of rape, particularly the resulting stigma. So powerful was the stigma that girls who had been raped felt they had no choice but to drop out of school and leave their home and the community where they lived. They were then at risk of engaging in work where they were more likely to be sexually abused:

When the girl is raped, she is different from the other girls. She feels that others will disclose her problem. And this mentally hurts her. And it causes her to move out of the school and sometimes to move to town or other places where their relatives live. (teenage boy, group discussion, urban area, Puntland)

HARD AND HEAVY WORK

Significant numbers of children engaged in "hard" or "heavy" work because of their family's poverty. Many children walked long distances carrying heavy water containers:

The children, when they are very young, are given a work load they cannot withstand. . . . A young boy who is carrying a sack full of rice or a young girl who is carrying a heavy sack on her back . . . Children take jerry cans on their back. (teenage boy, group discussion, urban area, Somaliland)

In urban areas, boys who shined shoes were often beaten and robbed in the course of work, and girls worked as servants or in the market where they were beaten or sexually abused. In rural areas, children tended the family livestock and faced considerable discomfort because they usually worked in very hot places far from water or alternately were subjected to cold when the temperatures changed. Typically, children in rural areas walked without shoes and suffered cut feet. In addition, their animals sometimes injured them.

Children's unhappiness with their burden of work led many girls and boys to run away to town. There, the girls often worked as servants or sought education in a madrassa. However, girls who went to town reportedly faced risks such as joining a group of girls with bad behavior or being beaten or sexually abused.

Young children's unhappiness with hard and heavy work was also evident in the body mapping activities, in which children described disliking being overworked or going to dangerous places such as the market at night or to boreholes to fetch water.

AGE AND GENDER DIFFERENCES

The seriousness of the harms varied by age and gender. Teenage girls and young women rated rape as one of the most serious harms, in contrast to teenage boys and young men who rated *khat* and drug use as most serious.

Adults and children differed in their views on beating. In Somali culture, beating children is commonplace and seen as necessary for teaching children proper behavior and values. However, teenagers reported that beatings demoralized children and made them run away from home, thereby exposing them to risks associated with living on the streets. For example, girls who were beaten and then ran away from home faced risks of becoming pregnant and engaging in substance abuse. Children also reported that being beaten by teachers was a reason why some children did not go to school:

> The parents insult their children and sometimes beat their children. After that the young child runs away from home. (teenage boy, group discussion, urban IDP camp, Somaliland)

> Now the girls mostly run from their houses. For example, the girl is working and the boy enters the house. So she says, "Wait, let me mop the house." And he says to her, "I don't care." And he slaps her. And if she fights back, the mother will say, "Why did you fight with the boy?" and beats her too. So the girl runs from that [abuse]. . . . She goes to her friend in Hargeisa and works at their house and becomes a servant. (teenage boy, group discussion, urban area, Somaliland)

Children were also beaten in the course of working in the markets, as servants in other people's houses, and on the street as shoe shiners. For example, boys who were shoe shiners faced brutal beatings from gangs and older children who stole their money and tools on their way from work. They also faced abuse from customers who would beat them instead of paying them. Beatings often occurred as children walked to or from work:

> Going to work from the town [is a serious harm] since the child is very young, they are seriously beaten when coming back from the town. (teenage girl, group discussion, urban area, Puntland)

The theme of beating also emerged in the body mapping activities (see table 7.3). Children aged 5–12 frequently reported that the head, hands, stomach, feet, and heart did not like being beaten.

The dislikes of younger children also varied according to age. Children between the ages of 5 and 8 did not like their parents fighting, being abused and insulted by parents and teachers, and living in dirty conditions, whereas older children did not like seeing dead and dying people, hearing gunfire, and being chased by bad people. Dislikes specific to young girls aged 5–8 included their mother being beaten and abused; dislikes among older girls included not going to school. Young boys disliked seeing car accidents and becoming a street child, whereas for older boys dislikes included heavy work and worry about having to get money.

DISCUSSION

The rapid ethnographic methodology proved to be quite useful in learning about children's, teenagers', and young adults' views of the harms to children. Overall the data indicate the importance of everyday stresses (Miller & Rasmussen, 2010). In Somaliland and Puntland, children face heavy burdens of risk related to being out of school, engaging in strenuous work, substance abuse, neglect, and beatings. In numerous respects, the physical dangers were less than those faced by children in zones of active fighting: The children in our study were not affected by direct attacks, bullets, bombs, or landmines. Nevertheless, the physical dangers were still extensive and took the form of beatings by parents and teachers, attacks on the streets, and sexual abuse. Accompanying this physical violence was psychological violence related to humiliation, discrimination, and fear. The fact that children in Somaliland and Puntland faced such a heavy burden of risks suggests that, in war-affected countries, children may suffer extensively and need support even if they are

TABLE 7.3 Children's Dislikes According to Body Parts, as Identified Through Body Mapping

	GIRLS 5–8	GIRLS 9–12	BOYS 5–8	BOYS 9–12
Eyes	Parents fighting	Mother angry	Children fighting	People fighting
	Mother shouting	Teacher shouting	Beating	Dead people
	Someone dying	Fighting	Guns	Dirty things
	Mother crying	Thieves	Car accidents	People crying
	Garbage	Mother shouting	Dead bodies	Guns
Ears	Mother being beaten	Abuses	Mother shouting	Father shouting at mother
	Brother shouting	Mother shouting	Father shouting	Listening to abuses
	Father shouting	Father shouting	Parents fighting	Sound of guns
	Teachers shouting	Teacher shouting	Insults	Shouting
	Sound of guns	Bad news	Sound of guns	
Nose	Feces	Feces	Feces	Feces
	Garbage	Garbage	Garbage	Garbage
	Urine	Dead animals	Dead bodies	Sewage
Heart	Not cared for	Chased from home	Being a street child	Being beaten
	Being beaten	Chased from school	Seeing a dead body	Being abused
	Abused	Being beaten	Mother shouting	Having to get money
	Mother sick	Being shouted at	Mother beating	Being hated
	Father dying	Being hated	Seeing fire	Lack of water
	Lack of pure water		Having pain	Having fear
Head	Overworking	Being boxed (hit)	Overworked	Falling into boreholes
	Being injured	Not being cared for	Beaten with stick	Being injured
	Being shouted at	Being confused	Injured	Being hit

	GIRLS 5–8	GIRLS 9–12	BOYS 5–8	BOYS 9–12
Mouth	Chewing *khat*	Speaking bad talk	Taking drugs	Taking alcohol
	Taking alcohol	Abusing friends	Insulting people	Abusing parents
	Abusing elders	Abusing elders	Eating donkey meat	Speaking abuses
	Abusing friends	Taking poison	Saying bad words	Eating rotten food
Hands	Given too much work	Not going to school	Being beaten	Excessive working
	Being beaten	Beaten by teacher	Beaten by father	Being beaten
	Touching fire	Burned while cooking	Beaten by mothers	Carrying heavy things
		Being beaten	Throwing stones	Being burnt
				Being cut
Feet	Going to dangerous places at night	Going to market at night	Walking without shoes	Walking without shoes
	Going to boreholes	Going to dangerous places	Stepping on nails	Being beaten
	Going to kitchen	Walking far distances	Stepping on thorns	Walking long distances
	Going to garbage dump		Being wounded	Being cut
				Being tied together
				Going to garbage dump

not in areas of active fighting. More broadly, the effects of war on children are not reducible to direct attacks, killings, and displacement. War weakens the social environment and necessitates holistic supports for all children, not just those who survive trauma and direct attack.

The gender dimensions of risks to children were significant. Because of discriminatory gender norms, girls were more likely than boys to be out of school, which increased their exposure to multiple risks. Girls were also reportedly subjected to rape and sexual assault more frequently than were boys. Boys were often at risk because they engaged in strenuous work or in jobs, such as shoe shining, that exposed them to violence. The importance of gender discrimination serves as a reminder that, in war-affected countries, the violence that affects children is likely to be a mixture of direct and structural violence (Christie, Tint, Wagner, & Winter, 2008).

Of note was that children's views of harms diverged in significant respects from those frequently put forth by child protection experts or adults. For example, FGM/C is widespread in Somalia and viewed by child protection analysts as highly injurious. In this study, FGM/C was seldom mentioned as a harm, possibly because participants viewed it as a normal and necessary practice for protecting women's marriageability and family honor. Children, however, did not respect all cultural norms, particularly that of child beating. Boys and girls were quick to point out the psychological and physical harms caused by such beating. This pattern of findings serves as an important reminder of the importance of learning from both girls and boys and of complementing expert-driven assessments with learning from the children themselves. This is not to imply that children's views trump those of child protection experts or adults, but to recognize that experts and adults could benefit from learning about children's perceptions that shape their behavior and worldview.

The findings have implications for efforts to strengthen national-level child protection systems, now the dominant approach in the global child protection sector (African Child Policy Forum et al., 2013: Davis, McCaffery, & Conticini, 2012; UNICEF, UNHCR, Save the Children, & World Vision, 2013). Specific recommendations include the following. First, efforts to strengthen child protection systems need to be contextual and varied. A single approach will not work in settings as different as rural areas, where nomadic pastoralists live, and urban areas, home to refugees and displaced people. Second, special attention should be given to gender differences in protecting the children of Somalia, with attention to the specific risks, threats, and supports that boys and girls have. Particularly needed are efforts to prevent gender discrimination and violence that promote the institutionalized inequities facing girls and women. Policies should be based on the principle of nondiscrimination, with equal attention given to girls.

Importantly, economic support should be integrated with child protection (Child Protection Livelihoods and Strengthening Task Force, 2013). Policy leaders should recognize that poverty is a fundamental driver of many of the most severe and prevalent risks to both boys and girls. In this research, some of the greatest harms to children—particularly being out of school and engagement in strenuous work—were related to severe poverty and an inability to meet basic needs. A priority is to strengthen economic supports for vulnerable children and families and to ensure through continuous monitoring that those supports actually reach the children at greatest risk. Efforts to develop child protection services and programs without integrating economic supports are unlikely to succeed because many of the biggest risks to children in this study stemmed from economic hardships. Finally, services to children need to attend to their everyday stresses and develop comprehensive supports for their psychosocial health and mental well-being. Although national-level plans frequently focus on clinical symptoms, which are important, supports to alleviate everyday distresses are also crucial.

CONCLUSIONS

The global child protection sector is becoming more systematic in its use of evidence to document which interventions work and to guide steps to strengthen practice and policy related to children. Although this is a positive trend, advocates of strengthening the evidence base for child protection sometimes privilege excessively quantitative methods. Indeed, quantitative methods are very important in addressing questions about the magnitude of problems, obtaining accurate measures of the prevalence of particular child protection issues, and measuring how impactful particular interventions are. However, mixed methods that use the complementary strengths of qualitative and quantitative approaches will be of greatest use in advancing our understanding of child protection.

The findings from this research and the points raised in the recommendations have significant implications for children in many different war zones. The need to listen in a grounded, gendered manner is universal. When doing research, it is always important to start with listening and open-ended learning. The use of elicitive, less structured methods makes it possible to learn about the perspectives of girls and boys of different ages and backgrounds. Without learning about such perspectives, there is a danger that measurement efforts will not assess children's lived experiences and perceptions of their greatest problems. Moreover, significant cultural differences are often overlooked when using methods that ask preconceived questions and use the categories and language of international child protection. A partial, limited understanding of the situation of children then results. Thus, in all contexts of work with children, careful attention must be paid to cultural considerations.

Ethnographic approaches may be useful in other contexts with war-affected children because they help give voice to children. Efforts to strengthen child protection systems need to be informed by the lived experiences of girls and boys, which may differ significantly from those of adults. These systems ought to enable the participation that is every child's right. When children have a voice, they are in a better position to contribute to efforts to strengthen child protection. In these respects, deeper listening to children must become a priority to strengthen child protection systems.

Note

The authors represented the Columbia Group for Children in Adversity and wish to thank Neil Boothby, who was co-principal investigator on this research; Rebecca Horn, who was lead trainer; and UNICEF/Somalia, which commissioned the research.

References

Accord. (2009). *Clans in Somalia*. Vienna: Austrian Red Cross.

African Child Policy Forum, African Network for the Prevention and Protection Against Child Abuse and Neglect, Environnement et Developpement du Tiersmonde, et al. (2013). *Strengthening child protection systems in sub-Saharan Africa: A call to action*. Dakar: Author.

Alderson, P., & Morrow, V. (2011). *The ethics of research with children and young people*. London: Sage.

Allden, K., Jones, L., Weissbecker, I., Wessells, M., Bolton, P., Betancourt, T., . . . Sumathipala, A. (2009). Mental health and psychosocial support in crisis and conflict: Report of the Mental Health Working Group—Humanitarian Action Summit. *Prehospital and Disaster Medicine*, 24 (Suppl. 2): 217–227.

Boyden, J. (2004). Anthropology under fire: Ethics, researchers and children in war. In J. Boyden & J. de Berry (Eds.), *Children and youth on the front line: Ethnography, armed conflict and displacement* (pp. 237–258). New York: Berghahn Books.

CESVI & Handicap International (2012). *Children with disabilities in Somalia: A knowledge, attitudes and practices household survey*. Hargeisa: Author.

Charmaz, K. (2006). *Constructing grounded theory: A practical guide through qualitative research*. Thousand Oaks, CA: Sage.

Child Protection Livelihoods and Strengthening Task Force. (2013). *Children and economic strengthening programs: Maximizing benefits and minimizing harm.* New York: Child Protection in Crisis Network for Research, Learning, & Action.

Christie, D., Tint, B., Wagner, R., & Winter, D. (2008). Peace psychology for a peaceful world. *American Psychologist, 63*(6), 540–552.

Columbia Group for Children in Adversity. (2013). *A rapid ethnographic study of community-based child protection mechanisms in Somaliland and Puntland and their linkage with national child protection systems.* New York: Author.

Davis, R., McCaffery, J., & Conticini, A. (2012). *Strengthening child protection systems in sub-Saharan Africa* (Working paper). Dakar: Inter-Agency Group on Child Protection Systems in Sub-Saharan Africa.

Gerstle, D. (2007). *2007 Justice for Children national survey for Somalia.* New York: UNDP.

Graham, A., Powell, M., Taylor, N., Anderson, D., & Fitzgerald, R. (2013). *Ethical research involving children.* Florence: UNICEF Office of Research-Innocenti.

Harper, M. (2012). *Getting Somalia wrong? Faith, war and hope in a shattered state.* London: Zed Books.

Miller, K., & Rasmussen, A. (2010). War exposure, daily stressors, and mental health in conflict and post-conflict settings: Bridging the divide between trauma-focused and psychosocial frameworks. *Social Science & Medicine, 70*(1), 7–16.

Puntland Development Research Center. (2004). *Report on socio-economic assessment in Puntland.* New York: UNDP/World Bank.

Strauss, A., & Corbin, J. (1990). *Basics of qualitative research: Grounded theory procedures and techniques.* Thousand Oaks, CA: Sage.

UNICEF/Somalia. (2003). *From perception to reality: A study on child protection in Somalia.* Hargeisa: Author.

UNICEF/Somalia. (2012). *Mapping and assessment of Somaliland's child protection system summary report: Strengths, weaknesses, and recommendations.* Hargeisa: Author.

UNICEF, UNHCR, Save the Children, & World Vision. (2013). *A better way to protect ALL children: The theory and practice of child protection systems* (conference report). New Delhi: Author.

United Nations. (2013). *Standards of conduct for the international civil service.* New York: Author.

U.S. Department of Labor. (2013). *Findings on worst forms of child labor.* Washington, DC: Author.

Wessells, M., Kostelny, K., & Ondoro, K. (2014). *A grounded view of community-based child protection mechanisms and their linkage with the wider child protection system in three urban and rural areas of Kenya: Summary and integrated analysis.* London: Save the Children.

Wessells, M., Lamin, D., King, D., Kostelny, K., Stark, L., & Lilley, S. (2012). The disconnect between community-based child protection mechanisms and the formal child protection system in rural Sierra Leone: Challenges to building an effective national child protection system. *Vulnerable Children and Youth Studies*, 7(31), 211–227.

8

SURVIVING DISORDER
Children, Violence, and War Stories in Liberia

Sukanya Podder

There are many ways to tell a story and there are also many ways to read a story. This is perhaps most true of war-stories.

—C. NORDSTROM, "FOUR WAYS TO TELL A STORY ON VIOLENCE"

THIS CHAPTER EXAMINES CHILDREN'S AGENCY and their relationship with violence through an in-depth exploration of their war stories. War stories are defined here as constructs that project the lives of children as atypical, violent, and extraordinary. These narratives tend to present personalized versions of survival and negotiation that suggest deviation from everything that can be viewed as "normal" and "appropriate" for a child. In this chapter, I argue that war stories narrated by children affected by war convey not only truths or partial truths but also that the process of their narration, compilation, and presentation can offer insights into children's perceptions of how their lives have changed because of war. In this sense, "war" itself becomes an episode in the "otherization" of the self; that is, telling war stories that reflect abnormal, powerful, imaginary, and thrilling experiences helps an individual present him- or herself in a different light by invoking virtues of heroism, courage, and survival. In this sense sharing war stories is more than storytelling: It also involves the creation of a particular type of self-image that privileges children's agency and capacity.

Liberia presents a pertinent case for understanding the implications of war stories narrated by child soldiers and other children affected by war. Eight different factions and splinter groups were active during the first civil war (1989–1996), and nearly every faction recruited soldiers from among children and youth. The first phase of the conflict traced its roots to the rise of an Americo-Liberian elite that strengthened an oligarchy and related discrimination in public life through the consolidation of the True Whig party regime. Shifts under President Tubman and the subsequent overthrow of his rule coincided with Samuel Doe's advent to power. This marked the beginning of ethnic polarization and favoritism toward the Krahn group. After a failed coup attempt by Captain Qwiwonkpa and the persecution of the Gio and Mano groups in Nimba County, the National Patriotic Front in Liberia (NPFL) insurgency led by Charles Taylor found support in Nimba, with many young men joining voluntarily in a revolutionary spirit. After intervention by a Nigerian-led Economic Community of West African States Monitoring Group (ECOMOG), in which the peacekeepers were party to the conflict, 14 short-lived peace accords between 1990 and 1995 culminated in the signing of 5 sets of peace agreements that preceded the Abuja II accord in 1996 and Taylor's electoral victory in 1997 (Dupuy & Detzel, 2007; Ellis, 1995; Jaye, 2003).

During the second civil war (1999–2002), opposition to Taylor crystallized at an international level. The United States and neighboring governments, especially Sierra Leone and Guinea, financed and provided bases for anti-Taylor elements, which resulted in the formation of two new insurgencies between 2000 and 2002: the Liberians United for Reconciliation and Development (LURD) and the Movement for Democracy in Liberia (MODEL; Brabazon, 2003; Reno, 2004). Fifty-three percent of an estimated 40,000 combatants were children (Achvarina & Reich, 2006, p. 143), but only 11,780 child soldiers formally demobilized after the conflict. Thousands of young people continued to experience injury, loss, and displacement (Podder, 2010). Since the Accra Accord (2003), a large amount of donor funding has supported an ambitious peace-building program with a selective focus on different aspects of children and youth's rehabilitation and capacity building.

Although the war is now officially over, the realities of poverty and violence remain. In 2013, Liberia ranked as the "second most miserable place to live" because of its unemployment and inflation prospects (Mahapatra, 2013). Its Human Development Index (HDI) value was 0.388 in 2012, based on three primary measures—life expectancy, school and adult education expectancy (3–25 years), and per capita national income that determines access to a decent standard of living (UNDP, n.d.). Liberalization and free trade policies, a weak state, and poor welfare provisions have resulted in a rapid privatization of basic service sectors, further weakening the state's capacity. Although youth (ages 15–35) constitute more than 60% of the population (Mutisi, 2012), Liberian society is dominated by a neo-patrimonial social ethos, where "big" men continue to control opportunities and demand unquestioned political loyalty and socioeconomic support from their youthful clients (Utas, 2012). It is within this postwar context that this chapter explores the relationship between children, violence, and war stories.

The chapter begins with a brief discussion of narrative research and the role of voice in exploring children's agency as transmitted through war stories. The second part of the chapter elaborates on the methodology used and then presents the two narratives—one of a former child soldier and another of a child who witnessed violence against her family—to explore some of these issues through the dual lenses of "otherization" and "ultra-experiences." The chapter concludes by exploring how the process of "storying"—of constructing these stories—creates opportunities for children to exercise agency. It reflects on the implications of the relationship between children and violence for children's agency and how human rights discourses approach child protection issues in conflict-affected environments.

NARRATION, VOICE, AND CHILDREN'S AGENCY

The use of narrative analysis has gained increasing momentum within social science research, particularly within social constructionist psychology. This approach takes the position that selves are formed, framed, and understood within language. How we talk about ourselves is highly dependent on the discourses available to us in our social settings; therefore, social constructionist psychology can be regarded as a subfield within the larger domain of discourse analysis in social sciences, in that the locus of the analysis is the individual and the discourse of the self (Burr, 1995). Sarbin (1986), Bruner (1985, 1990), Gergen (1994), and Polkinghorne (1988) argue that, epistemologically, the self is not an individual's personal or private structure, but rather is a form of relational discourse about the self, performed and framed through language available in the public sphere (Gergen, 2001). Thus "sense-making" in narrative studies is produced collaboratively in the course of social interactions between people (Wilkinson & Kitzinger, 2003). Further, the main function of the narrative is to unite the past with the present and signify future trajectories for the self. Therefore the terms "self" and "identity" are used interchangeably, both denoting processes of social construction (Gergen, 1994).

Stories are particularly useful for understanding children's experiences of war both individually and collectively because they offer a way to make sense of these experiences. By telling stories, children do more than simply relate a sequence of events; they also convey information about the context in which those events occurred and the meanings they derived from them. In particular, stories offer insights into the types and scale of violence to which children are exposed and how these experiences affect them, as well as how they navigate conflict-related dangers to survive in war zones. For example, telling stories may give them the opportunity to reflect on the reasons for joining an armed group and the types of violence to which they were exposed, as well as how they view their own use of violence. Stories can also be used to privilege self-representations of "victimhood" by presenting oneself as a powerless, passive recipient of violence, without any real ability to act (Kvist, 2002). In these forms, the perpetrator (or other) is portrayed as holding all the power with full freedom to act and with complete responsibility for the situation. Therefore, how children represent themselves through war stories can conform to a variety of imageries ranging from victim to perpetrator, from an active agent to more submissive or subjected forms.

At the same time, narratives are often organized so as to construct a preferred self-representation strategy. Davies and Harre (1990) highlight the importance of stories in people's construction of identity. Telling stories can be seen as a vital part of "creating perspectives for the self" (Dawson, 1994, p. 22). Therefore, throughout a narrative, identity has a fluid and dual nature of both being and becoming (Andersson, 2008; Saco, 1992). In this respect, narratives are constructed from the narrator's current social position (Wagner & Wodak, 2006) and are based on his or her understanding of "who I am" in combination with an understanding of "who I will become."[1]

Children can make meaning by creating and exploring their stories in concert with other interested parties. These stories can be influenced by policy frameworks on child protection and programming that depend on Western notions of childhood and advance a particular type of image of children in war zones. Indeed, the Global North and its aid apparatus "globalizes childhood" (Boyden, 2004), imposing criteria of legality and standards of human rights that may not be congruent with other cultural and social realities. The humanitarian discourse includes a familiar pattern of a plea for protection in the name of "all children" and a general characterization of all children as victims or innocents who are subject to forced recruitment or abduction or are forced to kill and slaughter their kin. Their participation is perceived as limited to being witnesses to extreme acts of violence, being abused or sexually assaulted, and being subjected to hunger and slavery. Within this framework, this passive role makes them unprepared for combat and therefore susceptible to injury and trauma through exposure to violence and witnessing death (Martins, 2011). As a result, the voice of young soldiers is often used to describe children's experiences of soldiering as a tragic life path. War stories may therefore be structured to conform to this dominant humanitarian narrative or to avoid being categorized as either victim or perpetrator, although they may simultaneously draw on both categories. In this sense, the study of stories and the storying process presents problems of validity that are inherent in self-reported data (Polkinghorne, 2010). Therefore, in exploring children's agency as represented through narratives about conflict, it is important to be aware that agency here can be double-edged. Not only does the narrative present instances of agency, but also children can engage in the process of storytelling to consciously filter or alter parts of their stories to suit specific audiences or to advance particular types of self-representation. In that it is both subjective (to the individual) and subject to interpretation by the person listening to the war story, the process of narration and construction can involve an element of agency and choice: The child decides what to say, what to leave out, and what to emphasize so that the story either conforms to mainstream projections of children's role in conflict or deviates from this "standard imagery" to present ultra-experiences that highlight the agency and capacity of young people caught up in conflict zones.

Wetherell and Edley (1999) discuss how male youth may construct themselves as "masculine" and "courageous"—capable of ultra-achievements—or as protagonists involved at the center of ultra-experiences by negotiating different imaginary positions. On the one hand, they may identify a heroic position in which they narrate particular productions of the self that coincide with a heroic masculine persona. This is done by describing the self in key adjectives of "what it means to be a man," such as courageous, physically tough, and able to keep one's cool (composure). In fact, according to Dawson (1994), virtues such as aggression, strength, courage, and endurance never simply convey a story of an individual adventure but rather characterize personal stories of soldiery, cultural stories, or social myths that are shared by all (Steedman, 1988). For young girls and women, conflict participation can be empowering and liberating, releasing them from patriarchal domination and enabling their political participation (Veale, 2003; West, 2000). They may take on more aggressive and masculine behaviors to assert themselves. Girls have been known to be fearless leaders across a range of recent conflicts such as Sri Lanka, Ethiopia, and Mozambique (Denov, 2010; Veale, 2003).

Therefore at the end of any conflict, it can be argued that there is no real self or authentic identity independent of the discursive environment; rather, individuals are positioned by particular discourses as coherent selves (Francis, 2002). They may consciously deploy arguments that enable them to construct a preferred image, which Wagner and Wodak (2006) refer to as "the enacted performance." Children may also use war stories to enable a process of otherization, in which war and its structural compulsions are seen as responsible for acts of violence and ultra-experiences.

METHODOLOGY

In the Liberian context, as in other West African countries, folklores have played an important role in the education of children and in the ongoing renewal of community life. Storytelling in African tradition is an improvised art form in that the teller adapts stories to the occasion, context, and the audience's expectation (Champion, 2003; Lenox, 2000). Fables that dramatize the effects of jealousy, greed, and disobedience tend to reinforce social norms. Most stories are participatory at multiple levels. The audience responds by punctuating stories with vocal affirmations and debate about how a story should end.

This chapter uses war stories as a methodological tool, elaborating on the stories of two young respondents: (1) Timothy Sunday, a young man I met in Nimba County, Liberia, who took part in the second Liberian civil war (1999–2002); and (2) Henrietta Sagbah, a 15-year-old girl I met in Monrovia who survived a MODEL attack in Margibi in 2002, but lost most of her family in the raid.[2] Timothy and Henrietta's stories enable us to understand to what degree war stories can be regarded as "enacted performances."

These stories were documented as part of a larger empirical study on child soldier recruitment and reintegration conducted during 2008–2012. Seven counties—Bong, Montserrado, Margibi, Nimba, Lofa, Grand Gedeh, Sinoe—and the capital city Monrovia were part of this study of conflict variables and ex-child soldier resettlement data provided by the UNDP/Joint Implementation Unit (part of the United Nations Mission in Liberia/UNMIL) and UNICEF Liberia. Due to logistical limitations and restricted access to communities, potential respondents were contacted through a number of international and local governmental and nongovernmental organizations working with ex-combatant youth in the areas of leadership, education, vocational training, and community recovery projects; these programs were funded by the United Nations Peacebuilding program, the United States Agency for International Development (USAID), and the Liberian Disarmament, Demobilization, Rehabilitation and Reintegration (DDRR) program.[3]

Respondents (those who were younger than 18 years of age when they first joined an armed group) were selected using a filter questionnaire and interviewed twice. A total of 126 ex-child soldiers were interviewed from November 2008 to October 2009. A follow-up study was conducted during December 2011 and January 2012. Several ethical concerns were central to the conduct of this research. The first issue was that of acquiring access in an ethical and safe manner. This process was negotiated through agencies and key informants who acted as gatekeepers, providing the necessary networks of trust through which respondents could be approached.

Second was the issue of my social identity—in terms of gender, age, physical appearance, and racial, ethnic, class, and national difference—and its impact on the respondent. With girls, being a woman proved to be an advantage because they felt comfortable in sharing issues about their sexual experiences, regrets, and hopes. With the male respondents, however, my gender proved to be a disadvantage: It tended to bottle up discussion on these issues. Most of the male respondents admitted to having witnessed incidents of sexual violence, but did not elaborate on their own role in those acts.

Third, my affiliation with a Western university, together with the disparities in economic and educational background between my respondents and me, created an unequal power relationship. As a result, interviews often served as a conduit for transmission of grievances, and some of my respondents asked whether I could help them study in the United Kingdom or give them money to buy books for school. These false expectations were addressed by honest discussion about the academic nature of the research and by the provision of small tokens of appreciation, such as pens, key chains, biscuits, or a cold drink during the interview, to make respondents feel rewarded for their participation.

To ensure accountability and facilitate the respondents' willingness to participate in the research, verbal informed consent was sought at all stages, and informants could refuse to answer any questions that caused them to feel uncomfortable or unwilling to talk about the issue. Efforts were made to adhere strictly to the requirements of confidentiality in the interviews because there was widespread acceptance of the fact that revelations of past deeds could have ramifications for the well-being of informants, especially when hearings held by the Truth and Reconciliation Commission (TRC) were ongoing in 2008.

Timothy was interviewed as part of the ex-child soldier survey, and Henrietta was a civilian whom I met at the Catholic bed and breakfast where I stayed in the capital. She was introduced to me by one of the nuns in the convent. Although Henrietta was not included in the study on child soldiers, her narrative was recorded as a civilian account of the Liberian civil war, following standard ethical procedures of describing the research purpose, securing informed consent, and sharing the final results. In this chapter, I draw on their two narratives to highlight how war stories as a methodology can help researchers use micro-data to develop a more accurate understanding of children's conflict experiences. These stories enable the researcher both to interrogate different coping strategies and to contextualize conflict experiences better by focusing on micro-level experiences of violence by civilians.

FINDINGS

TIMOTHY'S STORY

I met Timothy in the border town of Ganta in Nimba County. A Bassa boy born in Buchanan (a southern county in Liberia), he was part of the Taylor militia forces during the second civil war in 2002. Timothy took part in the DDRR program, receiving carpentry training at the Young Men's Christian Association (YMCA) in Buchanan. After nine months of training, he moved to Ganta as an ice-cream maker, a skill he had picked up during a short stint in Monrovia. When his business idea did not take off, he approached the Liberia Opportunities Industrialization Centers (LOIC) office in Ganta and presented himself as a war-affected youth so he could enroll in its eight-month training program to become a mason. Ganta offered opportunities for building and construction employment on the several infrastructure projects that were then ongoing.

Timothy's story presents interesting twists and turns that emphasize violence, magic, and reliance on unnatural powers to survive. His war story narrates a typical tale of coercive recruitment, with emphasis on issues of violence, feelings of regret, and reflections on moral conscience that shaped his experience of the war. These themes enable the reader to glean a particular type of self-representation—that of a victim of circumstance.

Timothy was in school in Grand Bassa when he was captured by one of the many Taylor militia groups roaming the countryside for recruits. In Timothy's words, "when I was in class, I was refusing to go with them, so the boys tied me and beat me . . . they wanted to kill me. My hand got affected—it still has marks [shows me the scar]."

After his capture in Grand Bassa, Timothy was taken to Grand Gedeh County for a period of 3 months. On his way "going" with the militia, Timothy tried to escape, but was recaptured and arrested at the ITI junction in Grand Gedeh County. Timothy was part of the Lion Group, which was from the Gbatala Base. His battalion commander was Red Devil. On the group's composition, Timothy said, "We were more than 250 in our group, we had about 125 small boys, 130 men and the girls had their own group called 'Wild Geese' battalion." In reflecting on his time spent in the group, Timothy recalled that he was badly treated (beaten), and as a result he can no longer fold or turn his hand. Beatings appeared to be a routine feature of his life in the group: "I was beaten for many days, and *tabayed* if I refuse to do things."[4] With such a violent start, one would expect Timothy to be bitter about his stay in the group. However, he suggested that, "after the first year, I was already used to the system and became relaxed . . . . There is a parable that says, where you tie a goat is where the goat will eat." He traveled to Sierra Leone, Guinea, Maryland County, Lofa County, River Gee, and Nimba County with the group.

Like most young recruits, Timothy witnessed extreme levels of violence, which later affected his mental health. He shared one incident that took place when his group came under attack:

On Saturday May 15, 2002, I can remember we were eating when someone roll grenade in our midst and it exploded. We fought from day to day night, non-stop for 24 hours. They called for small two-hour ceasefire but there was no resting. Most of our men got wounded, some lost their legs, some lost their sight, and as for me my finger burst. This fight was with the LURD rebels. We could not allow them to capture us because when they catch you they cut your skin while you are alive, cut your finger, or cut your arms as long or short sleeve and chicken wing sizes [cut arms off], and then they cut your foot. I saw these during the war.

From such a narrative, one would expect that Timothy may have also carried out similar forms of violent behavior. In his narrative, however, Timothy highlighted instances where he had the power to choose between right and wrong forms of violent action. For example, he referred to how the soldiers captured most of the girls in the group, but Timothy had only one woman with him:

> If I go to fight, I harass no one—it is sin to God to force. I did not rape. I did not eat human beings, because if I eat human beings, I will be sinning against God. Some of my friends did it—some of them even open pregnant woman's stomach. I was not able to do it.

He also recounted saving the life of a young girl and taking her into his safekeeping as a daughter:

> One time, I saw a girl child lying in the grass, and she put her head up, I thought it was an enemy so I wanted to fire, but when I got to know it was a child, I took her and carry her with me. She presently lives with my father in Grand Bassa County, and we call her Nene. I capture her in Gbarpolu in 2003 but keep her as my daughter.

Through such insights, Timothy emphasized feeling helpless and frustrated, unlike some of his friends in the group:

> At times, I would cry while on the frontline; I wondered how I managed to be on that side, especially when I thought about my family—to be arrested and captured and have no option. When I cry, my friends [in the group] would lock me up and tell me that I am no longer a child in the force, I should not cry, when I see people dying.

This sense of helplessness and exposure to violence had long-term postwar effects, including the possibility of physically harming his family members:

> Even while resting my heart could race hard and I could start hearing gunshots and get ready to fire. One time I was sitting near my mother with a knife in my hand; I suddenly jerked the knife and almost got her hurt, my mother got afraid. At other times, I would just sit and shout. My mother started to fear [me]. My violent outbursts scared her.

Timothy's war story helps us visualize how children and young people can participate in conflict through force and circumstance. His story aligns with the dominant "victim" images associated with child soldiers. In contrast, Henrietta's story is that of a survivor who escaped a deadly attack on her family in Margibi.

HENRIETTA'S STORY

I met Henrietta in Monrovia, at the Catholic bed and breakfast where I stayed during weekends spent away from the rural counties during my field research in 2009–2010. Henrietta was in seventh grade and struck me as a confident young person. Sister H., a nun who managed the establishment, introduced Henrietta to me as a good student who would be able to describe clearly her experience of the war. Although not a child soldier, her story illustrates how agency among young people in conflict-affected environments can be transmitted in various ways and how children perceive and communicate their survival strategies in a volatile environment.

Henrietta began by stating how she had suffered because of the war and that education had made a major difference in her ability to cope. She was grateful to the Catholic nuns for supporting her schooling, and she expressed an interest in pursuing nursing as a career. After initial introductions and a briefing regarding my research, we chose the time span for her experiences that she would share. We agreed that she would focus on the last episode of fighting in the counties in and around Monrovia.

Henrietta's war story takes us back to the time the second civil war broke out in 1999. She was living in Margibi County with relatives; her father lived in the same county, while her mother was residing in Bomi County. It was during a visit to her mother in Bomi "on a Sunday in 2001, that the LURD rebels attacked Tubmanburg."

Henrietta decided to escape and tried to reach her father.

Her memory may have been affected as a result of war: This "fog of war" effect is associated with experiencing extreme circumstances that can shift, alter, or fragment memory (McNamara, 2004); it may be responsible for the loopholes and discrepancies in her account. It was difficult to track her down for a second interview, and therefore her account is short and could not be elaborated on. Nonetheless, her story documents well her survival skills:

> When the LURD people come to Bomi, I decide to go to my father in Margibi with my mother. We were traveling with some people; when we got to Clay I decided to go get my oldest sister and her two children. When I got to the place

my sister lived [in Clay], I found the LURD rebels had already raped her and killed her husband and two children. I could not help her because she was already raped and she was bigger than me.

When asked what happened to her elder sister, Henrietta said she did not know. This seemed strange, because most internally displaced family members I met had been able to track down relatives after the war. Henrietta also did not shed much light on whether she had tried to get in touch with her sister after the war.

Returning to her story, she focused on how she managed to reach Margibi. A driver who was rescuing his children from Clay helped her with transport. She did not mention any further details of this travel, the difficulties she faced, what happened to her mother, and whether they traveled together or not. To allow her to present her story without interruptions, I let her continue.

The second part of Henrietta's story describes what happened after she reached Margibi:

In Margibi another rebel group called MODEL captured Kakata and started to target all the *money* [wealthy] *people* in the city. My father was the Managing Director of the Wealla Rubber Plantation, so they took my father and put tires on him with petrol and burned him. We fled and went to the SDA mission, and the rebels followed us and said they were in search of the Sagbah family. On their way to find us they asked our neighbors; in asking they killed lots of people claiming that the people were hiding us. While on their way to the SDA mission the rebels saw our oldest brother who had joined their ranks and was going to rescue father; they saw him and asked for his name; given that he was part of them and did not know what was going on he called his name and the commander told him, "you people are the ones we are looking for." They took him to the town that the mission was in and cut his ears and put it in his mouth to eat; later they killed him. When they got to the mission they asked for all the children names; when they got to us we said we were not Sagbah, but they caught our cousin and rape her right in front of us and then plug knife into her and killed her. They did all this because they killed our father and did not find any money. The head of the mission, a bishop, escaped with us and later sent my brother and I to Monrovia to our grandmother.

Such tales of atrocity are unfortunately common. Yet the account presented by Henrietta had few details and seemed to have gaps. It is well documented that rebel groups such as the MODEL used brutal tactics to terrorize the civilian population in areas far from their ethnic kin settlements in Grand Gedeh (TRC of Liberia, 2009). However, the abrupt nature of the story makes it seem less trustworthy and raises several questions. For example, how many other siblings were there in Margibi? Why were they all there at the same time? What happened to her mother? Why did Henrietta never go back to find her? Given that we were unable to arrange a second interview with Henrietta, we must take this story as a type of meta-data, a narrative that represents how young children experienced the war as civilians and choose to represent their experiences to researchers in the postconflict setting.

Children's stories (and by extension the children themselves) are not inherently untrustworthy. The premise of truth in studying subjects who participated in or witnessed violence during conflict is a gray area. As researchers, we are not in a position to judge whether a participant is telling the "truth," given that truth during the conflict itself is often dependent on affiliation (political, ethnic, economic) and can vary between groups. In research with war-affected children, accepting their truth as truth can result in a biased and subjective version of events. Yet, accepting the version presented by children as data helps illustrate how they elaborate or change details in an act of agency, navigation, and survival. Their accounts can be particularly powerful lenses through which to study their ability to understand and react to conflict and to understand the frames that define children and their role in conflict. They reveal how children's own understanding and capacity to navigate realities may differ from perceptions of international human rights agencies working with children in conflict-affected environments.

DISCUSSION

The process of "otherization" of the self through narrating ultra-experiences can take different forms. By creating a heroic position when storytelling, children can rely on a self-exalting strategy (Wetherell & Edley, 1999). Narrating their experiences as something extraordinary or fantastical, children engage in an imaginary process that uses a repertory of images (Zivkovic, 2011). Stories that children tell others about themselves can either conform to the structures of humanitarianism that deny children agency or use ultra-experiences and otherization to resist mainstream notions of victimhood and strengthen their ability to protect themselves and survive.

Recent studies highlight that the strategies civilians adopt in settings of on-going violence can be their first line of defense against recruitment or capture by armed groups (Baines & Paddon, 2012). Even projections of the self as "victim/survivor" or "subject/object of violence" can involve an element of agency geared toward captivating or appealing a particular audience. Often, this particular audience is the host of international child protection agencies that are drawn by the appeal of these ultra-experiences, which validate their desire to protect children from future harm.

The two narrators, Timothy and Henrietta, created distinct narrative plots in which their primary positioning in the story differed. Timothy's story has a victim plot characterized by helplessness and coercion, mediated by acts of kindness and morality, and containing reflections on violence and elements of regret. Despite being a subject of violence, Henrietta's story has a survivor plot characterized by courage interlaced with a feeling of helplessness at being unable to save members of her family and a feeling of pride in her ability to cope in the aftermath of their loss. The two narratives, however, suggest that storytelling is far from an unproblematic way to get things off one's chest. This is because each is in some way a victim and yet has demonstrated courage in coping with the banalities of war. Goffman (1981) talks extensively about playing multiple roles and presenting oneself in many different ways. For children and young people, war stories can offer a means of communicating and representing agency through the adoption of particular identities. Victims have the power to redefine their social identities in the postconflict sociopolitical space by accepting humanitarian standards of protection and support. Tailoring war stories to suit victim images reflects the material, social, and political reality in which they find themselves in the postconflict setting. In contrast, positioning themselves mainly as survivors enables intrapersonal, interpersonal, and societal relations that are more independent and that acknowledge young peoples' capacity for positive action, which can be facilitated by circumstances that help them overcome violence and loss (Curling, 2005).

A study of war stories also reveals that externally imposed narratives can be different from how child soldiers represent themselves. In this book, chapters 7 and 11 illustrate this point for war-affected children other than child soldiers in the contexts of Somaliland, Puntland, and northern Uganda. In regard to child soldiers, for the most part, the humanitarian discourse on child protection displays a lack of understanding of how the circumstances of war can render their participation in war meaningful rather than barbaric (Lee, 2009). Having both voice and responsibility as a subject and social actor is not exclusive to adults. Much like authors in the diaspora who exoticize their native land, reproducing Orientalist images in their writings, child soldiers can rely on an exoticized script of unnatural and ultra-experiences, thereby performing a process of self-otherization (Hayden, 2014).

Similarly, war stories may conform to and borrow from some form of fictionalization (Zulaika & Douglass, 1996), which has implications for how we researchers deal with discrepancies in oral testimonies. As Fujii (2009) suggests, when the truthfulness of the content is suspect, researchers can use such accounts for the collection of meta-data that enable a more nuanced understanding of how respondents in postconflict contexts construct and communicate their experiences. In this research, such an approach yielded a more accurate understanding of child recruitment and participation. Although war stories present images of abduction and coercive recruitment (to reflect the dominant narrative in the media and the humanitarian discourse of child recruitment practices), this study found that most children joined armed factions of their own volition. Timothy and Henrietta's stories enable us to piece together the real context of child soldiering and the nature of armed groups' interactions with civilians.

This study found that, for both Liberian civil wars, young people were often motivated to join armed groups by their search for security, access to food, family protection, and some form of work; this finding may explain some of the discrepancies in Timothy's story about how he joined and left the armed group. Henrietta's story captures the abusive relationship between armed factions and civilians and the ethnic nature of targeted violence documented during both episodes of the conflict, despite inconsistencies about the type of violence to which she was exposed.

There are three main policy implications of this research. First, it is important to apply humanitarian standards in a contextually sensitive manner to prevent children from using manipulation and cheating to gain access to programs aimed at supporting war-affected children. Second, both the positive and negative aspects of war participation need to be considered. Child-focused programming must acknowledge the positive aspects of protection from violence that membership in armed groups offered and must incorporate the postconflict utility of wartime affiliation and networks in terms of employment and support. Third, accepting the agency of children to voluntarily take part in violence is a key to developing more appropriate standards for dealing with juvenile crime in the context of war. Characterizing atrocities committed by children as merely a product of coercion or manipulation weakens the argument in favor of children's agency and ability to act in crises, both positively and negatively.

CONCLUSIONS

This chapter has explored how storytelling can be a means of exercising agency through a process of social construction. By seeing storytelling as a process whereby individuals can act as agents of change and by understanding that stories have intentions and purpose, it is possible to see the narratives of children affected by war as playing two roles. On the one hand, they can perpetuate a certain official script of war where children's role is assumed as intrinsically one of "passive victims" in the need of protection. On the other hand, they can present an alternative narrative that underlines thought, reflection, and decision-making capacity when faced with extreme adversity or "choiceless choices" (Langer, 1991, p. 83).

The findings and the war story methodology highlight the pitfalls of globalizing childhood experiences and encouraging a protection-driven child rights agenda in postconflict contexts. Such a discourse that relies on Western conceptions of human rights is limited in its utility. In addition, the war story methodology enables researchers to capture legacies of conflict in children's imagination. Despite the problems of authenticity in self-reports, it facilitates the collection of meta-data about how children experience conflict and choose to construct and communicate their experiences and feelings.

The war stories and storytelling methodology can enable more focused research of children in armed conflict. First, it encourages researchers to address discrepancies in narratives through the use of multiple forms of data collection that can triangulate stories. Ethnographic and participatory methodologies can help contextualize narratives and offer community-level insights into events. Second, this methodology encourages researchers to employ children's representation of violence and disorder as a unique lens for studying conflict narratives—as an actor and agent, both as participant and witness.

Listening to children's stories can not only offer us important insights into the experiences of conflict but can also help us assess the depth of an individual's character as represented through tales of survival, courage, and sacrifice. War stories help us visualize, construct, and relate power and status roles and develop more effective postconflict intervention policies.

The two narratives presented here show that "research into violence can confront Kipling's truism that the first casualty of war is truth, by misrepresenting the realities of violence" (Nordstrom, 1998, p. 158). These intensely personal tales offer not only snippets of reality but also insights into how the process of storytelling in itself can be an act of agency by putting forth the preferred self-representation as a victim or survivor.

Storytelling allows children to keep or regain "choice" and "control" (Frykman, 2003, p. 55) through the use of "voice" as communicated through narratives. In trying to relate the experience of disorder, violence, and war, children can reconstruct their preferred war-related experiences through a subjective lens. They can represent the "self" as something remarkable and extraordinary through the communication of stories about ultra-experiences involving survival, courage, or heroic deeds.

Through their storytelling, children's ability to influence how a particular audience perceives their role in war and relationship with violence has two main implications for how human rights discourses should approach child protection in conflict-affected environments in West Africa and elsewhere. First, these discourses ignore the existence of hierarchies of victims and that the politics underlying the construction of such a hierarchy may privilege certain groups as more deserving of victim status than other (Breen-Smyth, 2009, p. 28). Studies show that victims may resent such a label or use it to gain short-term benefits. In this sense, categories such as victim or perpetrator can be manipulated to suit both political and personal ends (Van Dijk, 2009, p. 2).

Second, storytelling enables children to exercise a subaltern form of agency that involves elements of diplomacy, self-representation, and choice, and can influence the tenor and direction of everyday social interactions as well as children's place in an evolving social context of recovery (Podder, 2015). The exercise of subaltern agency is one tactic used by children to navigate post-conflict social realities. It creates the space for positioning themselves to benefit from the flawed conceptions about childhood and children's role in war that continue to frame humanitarian and human rights approaches on children and conflict.

Notes

1. As an immigrant academic based in an UK research institution, my understanding of challenges for children in developing contexts is structured by my personal experiences of growing up in India.
2. Respondent names have been changed to retain privacy.
3. Agencies for negotiated community access included the International Organization for Migration, Child Fund Liberia, International Rescue Committee

and American Refugee Committee (Lofa); Save the Children (SC-UK), Liberian National Red Cross and Action Aid Liberia (Grand Gedeh); Young Men's Christian Association, and Equip (Nimba); Landmine Action and United Nations Mission in Liberia Civil Affairs (Sinoe) Mercy Corps (Margibi and Montserrado); and Save the Children UK and Justice and Peace Commission (Bong).

4. *Tabay* is a form of torture in which a person's elbows are tied together behind his or her back, causing severe pain and often leading to nerve damage in the arms (Hartjen & Priyadarsini, 2012).

References

Achvarina, V., & Reich, S. (2006). No place to hide: Refugees, displaced persons, and the recruitment of child soldiers. *International Security, 31*(1), 127–164.

Andersson, K. (2008). Constructing young masculinity: A case study of heroic discourse on violence. *Discourse & Society, 19*(2), 139–161.

Baines, E., & Paddon, E. (2012). "This is how we survived": Civilian agency and humanitarian protection. *Security Dialogue, 43*(3), 231–247.

Boyden, J. (2004). Anthropology under fire: Ethics, researchers and children in war. In J. Boyden & J. de Berry (Eds.), *Children and youth on the front line: Ethnography, armed conflict and displacement* (pp. 237–258). New York: Berghahn Books.

Brabazon, J. (2003). *Liberia: Liberians united for reconciliation and democracy* (Africa Program Armed Non-State Actors Project Briefing Paper 1). Retrieved from www.chathamhouse.org.uk/file/3733_brabazon_bp.pdf.

Breen-Smyth, M. (2009). Hierarchies of pain and responsibility: Victims and war by other means in Northern Ireland. *Trípodos, 25*, 27–40.

Bruner, J. (1985). Child's talk: Learning to use language. *Child Language Teaching and Therapy, 1*(1), 111–114.

Bruner, J. (1990). *Acts of meaning.* Cambridge, MA: Harvard University Press.

Burr, V. (1995). *An introduction to social constructionism.* London: Routledge.

Champion, T. B. (2003). *Understanding storytelling among African American children: A journey from Africa to America.* New York: Lawrence Erlbaum Associates, Inc.

Curling, P. (2005). Using testimonies as a method of early intervention for injured survivors of the bombing of the UN headquarters in Iraq. *Traumatology, 11*(1), 57–63.

Davies, B., & Harré, R. (1990). Positioning: The discursive production of selves. *Journal for the Theory of Social Behavior, 20*(1), 43–63.

Dawson, G. (1994). *Soldier hero: British adventures, empire and the imagining of masculinities.* London: Routledge.

Denov, M. (2008). Girl soldiers and human rights: Lessons from Angola, Mozambique, Sierra Leone and Northern Uganda. *International Journal of Human Rights, 12*(5), 813–836.

Dupuy, K., & Detzel, J. (2007). *Power-sharing and peace building in Liberia: Power-sharing agreements, negotiations and peace processes* (CSCW Papers). Oslo: Center for the Study of Civil War. Retrieved from www.priono/sptrans/623646343 /Liberia_full_report.pdf.

Ellis, S. (1995). Liberia, 1989–1994: A study of ethnic and spiritual violence. *African Affairs, 94,* 165–197.

Francis, B. (2002). Relativism, realism, and feminism: An analysis of some theoretical tensions in research on gender identity. *Journal of Gender Studies, 11,* 39–54.

Frykman, M. P. (2003). The war and after: On war-related anthropological research in Croatia and Bosnia-Herzegovina. *Etnološka tribina, 26*(33), 55–74.

Fujii, L.A. (2009). Interpreting truth and lies in stories of conflict and violence. In C. L. Sriram, J. C. King, J. A. Mertus, O. Martin-Ortega, & J. Herman (Eds.), *Surviving field research: Working in violent and difficult situations* (pp. 147–161). London: Routledge.

Gergen, K. J. (1994). *Toward transformation in social knowledge.* London: SAGE.

Gergen, K. J. (2001). Psychological science in a postmodern context. *American Psychologist, 56*(10), 803.

Goffman, E., 1981. *Forms of talk.* Philadelphia: University of Pennsylvania Press.

Hartjen, C. A., & Priyadarsini, S. (2012). *The global victimization of children: Problems and solutions.* New York: Springer.

Hayden, R. (2014). Self–othering: Stories about Serbia from externalized Belgrade insiders. *American Ethnologist, 41*(1), 187–192.

Jaye, T. (2003). Briefings Liberia: An analysis of post-Taylor politics. *Review of African Political Economy, 30*(98), 643–686.

Kvist, C. (2002). *Jeg er!—Er jeg? En fortælling om vold og væren* (Unpublished doctoral dissertation). Institute for Anthropology, Copenhagen.

Langer, L. L. (1991). *Holocaust testimonies: The ruins of memory.* New Haven, CT: Yale University Press.

Lee, A. (2009). *Understanding and addressing the phenomenon of 'child-soldiers': The gap between the global humanitarian discourse and the local understandings and experiences of young people's military recruitment* (Working Paper Series 52). Oxford: University of Oxford Refugee Studies Center.

Lenox, M. F. (2000). Storytelling for young children in a multicultural world. *Early Childhood Education Journal, 28*(2), 97–103.

Mahapatra, L. (2013, February 22). The 25 most miserable places in the world. *Business Insider.* Retrieved from www.businessinsider.com/most-miserable-countries -in-the-world-2013-2?op=1 2013.

Martins, C. (2011). The dangers of the single story: Child-soldiers in literary fiction and film. *Childhood, 18*(4), 434–446.

McNamara, R. (2004, April). Fog of war. *RUSI Journal, 149,* 76–88.

Mutisi, M. (2012). Interrogating traditional youth theory: Youth peacebuilding and engagement in post-conflict Liberia. *Africa Dialogue*, 87–120.

Nordstrom, C. (1998). Deadly myths of aggression. *Aggressive Behavior*, 24(2), 147–159.

Podder, S. (2010). *Child soldier reintegration outcomes in post-conflict environments: An analysis of the re-recruitment trends in the Liberian civil wars* (Unpublished doctoral dissertation). University of York, York, UK.

Podder, S. (2015). The power in-between: Youth's subaltern agency and the post-conflict everyday. *Peacebuilding*, 3(1), 36–57.

Polkinghorne, D. E. (1988). *Narrative knowing and the human sciences*. Albany: State University of New York Press.

Polkinghorne, D. E. (2010). Qualitative research. In J. C. Thomas & M. Hersen (Eds.), *Handbook of clinical psychology competencies* (pp. 425–436). New York: Springer.

Reno, W. (2004). Reconstructing peace in Liberia. In T. M. Ali & R. O. Matthews (Eds.), *Durable peace: Challenges for peace building in Africa* (pp. 115–141). Toronto: University of Toronto Press.

Saco, D. (1992). Masculinity as signs: Poststructuralist feminist approaches to the study of gender In S. Craig (Ed.), *Men, masculinity and the media* (pp. 23–39). Newbury Park, CA: Sage.

Sarbin, T. R. (1986). *Narrative psychology: The storied nature of human conduct*. Westport, CT: Praeger.

Steedman, C. (1988). *The radical soldier's tale*. London: Routledge.

Truth and Reconciliation Commission of Liberia. (2009). *Volume II: Consolidated final report*. Monrovia, Liberia: The TRC of Liberia. Retrieved from http://trcofliberia.org/resources/reports/final/volume-two_layout-1.pdf.

United Nations Development Program. (n.d.). *Liberia: Human development indicators*. Retrieved from http://hdrstats.undp.org/en/countries/profiles/LBR.html.

Utas, M. (2012). *African conflicts and informal power: Big men and networks*. New York: Zed Books.

van Dijk, J. J. M. (2009). Free the victim: A critique of the western conception of victimhood. *International Review of Victimology*, 16(1), 1–33.

Veale, A. (2003). *From child soldier to ex-fighter: Female fighters, demobilisation and reintegration in Ethiopia* (Monograph 85). Pretoria: Institute for Security Studies.

Wagner, I., & Wodak, R. (2006). Performing success: Identifying strategies of self-presentation in women's biographical narratives. *Discourse & Society*, 17(3), 385–411.

West, H. G. (2000). Girls with guns: Narrating the experience of war of FRELIMO's "female detachment." *Anthropological Quarterly*, 73(4), 180–194.

Wetherell, M., & Edley, N. (1999). Negotiating hegemonic masculinity: Imaginary positions and psycho-discursive practices. *Feminism & Psychology*, 9(3), 335–356.

Wilkinson, S., & Kitzinger, C. (2003). Constructing identities: A feminist conversation analytic approach to positioning in action. In R. Harré & F. M. Maghaddam (Eds.), *The self and others: Positioning individuals and groups in personal, political and cultural contexts* (pp. 157–180). Westport, CT: Praeger.

Zivkovic, B. (2011, February 11). Circadian clock without DNA—History and the power of metaphor. *Scientific American.* Retrieved from https://blogs.scientific american.com/observations/circadian-clock-without-dna-history-and-the-power -of-metaphor/.

Zulaika, J., & Douglass, W. A. (1996). *Terror and taboo: The follies, fables, and faces of terrorism.* London: Psychology Press.

9

REWEAVING RELATING IN SOCIAL REINTEGRATION

Participatory Action Research with War-Affected Young Mothers
and Their Children in Liberia, Sierra Leone, and Northern Uganda

Angela Veale, Miranda Worthen, and Susan McKay

*Social trauma affects individuals precisely in their social character; that is,
as a totality, as a system*

—I. MARTÍN-BARÓ, *WRITINGS FOR A LIBERATION PSYCHOLOGY*

ONE OF THE MOST PROFOUND consequences of prolonged conflict is its impact on the capacity of families and social systems to provide for the survival and protection of children, especially girls. In Sierra Leone, Liberia, and northern Uganda girls were among the many children recruited or abducted into armed forces or groups (CAFFAG) where they conceived or gave birth to children. On return to their communities as young mothers, they face many challenges. Their baby is evidence of "bush" relationships (McKay, Veale, Worthen, & Wessells, 2010), and they share similar experiences with other war-affected young mothers who become pregnant through unsanctioned relationships whereby the unknown or unacknowledged paternity of the child is a source of stigma (Baldi & MacKenzie, 2007). Many are forced to terminate their schooling or leave home (Sharkey, 2014). Girls formerly associated with armed groups grapple with managing a post-return identity within a "moral discourse" that sees them somehow as to blame for their sexual activity even if they were raped, and they try to "slink home" (Shepler, 2014, p. 18), seeking anonymity. Doing so is more difficult for young mothers who return with babies.

Although there are accounts of NGO staff trying to get former boys and girls associated with rebel groups to marry each other (Shepler, 2014), research indicates that the majority of returned young mothers do not wish to marry the "bush" fathers (SWAY, 2008). Because they refuse to slot back into their conditioned social position from before their involvement in an armed group, their presence is a challenge to communities that may be unsure how to relate to them. Their presence is also a symbol of the collective inability of their communities to provide for girls' protection and well-being. Sexual violence and sexual exploitation of girls in war have a collective impact on communities, including on men who may feel emasculated and even "useless" as a result of the violence perpetrated on girls and women (Shanahan & Veale, 2010).

Social reintegration interventions struggle to manage this dialectic of individual–community relations. For instance, a focus on CAFFAG returnees has frequently resulted in jealousy from those not formerly associated with armed groups (Wessells, 2006). A key question is how interventions can foreground the relational element of reintegration in a way that places girls *central* to the process, rather than engaging with "community" as an external, separate add-on activity such as in sensitization activities. This chapter discusses an innovative research methodology and an intervention that placed young mothers central in their relational networks and supported them to mobilize those networks for their reintegration, thereby addressing young mothers-in-communities in an embedded, ecological way.

Martín-Baró (1989, 1994) first drew attention to the socially embedded nature of trauma by introducing the term "social trauma" to capture the ways in which war directly or indirectly affects all the members of a society through its impact on relationships. Relationships mediate individual well-being, producing the possibility for growth or suffering. In this way, psychic trauma and social trauma are not separate, but are two sides of a single coin. Martín-Baró defined this dialectic relationship as psychosocial trauma:

> (a) the injury that affects people has been produced socially—i.e., its roots are not found in the individual, but in society; and (b) its very nature is nourished and maintained in the relationship between the individual and society, through various mediations by institutions, groups, and even individuals. (1989, p. 14)

At its core, psychosocial trauma is a process of dehumanization that brings about cognitive and behavioral changes that "impoverish" four key abilities: (1) to think clearly, (2) to communicate truthfully, (3) to be sensitive to the suffering of others, and (4) to hope (Martín-Baró, 1989, p. 14). Arguably, such processes are central to the stigma, discrimination, and marginalization experienced by former CAFFAG and "community" young mothers. This dehumanization process could be conceived as encompassing a breakdown in mentalizing capacity, which is a form of "imaginative mental activity about others or oneself, namely perceiving and interpreting human behavior in terms of intentional mental states—e.g. needs, drives, feelings, beliefs, goals, purposes and reasons" (Fonagy, Gergely, & Target, 2007, p.2 89). Community members often fail to stand in the shoes of war-affected young mothers and see the world through their eyes, but rather attribute blame to them and abdicate responsibility for their well-being. Fundamentally, there is a breakdown of relational processes. Yet one of the strongest predictors of positive outcomes for former CAFFAG including girls is community acceptance (Betancourt et al., 2010). How can this relational space in social reintegration be best conceptualized and addressed?

Martín-Baró's concept of psychosocial trauma resonates strongly with new paradigms in psychology on the social brain and on relating. Schore (2003, 2012) argues that psychological transitions and change occur through participation in relationships. The mechanism of change lies in right-brain to right-brain communication that can occur once joint attention or intersubjectivity is established. The right brain plays a key role in experience-dependent learning, emotional communication, self-regulation, empathy, and mentalizing. The intersubjective field is a site of action, a contact zone, where behavioral and emotional change occurs. For psychosocial interventions, it makes sense to give attention to how to create such moments of "being together" (Schore, 2012) as a way of mobilizing change both in the self and other. Gergen (2010) argues that relating occurs in sites of "joint action"—minds acting in social spaces. Knowledge, language, emotion, meaning making, and social action all come into being through communal activity and co-action—an action in relation to other actions. In this model, an utterance or action only makes sense in terms of the supplementary action: that which occurs when the other speaker or audience listens, deliberates, affirms, negates, or questions. An isolated act of asking does not have consequences; an outcome is only realized through a response from the other. The space of relating has to exist or be created. Gergen notes,

> If others do not treat one's utterances as communication, if they fail to coordinate themselves around the offering, one is reduced to nonsense. . . . Like a handshake, a kiss or a tango, the actions of the individual alone are empty . . . like the sound of one hand clapping. (2010, p. 76)

A challenge for psychosocial programming with war-affected young mothers is how to connect them with others in their communities so that their agentive activities for their well-being and that of their children are met and responded to in ways that create "joint actions." Doing so directly works at the site of stigma in which young mothers' agentive actions are marginalized or not met. This chapter presents an intervention that sought to act at such sites or moments.

CONTEXT

We selected Sierra Leone, Liberia, and northern Uganda for this study because girls and young mothers were documented in large numbers as serving in armed groups in these three countries (McKay & Mazurana, 2004). Northern Uganda experienced conflict from 1987 to 2006, when a ceasefire was negotiated with the Lord's Resistance Army (LRA). Girls had made up as much as 30% of the LRA fighting forces (McKay & Mazurana, 2004). In Liberia, the 2003 peace accord ended 14 years of civil war and brought about the resignation of former president Charles Taylor. Girls represented 10–30% of combatants across the three armed forces in Liberia (Specht, 2006). In Sierra Leone, the conflict began in 1991 and ended in 2002, and the Special Court of Sierra Leone acknowledged the extent of forcible recruitment of girls by all the fighting forces (except for the Economic Community of West African States Monitoring Group and UN peacekeeping missions).

When the study began in 2006, conflict was lessening or had ceased in all contexts. Yet all three countries continued to be affected by the direct impacts of conflict, including massive displacement and resettlement, social reintegration of former combatants, poverty, and gender-based violence (Advisory Consortium on Conflict Sensitivity [ACCS], 2013; Specht, 2006); all three presented challenging environments for social reintegration. In response, disarmament, demobilization, and reintegration programs (DDR) were active in all three countries.

METHODS

Participatory action research (PAR) is a methodology in which "communities of inquiry and action evolve and address questions and issues that are significant for those who participate as co-researchers" (Reason & Bradbury, 2008, p. 1). It recognizes the unique strengths of community participants and is well suited to promoting self-efficacy and empowerment after exposure to overwhelming events (Hobfoll et al., 2007). This PAR study evolved over a 4-year period through a partnership among international academics; local leaders in psychosocial policy; programming staff in Sierra Leone, Liberia, and northern Uganda; and in-country academics, government personnel, UNICEF officials, and donor representatives. The methodology developed over two meetings (October 2005 and October 2006) held at the Rockefeller Conference Center in Bellagio, Italy, to discuss the situation of girls who returned home from the fighting forces. At the 2005 meeting, significant reservations were voiced about working with girls as a separate group from boys. Others argued that more research was needed on how to support the reintegration of girls, in particular young mothers. A recommendation for further research was brought to a second meeting in October 2006, which was attended by NGO staff and regional UNICEF partners. A participatory research response to the challenges faced by returned young mothers and their children evolved in the final days of the meeting (see "Summary Notes from the Final Days of the Bellagio Meeting, October 2006").

This excerpt from our summary notes conveys the sense of excitement felt by participants about this participative approach to study and support war-affected young mothers. Rather than begin with a focus on appropriate training, livelihoods, skill building, or other forms of top-down interventions, the study was organized around one core concept: strengthening meaningful participation by young mothers in social relationships and in decision making. Existing structures that "weren't apparently helpful to the girls" would be supplemented by efforts to support the girls in creating and strengthening their own networks, which initially would be composed of those close to them. It was hoped and envisaged that these networks would broaden and strengthen in time; for example, by drawing in "peace-building women" and others who might be well disposed in their favor. There was also a vision that the outputs could help others in the community and not only women.

The PAR involved 658 young mothers and 1,200 of their children living in Liberia (n=111), Sierra Leone (n=226), and northern Uganda (n=281). The term "young mother" refers to youth between 14 and 30 years of age who are mothers, including former CAAFAG and other vulnerable young mothers in the community. A criterion of participation was that all participants had become pregnant while themselves a minor.

Two-thirds of the participants in the PAR were formerly associated with armed groups and became pregnant or had children during their association: The percentages for Sierra Leone, Liberia, and northern Uganda were 88%,

SUMMARY NOTES FROM THE FINAL DAYS OF THE BELLAGIO MEETING, OCTOBER 2006

Approaches and Methodology

- Highly interactive
- Include other vulnerable children but with focus on young mothers
- How will it work?
  - Team worker goes into community and reach out to families
    - In a family, there will be a young mother
    - Include all people in the household in the discussion
      - Elicit interest (win trust, build security and confidence)
      - Get the young mother and parents to participate
        - Discussion forums with parents and guardians and talk about issues affecting them but also other parents as well
  - Research becomes action oriented
    - Life skills as a point of action
    - Have interactive meetings, not a structured, formal meeting
      - Informal, in the community about how it used to be
      - Young mothers will be beneficiaries, as well as participants
    - Young mothers can become researchers
      - If (example) the question is about parenting, they can ask other people in the community about how it used to be; we will capture their perceptions of well-being
  - Young mothers or parents might come up with something, and we will develop that into something tangible to feed into the process
- The young mothers will take us into the community

Title of the project is: "Community-based Participatory Action Research to Empower Girl Mothers and Their Supportive Networks Toward Effective Reintegration." Bravo! Great stuff! What about young mothers' children?

- The young mothers and their supportive networks implies the child. Also, reintegration impacts the children. Dialogue approach will bring out children.

Supportive networks that already exist, or will you build new networks?

- Existing networks as identified by young mothers through participation with others. Through dialogue we hope the supportive networks will be expanded. For example, family would likely be a first supportive network.
- Are there peace-building women who can participate in support?
  - If the young mothers come out and identify these women, but we wouldn't want to impose them. So it'll come from the young mothers.
  - These structures used to exist, but aren't apparently helpful to the young mothers. They have their own networks they've created to support themselves.
  - Outputs could empower others in the community as well.
  - Imagine a participatory process for outputs relying on young mothers ingenuity—documents a story

The expertise is local: the young mothers themselves will tell us things.

80%, and 34%, respectively. One-third of participants were young mothers deemed vulnerable by their communities, but were not former CAFFAG: Most of these participants had been displaced due to the conflict, many had been orphaned, and others had physical disabilities.

The average age of participants at the beginning of the project was 20 years, 22 years, and 18 years in Liberia, Sierra Leone, and northern Uganda, respectively; 80% were between 16 and 24 years of age. At the start of the PAR, 22% had one child, 44% had two children, 25% had three children, and 9% had four or more children. Approximately 30 young mothers were enrolled in each of 20 sites across the three participating countries; project partners had identified these sites as having significant numbers of formerly associated young mothers and had established links with many of them. Sixty percent were rural sites, and 40% were urban or semi-urban sites. The proportion of young mothers who remained in communities where they had lived before the conflict was highest in northern Uganda (79%), followed by Liberia (65%) and Sierra Leone (56%). The percentage of formerly associated participants varied per site and was higher in Liberia and Sierra Leone (range, 71%–100%) than in northern Uganda (range, 15%–66%).

Ethical approval was granted through the University of Wyoming's Institutional Review Board. The informed consent procedure required that there would be no sharing of any information that participants regarded as sensitive and that there would be the collaborative development of educational messages from the project. Because only a minority of the young mothers could read and many were unable to write their names at the onset of the study, the consent form was read in the language of the participant and signed by the participant with an "X." In the case of minors who were living with parents or guardians, these adults also signed the form. As a research team, we reviewed ethical concerns and checked our "Do no harm" and participatory principles at each yearly meeting, as well as when we met within country-specific teams.

The PAR methodology in our project had four stages. The first stage involved community outreach, in particular to and by young mothers, inviting their participation. A significant focus of the first year was on supporting the participants in establishing their group meetings, during which they gathered information about their situation and needs. For this purpose, community advisory committees (CACs) were formed at each site, and they played a critical role in involving the community.

In the second stage, the young mothers identified, prioritized, and began implementing their livelihood activities and social action plans with community support. A key element of the project was a dedicated budget line for these activities, which were devised and implemented by the participants and over which they were the primary decision makers, supported by partner agency social workers and the CACs. Priorities across all sites included livelihoods, the health of young mothers and the health of their children, education, the challenge of being accused of "not being useful in the community," caring for their children, overwork of young mothers at home, mental disturbance of the girls, and their limited knowledge of family planning. In regard to the last challenge, one participant shared, "Many of us have small babies and are also pregnant. This means additional burdens are coming soon" (Kampala Team Meeting Notes, 2007).

In the third stage, supported by local academics, the girls learned to analyze the information gathered, which they could then share with their communities while they also developed and consolidated their social actions plans. The final stage involved working with participants to document and learn from their activities. A participatory survey was developed that consisted of 20 indicators of social reintegration and was completed by 434 participants who had registered in the project at its onset. Outcomes included better health for young mothers and their children, economic empowerment, reduced stigma, and improved family and community relations (McKay, Veale, Worthen, & Wessells, 2010, 2011; Veale, McKay, Worthen, & Wessells, 2013; Worthen, Veale, McKay, & Wessells, 2010).

The analysis presented here is based on monthly reports compiled by the young mothers' groups; ethnographic field notes, including interviews and focus group discussions conducted during regular site visits by the authors; the participative survey; and yearly international team meetings that brought together agency partners, national and international academics, and young mothers' representatives. Qualitative data were analyzed and reanalyzed to identify how the PAR acted within relational spaces to create sites of joint action, thus transforming the relational space occupied by young mothers-in-communities. This was a form of thematic analysis (Braun & Clarke, 2006), an inductive approach in which the identified themes emerged from the data.

FINDINGS AND DISCUSSION

"THE SOUND OF ONE HAND CLAPPING"

Although some young mothers and their children were welcomed back by family members, extreme poverty often meant that it was their responsibility to provide for themselves and their children. Lack of education and of child care, as well as few income-generating opportunities, meant that becoming a young mother was not a "one-off" event, but instead set up a developmental trajectory in which poverty and discrimination led to even greater poverty, stigma, and marginalization. Gergen (2010) notes that current relationships are shaped by experiences in previous relationships, and as time moves forward, these will be supplemented and transformed through other relationships. This developmental trajectory was leading many young mothers at the start of our study toward greater vulnerability. In northern Uganda, a local leader explained how teenage girls became young mothers in his community:

> This sub-county was entirely affected by the Karamojo from 1979 when the Karamojo began using firearms. There were lots of human rights abuses and extreme poverty. Then the LRA came. The UPDF mobilized the local militia to encounter the LRA. The life of girls and young women became very vulnerable. Some girls fell in love with soldiers. People were so vulnerable that they couldn't do the right thing at the right time for themselves. It introduced short-term survival, commercial sex. There were three UPDF battalions here. They had money. They sent for girls or their parents sent girls to them. It resulted in a number of young girls getting pregnant, and then they realized there was no further support for them.

Receiving "no further support" for themselves and their child was a common experience among study participants. As one Liberian young mother noted, "They see us as wasted, expired, useless." This comment captures Martín-Baró's concept of social trauma, sustained in an ongoing way by powerful, collective community dynamics. These dynamics set up a developmental trajectory that increasingly placed the young mothers outside of the circle of care they had experienced within their communities when identified as a child (not-mother). This trajectory placed them in situations of increased vulnerability, making it more likely that they would once again become mothers:

I had my first child in the bush. When I first came to Freetown my parents said they would not accept my child because it was from the bush. I pleaded with my mother to accept me because it was not my fault, so my mother accepted me and the child. I met a boyfriend and he assisted me. I was in love with the boyfriend, but when I became pregnant he stopped supporting me. He gave me no reason for stopping support. (young mother, Sierra Leone)

The first child is from the rape in the bush, second is from a boyfriend who I am no longer with, and the third is from my current boyfriend. I live with my family now, not the boyfriend. My friends said I should go stand where men could see me. I also would go to the beach and begged some small fish and sold them. (young mother, Sierra Leone)

Across our interviews, young mothers recounted their initial efforts to support themselves and their children: washing clothes, selling small fish, and prostitution. However, often their efforts were not met by supplementary action by others. Rather, like "the sound of one hand clapping" (Gergen, 2010), these young mothers failed to engage others with their efforts to care for themselves and their children. In a sense, they did not lack "individual" agency if this is defined as goal-directed, intentional action or the capacity to act in the world. However, their activity was often ineffective because what they lacked was *relational* agency, actions on their part that were then supplemented and supported by further action on the part of others.

RELATIONAL REINTEGRATION

At a fundamental level, the PAR created sites of joint action (Gergen, 2010), or minds acting in social spaces. Representatives of the young mothers participated in an international team meeting in Kampala in 2007 where they talked about their activities during their groups. One participant reported that their group played netball: "It relieves me and is relaxing." They visited each other's houses: "If one has a problem, then others go to visit and support her . . . we fetch water, or cook food and take it to that person's home, or fetch firewood." They met regularly in their groups, started small savings groups, and planned social activities (see McKay et al., 2010).

With the support of their community advisors, they began identifying and mobilizing social networks close to them:

It is of interest to note the zeal of a lady who has been identified by girls as their support network. According to her testimony to the girls and one member of advisory committee, she is HIV positive. Here is a lady who is always available to the girls at short notice and offers advice according to her capacity as a mother and also a victim of HIV/AIDS. She gives very supportive advice on sexual and reproductive health with wonderful understanding and a sense of humor. The girls are identifying similar people in the community. (field notes, Parabongo, June 2008)

In all three countries, the young mothers performed poems and plays. In Sierra Leone, they were even successful in obtaining a radio slot to broadcast their performances; these broadcasts attracted the attention of the community. A community leader in northern Uganda reflected, "Most of the families did not receive their daughters in a polite way as shown in the drama." An advisory committee member in Sierra Leone recalled that "the community themselves got guilty; they started coming to the girls." Community members began to patronize the small businesses created by the young mothers. The mothers' group meetings, plays, and activities enhanced their visibility and, with the support of advisers, became sites where social and income-generation projects slowly developed.

At the end of the first year of the project, representatives of the young mothers' groups attended the international team meeting in Kampala, where some voiced frustration. For instance, although groups had begun to receive a small amount of funding for their social activities, some young women felt it was insufficient and that their demands were not being met as they wished and expected. The agenda of the meeting was changed to create space for them to discuss their concerns. What emerged was a set of demands for "t-shirts, drums, and uniforms"—common status symbols of being linked to an organization—and greater funding to develop their activities:

> We volunteered to train ourselves and we have participated. We need t-shirts, drums, and uniforms. This encourages people and so it is important. We have reached a level where the project needs to assist us and to give us hope. I have nothing to come home with. I don't know what do to, what will we tell the people back home. We are going to lobby, to lobby—what is this? What has this project stated? What is the purpose of this project? (young mother representative, Kampala International Team Meeting notes, 2007)

This discussion was followed by sustained engagement and communication between the team academics and NGO partners and the young mothers' representatives over the following days, which required significant changes to the meeting schedule. The goal was not to meet their demands to provide drums and uniforms, but to create a relational space where a shared understanding of the goals and objectives of the project and the principles underpinning it could be achieved. Each party (the study team, the young mothers' representatives) had to try and see through the eyes of the other, a process of reflective functioning (Fonagy, 2014). An NGO partner shared the reality of the uncertainty that accompanies program development in all projects that receive seed money and are seeking further funding:

> The goal of this project is to work with your groups in your communities, to avoid a situation where you have food in your stomachs for the next two years but then at the end of two years it is gone. The international system works in such a way that we write proposals to attain funding. Some little funding is available based on your needs, but we are not sure of getting funds to continue in the future. This PAR project is different—you have been made part of it— you know the ins and outs of it. It is to empower you so that you will have the boldness and the ability to [go] out into the community—so that you can claim access to services and know your rights. (country team member, Kampala International Team Meeting notes, 2007)

This was a pivotal time for the project, and fortunately, the outcome was greater trust and respect between all parties. These discussions were an authentic experience of communication and "meeting," enabling young mothers to return to their communities and report to their groups in a way that renewed their commitment to work for their reintegration. Toward the end of the second year, there was evidence of a quantum leap forward at sites across the project as the scale and impact of their activities seemed to take off.

TWO HANDS CLAPPING

Throughout 2008 and 2009, participants continued to develop individual and group activities at their sites. With seed money in hand, young mothers began developing programs to support their livelihoods. Community advisors helped them carry out needs analysis on sustainability. Partner agencies provided relevant training at key points on skills requested by young mothers—managing group dynamics, bookkeeping, running a business, and handling specific tasks relevant to their projects, such as hygiene skills for running a restaurant or veterinary advice for pig rearing (Veale et al., 2013). Rural initiatives included individual or group agriculture projects, such as farming ground nuts and cassava on land provided by the community; they took into account seasonal changes by alternating agricultural work with small trading. Urban or semi-urban groups started small food-related businesses, which often demonstrated a degree of entrepreneurship; for example, selling tomatoes and onions at the entrance to a butcher stall with the permission of the butcher or establishing small businesses, such as pumping bicycle tires or renting tools. Some young mothers brewed alcohol, and some groups hired teachers to provide literacy training. One group used part of its funds to pay the tuition of a member to train as a nursery school teacher because it realized she could be a resource to their whole community. A number of their micro-businesses exhibited amazing dynamism and were responsive to the setting, time of year, resources they were able to access—for example, being given land or a building for a restaurant by local leaders—and their own ingenuity.

The extent to which all of this activity involved mobilizing and engaging with different community members is captured in the July monthly report from one Ugandan site.

In the 2009 international team meeting, a country team member noted the following:

> One of [the] things that developed that we hadn't anticipated [was] that girls started inviting their family members to the meetings and in some sites girls started making house visits, and they started taking up this responsibility. In programming terminology, it was follow-up. In this project this is something the girls took on. That is probably a key learning for dissemination.

EXAMPLES FROM A MONTHLY REPORT FROM A PAR SITE (JULY 2008)

- We conducted home visits based on issues discussed in meetings with parents on supporting girls to participate in the project.
- We massively held discussions with parents to lobby for support on agricultural and crop cultivation.
- We held several meetings with local leaders and parents within the villages for capacity building on farming to research marketable crops and good varieties of livestock.

Advocacy and lobbying was at family level to strengthen increased access to land. The aim is that when the young mothers get access to small pieces of land for cultivation then the future of their children will be assured with improved living conditions.

Increases in family and community acceptance were noted at every site. The following is an extended excerpt from a focus group discussion in northern Uganda in 2009 held with young mothers and their parents, husbands, and boyfriends 3 years into the project's lifespan. It captures the dynamics of action and follow-up actions that ultimately lead to social reintegration:

> *Sarah's mother* (pseudonym): When she came back, her behavior was not normal, not co-operative, not making sense. Now I can see the difference in the way she responds to issues, her mind is settled.
>
> *Sarah:* What I appreciate from my mother is she knew the days I was going to meetings—if I was relaxing, "Hey, are you not going for meeting?" She took responsibility for my babies. They would say "For you to ride bike, you don't need a child on your back. We will mind the child." They really helped me to be in this group.
>
> *A parent:* We were willing to remind them to come. First thing, we see there was a change in behavior—hygiene, becoming smart, clean, able to talk about what they taught her—oh today is your day, you seem to be not going—encouraging her one way or another.
>
> *Another young mother:* I was trained for 5 days in health training. Hygiene, how to care for yourself, your family, family planning methods, I am very happy I can space my children now, I have not had a second child.
>
> *Musee (grandfather):* We all encouraged her to go and come back. . . . She was abducted and people would say, "What will you do with that one, she is mentally ill, she will not marry." Now they compare her with their daughters—she serves well, kneels down [before elders].

In this exchange, it is clear that initially, Sarah's mother found her daughter's actions incomprehensible, and she did not understand her. However, in Sarah's and the other young mothers' families, action was followed by further actions, setting up a new developmental trajectory of inclusion, acceptance, and respect. Advisory committees and local leaders played a key role in advocating for young mothers in public spaces, particularly when they ran into difficulties with other community members, and in this way, their activities often flourished.

It is interesting that this excerpt captures the pressure on girls to conform to expected gender norms; for example, a "good girl" kneels down before her elders. Yet in many other ways, the young mothers were engaged actively in areas traditionally considered to be masculine. In northern Uganda, a group constructed a piggery, but twice during construction, boys in the community stole their sand. The authorities intervened on behalf of the young mothers, and a local leader wondered aloud, "Was it jealousy from the boys, or an attitude problem despising the girls' efforts because this kind of work is usually done by men?" In Sierra Leone, the metalworkers were more socioeconomically successful than other groups of young mothers. Their actions brought about remarked-on changes to traditionally gendered norms of income generation.

However, when it came to their reproductive health, young mothers' actions were situated within sociocultural constraints. One Sierra Leonean young mother told how, after years of war, there is a sense of an obligation to produce more children, as well as a taboo on the use of birth control. Many young mothers reported that they became pregnant even when they did not want to. However, another young mother insisted, "Some in the PAR have two or three children. . . . But girls outside the PAR have more."

As their economic initiatives developed and became more visible and successful, jealousies began to emerge in a number of communities. The young mothers and their partner agencies shared this problem at the international team meetings, where it was the focus of discussion. Inclusion of key actors from the onset was key to addressing these jealousies as CACs and local leaders advocated on their behalf. In addition, as the initiatives grew, the base of inclusion broadened: Boyfriends, parents, and those close to girls were often invited to participate in their meetings, and young mothers made home visits if a mother reported difficulties at home. A response from the young mothers themselves that was shared at the international meeting was to take up "no cost" community initiatives, such as organizing clean-up efforts in the community and community picnics, helping out at homes after the funerals of loved ones, and disinfecting a well, all of which contributed to community well-being and reduced jealousies.

"BEING A GIRL IS HARD, HARD . . ."

Toward the end of the PAR, we made field visits to each country to evaluate the study and its outcomes. One of these field visits was to Palabek Gem in northern Uganda. Palabek Gem, which is approximately 30 kilometers from the Ugandan border with Southern Sudan, was the site of LRA attacks, including child abductions, during the conflict. The young women in this group had been meeting for nearly three years; their main projects were individual

BEING A GIRL

It's easy being a girl . . .
It's hard being a girl, hard and it is really hard
When you see boys flocking to you like edible items in market
If you hear what they say you feel it's sweet and good
But it's easy being a girl . . .
It's hard being a girl, hard and it is really hard
Men has sweet lies words, sweet and nice like honey
You feel should accept and you really accept
But it's easy being a girl . . .
It's hard being a girl, hard and it is really hard my fellow women
You move at night without fear thinking that men are your king, God, everything you need is the man
But it's easy being a girl . . .
It's hard being a girl, hard and it is really hard
Once, twice your stomach is covered with a big calabash, today satisfied but who is responsible? No one
Being a girl is easy but bearing the pain is hard, hard, and hard
When you open your eyes you see the world and when you have pushed out the maggot you hear names *arach* (bad), *anywar* (abused), *akwero* (rejected) are the praises given to girls
Being a girl is easy . . .
Being a girl is hard, hard and it's really hard
Who think you are young, who?
Today you are a young beautiful girl tomorrow a mother, they don't sympathize with you
Being a girl is easy . . .
Being a girl is hard, hard and it's really hard
(Palabek Gem PAR Group, Uganda)

and group cultivation and small trading. Their group cultivation project had a record harvest, and they had sold their groundnuts on the local market for a handsome profit. Two of the authors participated in a meeting in Palabek Gem, which was attended by 27 young mothers (more than half of whom were former abductees of the LRA), three advisory committee members, a local government leader, and a social worker. During the meeting, one of the members chose to recite a poem she had composed, which has a call-and-response structure. In response to lines that claim that it is easy being a girl, the group responded with these words: "It is hard being a girl!" Thus, this poem does not exist in a vacuum, but is relational and engaged in a process of *negating* this "easy" perception and redescribing their reality as these young mothers experience it.

This reality is one of becoming pregnant for which no one is responsible. In one moment, you are beautiful, but once you become a mother, you lose the sympathy and protection that come from being thought of as young and beautiful. "You feel you should accept and you really accept" this introjected sense of self: "When you open your eyes you see the world and when you have pushed out the maggot you hear names *arach* (bad), *anywar* (abused), *akwero* (rejected) are the praises given to girls."

The social trauma as defined by Martín-Baró—the dehumanizing qualities that inhibit communication and being heard, that prevent others from being sensitive to the young mothers' suffering and seeing the world through their eyes—is evident in this poem. But "praises" given to girls show that this poem is not offered within a traditional feminine identity of being passive, submissive, and accepting, but rather reflects defiance, a refusal to be silenced. It situates the girls in relation to the men who impregnated them, who came "in sweetness," who called them bad, who abused and rejected them, who took no responsibility There is a mixture of voices—both those who were abducted and those who became pregnant "at a tender age" within their communities— in the poem. Unlike many young girls and mothers who return from armed groups and seek to "slink back" into communities (Shepler, 2014), the girls in the poem refuse to be silenced and are engaging with those who reject any constructive interaction with them, who see them as useless. This poem is a performative act that engages precisely at the site of dehumanization; it is reflective and aims to communicate truthfully, to stimulate the listener to think so that "when you open your eyes, you see the world" and to be sensitive to the ways in which their lives are "hard, really hard." Their collective and public performance of the poem brings into a social realm the space between people to help community members see life through their eyes.

Importantly, the poem also captures an element of "looking back." The poem was introduced by this short speech:

> [The PAR] has kept us so busy, but we are also forgetting the nasty things that happened in the past. Now we walk in public with pride. There used to be so much name-calling and stigmatizing—but this project has raised our level. We are able to dress well, take care of our children—we can now afford the salon and to make up our hair, these are the things we look forward to.

This speech was accompanied by a memorandum that listed the achievements of the group, including gaining leadership skills and being very involved in the community. Their refusal to be quiet and passive in a typically gendered way is wonderfully matched by their pride in their femininity: Dressing well, taking care of their children, and being able to afford visits to the hair salon are symbols of pride and success. Simultaneously they claim and rework being "a girl."

CONCLUSIONS

This chapter sought to understand *what happens in* and *through* relationships in a longitudinal social reintegration intervention, using PAR. The methodology made young mothers' meaningful participation in social relationships and in decision making central to all activities. The analysis captured how the PAR shaped young mothers' developmental trajectories by intervening at sites of action where dehumanizing and alienating processes occurred. This engagement enhanced the four core abilities "impoverished" by psychosocial trauma—the ability to think clearly, to communicate truthfully, to be sensitive to the suffering of others, and to hope (Martín-Baró, 1989). It also created sites of joint action (Gergen, 2010). The young mothers' actions fostered reflective functioning and mentalization (Fonagy, 2014) among community members, which better enabled them to see the world through their eyes and to join in their efforts to make their communities more hospitable places for themselves and their children.

In all three countries, the young mothers quickly understood participatory processes and wanted to be involved in improving their situation. The evaluation found that more than 90% of participants reported feeling involved in what their group was doing, 89% reported feeling more supported and respected by community members than before the project, and 75% felt that participation in the PAR resulted in better relationships with the broader community and that they were now able to better support their family by being able to buy basic necessities. Earning money enabled participants to become more self-sufficient and gain the respect of their communities. There were no significant differences between countries on these economic indicators.

However, there were significant differences in outcomes across countries on other indicators: "Involvement in the project has made me and my children more liked or loved by my family" (89%, 93%, and 80% for Sierra Leone, Liberia, and northern Uganda, respectively) and "Community members think worse of me now than before I joined the project" (1%, 2%, and 30% for Sierra Leone, Liberia, and northern Uganda, respectively). In Sierra Leone and Liberia, there may have been a greater emphasis in young mothers' groups of "giving back" to communities, which may have influenced these findings. Sampling may have also played a role because there were more community young mothers than CAFFAG young mothers in the northern Ugandan sample. The community mothers may have experienced less change in their level of acceptance or more jealousy because they may have been viewed as less entitled to special intervention. Furthermore, young mothers in northern Uganda reported that their boyfriends/husbands were supportive of their children less often than in the other countries (65%, 67%, and 33% for Sierra Leone, Liberia, and northern Uganda, respectively). Participants in northern Uganda were younger, and a greater proportion lived with parents than in the other countries; thus, they were less likely to live with husbands or boyfriends.

Although increasing their ability to earn a living was important across all countries, returning to school was a higher priority for Sierra Leonean participants. Macro-level postconflict educational policy in Sierra Leone advocates for and targets accelerated literacy education for girls and women; literacy was thus internalized as an expectation by participants, many of whom were able to establish links with literacy providers.

Our findings have implications for how participatory processes can evolve and be integrated with child protection policy, national-level development agendas, and resource allocation. In addition, the PAR highlights the importance to child protection policy and practice of enabling meaningful participation, enabling young mothers to mobilize their community networks to support their reintegration, and taking a slow, reflective, flexible approach that is responsive to emergent conditions. As we described, the first place where relatedness and joint action occurred was in the relationship between young mothers and the PAR staff and organizers, and then among the peer group of young mothers. Through experiencing trust, compassion, and shared meaning-making, the young mother participants in the PAR began to experience relatedness. This relatedness then expanded into other meaningful social relationships—with family, with community members, and with leaders. We recommend that practitioners consider their own social interactions with vulnerable young people as locations where this type of social transformation can begin.

Although reintegration policy often emphasizes transactional processes—give up your weapon and get this package of training—policy makers would do well to consider the social fabric that must be rewoven for hostilities to fundamentally cease. They should provide funding and time for socially transformative programming to assist communities with the community-level healing that must occur for social trauma to be addressed (Martín-Baró, 1994). The PAR demonstrated that vulnerable young mothers have the capacity to do this socially transformative work when well supported to address their priorities in their own lives.

A limitation of this study is that the distinctive conditions under which it was conducted decrease the ability to generalize its findings to other contexts. The project was conducted months, and in West African cases, years after the end of armed conflict. By this time there were reasonable levels of security and mobility that allowed young mothers to engage in regular group support and livelihood activities. The methodology is also intensive and therefore demanding of staff resources. Thus, this approach may be less suited to active conflict zones where security concerns may make it difficult to convene groups of young mothers or where fast responses are needed. Additional research is needed to explore these factors.

Note

We would like to acknowledge our partner agencies and academics. In Liberia the partners are Save the Children UK, Touching Humanity in Need of Kindness, and Debey Sayndee at the University of Liberia; in Sierra Leone the partners are Christian Brothers, Christian Children's Fund, Council of Churches in Sierra Leone, National Network for Psychosocial Care, and Samuel Beresford Weekes at Fourah Bay College; in Uganda the partners are Caritas, Concerned Parents Association, Transcultural Psychosocial Organization, World Vision, and Stella Nema at Makerere University. Primary funding for the PAR was provided by the Oak Foundation and the ProVictimis Foundation. Additional funding was provided by the Compton Foundation, UNICEF West Africa, and the Rockefeller Bellagio Study Center.

References

Advisory Consortium on Conflict Sensitivity (ACCS). (2013). *Northern Uganda conflict analysis.* Retrieved from http://reliefweb.int/sites/reliefweb.int/files/resources/ACCS_Northern_Uganda_Conflict_Analysis_Report.pdf.

Baldi, S., & MacKenzie, M. (2007). Silent identities: Children born of war in Sierra Leone. In R. Carpenter (Ed.), *Born of war: Protecting children of sexual abuse survivors in conflict zones* (pp. 78–93). Bloomfield, CT: Kumarian Press.

Betancourt, T., Borisova, I., Williams, T., Brennan, R., Whitfield, H., de la Soudiere, M., . . . Gilman, S. (2010). Sierra Leone's former child soldiers: A follow up study of psychosocial adjustment and community reintegration. *Child Development, 81*(4), 1077–1095.

Braun, V., & Clarke, V. (2006). Using thematic analysis in psychology. *Qualitative Research in Psychology, 3*(2), 77–101.

Fonagy, P. (2014, December 12). *Parenting interventions and epistemic trust*. Presentation to the Parenting Neuroscience Intervention Conference, Anna Freud Center/University College London.

Fonagy, P., Gergely, G., & Target, M. (2007). The parent-infant dyad and the construction of the subjective self. *Journal of Child Psychology and Psychiatry, 48*, 288–328.

Gergen, K. (2010). Beyond the enlightenment: Relational being. In S. Kirschner & J. Martin (Eds.), *The sociocultural turn in psychology: The contextual emergence of mind and self* (pp. 68–87). New York: Columbia University Press.

Hobfoll, S. E., Watson, P., Bell, C. C., Bryant, R. A., Brymer, M. J., Friedman, M. J., . . . Ursano, R. J. (2007). Five essential elements of immediate and mid-term mass trauma intervention: Empirical evidence. *Psychiatry, 70*(4), 283–315.

Martín-Baró, I. (1989). Political violence and war as causes of psychosocial trauma in El Salvador. *International Journal of Mental Health, 18*(1), 3–20.

Martín-Baró, I. (1994). *Writings for a liberation psychology*. Cambridge, MA: Harvard University Press.

McKay, S., & Mazurana, D. (2004). *Where are the girls? Girls in fighting forces in Northern Uganda, Sierra Leone and Mozambique: Their lives during and after war*. Québec: Rights & Democracy.

McKay, S., Veale, A., Worthen, M., & Wessells, M. (2010). *Community-based reintegration of war-affected young mothers: Participatory action research (PAR) in Liberia, Sierra Leone & Northern Uganda*. Retrieved from http://www.uwyo.edu/girlmotherspar/.

McKay, S., Veale, A., Worthen, M., & Wessells, M. (2011). Building meaningful participation in (re)integration among war-affected young mothers in Liberia, Sierra Leone and northern Uganda. *Intervention: International Journal of Mental Health, Psychosocial Work and Counselling in Areas of Armed Conflict, 9*(2), 108–124.

Reason, P., & Bradbury, H. (2008). Introduction. In P. Reason & H. Bradbury (Eds.), *The Sage handbook of action research: Participative inquiry and practice* (pp. 5–10). Thousand Oaks, CA: Sage.

Schore, A. (2003). *Affect regulation and repair of the self*. New York: Norton.

Schore, A. (2012). *The science of the art of psychotherapy.* Norton Series on Interpersonal Neurobiology. New York: Norton.

Shanahan, F., & Veale, A. (2010). The girl is the core of life: Violence & the sacred in social reintegration, northern Uganda. In B. Maeland (Ed.), *Culture, religion & the reintegration of former child soldiers in Northern Uganda* (pp. 115–132). Geneva: Peter Lang.

Sharkey, D. (2014). Through war to peace: Sexual violence and adolescent girls. In D. Buss, J. Lebert, B. Rutherford, D. Sharkey, & A. Obijiofor (Eds.), *Sexual violence in conflict and post-conflict societies: International agendas and African contexts* (pp. 86–98). New York: Routledge.

Shepler, S. (2014). *Childhood deployed: Remaking child soldiers in Sierra Leone.* New York: New York University Press.

Specht, L. (2006). *Red shoes: Experiences of girl combatants in Liberia.* Geneva: International Labor Organization. Retrieved from www.ilo.org/wcmsp5/groups /public/—ed_emp/—emp_ent/—ifp_crisis/documents/publication/wcms_116435 .pdf.

SWAY. (2008). *A way forward for assisting women and girls in northern Uganda.* Retrieved from http://chrisblattman.com/projects/sway/.

Veale, A., McKay, S., Worthen, M., & Wessells, M. (2013). Participation as principle and tool in reintegration of war-affected young mothers. *Journal of Aggression, Maltreatment & Trauma, 22*(7), 829–848.

Wessells, M. (2006). *Child soldiers: From violence to protection.* Cambridge, MA: Harvard University Press.

Worthen, M., Veale, A., McKay, S., & Wessells, M. (2010). "I stand like a woman": Empowerment and human rights in the context of community-based reintegration of girl mothers formerly associated with fighting forces and armed groups. *Journal of Human Rights Practice, 2*(1), 49–70.

PART THREE

PRACTICE AND SERVICE DELIVERY

Professional Applications to Address the Realities of Children Affected by Armed Conflict

THIS FINAL SECTION OF THE collection examines practice and services in relation to war-affected children. We adapt NASW's (2016) definition of practice to include the application of techniques to help war-affected children, families, and communities obtain and improve social and health services. Reflecting a socioecological approach, practice requires knowledge of culture, context, and human development and of their interaction.

In chapter 10, "Health Care Services to War-Affected Children in Northern Uganda: Accounting for Discrepancies Between Interventions and Children's Needs," Grace Akello investigates the mismatch between health care service provision and what wartime preadolescent children identified as their actual health needs in Gulu District in northern Uganda. She argues that both framing health care service provision to children within the meso-level national health policy guidelines and the provision of trauma-focused support by emergency aid organizations led to discrepancies between what was provided and what children regarded as their health priorities in the context of war. Akello presents children's narratives that capture the complex forms of psychosocial suffering during war and their subsequent coping strategies. She shows that meso-level discourses—including the national health policy and various emergency aid interventions—significantly affected the extent to which children accessed health care by muting their voices and agency. Akello illustrates how even so-called culturally appropriate interventions can be inappropriate in a context of armed conflict when they fail to address the identified needs and priorities voiced by the children themselves.

In chapter 11—"When the System 'Works': Exploring the Experiences of Girl Survivors of Sexual Violence in Postconflict Liberia"—Debbie Landis and Lindsay Stark explore the effectiveness of the formal system in Liberia in addressing the issue of sexual violence against children. They show that participants had positive experiences with several services in the referral pathway. However, by comparing these experiences with national statistics, Landis and Stark highlight that this system serves only a minority of young sexual violence survivors in Liberia. The authors argue that the site of the study—the capital Monrovia—is one in which children have disproportionately greater access to the formal system and receive a substantial degree of support from service providers. The authors also point out that, despite the strength of the formal system, weaknesses remain, particularly in its effectiveness in responding to social stigma and harmful treatment of young survivors by relatives, friends, and community members.

In chapter 12, Ghada Kachachi draws from practical experience in working for the protection of children in the Darfur region of Sudan with the United Nations Children's Fund (UNICEF) and its partners. Titled "Working with Children Affected by Armed Conflict: Practical Protection Work During the Darfur Crisis in the Sudan," the chapter outlines key approaches and thematic areas of interventions for the protection of children, focusing on establishing measures, systems, and services to protect all vulnerable children. Importantly, this work sought to maximize the participation and empowerment of children by including them in the program process and activities, with particular attention to gender issues. Kachachi discusses the effectiveness and relevance of the overall work during this period and argues that a collective and holistic response of government, nonstate actors, communities, and the children themselves can provide a safety net for children even in the most difficult situations.

In chapter 13, "Meeting the Needs of Children Affected by Conflict: Teacher Training and Development in South Sudan," Jan Stewart presents an ongoing research program that focuses on the development and implementation of teacher training to meet the educational and psychosocial needs of war-affected children and youth in South Sudan. Her model of engagement highlights the need for a comprehensive consultation process involving actors in multiple ecological systems that influence the development of children. To achieve a sustainable future, Stewart argues that the goal of this model should be providing specialized peace education and conflict sensitivity training for teachers to facilitate the widespread implementation of comprehensive peace education for all students. Furthermore, the findings suggest that peace education was a catalyst for teachers' own healing and recovery from the effects of war.

These chapters highlight the ways in which multiple systems at the micro-, meso-, and macro-levels within the realms of justice, education, health care, and child protection can work toward the betterment of war-affected children's lives.

10

HEALTH CARE SERVICES TO WAR-AFFECTED CHILDREN IN NORTHERN UGANDA

Accounting for Discrepancies Between Interventions and Children's Needs

Grace Akello

THE CONFLICT BETWEEN THE Lord's Resistance Army (LRA) and Ugandan government forces beginning in 1986 resulted in the displacement of approximately two million people (Okot, Amony, & Otim, 2005). They were resettled in the relatively safe Gulu municipality, as well as in "protected villages" known as internally displaced persons (IDP) camps, where violence, idleness, and exposure to preventable infectious diseases such as malaria, cholera, and HIV/AIDS were rampant compared with other parts of the country unaffected by war (MOH, 2011). Women and children comprised most of the war-affected population (Okot, Amony, & Otim, 2005; WFP, 2003).

Between 2004 and 2006, when the research for this chapter was conducted, humanitarian agencies tended to frame the services they provided within the model of trauma-focused psychosocial support. At the same time, national health policy guidelines assumed that children older than 5 years of age had developed significant immunity and were therefore considered a "healthy group" whose major health needs included deworming, oral hygiene, and tetanus vaccination of girls of reproductive age (MOH, 1999). However, this chapter shows that children suffered at that time not only from infectious diseases but also from complex forms of psychosocial suffering—resulting in significant discrepancies between the services provided and children's actual self-identified needs.

In this chapter, I examine the reasons for these discrepancies. Needs or self-identified priorities refer to issues that children named and for which they suggested they required urgent external (or outside the family) assistance. I distinguish needs from daily challenges to imply that there are issues that war-affected children deal with on their own. For instance, children used herbal remedies for many of their daily stressors, even though they were often encouraged to seek free counseling services. The counseling reportedly had a minimal impact because of the chronicity of the health complaint or because the new approaches were not consistent with what the children deemed useful and effective.

The main argument in this chapter is that framing health care service provision to children older than 5 years within the meso-level national health policy guidelines—which, in fact, are adapted from macro-level World Health Organization (WHO) guidelines for school health (Jamison, 1999)—and the provision of trauma-focused psychosocial support led to important discrepancies between the health care services provided and what wartime children regarded as their priority health needs. I first present information about humanitarian aid and state policy–guided interventions during wartime northern Uganda from 1986 to 2007. After presenting an overview of the setting and the methodology, I then discuss the health complaints identified by children as common illnesses that affected them, presenting data that reflect a quantitative summary of children's responses. Then I analyze war-affected children's narratives, which capture complex forms of psychosocial suffering, as well as coping mechanisms. My analysis shows that the meso-level discourses, including the mandates guiding humanitarian aid interventions and the national health policy for schoolchildren, influenced the extent to which children were able to gain access to services that met their health care needs. Theories from Bronfenbrenner (1979) and Belsky (1999) support the notion that the mental health of children is affected by the relationship between the caregiver and child, the socioeconomic position of the caregiver (and child), the availability of formal and informal support systems, and the security of the environment in which they live.

CONTEXT: HUMANITARIAN INTERVENTIONS FOR WAR-AFFECTED CHILDREN

In 2005, approximately 265 national and international humanitarian agencies provided psychosocial support to war-affected people in northern Uganda, with the primary aim of ensuring their mental well-being (Gulu District NGO-Forum, 2006). During the war, people often lacked basic necessities and lived in fetid and congested camps (Otunnu, 2006). Research conducted in Lacor

Hospital, located within the Gulu municipality, found that children and parents from Unyama and Koro subcounties within Gulu District had higher rates of infection and abductions by rebel groups than children in other subcounties. Accordingly, they presented with severe distress and fear.

Many humanitarian organizations focused on promoting children's well-being through trauma-focused interventions (Akello, 2010; Summerfield, 1999). They also established programs such as rehabilitation centers for former child soldiers, night shelters for commuters, and primary schools designed to ensure the safety of displaced children. They implemented a wide range of trauma-focused interventions in which children aged 5–17 were encouraged to talk about their extreme experiences and engage in creative play therapy and other culturally adapted trauma-focused activities, such as dancing Acholi cultural dances.[1] This focus on the cultural adaptation of interventions has been critiqued for diverting attention from social and political determinants of disease (Metzl & Hansen, 2014). Although some studies showed the promise of cognitive behavioral therapy (Betancourt & Williams, 2008; Okello & Ekblad, 2003), talk and interpersonal therapy (Bolton et al., 2003; Patel et al., 2010; Schauer et al., 2004), problem-solving therapy (Chibanda et al., 2011), cognitive-processing therapy (Bass et al., 2013), and narrative exposure therapy (Neuner, Schauer, Klaschik, Karunakara, & Thomas, 2004) in helping war-affected people in northern Uganda cope with extreme experiences, children frequently opted for local coping mechanisms that they believed to be more effective. This section shows how humanitarian interventions depoliticized children's suffering by promoting personal healing through individual self-expression and reframing suffering and sociopolitical experiences as a set of bodily symptoms to be treated—as a medical problem (Fassin, 2012; Marshall, 2014; Summerfield, 1999).

Some humanitarian aid workers subscribe to the belief that people exposed to wartime events suffer from adverse mental health consequences (including trauma) and that the solution lies in psychosocial, trauma-focused projects (Akello, Richters, & Reis, 2010; Apfel & Simon, 1996; De Berry et al., 2003; Galappatti, 2003; Summerfield, 1999). Proponents of trauma-focused psychosocial interventions, which are costly and dependent on specialized expertise (De Berry et al., 2003), assume not only that these interventions are widely applicable for war-affected children but also that they are the only way such children can be helped (Bolton et al., 2003; Schauer et al., 2004). Some scholars have indeed shown how trauma-focused interventions can be useful for war-affected children (Bolton et al., 2003; Schauer et al., 2004). For example, in a randomized trial, Bolton et al. (2003) found that talk therapy promoted healing in wartime adolescent girls but not in boys in northern Uganda.

However, these projects privilege mental health services and interventions by mental health professionals while downplaying community-based and grassroots approaches (Apfel & Simon, 1996; De Berry et al., 2003; De Jong, Kleber, & Puratic, 2003; Fernando, 2012; Sax, 2014). Although war affects a community's mental and physical health, as well as its socioeconomic and political fabric, in northern Uganda, many agencies prioritized individually and trauma-focused psychosocial interventions. Such interventions can, in certain contexts, effectively mute the voices and agency of beneficiaries (Akello et al., 2010; Wessells, 2009). For example, Akello et al. (2010) discuss how some counselors often told child clients about some of their other clients who had comparatively "worse" problems and how these "others" had managed to cope effectively.

Kirmayer (2012) critiques evidence-based practices (such as trauma-focused interventions in complex emergencies) as developed in Western countries as not being culturally appropriate, feasible, or effective in other contexts. Although these practices are easy to implement through simple, standardized behavioral interventions, there is a danger that focusing primarily on promoting mental well-being limits more complex psychosocial interventions (Kirmayer & Pedersen, 2014). Another unintended consequence is that trauma-focused interventions divert children's attention from their local coping mechanisms or local approaches employed in managing such challenges.

In response to vulnerable people's needs in disaster settings, some scholars recommend a hybrid framework for mental health care that encompasses community- and facility-based care (Jordans, Tol, Komproe, & De Jon, 2013), whereas others recommend the incorporation of children's agency and resilience into the design of emergency interventions (Tol, Song, & Jordans, 2013). Unfortunately, in war-affected northern Uganda, psychological approaches such as trauma-focused interventions have been used in ways that have caused unintended harm (Apfel & Simon, 1996). Such approaches largely neglected the resilience of war-affected children in dealing with their socioeconomic challenges by engaging in income-generating activities, taking herbal medicines and pharmaceuticals for health complaints, and using what they considered to be effective coping mechanisms within the context of their personal experiences, relationships, values, culture, and understandings (Akello et al., 2010; De Berry et al., 2003; Giller, 1998; Richters, 1998).

Compounding the problem, the variety of support modalities in northern Uganda presented a source of confusion for children, social workers, policy makers, and researchers alike (Akello, Richters, & Reis, 2006; USAID/UNICEF, 2006). Because interventions termed "psychosocial support" varied to a great extent in quality, and there was little coordination by humanitarian agencies, appropriate guidelines were critically needed. In fact, interventions as varied as sensitizing adults and children about trauma, organizing games and sports for schoolchildren, distributing footballs, offering primary schools costumes for traditional dances, and training teachers to identify traumatized children were all termed "psychosocial support." Given such realities, the Inter-Agency Standing Committee *Guidelines on Mental Health and Psychosocial Support in Emergency Settings* (IASC, 2007) was created. Thorough evaluations of these guidelines, both analytically and in the field, were conducted so that interventions could better reflect the needs of beneficiaries.

Health care services for children older than 5 years of age were provided through the schools within the framework of the Ugandan National Health Policy. School health programs provided regular deworming, sporadic oral hygiene checks, and frequent vaccination of older primary school-age girls (Akello, 2010; DDHS-Gulu, 2006; Jamison, 1999; MOH, 1999). Health care provision for children younger than 5 years old was provided primarily by pediatric units in Ugandan hospitals, although medical personnel, at their own discretion, might recommend that children older than 5 seek care in adult units, where their specific needs were often not addressed (Akello, 2010).

THE RESEARCH STUDY

METHODOLOGY

This chapter is based on an ethnographic study I conducted over a 12-month period from 2004–2005 with 9- to 16-year-old children. To select a manageable sample for this study, I recruited children who met one of the following criteria: (1) they had been displaced from their home villages and livelihoods; (2) they attended schools specifically built for wartime children and spent nights in night commuter shelters (designated areas where tents were erected at night and security was guaranteed for children affected by war); (3) they lived in child-headed households and experienced abject poverty; (4) they took

TABLE 10.1 Sociodemographic Characteristics of the Ethnographic Sample (N=415)

CHARACTERISTICS	BOYS (N = 212)	GIRLS (N = 213)
Age range (years)	10–15	10–15
Average age (years)	13.8	13.4
Education (years)	3–7	4–7
Average household size	4.9	4.5
Average number of years living in camps	6.2	6
Number of child-headed households	72	86
Number of children with parents living in camps	140	127

care of adult relatives living with HIV/AIDS; or (5) they were former child soldiers.

More than 400 war-affected children participated in the full study, and 24 children were recruited as a subsample engaged in multiple follow-ups over a one-year period. The small size of the subsample enabled me to focus intensively on their narratives and understand their health care challenges. Although I had planned to meet with the subsample of children twice a month at their homes, churches, schools, and night commuter shelters, the children invited me to their homes more frequently as a guest or when they had challenges and unmet needs. For instance, two children often invited me to their home to help when their sick parents required hospital admission. On average, I interacted approximately five times a month with each of the 24 children over the 12-month period. Table 10.1 provides the sociodemographic details of the participants.

I used child-adapted qualitative methodological techniques including life histories, focus group discussions, interviews, and workshops to discuss the children's traumatic events experienced during war and to explore their coping mechanisms. Table 10.2 shows the different techniques used with the entire sample.

In the workshops, children engaged in participatory approaches and role playing to present their experiences, including showing peers the pharmaceuticals they commonly took and the local medicines they used to exorcise *cen* (evil spirits). I conducted 165 semi-structured interviews with open-ended

TABLE 10.2 Child-Adapted Techniques and Number of Participants Studied by Each Method (N=415)

RESEARCH METHOD	SUB-SAMPLE	TOTAL PARTICIPANTS
Writing compositions/stories	150	150
Interview with interview guides	165	315
Drawing of illness	100	415
Focus group discussions	108	415
Workshops	24	415
In-depth interviews	24	415
Participant observation	24	415
Detailed narratives	24	415
Ethnographic sample	24	415

questions to find out more about children's experiences and medicine used within a one-month period.

Through a comprehensive assessment of children's experiences in various social contexts (see Akello, 2015) it was possible to ascertain their priority needs, local resources in coping, and what they regarded as appropriate interventions. In addition, I conducted key informant interviews with 2 pediatricians, 5 nurses, 2 clinical officers, 15 counselors (some of whom also coordinated humanitarian interventions), 2 psychiatrists, and 28 primary schoolteachers. Schoolteachers who taught in schools for displaced children were interviewed to triangulate children's narratives and gain further insight into their life histories. I interviewed health care workers using an interview guide created to find out the common health complaints of children older than 5 and the medicines prescribed for those health complaints. These interviews lasted an average of 30 minutes. Most importantly, I observed processes of "treating" children in pharmacies, drug shops (where medicines are sold by individuals who have no medical training), outpatient clinics, psychiatric clinics, and rehabilitation centers.

DATA ANALYSIS

At the end of each day of interviews, I typed field notes highlighting recurring themes from different respondents. I also listened to the audio recordings of the participant interviews while noting pertinent themes about children's health complaints and quests for therapy. Later, I coded the highlighted and recurring themes. For example, when children talked about their experience with malaria, I assigned the number 1; their purchase of anti-malarials such as Chloroquine was coded with a number 2; and when they mentioned Fansidar, I coded it as a 3. To minimize researcher bias, I emailed transcribed and typed data to two of my doctoral study supervisors for critical review (Lincoln & Guba, 1985). The two supervisors also visited northern Uganda to see the study site and engage in discussions about the findings. I later inputted the different codes I assigned to recurring responses into SPSS for analysis, generating simple statistical information and inferences as shown in table 10.3.

ETHICAL CONSIDERATIONS

This study was approved by the Uganda National Council of Science and Technology, as well as the resident district commissioner, the district director of health services, and the district education officer in Gulu District. Additionally, I sought permission from primary school head teachers, coordinators at the night commuter shelters, and humanitarian aid organizations that had specific intervention objectives and offered psychosocial support for school-aged children.

I also obtained permission from the children who participated in the study, after explaining the study objectives, assuring them anonymity, and informing them about the research process. All children who participated in this study gave their verbal assent and reinforced their willingness to participate by engaging in other activities relevant to this research, such as weekend workshops, peer-educator sessions, and role playing about their past illness experiences. I used pseudonyms to ensure anonymity.

In the following section, I present a summary of data obtained through open-ended interviews inquiring into children's illness experiences (see table 10.3). I then present qualitative data, which are mainly in the form of verbatim reports.

FINDINGS

COMMON HEALTH COMPLAINTS IDENTIFIED BY CHILDREN

Health complaints that children identified as common were consistent with records in the outpatient unit and the district health report (DDHS-Gulu, 2005). As shown in table 10.3, more than 70% of the complaints were of infectious diseases including malaria, diarrhea, and eye and skin infections.

In 2005, Gulu district experienced three major epidemics: two cholera epidemics and a skin infection epidemic. Popularly referred to as scabies, the skin infection epidemic affected many children until Doctors Without Borders administered mass treatments in infected settlements and schools.

Although children mentioned having malaria and *malaria madongo* (severe malaria) during the study, they explained that there were no specific interventions for malaria prevention or treatment. In health centers where they sought medical attention, they were offered prescriptions for anti-malarial medication, but those drugs were rarely stocked in the hospital pharmacy. Many children therefore resorted to self-medication with medicines of different quality and quantity, which could be obtained over the counter for a small amount of money. Furthermore, within the category of *malaria*, children also discussed their experiences with headache, fever, and vomiting. Thus, those who took anti-malarial medication were likely overusing pharmaceuticals that may not have addressed their presenting symptoms. Reyburn et al. (2004) found similar results in Tanzania, where all febrile illnesses were managed with anti-malarials and there was a high risk of ignoring illnesses that could be effectively treated with antibiotics.

If children did not recover after treating their health complaints with pharmaceuticals, they engaged in quests for effective therapy—consulting religious healers, using herbal medicines, purchasing stronger medicines, or leaving illnesses to heal over time. They rarely engaged in preventive measures such as weekly prophylaxis and sleeping under treated insecticide mosquito nets. In addition to using pharmaceuticals for common illnesses, children discussed having used the *atika* plant (Labiate species) to treat illnesses. The *atika* plant is applied through a ritual that involves making incisions on the forehead and spreading the plant seeds in the incisions before going to sleep.

During interviews, children discussed their experiences with persistent headaches, sleeplessness, stomachaches, and nightmares caused by *cen*. They mentioned having "picked up" *cen* during the war by accidentally stepping on

TABLE 10.3 Prevalence of Health Complaints Within a One-Month Recall Period (N=165)

ILLNESS	BOYS	GIRLS	TOTAL	P-VALUE
Diarrheal diseases	81	69	150	0.59
Aona ki avuru (cough and flu)	76	68	144	0.71
Cado (diarrhea)	40	35	75	1.00
Cadopiipii (diarrhea with watery stools)	32	30	62	0.73
Cadomarac / remo (diarrhea with blood)	9	4	13	0.23
Eye infections	32	35	67	0.24
Lit wang (red eye)	15	23	38	0.05
Trachoma (for those who went to health centers)	17	12	29	0.53
Malaria	84	74	158	0.84
Lyeto (fever)	35	24	59	0.25
Malaria (generalized malaria symptoms)	20	21	41	0.50
Koyo (coldness)	13	12	25	0.88
Abaawic (headache)	11	14	25	0.31
Malaria madongo (severe malaria)	5	3	8	0.59
Gwinyo (scabies)	83	33	116	<0.005
Tyenalit / wang vu (wounds and injuries)	38	57	95	<0.005
Amwodaici (stomachache)	22	61	83	<0.005
Twolokayan (snakebite)	17	2	19	0.001
Twocimu (epilepsy)	1	1	2	0.35
Total	434	400	834	

dead bodies or witnessing violent scenes including the murder of close relatives. Because children's complaints were nonspecific and those who had frequent nightmares exhibited symptoms such as persistent headaches, such somatic symptoms may have reflected forms of psychosocial suffering. Children's reference to *atika*, an herbal remedy for *cen*, is significant because many interventions that aimed to promote their psychosocial well-being encouraged counseling services such as play therapy and traditional dances. Recognizing local resources in coping, I argue, is one way to reduce funds used to design and implement interventions that the target population will not find useful. I return to the importance of recognizing local coping strategies.

CHILDREN'S STRESS FACTORS AND COPING

Children actively engaged with many daily challenges and stressors, for which they sometimes attempted to obtain help from humanitarian organizations. Ojwiya, a 14-year-old schoolboy, discussed his experience:

> I lost both parents to abductions and Lord's Resistance Army (LRA) killings. Within a few months, my elder brother also died in a motorcycle accident. I have since then become like a father and mother to my younger sisters. There are many times when we do not have food to eat. Twice we have been told to leave the huts where we were staying due to our inability to pay monthly rent. In both cases, the hut owners just threw away our belongings while insulting us.

Fifteen-year-old Omony also endured many stressful experiences, including witnessing the brutal killing of his father; he frequently complained of nightmares in which his deceased father's *cen* demanded a ceremony for his last funeral rites. Omony explained,

> The saddest moment this year was when our hut was accidentally burnt down. In it were the harvested crops, all the money we had earned, clothes and utensils. But I had to be strong. This is because people even praise you if you can ignore your problems and not disturb them with misery. I think it is because so many people have seen problems with this war that even when someone dies, they spend there [at the funeral] a very short time and then go about their business.

Omony's narrative indicates local mechanisms of coping with extreme stressors, such as performing last funeral rites, not expressing one's misery, and ignoring one's current problems. Akello et al. (2010) also show how the community's silencing of distressed children was a way of coping with extreme events during the war in northern Uganda. Although this approach was not ubiquitous, in contexts where large groups of people have to deal with profound personal stressors, it can be perceived as the best available means of coping.

In one workshop held to discuss extremely disturbing events that occurred during the war, 14-year-old Apio shared her account of the source of her own severe emotional distress. She also emphasized the need for children to be strong—ignoring intimidation from the community and not dwelling on their own challenges, the role of her supportive father in coping with stressors, and the importance of using *atika*:

> I had to be strong when my mother became mad due to *malaria madongo* [severe malaria]. Children in the Abili camp frequently laughed at us, saying my mother was not ashamed anymore of walking naked where people were. I and my younger brother Bernard suffered a lot during that time. My father requested relatives to host us, but they all mistreated us. That is how my father rented a hut for us in Layibi. In Layibi, we have many problems, but I never sit down to cry or refuse to eat food! I can have *par madongo* [deep painful thoughts], *can dwongataa* [deep emotional pain] and *cwercwiny* [sadness], but I cannot show it to people. I sometimes simply close myself in the hut in order to cry about all these problems. My father always tells us to burn *atika* plants at the fireplace in the hut. I make sure each night we place branches of *atika* also at the doorposts and on the roof to ward off *cen*.

Another girl, who was 12 years old, discussed her mother's persistent cough, which made her elder brothers go to a night commuters shelter to sleep:

> My mother has *aona opiu* [tuberculosis]. Although she has been taking medicines, she does not recover. Sometimes she coughs throughout the night. You do not know what to do. I get scared when I see her vomiting blood due to that cough. The landlady threatened to chase us from her hut due to that cough. At World Vision, they always tell us not to share plates, cups, food, or a hut with people with *aona opiu*. But we have only one hut and a few cups and plates. We share all these with my mother. I cannot go to sleep at the night commuters' shelter because it is at night when my mother needs someone to light the lamp for her, to clean her, and to give her medicines.

As shown in this narrative, humanitarian organizations' approach of educating community members to deal with complex emergencies was mostly ineffective and reflected a lack of understanding of children's realities, needs, and appropriate coping mechanisms. For instance, for that 12-year-old girl's family, providing material support would have been a more appropriate intervention than disseminating information about pathogens.

In a discussion of nightmares held in a workshop to discuss extreme war events, two children referred to disturbances by *cen* and *tipo* and also brought in *atika* plants to demonstrate their use as medicines for chasing *cen*. In the workshop, children discussed how *tipo*, the spirit of a deceased kin member, can turn into an evil spirit depending on the frequency with which it appears and the disturbance it causes. Although children acknowledged counseling and counselors as avenues that can provide help for getting rid of nightmares, on inquiry, none confirmed that they had sought the advice and assistance of counselors. It is likely that children did not seek professional help to deal with *cen* because of their ability to deal with the issue and a preference for local coping mechanisms. Fifteen-year-old Akello explained this distinction between *cen* and *tipo* when describing the persistent nightmares caused by her deceased father's spirit:

> At home, my mother often corrected me if I talked about seeing [the] *cen* of my late father in my dream. She always told me that the spirit of someone I knew and close relatives who did not want to harm me is *tipo* and not *cen*. But since I had reached a level of not sleeping and screaming in my sleep, even during the day, due to my late father's disturbance and his demand for *guru lyel* [last funeral rites], even my mother started referring to it as *cen*. I suffered very much during that time due to that *tipo*, until my mother and *lodito* [clan elders] organized the ceremony of *ryemocen/tipo* [to chase away evil spirits] at Karuma, involving the strongest indigenous healer].

Many children considered *atika* plants to be important and effective medicine. If they had come across a dead body and were subsequently haunted by the scene, they would spread the plants around their sleeping place, attesting to its power to ensure that the *cen* they had picked up would not disturb them anymore. In one workshop, two girls, who often talked about having persistent stomachaches, presented *atika* plants as the recommended medicine for such problems. During this workshop, they both also recounted their nightmares about violent men wanting to rape them in their sleep. A 13-year-old girl gave this account:

> For a year now I have been having bad sleep. The moment I close myself in the hut at night, even before I sleep, I see a very huge man who wants to attack me. Sometimes he comes with a knife. The moment I fall asleep, that same man comes to rape me. In such moments, I scream and wake up. My two younger brothers also wake me up when I keep shouting in my sleep. When I

told our landlady about it, she advised me to put branches of *atika* plant at the doorpost and window, to smear its seeds over my head and around the mat. When I am going to sleep, I should burn some *atika* plants in a partially broken pot.

It is plausible that in these two girls' narratives, their reference to stomachaches represented past experiences of rape. Many girls who complained of stomachaches also disclosed during workshops their experiences of being raped as they fled to safer areas. Indeed, some children described somatic symptoms that were perhaps more likely to be manifestations of distress rather than of physical ailments. For some children, the most effective approach was to first treat the physical pain, such as stomachaches, and then deal with psychological issues, which were also expressed somatically. It was often noted that coping solely through the use of pharmaceuticals was not effective, as exemplified in the following narrative:

This headache I have been having for the last three months is not the one for malaria. It starts with something moving around my body. Such a thing is painful and when it reaches my head, I feel intense headache. I often swallow Hedex or Action,[2] sometimes three of them at a go, but the headache only subsides. A week ago when I went to Layibi Health Center, I told the *daktar* [healthcare provider] that instead of giving me medicine for malaria, let them perform all possible laboratory tests to find out the illness causing the headache. Instead, he wrote for me to buy chloroquine, Panadol, and Fansidar for malaria.

Generally speaking, children and adults in war-affected northern Uganda presented their psychological suffering using somatic idioms. As mentioned ealier, Akello et al. (2010) show that the silencing of distressed children contributes to this phenomenon. In the previous narrative, the health care worker treated the presenting complaint as malaria because the symptoms the boy discussed were similar to those of malaria. However, when the child explained his reservations about the malaria diagnosis, it would have been prudent to have performed the necessary diagnostic tests and assess further the presence of psychological and mental stressors in this child's life. The health worker may have missed an important opportunity to identify the actual complaint because of a failure to see distressed children as independent health care seekers.

In another case, 14-year-old Akello presented at the hospital with a stomach-ache and was diagnosed with a urinary tract infection. She was prescribed Amoxicillin and Indocid, which she bought in a drug shop and took. Yet she experienced the same stomachache two weeks later. This is her explanation for the persistence of her pains:

> This stomachache has been disturbing me for a long time. Since *mony* [LRA soldiers] attacked our home in Anaka and also took with them my elder brother Odokorach, I have been having this stomachache. There is no medicine that I have not tried. My mother used to buy Panadol, Hedex, Action, Indocid and Amoxicillin . . . and in one clinic I was told if I buy *cipro* [Ciprofloxacin] I would get better. But after using *cipro* I was not okay. The pain is still there, as I told you.

Because Akello's complaint was primarily couched in somatic descriptions, it was difficult for the health worker to diagnose her pain. If she had told the health worker about her wartime experiences, it would have been easier to categorize and prioritize what medical condition to treat first. In this narrative it appears that only physical complaints were managed throughout the treat-ment trajectory. In complex emergencies, medical workers should be trained with skills to listen not only to physical complaints but also to psychological suffering, even when clients present their experience with stressors as somatic complaints.

In summary, living in the context of war affected not only children's mental well-being but also their socioeconomic, cultural, and physical health. They were, however, resilient, engaging with their daily challenges through their own local coping strategies and seeking help where possible, which included visiting humanitarian agencies.

TRAUMA-FOCUSED COUNSELING

One child participant complained of persistently lacking sleep, being disturbed by *cen*, and living in abject poverty and misery. He went to the counseling center and discussed his experience:

> The counselor told me that she also suffered like me. She comes from a simi-lar family like mine, but for them they were nine children compared to only five of us. Unlike me, she was the oldest in the family. When her father died,

she was younger than me, but she managed to take care of her siblings. She told me that I should know that there were numerous people with problems just like or more than mine.

Earlier, I alluded to the distinction between children's needs and their daily challenges. In this narrative, the counselor attempted to address the child's needs by making him aware that there are people with more complex challenges, thereby minimizing his experience. This technique may cause some children to believe that they are inadequate to handle common life stressors and therefore unable to take care of themselves and their dependents. To ameliorate a stressor such as living in poverty, research recommends the provision of material needs, avoiding medicalization, and recognizing local resources of coping—and not trauma-focused interventions (Richters, 1998; Ventevogel, 2014; Weyermann, 2007).

The ineffectiveness of trauma-focused interventions can be seen in the experience of two primary schools for displaced children, which most of the child respondents attended. The administrators of both schools invited a humanitarian organization to provide counseling. The invitation letter stated that the children's identified needs included lack of food, inadequate shelter, and inability to pay school fees. Three local counselors came to the schools where they offered a group counseling session, tackling various topics that included the challenges of living in IDP camps, the causes of nightmares and how to deal with them, and the challenges of growing up.

In the group counseling session, the topic discussed most extensively was the presence and causes of nightmares. One counselor elaborated on the causes of nightmares and how to avoid or deal with them, noting that nightmares are "playbacks" of events experienced, seen, heard, or thought about. Such events included witnessing, hearing, and discussing killings and shootings and watching violent videos. The advice given to the children was that it is "normal" to have nightmares and that people who have such dreams should be left alone and not woken up or interrupted. However, the counselor's recommendation that the children start to view their problems of nightmares as normal was contrary to the belief among the Acholi people that dreams have particular meanings; it therefore violated important cultural practices. For example, when a child is constantly confronted in a dream by his or her deceased kin demanding *guru lyel*, Acholi culture believes that there is a pressing need to conduct the ceremony whereby the bereaved family visits the burial site and performs rituals to appease the deceased. Because of the various interpretations and implications of dreams and nightmares within Acholi culture, it was both problematic and counterproductive for the counselors to describe such dreams simply as "normal playbacks" and therefore "nothing to worry about." In reality, the children worried constantly about sleep disturbances and *cen*. They even had local coping mechanisms that counselors should have acknowledged, if only to reinforce the children's own coping and resilience in dealing with daily challenges.

In the same group session, another counselor discussed the challenges of growing up, and much to the children's amusement, his discussion included detailed description of bodily changes during adolescence. He first sent away more than three-quarters of the participants who were preadolescent children, because he believed they were too young to hear the discussion. Those who remained preferred, however, to ask him questions about how to address material problems, such as the lack of school fees and money for food, and whether there was material assistance available to children in child-headed households if they went to local counseling centers and talked about their problems.

The counselors' choices of topic and decision to address the children's complaints through group counseling were problematic, missing the priorities that individual children themselves identified and that were expressed clearly in the invitation letter sent to the organization. Furthermore, because of the way in which treatment and support were administered in these sessions, the counseling was often prescriptive, rather than allowing for the children's involvement in addressing what they regarded as priority needs. In addition, counselors frequently told children about others who had experienced more complex problems than they had (e.g., Omony's account), which could imply that the children had no right to complain. The fact that the counselors were Ugandan is especially interesting, showing how Western approaches have been propagated and integrated into the daily practice of Ugandan practitioners.

CONCLUSIONS AND RECOMMENDATIONS

In sum, during the conflict in northern Uganda, there was a discrepancy between what wartime children identified as their needs and the health care services provided by the state and humanitarian organizations. The national health policy guided implementation of school health programs, which focused on deworming, oral hygiene, and tetanus vaccination to adolescent girls, rather than addressing the social determinants of commonly experienced infectious diseases that sometimes occurred as epidemics and the grave lack of material and psychological support for children in wartime northern Uganda. In addition, many interventions were given in the primary schools, which not all preadolescent children attended. As is common in rural settings and contexts affected by armed conflict, many school-aged children did not attend school and therefore did not receive any support at all. Furthermore, humanitarian interventions were primarily trauma focused, ignoring specific cultural constructs of illness and not acknowledging the existence of local ways of coping with stressors. These factors affected the nature, quality, and quantity of health services.

In light of these findings, there is a need to redesign school health policy to take into account the immediate health care needs of older children (older than 5 years of age), including infectious diseases and social suffering. In addition, a broader target population should include both in-school and out-of-school children. I thereby propose a radical approach whereby stakeholders from the macro-level systems such as the World Health Organization, Ministry of Health of Uganda, and the Ugandan District Health Services view preadolescent children as a unique group with self-identified health needs. In addition to offering pediatric services, health centers need to have preadolescent and adolescent units with qualified health care workers who have been trained in providing mental health care for that age group.

This chapter also highlights the importance of local resources in coping with everyday extreme experiences. For example, where children lived in fear of abduction and therefore were reluctant to participate in activities aimed to help them deal with this trauma, other acceptable activities (consistent with their priorities and that recognize local resources in coping) can be recommended. Yet in the sites I studied in northern Uganda, a top-down prescription of talk and play therapy was enacted, rather than culturally adapted ways of coping with trauma. Other researchers mention the importance of recognizing local resources (Kirmayer, 2012; Tol et al., 2003) and support in complex settings. For example, children named *atika* plants as a therapy for individuals who experienced *cen*, a local idiom of distress. Children who accidentally stepped on dead bodies were advised to rub leaves and seeds of these plants on their foreheads to minimize nightmares.

In conclusion, this research suggests that a relevant health care service delivery framework for war-affected preadolescent children needs to include prevention and treatment of common infectious diseases, as well as general local response mechanisms, and to provide psychosocial support that is responsive to children's identified needs and priorities.

Notes

1. The Acholi people are a Luo-speaking group who originated from Southern Sudan. In Uganda, most live in districts in the northern region: Agago, Amuru, Gulu, Kitgum, and Pader. This ethnic group has a variety of traditional dances, which some humanitarian organizations regarded as cultural ways of coping with extreme stressors during war.
2. Hedex and Action contain paracetamol-acetyl salicylic acid-caffeine for treatment of aches and pains including headaches.

References

Akello, G. (2010). *Wartime children's suffering and quests for therapy in northern Uganda*. Leiden: African Studies Center.

Akello, G. (2015). The impact of the Paris Principles on reintegration processes of former child soldiers in northern Uganda. *Annals of Psychiatry and Mental Health*, 3(5), 1038–1047.

Akello, G., Richters, A., & Reis, R. (2006). Reintegration of former child-soldiers in northern Uganda: Coming to terms with children's agency and accountability. *Intervention*, 4(3), 229–243.

Akello, G., Richters, A., & Reis, R. (2010). Silencing distressed children in the context of war: An analysis of its causes and health consequences. *Social Science and Medicine*, 71(2), 213–220.

Apfel, R. J., & Simon, B. (1996). Psychosocial interventions for children of war: The value of a model of resiliency. *Medicine and Global Survival*, 3(1), 1–16.

Bass, J. K., Annan, J., Murray, S. M., Kaysen, D., Griffiths, S., Cetinoglu, T., . . . Bolton, P. A. (2013). Controlled trial of psychotherapy for Congolese survivors of sexual violence. *New England Journal of Medicine*, 368(2), 2182–2191.

Belsky, J. (1999). International and contextual determinants of attachment security. In J. Cassidy & P. Shaver (Eds.), *Handbook of attachment theory, research and clinical application* (pp. 249–264). New York: Guilford.

Betancourt, T. S., & Williams, T. (2008). Building an evidence base on mental health interventions for children affected by armed conflict. *Intervention*, 6(1), 39–56.

Bolton, P., Bass, T., Neugebauer, R., Verdi, H., Clougherty, K. F., Wickramaratne, P., . . . Weissman, M. (2003). Group interpersonal psychotherapy for depression in rural Uganda: A randomized controlled trial. *Journal of the American Medical Association*, 289(23), 3117–3124.

Bronfenbrenner, U. (1979). *The ecology of human development experiments by nature and design.* Cambridge, MA: Harvard University Press.

Chibanda, D., Mesu, P., Kajawu, L., Cowan, F., Araya, R., & Abas, M. A. (2011). Problem-solving therapy for depression and common mental disorders in Zimbabwe: Piloting a task-shifting primary mental health care intervention in a population with a high prevalence of people living with HIV. *BMC Public Health,* 11(1), 8–28.

DDHS-Gulu. (2005). *Health sector strategic plan for 2005/2006.* Unpublished manuscript.

DDHS-Gulu. (2006). *Health sector strategic plan 2006–2007.* Unpublished manuscript.

De Berry, J., Nasiry, F., Fazili, A., Hashemi, S., Fahad, S., & Hakimi, M. (2003). *The children of Kabul discussion with Afghan families.* Dakar. Save the Children & UNICEF.

De Jong, K., Kleber, R., & Puratic, V. (2003). Mental health programs in areas of armed conflict: The Médecins Sans Frontières counselling centers in Bosnia-Hercegovina. *Intervention,* 1(1), 14–32.

Fassin, D. (2012). *Humanitarian reason: A moral history of the present.* Berkeley: University of California Press.

Fernando, G. A. (2012). The roads less travelled: Mapping some pathways on the global mental health research roadmap. *Transcultural Psychiatry,* 49(3–4), 396–417.

Galappatti, A. (2003). What is psychological intervention? Mapping the field in Sri Lanka. *Intervention,* 1(1), 3–17.

Giller, J. (1998). Caring for "victims of torture" in Uganda: Some personal reflections. In P. J. Bracken & C. Petty (Eds.), *Rethinking the trauma of war* (pp. 113–128). London: Free Association Books.

Gulu District NGO-Forum. (2006). *List of registered NGOs in Gulu.* Unpublished manuscript.

Inter-Agency Standing Committee (IASC). (2007). *Guidelines on mental health and psychosocial support in emergency settings.* Geneva: Author.

Jamison, T. J. (1999). Investing in health. In D. T. Jamison, J. G. Breman, A. R. Measham, G. Alleyne, M. Claeson, D. B. Evans, P. Jha, A. Mills, and P. Musgrove (Eds.), *Disease control priorities in developing countries* (pp. 1–34). Washington, DC: World Bank.

Jordans, M. J., Tol, W. A., Komproe, I. H., & De Jong, J. V. (2013). Systematic review of evidence and treatment approaches: Psychosocial and mental healthcare for children in war. *Child and Adolescent Mental Health,* 14(1), 2–14.

Kirmayer, L. J. (2012). Cultural competence and evidence-based practice in mental health: Epistemic communities and the politics of pluralism. *Social Science and Medicine,* 75(2), 249–256.

Kirmayer, L. J., & Pedersen, D. (2014). Toward a new architecture for global mental health. *Transcultural Psychiatry, 51*(6), 759–776.

Lincoln, Y. S., & Guba, E. G. (1985). *Naturalistic inquiry.* Beverly Hills, CA: Sage.

Marshall, D. J. (2014). Save (us from) the children: Trauma, Palestinian childhood, and the production of governable subjects. *Children's Geographies, 12*(3), 281–296.

Metzl, J. M., & Hansen, H. (2014). Structural competency: Theorizing a new medical engagement with stigma and inequality. *Social Science and Medicine, 103,* 126–133.

Ministry of Health, Uganda (MOH). (1999). *National health policy.* Entebbe: Author.

Ministry of Health, Uganda (MOH). (2011). Uganda malaria control strategic plan, 2005/06–2009/10. Kampala: Author.

Neuner, F., Schauer, M., Klaschik, C., Karunakara, U., & Thomas, E. (2004). A comparison of narrative exposure therapy, supportive counselling and psychoeducation for treating Posttraumatic Stress Disorder in an African refugee settlement. *Journal of Counselling and Clinical Psychology, 72*(4), 579–582.

Okello E., & Ekblad, C. (2006). Lay concepts of depression among the Baganda of Uganda: A pilot study. *Transcultural Psychiatry, 43*(2), 287–313.

Okot, A.C., Amony, I., & Otim, G. (2005). *Suffering in silence: A study of sexual and gender based violence (SGBV) in Pabbo camp, Gulu district, northern Uganda.* Gulu: Gulu District Sub Working Group on SGBV. Retrieved from http://reliefweb .int/sites/reliefweb.int/files/resources/BEFB77D29CC17FE74925702200095601 -unicef-uga-15jun.pdf.

Otunnu, O. A. (2006, January 8). Northern Uganda: Profile of a genocide. *Daily Monitor.* Retrieved from www.essex.ac.uk/armedcon/story_id/000290.html.

Patel, V., Weiss, H. A., Chowdhary, N., Naik, S., Pednekar, S., Chatterjee, S., . . . & Simon, G. (2010). Effectiveness of an intervention led by lay health counsellors for depressive and anxiety disorders in primary care in Goa, India (MANAS): A cluster randomized controlled trial. *The Lancet, 376*(9758), 2086–2095.

Reyburn, H., Mbatia, R., Drakeley, C., Carneiro, I., Mwakasungula, E., Mwerinde, O., . . . Greenwood, B. M. (2004). Overdiagnosis of malaria in patients with severe febrile illness in Tanzania: A prospective study. *British Medical Journal, 329*(7476), 1212–1214.

Richters, A. (1998). Sexual violence in wartime. Psychosociocultural wounds and healing processes: The example of the former Yugoslavia. In P. J. Bracken & C. Petty (Eds.), *Rethinking the trauma of war* (pp. 77–112). London: Free Association Books.

Sax, W. (2014). Ritual healing and mental health in India. *Transcultural Psychiatry, 51*(6), 829–849.

Schauer, E., Neuer F., Elbert J., Erti V., Onyut P. L., Odenwald, M., & Schauer, M. (2004). Narrative exposure therapy in children: A case study. *Intervention, 2*(1), 18–32.

Summerfield, D. (1999). A critique of seven assumptions behind psychological trauma programs in war-affected areas. *Social Science and Medicine, 48*(10), 1449–1462.

Tol, W. A., Song, S., & Jordans, M. J. (2013). Annual research review: Resilience and mental health in children and adolescents living in areas of armed conflict—A systematic review of findings in low- and middle-income countries. *Journal of Child Psychology and Psychiatry, and Allied Disciplines, 54*(4), 445–460.

USAID/UNICEF. (2006). *A hard homecoming lessons learned from the reception center process in northern Uganda: An independent study.* Washington, DC: Author.

Ventevogel, P. (2014). Integration of mental health into primary healthcare in low-income countries: Avoiding medicalization. *International Review of Psychiatry, 26*(6), 669–679.

Wessells, M. G. (2009). Do no harm: Toward contextually appropriate support in international emergencies. *American Psychological Association, 64*(8), 842–854.

Weyermann, R. (2007). Linking economic and emotions towards a more integrated understanding of empowerment in conflict areas. *Intervention, 5*, 83–96.

World Food Programme (WFP). (2003). *Northern Uganda emergency assessment report.* New York: Author.

11

WHEN THE SYSTEM "WORKS"

Exploring the Experiences of Girl Survivors of Sexual Violence in Postconflict Liberia

Debbie Landis and Lindsay Stark

THE LINKAGES BETWEEN SEXUAL VIOLENCE and armed conflict have been well documented (Krug, Dahlberg, Mercy, Zwi, & Lozano, 2002; Potts, Myer, & Roberts, 2011; Stark & Wessells, 2012; Swiss et al., 1998; Vu et al., 2014). Within the context of war, children are often among those most affected by sexual violence, because conflict disrupts social structures that are typically in place to protect them and creates circumstances within which violence and abuse can occur (Apfel & Simon, 1996; Boothby, Strang, & Wessells, 2006; Machel, 2001; Montgomery & Foldspang, 2005). In the aftermath of war, sexual violence often remains pervasive, as shifting social norms and patterns of behavior that emerged during the conflict continue, coupled with new stressors experienced by families and communities. In some cases, high rates of sexual violence during protracted armed conflicts result in the practice of violence becoming "normalized' in postconflict societies (Spangaro et al., 2013; Stark & Ager, 2011; United Nations, 2013; Ward, 2002).

Sexual violence was an issue of grave concern during Liberia's years of civil war (Okereke, 2013; Specht, 2006; Swiss et al., 1998). Since the war ended, rape and other forms of sexual violence have continued to be widespread (GoL/UN Joint Program on SGBV, 2011; Human Rights Watch, 2011; Save the Children, 2006, 2008, 2009; Stark, Warner, Lehman, Boothby, & Ager, 2013; UNMIL, 2008). In August 2011, the UN secretary-general expressed concern about the high number of reported rapes in Liberia, particularly those involving young survivors (United Nations, 2011). In 2011, Human Rights Watch reported that the majority of survivors of reported cases of rape in Liberia were younger than age 16. These assertions are supported by data from the Liberian Ministry of Gender and Development (MoGD), which suggest that, in 2011, almost 50% of all reported cases of gender-based violence (GBV) involved survivors between the ages of 5 and 14 and approximately 5% involved survivors 4 years old and younger (MoGD, 2011a). Of the total number of GBV cases reported in 2011, 61.9% were rape, 5.8% were sexual assault, and 5.5% were gang rape. Seventy-five percent of the perpetrators were reported to be the relatives, neighbors, or intimate partners of the survivors (MoGD, 2011a). Rape remains the most commonly reported crime to the Liberian National Police (LNP) (GoL/UN Joint Program on SGBV, 2011). Given that reported data do not capture complete incidence or prevalence rates, the figures presented here are underestimates at best.

The notion of sexual violence becoming normalized in the postconflict period as a result of the war is arguably evident in Liberia. In 2011, a study investigating the reasons behind the continued high rates of sexual violence and other forms of GBV in postconflict Liberia found that the years of armed conflict had far-reaching effects on the nation's social fabric—causing changes in social structures, beliefs surrounding sex and gender, traditional protective mechanisms, behavioral norms, and larger economic and government systems—all of which have contributed to ongoing sexual violence on a large scale despite the fact that the war has ended. In addition, challenges with implementing legal and judicial reforms have enabled perpetrators to commit sexual violence with impunity, contributing to its occurrence (GoL/UN Joint Program on SGBV, 2011).

In response to these issues, the government of Liberia (GoL) has placed the prevention of sexual violence and the development of comprehensive response initiatives among its top priorities as it engages in the postconflict reconstruction process. The GoL has adopted a national action plan for addressing gender-based violence and established a GBV Unit at the Ministry of Gender and Development (MoGD) along with other government structures to handle national prevention and response initiatives (MoGD, 2011b). In addition, in 2008, the GOL/UN Joint Program on SGBV, which brings together key UN agencies and government ministries working to address the issue of sexual and gender-based violence, was established (GoL/UN Joint Program on SGBV, 2009). In recent years, the GoL and its partners have also sought to make the formal system more child friendly to better address the needs of the large number of children reporting cases of sexual violence. These efforts are particularly notable, because initiatives to address GBV in Liberia have historically focused on the needs of adult female survivors rather than those of children.

Liberia represents a particularly interesting context within which to investigate the services provided to child survivors in postconflict environments, both because of the gravity of the problem of sexual violence during and since the war and the substantial level of investment that the Liberian government and international and national partners have made in addressing this issue as a central component of its postconflict rebuilding strategy.

This chapter argues that, although a strong formal system has been established to respond to the issue of sexual violence against children in Liberia, significant gaps exist, particularly with regard to the ability of the formal system to effectively respond to social stigma and harmful treatment of young survivors by relatives, friends, and community members. Because of the high rates of sexual violence that occurred during the war, this chapter argues that social norms have shifted in ways that have allowed sexual violence to often become normalized—despite the strong prohibition against it under national and international law. This chapter first describes the methods used in this study and gives an overview of the experiences of young survivors with core services following their experiences with sexual violence. Finally, the chapter discusses implications for program and policy development.

Although this study features the perspectives of young survivors, it is important to note that the children interviewed for this study do not reflect a representative sample of all child survivors in Liberia. Research activities were carried out in the capital city of Monrovia, where access to essential services is far greater than in many parts of the country. Additionally, all interviews were conducted with children at a single organization—one that was selected based on its reputation among GBV actors for providing comprehensive case management and assistance to children who have experienced sexual violence. Thus, the study findings do not reflect the experiences of children living in other parts of the country, those who have not accessed services, or those with cases that may have fallen through the cracks of the formal system. Instead, this study represents an investigation into what happens in what can arguably be called a "best case" scenario for child survivors of sexual violence in Liberia—one in which cases are reported, access to needed services exists, and supportive providers are present to facilitate children's rehabilitation and care.

Examining the experiences of children within this context enables "success stories" to be highlighted—in which the formal system works as it was intended—and to feature the ongoing challenges that remain. Findings from this study can be used to inform program and policy development for child survivors in Monrovia and throughout Liberia as a whole, with the ultimate goal of seeking to make supportive services accessible to all children—not just a small minority.

METHODS

In 2012, the Child Protection in Crisis (CPC) Learning Network[1] conducted a review of services for child survivors of sexual violence in Liberia to identify promising practices, challenges with implementation, and areas for further research and program development. The study involved both a document review of program-related materials and interviews with key informants from government ministries, UN agencies, and national and international nongovernmental organizations (INGOs), the findings of which are published elsewhere (Landis & Stark, 2014). In addition, interviews were also conducted with young survivors to understand their perspectives on the types of services they received and their experiences with the formal system.[2]

All the children interviewed had experienced some form of sexual violence, broadly defined for the purposes of this study as rape or any other form of sexual abuse that prompted them to report their cases and use formal services. They all were receiving support from a local NGO in Monrovia that provides case management, psychosocial care, and referrals to service providers, such as medical treatment and access to the justice system. The organization was identified in consultation with members of the GBV Unit and the GBV Interagency Taskforce and was selected for its primary role in providing services for child survivors. It only serves female survivors, and so no male survivors were included in this sample. Girls included in this study were between the ages of 11–17.

Research activities consisted of site visits, participant observation, and formal and informal interviews with children over a 4-week period. Interviews did not probe directly the survivors' experiences with violence, but rather focused on their perspectives on service provision. However, if children chose to discuss their abuse, the researcher created space for them to do so to the extent that they were comfortable.

In keeping with the "Do No Harm" imperative (Anderson, 1999), interviews were not conducted with children who were currently experiencing symptoms of psychosocial distress. Furthermore, the study protocol included measures to refer children for follow-up support if their participation in the study triggered emotional discomfort. To protect the confidentiality of all child participants, no names or identifying information were included in the study, and the name of the organization where the research was conducted was excluded. The protocol for this study was approved by the Institutional Review Board (IRB) at the University of Liberia before the start of data collection.

RESULTS

GENERAL CASE DETAILS

As previously mentioned, all the girls selected for the study had experienced and reported some form of sexual violence. Although the researcher did not probe directly their experiences with violence, in the interviews the girls all voluntarily disclosed certain details about their case, including the type of abuse experienced and information on the perpetrator(s). Although they reported various forms of abuse, rape was mentioned the most frequently, with the majority of girls experiencing rape on a single occasion by one or more perpetrators or, in some cases, by the same perpetrator over an extended period of time.

The majority of girls reported experiencing sexual violence in or near their homes and by a perpetrator who was a relative—with fathers mentioned most frequently, followed by uncles. A 13-year-old girl, for example, described being raped by her father, saying,

> It was in the night my father called me in the room and I go and he was sleeping and he say, "Come, let me check you," and I started crying and he get on me. He hold my clothes and get on me. . . . He say if I crying, he kill me. When he get off [of me], I run away.

A few girls reported violence perpetrated by others in the community or by unknown men, with one 13-year-old girl reporting being raped by two men on the same occasion. She said, "The thing that brought me here. . . . Two men. Two men, they raped me. . . . They raped in the house. They took off my clothes." For one survivor, her abuse occurred in the form of forced/early marriage at the age of 13 to a 63-year-old man. Although early marriage has historically been practiced in certain parts of Liberia, the custom was criminalized as statutory rape under Liberia's new rape law, which holds that sexual activity between an adult and anyone under the age of 18 is illegal (Government of Liberia, 2006).

EXPERIENCE WITH CORE SERVICES

Findings from the interviews were structured around the ways survivors navigated the national "referral pathway," which was established by the Ministry of Gender and Development (MoGD) in 2009. This protocol mandates the essential services that survivors should receive, dividing interventions between those that should take place within the first 72 hours after an incident and those connected to longer term care (MoGD, 2009). Services outlined in the referral pathway focus on the following key areas: the police, medical care, the courts, and psychosocial support.

Survivors, who may report their cases at any point along the pathway (i.e., to a medical provider, the police, etc.), are given a "survivor card" that provides them with a unique ID number and contains codes that represent the particular form(s) of gender-based violence that they experienced. To protect the confidentiality of survivors, these cards do not contain personal information, and the coding system is structured in such a way that only those involved in the provision of services through the formal system are aware of the meanings of particular codes. Survivors are supposed to carry their cards to all appointments associated with their case to facilitate data harmonization across actors and enable service providers to make appropriate referrals as needed.

POLICE Girls reported almost unanimously that the police were their first access point along the referral pathway, typically through interaction with the Women and Children Protection Section (WACPS) of the Liberian National Police (LNP). WACPS, formed in 2005, handles cases of abuse, neglect, or other protection concerns involving women and children (UNICEF, 2005). It places a priority on hiring female officers, thereby providing a greater level of sensitivity in cases of violence and abuse encountered by women and children. In addition, the WACPS headquarters in Monrovia is not located in the main police station, thus providing a greater level of confidentiality to those making reports. The WACPS building is equipped with private rooms for case consultation and has living quarters with child-friendly amenities for children in need of temporary shelter. Police from the United Nations Mission in Liberia (UNMIL) serve in an advisory capacity to WACPS and provide additional support on especially sensitive cases. As part of this process, special protocols have been developed for responding to instances of sexual violence, particularly cases involving children. UNICEF and NGO partners have also provided training for WACPS on GBV and case management for survivors. Although the headquarters for WACPS is located in Monrovia, WACPS units have been placed in police stations throughout Liberia.

In most instances, girls first told a family member or another adult what had happened to them, and that individual went with them to the police station to file a report. In one instance, a 14-year-old girl who was raped by her father described reporting the incident to an older brother, who subsequently took her to the police. As she said, "I told my brother. My brother didn't go to work [after hearing about her abuse]. He go to the police station with me and we tell the police people." In some cases, however, the initial adult whom the girls approached did not help them file a report with the police. A 17-year-old girl who was raped on multiple occasions by her father, for example, described that she initially informed other adults in her household about what was happening, but they told her to keep quiet:

> Somebody did know about it. They used to be in the house when he used to be doing it. . . . But they said they know but told me not to talk about it. They told me to keep it as a secret.

When the abuse continued, however, she eventually ran away and was taken to the police by a stranger who found her on the street:

> Actually I ran away, but I didn't really know the right place to go. I was on the street near the market. So, one time a girl took me to the [police] station . . . and they were asking me what happened.

Although the majority of girls described going to the police with the assistance of someone else, in some cases, girls went directly to the police on their own. For example, a 16-year-old survivor noted that she and her three sisters had experienced repeated sexual abuse at the hands of one of their uncles. Her oldest sister was eventually able to get away and file a report with the police, who then came to the house to arrest the uncle and take the other sisters to begin receiving services. The oldest sister first filed a report with UNMIL police, who worked in coordination with WACPS officers to respond. The younger sister said,

> First my big sister came [to the police]. She launched a complaint to UNMIL. Now they went to the police station. Now the police say they will come for us— for my sisters and I. The UNMIL wait for us at our house. . . . I was home. They came and said we have to carry you to a safe area to be able to help you and let you go to school and be a good person for tomorrow.

Girls also described the police as playing an integral role in arranging lodging for the girls in safe homes or other secure locations. Safe homes provide temporary shelter and access to counseling and other essential services for survivors until more permanent care and living arrangements can be identified. The location of safe homes is kept secret, except to agency staff and other key implementing partners, and detailed protocols are put in place to ensure that the safety and security of survivors are preserved at all times. A 13-year-old girl, for example, stated that police had brought her to a safe home, because her father was on the run and had reportedly threatened to kill her if she came forward about her abuse. Although the girl originally reported her case in another location, the police relocated her to Monrovia until they could apprehend her father. She said, "He [her father] tell the people anyplace I am, he will kill me. So I will be here [in Monrovia] until they find him."

When asked about their experiences with the police, girls described them as generally helpful and reassuring. The 16-year-old girl mentioned earlier, who came to the attention of the police along with her sisters, said that she was initially afraid of the police, but during a follow-up visit felt more comfortable. She said, "I gave a statement to the police. I feel good. At first I was scared, but the second time I was not scared to talk." The majority of girls reported that their perpetrators had been arrested by the police and were currently in jail, and they talked freely about the outcomes of police investigations. For the girls who did not report that their perpetrator had been arrested, their cases had still been referred to the police and were currently under investigation.

MEDICAL CARE National-level protocols in Liberia for handling cases of sexual violence urge survivors to seek medical care as soon as possible after an incident, with a strong priority placed on accessing care within the first 72 hours. For the majority of girls in the study, reporting their case to the police was their first encounter with the judicial system, and most were then brought to a hospital or clinic. For example, a 16-year-old girl said, "After I went to the police they carried me to the hospital and they gave me medicine for any sickness in my body to come out." Girls often mentioned receiving medical services at a major clinic in Monrovia designated by the referral pathway to provide care to survivors of sexual violence. This clinic is designed to enable survivors to come and go discreetly and so is located in a separate building behind the main hospital. It is also set up in a manner that is intended to be child friendly, with books, toys, and other decorations intended to make children feel as comfortable as possible. Medical providers at the clinic have dolls and visual aids that children can use if desired to help them describe the types of abuse they experienced, thereby making the case consultation and exam process more accessible for children of younger ages and developmental stages. The clinic also has psychosocial staff on site, so that survivors can receive counseling along with medical care. The GoL has sought to replicate the comprehensive on-site approach of this clinic in other locations, although access to these types of services is not available in many areas.

Girls reported receiving a range of treatments depending on the nature of their cases, although services described in almost all instances included receiving postexposure prophylaxis and being tested for pregnancy, HIV/AIDS, and other sexually transmitted infections. Regardless of the duration or type of medical care they received, girls reported feeling physically better as a result of their treatment. For example, a 14-year-old said, "I went to the hospital. They say my father finished hurting me. I felt bad. They checked me. The medicine made my body feel fine [better]." Girls regularly mentioned feeling encouraged by the ways in which medical staff engaged with them and noted that they often received counseling in addition to medical care. One 15-year-old girl noted,

They talked to me in a nice way. . . . They asked me what happened and said they should check me. They checked me and said I'm not pregnant. They gave me an AIDS test and said I don't have AIDS. I feel fine. . . . I was happy [on hearing the test results]!

Similarly, a 17-year-old girl said,

I was sick! So, so sick. So they've been treating me until I come back to myself. . . . They gave me some treatment with a drip [IV treatment]. When I came to myself, they started counseling me, talking to me. . . . They said some encouraging words. I shouldn't feel bad about the unfortunate thing. Other people have passed through it. . . . They gave me medical support. All the things you go through, they can be hard. But they give you encouraging words. They talk to you. They can check you. They take care of you.

COURT All the study participants reported having some form of contact with the judicial system, most commonly when their cases were handled by the SGBV Crimes Unit—established in 2009 as the designated branch of the Ministry of Justice for the prosecution of sexual violence cases. Prosecutors and

case liaison officers in this unit work with the police and other actors to ensure that evidence is collected correctly and that cases are prepared for court
(Abdulai, 2010). In addition, the unit employs victim support officers who provide direct services and psychosocial support to survivors. Girls described
going to the SGBV Crimes Unit on multiple occasions while their cases were
being prepared.

During these visits, girls received assistance with preparing their statements, were told what to expect at their trial, and were informed of other
issues they might encounter with the judicial process. For example, a 17-year-old
girl said,

> The Crimes Unit too, when you go there they can talk to you. They can take
> statement from you. When they finish talking to you and take statement from
> you, they will send you to court. . . . They talk to you about how it happened to
> you, the year, the month, the date, and you when you enter the court, no one
> can speak for you, you have to do your talking for yourself, and you shouldn't
> be shy. Everything you say, it should be the truth, and you can't go and change
> your statement two times. You have to say one statement and when they check
> it with other statements it has to be the same.

A 15-year-old girl described the way in which those working on her case emphasized her role in the legal process, stating that it was her choice whether to
press charges and that the case would not move forward if she did not want it
to. She said,

> Oh, they told me that when you go to court, you're the one that will get the final
> say. And when you say the man will go to jail, he will go to jail, and if you decide
> he will not go to jail, he will not go to jail. You are the one who will decide.

All cases involving survivors who participated in this study were heard by
Criminal Court E, established in 2008 as a specialized court to hear and process
sexual violence cases (Government of Liberia, 2008). Housed in the Temple
of Justice in Monrovia, Criminal Court E was designed to expedite the prosecution of cases and to provide a greater level of sensitivity to the needs of
survivors; for example, by using "in camera" hearings, which make it possible
for survivors not to physically appear in court or be seen by perpetrators during their trial. Although the primary court is located in Monrovia, special divi-

sions of the court have been established at the circuit court level to hear cases in other regions of the country.

The majority of survivors reported that their perpetrators had been convicted in court. Among those who did not report convictions, their cases were still under investigation by the police, or their court proceedings were still in progress.

Although girls reported high rates of conviction, they also described significant challenges with the justice system. For example, the 16-year-old girl whose case was taken up on behalf of her sisters and her reported experiencing significant delays, and the proceedings were suspended for long periods of time because the girls did not have sufficient legal counsel. She said,

> Our case stayed long. When our case raised, then one year passed and our case was [still] going. . . . Today we would go to court, then tomorrow we would go to court. Then it would stop. It stayed long.

Eventually, the girl's case was taken up with the support of an expatriate lawyer who was in Liberia, had heard about the girls' situation, and decided to take up their case. As the girl described,

> A lawyer heard about our case. She was in Liberia and she said she would be on our case. She stayed and called some of her friends and they helped with money. . . . We talked about what happened to us and the thing that he used to do to us and what happened . . . And they asked us if he should go to jail, and we said, "yes."

Although the girl's case went on for more than a year and experienced numerous roadblocks before the new lawyer provided representation, it ultimately resulted in the conviction of her uncle. The girl described her emotions at the moment that the verdict was given in court: "I was happy! They knocked on the table and said, 'Person guilty' and that the case was finished. I was feeling good!"

In addition to procedural or resource-related challenges with the judicial system, a primary issue reported by girls involved negative reactions from their families once the case had been taken to trial. Girls frequently reported that their relatives or other community members accused them of lying about the abuse they experienced or turned against them if the perpetrator was convicted.

For example, the 16-year-old girl whose uncle was convicted of abusing her sisters and her said,

> Since the case happened, our family thinking bad on us. They didn't get time for us. They said we're lying. So they didn't get time for us. . . . I feel bad because my own parents talking bad things. I feel bad. They said they don't have time for us.

A 17-year-old girl described a similar stigmatization by her relatives after her father was convicted in court for sexually abusing her. He then committed suicide in jail, increasing the level of hostility from her relatives. As she described,

> They [the court] found him guilty, so they said they put him in jail. And he killed himself. . . . And since then, all my relatives, they turned their back on me. They said the wrong thing I did. . . . They're still chasing after me.

This stigma and disbelief of girls' stories by families and communities led one 15-year-old girl, whose case was still in its early stages, to say she was going to change her story when she went back to court. She had initially reported that her uncle raped her, but said she wanted to tell the authorities he was innocent because he had a family and she did not want him to be in jail. She said,

> I feel selfish because my Ma brother [her uncle] has eight children. They will suffer. That's why I say I feel selfish, so I want to say he did not do nothing to me. . . . I don't want him to be in jail. I want him to be free. I'm going to explain that he did not do anything to me.

PSYCHOSOCIAL SUPPORT All the participants reported receiving psychosocial support as part of their recovery process, often in the form of individual counseling. The girls received counseling at various locations, including from medical staff and from caseworkers of the SGBV Crimes Unit. In addition, they reported receiving individual and group counseling on an ongoing basis at the organization where research activities were conducted. The girls described the need for this type of support and the significant impact it had over time in helping them work through their experiences. For example, a 16-year-old girl said, "First, I came, I was crying, but they talked to me, and I forget about the past. . . . They counseled me. I feel good." Similarly, a 15-year-old girl noted,

> At first when I came it was hard. . . . I liked to sit on my own. . . . When I first came, I used to not speak. I was not able. . . . I come here at first, I was not happy. For nearly a year. So people came around me and started talking, and having advice for me. They were counseling me, and I start coming to myself and would start going to play, small, small . . .

Often girls described the positive role that peer relationships played in their recovery, particularly their interactions with fellow survivors at the organization where they were receiving services. For example, a 17-year-old girl said, "When I came here, I saw other people, and my friends who had the same problem I had. . . . So people used to talk to me, and counsel me. . . . And I associate myself with my friends." By interacting with other girls who had also experienced sexual abuse and had been able to move forward, girls reported feeling more empowered and hopeful about the future. For example, the 15-year-old girl quoted earlier said,

> They [other survivors] would say that anything you have passed through, myself I have passed through. Don't sit down and worry. Come with your friends, they be playing. I've passed through so many things too, the same as you; I've passed through it too, but God will make me someone in the future, and so God will make you someone in the future. One day, you will be more than Ellen Johnson [the president of Liberia]. So I say, "Oh yes, by the grace of God, I will be more than Ellen Johnson!"

Looking toward the future was a commonly reported theme among survivors, with many of them focusing on the types of careers they wanted to have and on attending school. A number of girls expressed a desire to engage in public service or to enter into a career that would help other survivors of sexual violence. For example, a 16-year-old girl said,

> I want to become a journalist. Or, if I don't become a journalist I want to become a lawyer. . . . I want to become a lawyer because the things that happen to me, I want to preach [about the issue of abuse]. I want to speak on it. But if I don't become a lawyer, God will make me to become president. I want to

become president of the country so that if any man play on a woman, he will go in jail. . . . They should clean the country. . . . I would help them.

DISCUSSION

As mentioned, this study can best be viewed as an exploration of the experiences of child survivors of sexual violence in Liberia who have been provided with a higher than usual level of access to the formal system and a substantial degree of support from service providers. All the participants in this study reported access to all key elements of the referral pathway: police, medical care, the courts, and psychosocial support. This rate of access differs significantly from national data, which suggest that, among reported cases of GBV in 2011, only 52% reported access to medical care and 46% reported accessing support from the police, with equal rates of access reported for the court (22%) and psychosocial support (22%; MoGD, 2011a). As these data suggest, the majority of survivors in Liberia go without the essential services that girls participating in this study received.

With regard to the police, the girls consistently described the role that WACPS officers played in responding to cases of abuse and making referrals to needed services. In addition, the majority reported that their perpetrators had been arrested. This finding differs significantly from national data, which suggest that only 20% of reported cases of GBV in 2011 resulted in the perpetrator's arrest (MoGD, 2011a). Girls' positive encounters with WACPS were likely due to the fact that they were seen in Monrovia, where access is significantly greater than in many locations. For example, police stations in rural areas are often underfunded and understaffed, lacking the resources to investigate cases of sexual violence effectively (De Carvalho & Schia, 2009; Schia & De Carvalho, 2009). In addition, they often lack the private rooms for confidentiality and other child-friendly amenities of the WACPS headquarters in Monrovia, which could significantly affect girls' experiences with rural police.

It is particularly significant that the majority of girls who participated in this study reported that their perpetrators had been convicted in court: This finding runs counter to national data on the judicial process for GBV cases in Liberia. According to 2011 data from the Liberian Ministry of Gender and Development, for example, 22% of the total reported cases of GBV in 2011 were taken to court, and only 1% resulted in the conviction of a perpetrator

(MoGD, 2011a). Other studies of GBV cases in Liberia have found similarly low rates of prosecution, highlighting significant inefficiencies with the justice system, such as insufficient resources, corruption, and lack of access in rural areas (De Carvalho & Schia, 2009; Sarkar, Syed, & Nzau, 2009; Schia & De Carvalho, 2009).

The girls in the study had their cases heard in Monrovia, where access to legal services is greater than in rural areas, and they received intensive case management and follow-up from the organization where research activities took place. Survivors in remote locations or those who are not provided with the same level of monitoring and follow-up on their cases are likely to experience outcomes in court that are more in line with national statistics. It is also notable that one of the girls described having her case put on hold for more than a year because she and her sisters were unable to secure adequate legal representation. Although it is very fortunate that adequate legal counsel could be obtained in this case, this type of specialized assistance is not available to the vast majority of survivors.

Similarly, although girls consistently described the medical care and psychosocial support they received to be healing and transformative, their experiences were also largely influenced by the fact that they were seen in Monrovia where specialized clinics and programs have been devised with the unique needs of child survivors in mind. Although the GOL is actively working to replicate these types of initiatives, scaling up at the national level has not yet taken place. In many parts of the country, survivors must often walk long distances to obtain medical care, and existing facilities are often short-staffed and face significant resource constraints (Landis & Stark, 2014; Sarkar et al., 2009).

As previously mentioned, all the participants in this study voluntarily chose to disclose their relationship to their perpetrator(s). It is notable that the majority of girls reported being abused by relatives—such as fathers or uncles—or other individuals known to them and that instances of sexual violence typically took place in or near girls' homes. These findings are consistent with the previously mentioned data from the Ministry of Gender and Development, which reveal that, among reported cases of GBV in Liberia in 2011, 75% involved perpetrators who were either relatives, neighbors, or intimate partners of the survivors (MoGD, 2011a). These figures are also in line with earlier studies of GBV in postconflict environments, which found rates of violence carried out by relatives or intimate partners to be higher than those involving strangers (Hynes, Robertson, Ward, & Crouse, 2004; Stark, Warner, Lehman, Boothby, & Ager, 2013).

That available data suggest that a trend toward violence against children by family members and others they know remains highly problematic. This is because earlier research found that child survivors are more likely to disclose their abuse to relatives or those they know than to report cases to formal authorities (UNICEF, 2014). Within this context, there is a great risk that children will be urged not to report the violence, as when a young survivor was told by adults in her house to "keep quiet" about her repeated abuse.

Similarly, although the majority of girls who participated in this study went to the police with the help of a relative or another adult, girls also reported experiencing significant stigma and in some cases threats of additional harm from other relatives and community members once charges were made, particularly after their perpetrators had been convicted in court. Within Liberia, pressure is commonly placed on survivors not to press charges against perpetrators if they are relatives or neighbors, because of the impact that a conviction would have on a perpetrator and his or her family. Girls are frequently told by relatives or community members to "just move forward" and that rape is a common, and therefore almost normal, occurrence in Liberia (Landis & Stark, 2014).

Referred to as "compromising cases," this practice has been widely reported in Liberia and represents a significant threat to the ability of survivors to gain justice (Landis & Stark, 2014). This type of pressure has increased in recent years because of the new rape law, which, as previously mentioned, criminalizes all sexual activity between adults and those under the age of 18. It also calls for harsh penalties for those who are convicted, including a maximum penalty of life in prison for first-degree sexual offenses (Government of Liberia, 2006).

Child survivors in Liberia face not only the physical and psychosocial consequences of their abuse but also the added challenges of rejection and additional harm at the hands of their family members and close acquaintances if they choose to move forward with prosecution. Girls who do not report their cases and do not receive the necessary care will suffer well-documented adverse consequences to their physical and emotional health and development (Chen, 2010; Dinwiddie et al., 2000; Krahe, Scheinberger-Olwig, Waizenhofer, & Kolpin, 1999; UNICEF, 2014). And yet, if they come forward, survivors often risk being alienated from their families and facing life-altering stigma that further exacerbates the abuse they have already experienced.

In light of these dynamics, findings from this study suggest an urgent need for program and policy initiatives aimed at addressing the root causes of sexual violence against children—with a particular emphasis on the contributing factors associated with violence within the home or community, rather than focusing on preventing violence carried out by strangers. To explore these issues, policy makers and service providers should engage in further research to examine the root causes of sexual violence against children. In light of the limited evidence base by which to determine promising practices in this area (Landis & Stark, 2014), efforts should be made by policy makers and practitioners to rigorously evaluate existing program and policy initiatives. Findings from these efforts should be used to inform the development of interventions that seek to reduce sexual violence against children and create a shift in harmful attitudes, beliefs, and practices that contribute to its occurrence.

In addition, the study findings suggest the need to raise awareness among families and communities about the short- and long-term consequences of sexual violence on children and the need for children to receive supportive care after experiencing incidents of abuse. These efforts are particularly important to combat the commonly held perception of rape as being somehow normalized or something that children can simply "get over" without external support. These perceptions create significant barriers to the ability of survivors to obtain justice and needed services and can serve as a disincentive for children to report cases of sexual violence when they occur. As such, policy makers and practitioners should prioritize social norms change initiatives with diverse community stakeholders and work to ensure that referral pathways for cases of sexual violence against children are well known and accessible.

Findings from this study also suggest the need for reintegration programming that helps survivors navigate short- and long-term solutions that are safe and appropriate after their cases have been reported. Such programming is particularly important in addressing the type of stigma experienced by the survivors who participated in this study. Without necessary support at the family and community levels, even the most well-developed referral pathways and formal services will remain insufficient.

This focus on the involvement of survivors' families and communities is consistent with ecological theory (Bronfenbrenner, 1979), which views individuals as existing in nested systems of protection and care. Based on this framework, family and friends hold the potential to provide the greatest level of support—or harm—for girls affected by sexual violence, and so efforts to promote their active involvement in the care and rehabilitation of young survivors of sexual violence in Liberia are particularly crucial.

Finally, findings suggest that, although the GOL has put substantial laws and national structures in place to address the legal, medical, and psychosocial needs of child survivors, additional resources and capacity-building efforts are urgently needed to increase the impact of these initiatives. Significant work is also needed to expand access to child-friendly and essential services to survivors in all regions of the country—particularly those outside of Monrovia.

CONCLUSIONS

Taken cumulatively, findings from this study suggest that the formal system established by the Liberian government to meet the needs of survivors of sexual violence can work, if the necessary resources and personnel are in place to handle cases effectively. However, these conditions are not in place for the large majority of survivors, and even for those who can successfully navigate the formal system, challenges remain. The close relationship that often exists between perpetrators and survivors has been shown to deter the reporting of cases and exposes children to stigma and threats of additional harm once they decide to come forward.

Despite these challenges, findings from the study also highlight the positive role that effective service provision can play in promoting the health, well-being, and recovery of child survivors. Girls participating in the study described moving from feeling hopeless and distressed as a result of the violence they encountered to being able to embrace positive ambitions for the future. This outcome shows both the ongoing need for appropriate care and the crucial role that these initiatives can play in transforming the lives of children affected by sexual violence. In the process, promoting the healing of survivors can contribute to the recovery of the Liberian nation as a whole.

These initiatives are particularly essential because of the pervasive nature of sexual violence both during and since the war. The case of Liberia also exemplifies the ways in which shifting social norms and patterns of behavior that emerged during wartime have continued in the postconflict period. As a result, rape and other forms of sexual violence have in some cases become normalized, creating further challenges not only for survivors but also for those seeking to engage in effective prevention and response initiatives.

Although this study focuses on the experiences of child survivors in Liberia, its findings have direct relevance to conflict-affected societies more broadly, given the common—yet deeply troubling—occurrence of sexual violence against children in the aftermath of war. The challenges to effective service provision, along with the issues of stigma and harmful treatment experienced by survivors in this sample, are also common in conflict-affected states. Sexual violence against children—in Liberia and beyond—represents a public health and human rights abuse of grave concern. In light of its detrimental impact on children's healthy growth, development, and well-being, efforts to combat the root causes of sexual violence against children are urgently needed, as well as continued work to make existing programs and services for survivors even more effective.

Notes

1. The Child Protection in Crisis (CPC) Learning Network is "a collaboration of humanitarian agencies, local institutions, and academic partners working to improve the protection of children in crisis-affected settings" (CPC website, www.cpcnetwork.org). The global secretariat of the CPC Learning Network is based in the Program on Forced Migration and Health at the Mailman School of Public Health at Columbia University.
2. For the purposes of this chapter, the term "formal system" refers to government-led prevention and response initiatives, as well as the contribution to these efforts provided by UN agencies and NGOs.

References

Abdulai, E. (2010, November). *Strengthening of prosecution of SGBV offenses through support to the Sexual and Gender Based Violence Crimes Unit (SGBV CU)*. Monrovia: UNFPA.

Anderson, M. (1999). *Do no harm: How aid can support peace—or war*. Boulder, CO: Lynne Rienner.

Apfel, R., & Simon, B. (Eds). (1996). *Minefields in their hearts: The mental health of children in war and communal violence*. New Haven, CT: Yale University Press.

Boothby, N., Strang, A., & Wessells, M. (Eds). (2006). *A world turned upside down: Social ecological approaches to children in war zones*. Bloomfield, CT: Kumarian Press.

Bronfenbrenner, U. (1979). *The ecology of human development: Experiments by nature and design*. Cambridge, MA: Harvard University Press.

Chen, L. (2010). Sexual abuse and lifetime diagnosis of psychiatric disorders: Systematic review and meta-analysis. *Mayo Clinic Proceedings, 85*(7), 618–629.

De Carvalho, B., & Schia, N. (2009). *The protection of women and children in Liberia* (NUPI Policy Briefs). Oslo: Norwegian Institute for International Affairs.

Dinwiddie, S., Heath, A., Dunne, M., Bucholz, K., Madden, P., Slutske, W., . . . Martin, N. (2000). Early sexual abuse and lifetime psychopathology: A co-twin-control study. *Psychological Medicine, 30*(1), 41–52.

Government of Liberia (GoL). (2006, January 17). *An act to amend the New Penal Code Chapter 14 Section 14.70 and to provide for gang rape.* Monrovia: Ministry of Foreign Affairs.

Government of Liberia (GoL). (2008, September 23). *An act amending Title 17 of the Revised Code of Laws of Liberia, known as the Judiciary Law of 1972 by adding thereto a new chapter to be known as Chapter 25 establishing Criminal Court "E" of the First Judicial Circuit, Montserrado County, and Special Divisions of the Circuit Courts of other counties of the republic to have exclusive original jurisdiction over the crimes of rape, gang rape, aggravated involuntary sodomy, involuntary sodomy, voluntary sodomy, corruption of minors, sexual abuse of wards and sexual assault respectively.* Monrovia: Ministry of Foreign Affairs.

Government of Liberia (GoL)/United Nations (UN) Joint Program on Sexual and Gender-Based Violence [GOL/UN Joint Program on SGBV]. (2008, June 13). *Government and UN joint program to prevent and respond to sexual gender based violence.* Monrovia: Author.

GoL/UN Joint Program on SGBV. (2011). *In-depth study on reasons for high incidence of sexual and gender based violence in Liberia—Recommendations on prevention and response.* Stockholm: SIDA.

Human Rights Watch. (2011). *Country summary: Liberia* (World Report, 2011). New York: Author.

Hynes, M., Robertson, K., Ward, J., & Crouse, C. (2004). A determination of the prevalence of gender-based violence among conflict-affected populations in East Timor. *Disasters, 28,* 294–321.

Krahe, B., Scheinberger-Olwig, R., Waizenhofer, E., & Kolpin, S. (1999). Childhood sexual abuse and revictimization in adolescence. *Child Abuse and Neglect, 23*(4), 383–394.

Krug, E., Dahlberg, L., Mercy, J., Zwi, A., & Lozano, R. (Eds.). (2002). *World report on violence and health.* Geneva: World Health Organization.

Landis, D., & Stark, L. (2014). Examining promising practice: An integrated review of services for young survivors of sexual violence in Liberia. *Intervention, 12*(3), 430–441.

Machel, G. (2001). *The impact of war on children.* London: Hurst & Company.

Ministry of Gender and Development, Liberia (MoGD). (2009). *National standard operating procedures for prevention and response to sexual gender-based violence in Liberia*. Monrovia: Author.

Ministry of Gender and Development, Liberia (MoGD). (2011a). *Gender-based violence annual statistical report for 2011*. Monrovia: Author.

Ministry of Gender and Development, Liberia (MoGD). (2011b). *National action plan for the prevention and management of gender-based violence in Liberia (2nd phase), 2011–2015*. Monrovia: Author.

Montgomery, E., & Foldspang, A. (2005). Seeking asylum in Denmark: Refugee children's mental health and exposure to violence. *European Journal of Public Health, 15*(3), 233–237.

Okereke, G. (2013). Crime and punishment in Liberia. *International Journal of Comparative and Applied Criminal Justice, 37*(1), 63–74.

Potts, A., Myer, K., & Roberts, L. (2011). Measuring human rights violations in a conflict-affected country: Results from a nationwide cluster survey in Central African Republic. *Conflict and Health, 5*(1): 4.

Sarkar, M., Syed, S., & Nzau, M. (2009). *Strategic inquiry on prevention and response to gender based violence (GBV) in Liberia*. Monrovia: Government of Liberia and United Nations Joint Program.

Save the Children. (2006). *From camp to community: Liberia study on exploitation of children*. Monrovia: Author.

Save the Children. (2008). *Multi-sectorial GBV assessment: Cote d'Ivoire and Liberia border communities*. London: Author.

Save the Children. (2009). *In-country network assessment into sexual exploitation and abuse of women and children in border communities in Liberia*. London: Author.

Schia, N., & De Carvalho, B. (2009). Nobody gets justice here! Addressing sexual and gender based violence and the rule of law in Liberia. *Security in Practice, 5* (NUPI Working Paper 761). Oslo: Norwegian Institute for International Affairs.

Spangaro, J., Adogu, C., Ranmuthugala, G., Powell Davies, G., Steinacker, L., & Zwi, A. (2013). What evidence exists for initiatives to reduce risk and incidence of sexual violence in armed conflict and other humanitarian crises? A systematic review. *PLoS One, 8*(5).

Specht, I. (2006). *Red shoes: Experiences of girl combatants in Liberia*. Geneva: International Labor Organization (ILO).

Stark, L., & Ager, A. (2011). A systematic review of prevalence studies of gender-based violence in complex emergencies. *Trauma, Violence and Abuse, 12*(3), 127–134.

Stark, L., Warner, A., Lehman, H., Boothby, N., & Ager, A. (2013). Measuring the incidence and reporting of violence against women and girls in Liberia using the Neighborhood Method. *Conflict and Health, 7*(20).

Stark L., & Wessells, M. (2012). Sexual violence as a weapon of war. *Journal of the American Medical Association, 308*(7), 677–678.

Swiss, S., Jennings, P., Aryee, G., Brown, G., Jappah-Samukai, R., Kamara, M. S., Schaack, R. D., & Turay-Kanneh, R. (1998). Violence against women during the Liberian civil conflict. *Journal of the American Medical Association, 279*(8), 625–629.

UNICEF. (2005, September 1). *New women and children protection section for Liberia's police.* New York: Author.

UNICEF. (2014). *Hidden in plain sight: A statistical analysis of violence against children.* New York: Author.

United Nations. (2011). *Twenty-third progress report of the Secretary-General on the United Nations Mission in Liberia* (United Nations Security Council S/2011/497). New York: Author.

United Nations. (2013). *Sexual violence in conflict: Report of the Secretary-General* (A/67/792-S/2013/149). New York: Author.

United Nations Mission in Liberia (UNMIL). (2008). *Research on prevalence and attitudes to rape in Liberia* (Legal and Judicial System Support Division). Monrovia: Author.

Vu, A., Adam, A., Wirtz, A., Pham, K., Rubenstein, L., Glass, N., . . . Singh, S. (2014). The prevalence of sexual violence among female refugees in complex humanitarian emergencies: A systematic review and meta-analysis. *PLoS Currents, 6.*

Ward, J. (2002). *If not now, when? Addressing gender-based violence in refugee, internally displaced, and post-conflict settings: A global overview.* New York: Reproductive Health for Refugees Consortium.

12

WORKING WITH CHILDREN AFFECTED BY ARMED CONFLICT

Practical Protection Work During the Darfur Crisis in the Sudan

Ghada Kachachi

A HOLISTIC APPROACH TO CHILD protection issues is one that takes into account all vulnerabilities faced by children of all ages and deals with them by strengthening protective factors in all layers of a child's environment—including the individuals who deal with a child, their family, their schools, their wider communities, and policies and services at national and international levels.[1] In this chapter, I provide an analysis of children's experiences of armed conflict in the Darfur region of Sudan and the national and international responses to those children's critical needs. To develop this analysis, I have drawn on my experience as a humanitarian worker during the implementation of a child protection program in Darfur from 2005–2010. The United Nations Children's Fund (UNICEF) and partners in the Darfur region provided support for the implementation of that program, but the views I express here do not necessarily represent the position of UNICEF or its partners.

Even in the midst of conflict, a holistic approach to child protection services is essential. I base my arguments in this chapter on a child rights perspective and framework informed by the United Nations Convention on the Rights of the Child (CRC, 1989). The CRC establishes a focus on the whole child and a global commitment to the principles of children's rights, including universality, nondiscrimination, and participation. It sets out the protection rights that must be realized for children to develop their full potential free from violence, abuse, exploitation, and neglect.

In this chapter I first provide a child rights and gendered-based analysis of the experiences of children during the armed conflict in Darfur. It builds on children's involvement in the child protection program through their participation in individual interviews and focus group discussions, both in the program assessment and planning stages. Their participation continued throughout the program implementation and evaluation stages. In addition, UNICEF, in partnership with the Ministry of Youth, Culture and Sports, conducted a National and Baseline Study on Children and Youth (UNICEF & Government of Sudan [GoS], 2008). It involved 529 children and youth (ages 12–25) of both genders from North, South, and West Darfur.

In the second part of the chapter, I examine national and international responses to the conflict, focusing on the implementation of a child protection program in Darfur. By taking into account multiple intersecting systems that affect child protection, the program took a holistic approach to child protection, supporting the reintegration of child soldiers and the needs of children who experienced violence. I also describe the restructuring of the legislative and policy environments in the area of child protection in Sudan, the strengthening of capacities and systems to implement the child protection program and enforce laws in Darfur, and the building of understanding and awareness among families and wider communities.

METHODOLOGY

The data in this chapter are drawn from several key documents, assessments, program evaluations, and studies of the risks and vulnerabilities Darfurian children experienced. The majority of these assessments involved field research, interviews and focus group discussions with relevant stakeholders, including both male and female children. The *Situation Analysis of Child Protection in Darfur* (Bremer, Ager, & Boothby, 2006), commissioned by UNICEF and conducted in March 2006 by researchers from Columbia University, was the most comprehensive study in shaping the child protection program (United Nations Secretary General [UNSG], 2006, art. 48). Other evaluations and studies that informed this chapter include the *Evaluation to Improve the Quality of Psychosocial Support for Children and Adolescents in the Darfur Refugee Camps* (De Winter, 2005–2006), a real-time evaluation of the quality of psychosocial support provided in the child protection program, and the *Assessment of UNICEF Supported Programs for Reintegration of Children Formerly Associated with Armed Groups and Forces in Sudan* (Bremer, 2008). These assessments helped shape the program, enhance its effectiveness, and measure its impact.

The UN Mechanism to Monitor and Report on Grave Child Rights Violations (MRM) has also provided real-time information on the situation of children and child protection issues in armed conflict in Sudan. This mechanism was established in response to UN Security Council Resolution 1612 to help protect children in conflict-affected areas. It provides for the systematic gathering of accurate and timely information on grave violations committed against children in situations of armed conflict, including in Darfur. These violations include the killing or maiming of children, the recruitment or use of child soldiers, rapes and grave sexual violence against children, abduction of children, attacks against schools or hospitals, and the denial of humanitarian access. Several reports from the UN secretary-general addressing MRM helped inform this chapter (UNSG, 2006, 2007, 2009, 2010).

In the annual reports on children and armed conflicts, the UN secretary-general lists the names of groups/parties to conflict that commit such violations: Darfur has been included each year during the reporting period of this chapter. The Security Council asks listed parties to develop action plans—written and signed commitments between the United Nations and those parties—outlining concrete and time-bound steps to ensure compliance with international law and a more protected future for children. Once a party's full compliance with its action plan has been verified, the party is removed and delisted from the annexes of the secretary-general's report.[2]

In drawing on these documents and assessments of the experiences of children in the armed conflict in Darfur and of the child protection program that has been implemented to meet their needs, I highlight the importance of taking a holistic approach to supporting children in contexts of armed conflict. Even—and perhaps especially—in the midst of ongoing conflict, children need a strong child protection program that is shaped by their voices and designed to comprehensively build the capacity of state and nonstate actors, communities, families, and children themselves to deal with child protection issues. Lessons learned in Darfur have the potential to inform the development and implementation of child protection programs in other regions affected by armed conflict.

THE CONFLICT IN DARFUR: A CHILD RIGHTS AND GENDER-BASED ANALYSIS

The humanitarian situation in Sudan remains complex and volatile, with wide variations in vulnerabilities, needs, and challenges. The conflict in Darfur, the western region of Sudan, has been framed as one between pro-government

Arab tribes and African rebels. The pro-government tribes are referred to as the Janjaweed. Because these ethnic groups are native Arabic speaking, and some of their neighbors speak African languages in addition to Arabic, they are often called Arabs (UNSG, 2006). They have a nomadic lifestyle that involves the herding of camels and cattle. The Janjaweed are fighting African rebels, most of whom are farmers who reside in one geographical location.

A series of droughts in recent decades led to dwindling resources and, consequently, increased competition and conflict between farmers and herders. In this context, underdevelopment, neglect, and marginalization sparked localized conflicts in 2003 between the African tribes and the government and Janjaweed. After a report by the International Commission of Inquiry on Darfur (ICoI, 2005) documented violations of international human rights and humanitarian law perpetrated against civilian populations, the UN was called on to provide emergency support. A wide array of international actors has since become involved in the resulting humanitarian operation, delivering relief and deploying protective forces to establish areas of security.[3] However, humanitarian access has been seriously hampered by ongoing fighting in the region, attacks on humanitarian workers, and restrictions on movement imposed by the government in some parts of Darfur (UNSG, 2009).

As of 2009, this complex emergency was estimated to have affected some 4.7 million people, including more than 2.7 million people forced to leave their homes (UNICEF, 2010a). Most internally displaced persons (IDPs) have been accommodated in some 200 organized camps throughout Darfur. Some IDPs who are better off financially or have relatives in urban areas have moved to urban centers. Others have been scattered across small informal settlements around towns and near the border with Chad. More than 200,000 refugees have moved across the border to Chad (Government of National Unity & Government of Southern Sudan, 2008).

Children, representing nearly half of the population (UN & Partners, 2010), have been most severely affected by this crisis. They have been maimed and killed during aerial bombardments, bombings, attacks, and clashes by and between government forces and armed groups. They have been seriously injured and killed by landmines and unexploded ordnance (UNSG, 2006, 2007, 2009, 2010). They have also been subjected to sexual violence and recruitment into armed groups.

SEXUAL VIOLENCE AGAINST CHILDREN

Rape and other forms of sexual violence against children, particularly girls, have been widespread and systematic throughout the Darfur conflict (UNSG, 2009, art. 72) and are considered methods of warfare used to deliberately humiliate and forcibly displace girls and their families. Younger girls have been increasingly targeted (UNSG, 2007, art. 8, 103). In 2006, the UN secretary-general reported that an estimated 40% of victims were under 18 years old (UNSG, 2006, art. 33).

> While daily reports help illustrate the scope of sexual violence against children in Sudan, the majority of cases go unreported. Women report that most victims of sexual violence do not report the incident, in order to avoid scandals in their communities. For example: "When women are raped they do not scream because they are afraid and want to avoid a scandal; she begs the perpetrator not to rape her—if he does, she tells her husband, but he cannot do anything." (United Nations Population Fund [UNFPA] & UNICEF, 2005)

Social stigma and cultural taboos pose significant barriers to reporting of sexual violence. Victims of sexual- and gender-based violence also avoid filing police complaints because of lack of confidence in the police and justice system (Samar, 2009; see also Bremer et al., 2006). In some cases, victims who report being raped even face capital charges, including the capital charge of adultery, or *zina*. This risk is particularly high for unmarried pregnant females who cannot prove they were raped. To convict a man of rape, the testimony of four witnesses is required (United Nations High Commissioner for Human Rights [UNHCHR], 2005). As a result, very few victims have lodged official complaints regarding crimes committed against them or their families. Of the few cases where complaints have been made, most have not been properly pursued (ICoI, 2005). This illustrates the need for interventions that approach sexual violence holistically.

RECRUITMENT OF CHILD SOLDIERS

In Darfur, thousands of children—mostly male—have been recruited and used in the conflict by the military, paramilitary, and rebels/armed groups. The recruitment of children continues despite international law, including the UN Convention of the Rights of the Child (CRC, 1989), which calls for state parties to set up measures to prohibit and end this practice (UNSG, 2006, art. 19; UNSG, 2009, 2010).[4] In Darfur, almost all of the children recruited have been boys; however, girls have also been associated with armed groups in limited numbers (UNSG, 2009, art. 15). Girls who have been recruited have mainly filled military support roles, such as bringing food to soldiers (Bremer et al., 2006, p. 5). With the presence of a considerable number of armed forces and groups in the region, many of which have no clear legal status, it has been very difficult to allocate responsibility to specific groups for grave violations against children's rights.

Children as young as 12 years old have been recruited as soldiers in Darfur (UNSG, 2009, art. 15). The opportunity to earn an income provides an incentive for many children to join the armed forces and other armed groups. There is a cultural expectation in Darfur that all members, including children, play a role in protecting their community. The lack of alternative activities, such as secondary education and employment opportunities, also increases the risk of children joining armed groups (Bremer et al., 2006). Research with child soldiers in other contexts has also found that adolescents often join military or paramilitary forces to gain access to food, shelter, and safety (Rosen, 2007). Any child protection response must therefore consider the complex circumstances surrounding the child to successfully prevent the recruitment of child soldiers and reintegrate them back into communities, as discussed in the next section.

CHILDREN WITNESSING VIOLENCE

A significant number of children have been victims of violence or witnessed violent acts in Darfur. Many children have witnessed members of their family and community being raped, maimed, or killed during attacks on their villages. For instance, the following is a testimony collected from a young girl describing her run to safety:

> When we heard the guns and the screaming we ran as quickly as we could to the fields. . . . It was the right season for sorghum and so the plants were high enough to hide behind. But not for my father . . . he was killed as we escaped. (12-year-old internally displaced girl, Kalma Camp, Nyala, South Darfur; Elder, 2004)

Witnessing such violence can have long-lasting psychosocial impacts. In their study of children exposed to violence in southern Darfur, Morgos, Worden, and Gupta (2007) found a direct relationship between the number of violent war exposures and the negative impact on children's psychological well-being. Many children in their study had symptoms associated with traumatic reactions, depression, and grief. Separation from family members can be particularly traumatic for children, because it often results in the loss of primary caregivers, who play a crucial protective role in times of war (Morgos et al., 2007).

The psychosocial impacts of witnessing violence were evident in the stories of children. A 12-year-old boy discussed the effects of the violence on his daily life: "I sometimes have trouble sleeping at night because I remember the burning of my village" (Bremer et al., 2006). Community leaders in Darfur reported how they often heard a small boy who had been with his mother when she was killed crying out in the middle of the night (Bremer et al., 2006). The situation analysis in Darfur has found that children are at heightened risk of experiencing nightmares, trouble sleeping, restlessness, and anxiety, with aggression as the most common and visible sign of stress among children (Bremer et al., 2006).

In sum, girls and boys in the Darfur region have experienced and witnessed persistent violence in their communities. Many children, particularly girls, have been the victims of sexual violence. Many boys have been recruited into the military and other armed groups and have witnessed and participated in rapes, maiming, and killings. These experiences have negative psychosocial effects on children's lives, increasing their risk of distress, depression, and aggression. Studies from around the world suggest that the mental and social ramifications of conflict and violence can last for decades and have transgenerational impacts on the families of victims (UNICEF, 2013).

Because of the lack of child protection services and preventive measures in Sudan, the development and implementation of the program featured in this chapter required a holistic approach to child protection. This approach needed to consider the individual, family, and community levels in the reintegration of child soldiers and the prevention of children from joining military groups. It also needed to address the development of laws and policies in the area of child protection. To implement and enforce these laws and strengthen policies, both national systems and national capacity and local services were essential. Finally, it was critical that there be an educational component to build awareness of child protection issues among families and communities. These issues are explored in the next section.

INTERNATIONAL AND NATIONAL RESPONSES TO CHILD PROTECTION IN DARFUR

In this section, I examine national and international efforts to establish an effective "protective environment" and address the protection needs of children in an integrated, holistic, and systematic manner through the development and implementation of a child protection program in Darfur. These efforts entailed a variety of approaches and strategies, including the reintegration of child soldiers and support for children who have experienced violence, the reform of legislative and policy environments, strengthening the capacities of service providers, and transforming the knowledge and attitudes of families and communities.

REINTEGRATION OF CHILD SOLDIERS AND SUPPORT OF CHILDREN

Approaches to the reintegration of child soldiers and the provision of support to develop the skills of children and thereby prevent them from joining the military included educational interventions, designed to enable the local schools to expand access to education and skills training. This effort was accompanied by improving the quality of education by building the capacity of service providers, such as teachers. Education kits with materials to assist teachers in setting up schools and organize learning were provided and schools were rehabilitated. Educational interventions also occurred outside of the formal school system and included remedial education programs, accelerated learning programs, vocational training, and apprenticeships with local traders (UNICEF, 2010a). Children who had missed several years of schooling were able to register and attend remedial or accelerated classes or programs designed to help them catch up or advance their learning, respectively. For example, former child soldiers who participated in accelerated learning programs were able to enroll and complete their primary and intermediate schooling without age requirements and in a shorter period of time than normal by completing a condensed curriculum.

There were also efforts to prevent rape and sexual violence by offering skills training to girls and women and empowering them to engage in income-generating activities, such as handicrafts and sewing. Prevention efforts also included promoting the production and usage of fuel-efficient stoves, thereby reducing the number of times that women and girls would need to walk long distances outside the camps to collect firewood (UN & Partners, 2006a, 2006b).

Protective factors within families, schools, and communities have been shown to increase resilience in children who have experienced adversity (Boyden, 2009; United Nations, 2008a). In Darfur, there was a need for child-friendly centers and community or school activities to promote children's socialization, play, and learning, as well as places where children could obtain counseling (De Winter, 2005–2006, 2007; UN & Partners, 2008). Within these child-friendly centers, interventions focused on building the capacity of teachers and animators (e.g., program facilitators who directly engage in psychosocial activities with participants) through skills training. Children were provided with access to peer groups and other forms of social support. Children with more severe mental health needs were sometimes referred to professional psychosocial counseling and mental health services (De Winter, 2005–2006, 2007).

ADDRESSING GENDER INEQUALITY

There were challenges in addressing gender equality. Although the holistic intervention was planned to have equal participation of boys and girls, this goal was not easily achieved in many communities in Darfur, where cultural norms often limit girls' participation in school and other social activities (De Winter, 2005–2006, 2007). A general lack of interest in and attention to adolescent needs, particularly those of girls, and insufficient possibilities for community participation were highlighted as critical gaps and barriers to child protection. Efforts to address these issues focused on capacity-building initiatives. Core groups of skilled and highly motivated "model-animators" were trained in close cooperation with local and international partners, and creative and culturally appropriate activities were identified to promote the participation of girls and adolescents (De Winter, 2005–2006, 2007). After the training, "model-animators" were responsible for training and supervising other animators in providing psychosocial support to children (De Winter, 2007).

Although all children face problems in situations of armed conflict, girls often face greater challenges than boys in securing support for their rights. Girls are frequently rendered "invisible" and difficult to reach. The combination of traditional gender roles and the potential stigma of having been associated with armed forces keeps many girls out of the public sphere where services are provided. Therefore, interventions should encompass specific strategies to engage girls (Bremer, 2008). Programs for recovery and reintegration must be comprehensive and holistic to address all types of violence and abuse that girls may experience in contexts of armed conflict.

Reintegration is a long, ongoing process. The sources of funding and the programs supporting it must be rooted in permanent government institutions, such as national and state ministries and local authorities, as well as local civil society organizations (Bremer, 2008). An accurate technical analysis of the livelihood systems, market opportunities, and predictions for future demands is required to develop economically relevant training, alternative forms of education, and opportunities for economic reintegration. Providing long-lasting employment opportunities is increasingly being recognized as a key strategy to ensure sustainable reintegration that will not only help both boys and girls meet their needs and achieve personal goals but will also contribute to peace, stability and growth in their community (International Labour Organization [ILO], 2011)

LEGISLATIVE AND POLICY ENVIRONMENTS

UNICEF, the UN, and other stakeholders advocated successfully for the inclusion of specific provisions for the protection of children in the Darfur Peace Agreement (DPA, 2006). The DPA called for special protection for women, children, and vulnerable and disabled persons while placing an emphasis on gender (GoS, 2009, arts. 14, 15; UNSG, 2007, art. 105). It allowed UNICEF to continue its engagement with signatory armed groups in order to realize their commitments to protect children; UNICEF successfully negotiated and signed an Action Plan with the Sudan Liberation Army (SLA) Minnawi for the release and reintegration of children associated with this group ("SLM-Minawi Agrees to Hand over Darfur 'Children Soldiers'—UN," 2007; UN, 2009; UNSG, 2007, art. 105).

The technical support provided by UNICEF and its collaboration with the Sudanese government, particularly the National Council for Child Welfare, were also essential to address the protection gaps as part of the efforts to harmonize and bring Sudan's legislation in line with international standards. These international standards included the UN Convention on the Rights of Children (CRC, 1989) and its two optional protocols on the involvement of children in armed conflict and the sale of children, child prostitution, and child pornography. Among other reforms, the death penalty was abolished in Sudan for anyone under 18 years of age (UNICEF, 2010b). The reforms also established 18 years as the minimum age for recruitment into armed forces, while stipulating criminal penalties for individuals who recruit children and outlining penalties for other violations of humanitarian and human rights law.

STRENGTHENING CAPACITIES

Although quite challenging, efforts to strengthen coordination and promote leadership have been vital to developing better protection for children in Darfur. Effective interventions and approaches to child protection require integration across multiple sectors and actors, including social welfare, education, health, law enforcement, justice, and civil authorities. Building a durable protective environment also requires the mobilization and involvement of families, communities, and other nonstate actors. Cross-border coordination is very important in the context of the Darfurian conflict, given the distribution and movement of tribes across borders, as well as the movement of refugees from Darfur to neighboring countries.

HOLDING PERPETRATORS OF GRAVE VIOLATIONS AGAINST CHILDREN ACCOUNTABLE

The MRM has helped strengthen Darfur's capacity for child protection and supported the sustainability of the child protection program. Because of its political nature and the punitive measures that the Security Council can take to bring offending parties into compliance with international child rights standards, this monitoring mechanism has drawn attention to groups that have committed grave violations against children (Samar, 2009, arts. 14–16; UNSG, 2006, arts. 3, 31, 42, 44, 49, 50). Information on grave violations against children has been shared in global bimonthly notes, annual reports of the UN secretary-general on children and armed conflict, and two reports on Sudan. These annual reports have listed parties in Darfur that have recruited or used children and noted their involvement in other violations against children. The listing process has functioned as a naming exercise that indicates who the perpetrators have been and where they have been active (UN, 2007, arts. 3.6, 3.7).

However, progress in addressing violations against children has been slow, and no party to the conflict in Darfur has yet been delisted. The continued splintering and reorganization of armed groups and the lack of clear leadership in some groups have posed many challenges. Distinctions between legal and nonlegal militias are blurred, undermining the potential to hold armed groups responsible for child rights violations.

For child soldiers themselves, a focus on their reintegration has been maintained, even when they have been accused of crimes. The *Paris Principles and Guidelines on Children Associated with Armed Forces and Groups* (UN, 2007) specifies that children who are accused of crimes under international law should be considered primarily as victims of offenses against international law. They must be treated using a framework of restorative justice and social rehabilitation, consistent with international law, and alternatives to judicial proceedings must be sought (ICCPR, 1967; UN, 1985, 1990).

BUILDING NATIONAL CAPACITY TO IMPLEMENT LAWS, POLICIES, AND SYSTEMS IN CHILD PROTECTION

A focus on strengthening the social welfare system at state and national levels has also been critical to building capacity for child protection in Sudan. UNICEF has deployed international social workers to government ministries to assess the effectiveness of the existing system in each state of Darfur and to provide technical assistance (Bowring, 2008). A case management model has been developed, and on-the-job training has been provided to help build capacity (UNICEF, 2010a, p. 139; UNICEF, 2010c; UNSG, 2009, art. 65). Recommendations have also been made for restructuring the Department for Child and Family within the Ministry of Social Welfare, clarifying roles and responsibilities and setting up referral mechanisms (Bowring, 2008).

Emphasis has been placed on the establishment of a holistic system for children and women in conflict with the law, including child offenders, victims, and witnesses. The Police Higher Authority/Director General requires all states to establish Child and Family Protection Units, including in areas where women and girls are especially vulnerable, such as Darfur (UNSG, 2009, art. 64); these efforts have scaled up rapidly (UNICEF, 2008c). These units offer a "one-stop-shop," providing specialized and professional services to help manage cases involving different types of violence, abuse, and exploitation against children and women (UNICEF, 2008c). Emphasis has been placed on developing child-friendly and gender-sensitive procedures. Female police have been deployed to work in these units, and the number of female police officers working in the units and more broadly within the police forces has also been gradually increased (UNICEF, 2008c). Capacity building and on-the-job training have been provided for female police deployed as part of this cadre, as well as for other members of police forces who manage cases involving children and women (UNICEF, 2008c). Connections have also been established between these special units and other service providers.

Efforts have also been made to promote key institutional developments within the judicial system, including the establishment of a special court and prosecution office for children in each state that ensures confidentiality and privacy for children and reduces their risk of intimidation during court proceedings (GoS, 2009, arts. 95, 96; UNSG, 2009, art. 64). Fostering a protective environment requires collaboration between government institutions and the humanitarian community. Efforts to build capacity are more effective when they are geared toward organizational and institutional development.

BUILDING AWARENESS OF CHILD PROTECTION

The child protection program has helped build awareness of relevant laws, international standards, and existing services among children, communities, service providers, and peacekeeping personnel in Sudan (GoS, 2009, arts. 35–39; UNSG, 2009, art. 65). Commanders and other members of armed forces, including military groups, paramilitary groups, armed groups, and peacekeeping missions, have received training on international legal instruments, standards for protecting children in armed conflict, and the monitoring and reporting of child rights violations. They have also received training on codes of conduct related to sexual violence and exploitation, as well as on how to interview and care for survivors of gender-based violence. A child rights unit has been created within the Sudan Armed Forces (SAF) to strengthen the protection of children within the armed forces (UNICEF, 2008b).

A public multimedia awareness campaign, "Watch-Listen-Talk," was also launched in 2008 to address a wide range of protection concerns. It targeted a core audience of family- and community-level actors, focusing on child recruitment, children in contact with the law, and sexual violence. It aimed to raise awareness and understanding of the dangers and harms that children face in the conflict, the effective actions that families and communities can take to protect children, and the available support services (GoS, 2009, arts. 41, 42; UNSG, 2009, art. 64). Key messages were communicated through radio, television, mass print media (e.g., newspapers, magazines), and small print media (e.g., posters, banners, leaflets, outdoor notice boards). Children and other community members also participated in a wide range of awareness-raising activities, including dance, drama, poetry, sports, and music initiatives (UNICEF, 2008a). Engaging children in active dialogue and promoting respect for their perspectives are critical to empowering them as actors in their own protection and that of their peers (UN, 2008).

A coherent and holistic response to the protection risks and vulnerabilities that children face requires systematic consideration of the factors contributing to the establishment of an effective "protective environment" for children.

Protection programming cannot be successful if those who develop and implement it do not understand and address the interacting risks and vulnerabilities that children face as a result not only of political violence, conflict, and displacement but also of preexisting customs and practices (Bremer et al., 2006). Harmful practices and beliefs can be deeply entrenched in communities. Some forms of violence are rooted in unequal and discriminatory gender dynamics and are exacerbated by societal acceptance.

To enact widespread social change requires communication and social mobilization across a broad range of actors, with an emphasis on influencing attitudes and social norms to promote understanding and support for child protection efforts. Open discussion and the engagement of children themselves require strong support from communities and civil society (UN, 2008). Legislation can contribute to changes in social norms, and regulations and training aiming to reduce violence and abuse against children are more effective when backed by social consensus (UN, 2008).

REFLECTIONS ON LESSONS LEARNED

The child protection program in Darfur yields lessons that may be helpful to policy makers and practitioners in other contexts of armed conflict. Child protection work, by its very nature, is extremely complex, requiring cultural awareness and sensitivity. It is made even more difficult in contexts of ongoing armed conflict because of political violence and displacement. In the Darfurian context, a lack of existing services meant that systems and local capacity had to be built from the ground up. For instance, a lack of birth registration data made it difficult to enforce laws against child recruitment when they were implemented. As a result, a civil birth registry had to be developed.

Child protection implicates other systems as well, such as health care, education, and justice systems, all of which need to be brought into line with international standards. At the inception of the child protection program in Darfur, the justice system was not set up to deal with children as children: It treated them as adults, and specific legal and administrative services and frameworks were not available to grant children access to age-appropriate processes and justice. Children under 18 faced the same risk as adults of being arrested and detained for certain offenses and of being sentenced to death by capital punishment. Legislative and institutional changes and policies had to be developed and implemented to address these issues. Moreover, during the process of program development and implementation, formalized training courses were initially used to build capacity within relevant ministries or institutions. However, over time it was found that it was more effective to place experts within the specific ministry or institution, where they could work with staff on a daily basis and in a practical manner.

Developing and strengthening the child protection program in Darfur also meant confronting social and cultural norms and ideas regarding childhood that may not be congruent with international standards—for example, sociocultural norms that limit girls' participation in certain activities that are considered appropriate for boys only, as well as norms that look positively on boys wearing a uniform. From the outset of any child protection program, a gendered analysis must be coupled with an understanding of local cultural and political contexts. Education is essential to raise awareness and acceptance among families and wider community members of international standards for children's rights.

Another challenge relates to the engagement of local, state, and national governments, which is made especially difficult and contentious in times of armed conflict. Fostering ownership of government agencies over child protection programs is essential to assuring their long-term sustainability. The MRM has been vital to this process in Darfur because it has provided evidence-based information to guide advocacy efforts, help hold parties to the conflict accountable to international standards, and enhance protection responses. Yet despite the significant progress made by the child protection program in Darfur, challenges remain. Services must be integrated, an effective referral system must be developed, psychosocial support must be mainstreamed within the education system, mobile services must be established to reach remote localities, and communities and families need ongoing education to change harmful attitudes and practices and increase their understanding of child protection issues. Developing and implementing a national child protection program requires a great deal of investment—not only in monetary terms but also in time and effort. Sustainability must be a priority.

CONCLUSIONS

In this chapter, I argued that a holistic approach to child protection in conflict-affected areas is essential. It is critically important to include the perspectives and experiences of children in the planning, development, implementation, and evaluation of programs for child protection.

In general, child protection work is extremely complex and staff intensive because of the politically and culturally sensitive nature of child protection issues. It was made more difficult in Darfur during the reporting period (2005–2010) because of the numerous and wide-ranging protection issues that existed, as well as the tense political environment. During this period, the Sudanese government expelled 13 international nongovernmental organizations (INGOs), the majority of which focused on protection issues, from the region after the International Criminal Court issued an arrest warrant for the president of Sudan. This added to the challenges of establishing, maintaining, and evaluating a protection program for children. Nonetheless, even in this difficult context, it was possible to highlight and address sensitive child protection issues through investments in supporting assessments, research, analysis, and evaluations of the situation and the programming.

Providing a holistic protection response has been critical. Social services, including psychosocial support and case management, were nonexistent in most of the conflict-affected areas of Darfur prior to the emergency. There were also huge gaps in the country's legal and administrative frameworks, and as a result, specific services for children were not available to ensure their access to justice. Similarly, the number of educational facilities and schools was insufficient to accommodate the huge influx of displaced children. The emergency has provided an opportunity to adopt new protective legislation for children and build up basic social services in a comprehensive manner. As this work continues, a holistic response can help ensure that children receive the services and support they need to address child protection issues. Challenges remain in establishing systems for quality assurance, including supervision and oversight.

Notes

The opinions expressed in this chapter represent mine alone. Although I have worked with the United Nations Children's Fund (UNICEF), the views expressed in this chapter are not necessarily shared by UNICEF or the UN. I would like to thank Dr. Bo Viktor Nylund for reviewing this chapter and providing valuable and constructive comments and suggestions. Dr. Nylund served as Chief of Child Protection in UNICEF Sudan from 2006–2008.

1. "Children" refers to every person younger than 18 years old.
2. Delisting can be granted only after the United Nations verifies that all activities included in the signed action plan have been successfully implemented and those responsible are held accountable.

3. This included the African Union Peace Keeping Mission (AU) followed by the deployment of the United Nations–African Union Mission in Darfur (UNAMID).

4. The term *child soldier* is defined as "a child associated with an armed force or group." According to the UN Paris Principles and Guidelines on Children Associated with Armed Forces and Groups (2007), this includes any person younger than 18 years of age who is or has been recruited or used by an armed force or group in any capacity, including but not limited to children used as fighters, cooks, porters, messengers, spies, or for sexual purposes. It does not only refer to a child who is taking or has taken a direct part in hostilities.

References

Bremer, M. (2008). *Assessment of UNICEF supported programs for reintegration of children formerly associated with armed groups and forces in Sudan*. Khartoum: UNICEF.

Bremer, M., Ager, A., & Boothby, N. (2006). *Situation analysis of child protection in Darfur*. Khartoum: UNICEF & Columbia University.

Bowring, L. (2008). *An analysis of the knowledge, attitudes and practices of social workers*. West Darfur, Sudan: UNICEF.

Boyden. J. (2009). Risk and capability in the context of adversity: Children's contributions to household livelihoods in Ethiopia. *Children, Youth and Environments, 19*(2), 111–137.

Convention on the Rights of the Child (CRC). (1989, November 20). 1577 U.N.T.S. 3. Retrieved from www.ohchr.org/en/professionalinterest/pages/crc.aspx.

Darfur Peace Agreement (DPA). (2006, May 5). SDN-SLM/A. Retrieved from www .un.org/zh/focus/southernsudan/pdf/dpa.pdf.

De Winter, M. (2005–2006). *Evaluation to improve the quality of psychosocial support for children and adolescents in the Darfur refugee camps*. Khartoum: UNICEF.

De Winter, M. (2007). Improving the quality of psychosocial support for children and adolescents in the Darfur refugee camps. *Intervention, 5*(1), 61–66.

Elder, J. (2004, June 29). A child's story of horrific attack. *Frontline Diary*. Retrieved from www2.unicef.org:60090/infobycountry/sudan_22054.html.

Government of National Unity & Government of Southern Sudan. (2008). *A situation analysis of children in Sudan*: Khartoum: UNICEF.

Government of Sudan (GoS). (2009). *Consideration of reports submitted by states parties under article 8 (1) of the Optional Protocol to the Convention on the Rights of the Child on the involvement of children in armed conflict: Initial report: Sudan* (CRC/C/OPAC/SDN/1). Geneva: UN Committee on the Rights of the Child.

International Commission of Inquiry on Darfur (ICoI). (2005). *Report of the International Commission of Inquiry on Darfur to the United Nations Secretary-General*.

Geneva: United Nations. Retrieved from www.un.org/news/dh/sudan/com_inq _darfur.pdf.

International Covenant on Civil and Political Rights (ICCPR). (1966, December 16). 999 U.N.T.S. 171. Retrieved from www.ohchr.org/en/professionalinterest/pages /ccpr.aspx.

International Labour Organization (ILO). (2011). *Economic reintegration of children formerly associated with armed forces and armed groups.* Geneva: ILO International Programme on the Elimination of Child Labour.

Morgos, D., Worden, J. W., & Gupta, L. (2007). Psychosocial effects of war experiences among displaced children in southern Darfur. *OMEGA: Journal of Death and Dying, 56*(3), 229–253.

Rosen, D.M. (2007). Child soldiers, international humanitarian law, and the globalization of childhood. *American Anthropologist, 109*(2), 296–306.

Samar, S. (2009). *Report of the special rapporteur on the situation of human rights in the Sudan* (A/Hrc/11/14). Geneva: Human Rights Council. Retrieved from www2 .ohchr.org/english/bodies/hrcouncil/docs/11session/A.HRC.11.14_AUV.pdf.

SLM-Minawi agrees to hand over Darfur "children soldiers"—UN. (2007, June 11). *Sudan Tribune.* Retrieved from www.sudantribune.com/spip.php?article22334.

UNICEF. (2008a, June 16). *On the Day of African Child, UNICEF in Sudan calls for children to be heard and better protected* [Press release]. Retrieved from www .unicef.org/media/files/Day_of_the_African_Child.doc.

UNICEF. (2008b, December 23). *UNICEF signs agreement with Sudanese government and partners to work together to protect children in Sudan* [Press release]. Retrieved from www.unicef.org/media/media_46933.html.

UNICEF. (2008c). *UNICEF Sudan: Family and child protection units* (Technical Briefing Paper 3). Khartoum: Author. Retrieved from www.unicef.org/sudan /Briefing_paper3-CP_Units.pdf.

UNICEF. (2010a). *Humanitarian action report, 2010: Partnering for children in emergencies.* Geneva: Author. Retrieved from www.unicef.org/har2010/.

UNICEF. (2010b, January 7). *Statement by UNICEF's representative in Sudan to mark the official celebration of the ratification of the Federal Child Act* [Press release]. Retrieved from www.unicef.org/sudan/media_5990.html.

UNICEF. (2010c). *UNICEF annual report for Sudan.* Retrieved from www.unicef .org/about/annualreport/files/Sudan_COAR_2010.pdf.

UNICEF. (2013). *A post-2015 world fit for children: Sustainable development starts and ends with safe, healthy and well-educated children.* New York: Author.

UNICEF & Government of Sudan (GoS). (2008). *National and baseline study on children and youth in Sudan.* Khartoum: Author.

United Nations. (1985, November 29). *United Nations standard minimum rules for the administration of juvenile justice ("the Beijing rules")* (A/RES/40/33). New York:

UN General Assembly. Retrieved from www.ohchr.org/en/professionalinterest/pages/ccpr.aspx.

United Nations. (1990, Dec. 14). *United Nations guidelines for the prevention of juvenile delinquency (the Riyadh guidelines)* (A/RES/45/112). New York: UN General Assembly. Retrieved from www.un.org/documents/ga/res/45/a45r112.htm.

United Nations. (2007). *The Paris principles and guidelines for children associated with armed forces or armed groups.* Paris: Author.

United Nations. (2008). *UNICEF child protection strategy.* New York: UN Economic and Social Council. Retrieved from www.unicef.org/protection/files/CP_Strategy_English.pdf.

United Nations. (2009, July 27). *UN demobilizes first batch of child soldiers in Darfur* [Press release]. Retrieved from www.un.org/apps/news/story.asp?NewsID=31597#.VXZavaTbLIU.

United Nations & Partners. (2006a). *2006 work plan for Sudan: Mid-year review.* Geneva: UN Office for the Coordination of Humanitarian Affairs.

United Nations & Partners. (2006b). *2007 work plan for Sudan.* Geneva: UN Office for the Coordination of Humanitarian Affairs.

United Nations & Partners. (2008). *2008 work plan for Sudan: Mid-year review.* Geneva: UN Office for the Coordination of Humanitarian Affairs.

United Nations & Partners. (2010). *2011 work plan for Sudan.* Geneva: UN Office for the Coordination of Humanitarian Affairs.

United Nations High Commissioner for Human Rights (UNHCR). (2005). *Access to justice for victims of sexual violence: Report of the United Nations High Commissioner for Human Rights.* Geneva: UN Human Rights Council.

United Nations Populations Fund (UNFPA) & UNICEF. (2005). *The effects of conflict on the health and well-being of women and girls in Darfur.* Khartoum: Author.

United Nations Secretary-General (UNSG). (2006). *Children and armed conflict in the Sudan* (S/2006/662). New York: UN Security Council. Retrieved from www.un.org/ga/search/view_doc.asp?symbol=S/2006/662&Lang=E&Area=UNDOC.

United Nations Secretary-General (UNSG). (2007). *Children and armed conflict* (A/62/609–S/2007/757). New York: UN Security Council. Retrieved from www.un.org/ga/search/view_doc.asp?symbol=A/62/609&Lang=E&Area=UNDOC.

United Nations Secretary-General (UNSG). (2009). *Children and armed conflict in the Sudan* (S/2009/84). New York: UN Security Council. Retrieved from www.un.org/ga/search/view_doc.asp?symbol=S/2009/84&Lang=E&Area=UNDOC.

United Nations Secretary-General (UNSG). (2010). *Children and armed conflict* (A/64/742–S/2010/181). New York: UN Security Council. Retrieved from www.un.org/ga/search/view_doc.asp?symbol=A/64/742&Lang=E&Area=UNDOC.

13

MEETING THE NEEDS OF CHILDREN AFFECTED BY CONFLICT
Teacher Training and Development in South Sudan

Jan Stewart

EDUCATION IN POSTCONFLICT AND FRAGILE ENVIRONMENTS

Increasing attention has been given to education and its critical role in reconstruction and peace-building process in postconflict societies (Barakat, Connolly, Hardman, & Sundaram, 2013; Bush & Saltarelli, 2000; Davies, 2004; Paulson, 2011). International guidelines such as Education for All (EFA) and the Millennium Development Goals (MDG) have focused on the function of education and how it contributes to peace building (Smith Ellison, 2014). Studies have highlighted the two sides or faces of education and the role it has in both fueling and mitigating conflict (Bush & Saltarelli, 2000), as well as the links and influences between conflict and education (Brown, 2011); for example, the ways that school systems have reinforced gender inequalities and subsequently contributed to conflicts (Davies, 2002, 2004). Despite the conflicting discourse, education can play a critical role in facilitating stability, establishing a sense of routine or normalcy, and inspiring hope for a peaceful future (Mendenhall, 2014). Thus, the World Bank (2005) emphasizes education as a critical postconflict intervention for "reshaping the future" with the potential to shore up support for peace and provide a "peace dividend." As Kirk (2007) notes, if a lack of education leads to instability, then the imperative to prioritize education in fragile states is essential.

Conflict has a devastating impact on the infrastructure of educational institutions and community structures, and it has a direct influence on the psychosocial and mental health of students and teaching staff (Bretherton, Weston, & Zbar, 2005; World Bank, 2005). Conflict leaves schools weakened, damaged, and underresourced (World Bank, 2005) at a time when children and youth need schooling most to help support and rebuild their lives. War can burden children with physical injuries and disabilities, as well as psychological issues related to loss, displacement, and traumatic memories of violence (Denov, 2010). Some children have only lived during times of war, and the psychosocial effects of trauma can last for decades (Cheney, 2005). There is consensus on the need to get schools functioning following a crisis and for building sustainable community capacity that can support complementary programs such as those addressing psychosocial and livelihoods issues (Barakat et al., 2013; Davies, 2011). Although researchers have largely been concerned with conflict analysis, they have paid attention more recently to the concepts of peace building and peace education (Smith, 2011).

This chapter first examines how conflict has affected both the teachers and the students of South Sudan, demonstrating the need for comprehensive peace education for all students and specialized peace education and conflict sensitivity training for teachers. This discussion is followed by an overview of an ongoing research program in South Sudan and the development and implementation of a professional development workshop for pre-service (student) teachers and in-service (practicing) teachers held in Juba, South Sudan. The chapter concludes with some reflective comments on the approach used in the training, the impact that the training had on both facilitators and participants, and the need for widespread peace education training and relevant research in the area of education in postconflict environments. Peace education, as conceptualized herein, not only provided teachers with strategies for teaching and building peace but it was also a catalyst for teachers' own healing and recovery from the effects of war.

The research program was guided by the following four questions: (1) How has conflict affected the teachers and students in South Sudan? (2) What is currently being implemented in the area of peace education? (3) How might educators more effectively respond to the needs of students who have been affected by war? (4) What training do teachers need to provide support to students in South Sudan? Combining the voices of teachers, university students, secondary students, nongovernmental organization (NGO) representatives, and ministry officials, the inquiry included semi-structured interviews, focus group discussions, and pre- and post-workshop questionnaires given to teachers who participated in the training course.

CONTEXT: SOUTH SUDAN

Emerging after more than 20 years of civil war and conflict, South Sudan became the world's newest country in July 2011, reporting some of the lowest poverty, education, and development indicators in the world (UNICEF, 2011, 2014; World Bank, 2013). It is estimated that more than 2.5 million people died and more than 4 million people were displaced from their homes during the years of war (UNHCR, 2014a). Schools and health facilities were burned down or forced to close, teachers were displaced or fled the country, and generations of children were denied the basic right to an education (Ministry of General Education and Instruction, 2012). Brown (2012) reports that more than one million of the children eligible for primary school are not enrolled in school, and enrollment in secondary level is below 10% of eligible teens. The primary school dropout rate is around 23%, and the secondary school dropout rate is at 61%. Gender inequalities are pronounced, with only 6% of 13-year-old girls completing primary school. Brown (2012) further notes that girls in South Sudan are twice as likely to die in childbirth than they are to finish secondary school. The South Sudan Household Health Survey in 2010 reported a country-wide literacy rate for women of 13.4% (Republic of South Sudan, 2010).

In December 2013, President Kiir ousted Vice-President Riek Machar, which led to massive violence between the Nuer and Dinka tribes and resulted in over 100,000 deaths and more than 155,000 internally displaced persons (IDPs) or people living in IDP-like situations (UNHCR, 2014a). More than 167,000 have fled to Ethiopia since the conflict erupted in December 2013 (UNHCR, 2014b). Despite a peace agreement signed in May 2014, ethnic-based political violence continues in several states, and many South Sudanese people remain in camps, too afraid to return to their communities. Border disputes with Sudan persist, and arguments over land and cattle continue to fuel intra-state and interstate conflicts. Youth, parents, and community members see education as the most important peace dividend, and emphasis has been placed on the development of life skills and peace-building programs at all levels, ranging from early childhood initiatives to secondary education and programs for children not formally enrolled in school (UNICEF, 2014). Combining skills, resources, and professional networks, I collaborated with a country-based NGO to create and implement a research and development program to build teacher capacity for teaching peace education and sustainable development in South Sudan. In this chapter the NGO is assigned a pseudonym (EDUCARE) to protect the anonymity of the participants and facilitators.

As both a philosophy and a practice (Harris & Morrison, 2013), peace education needs to be a collaborative and evolving process that extends beyond the school context to include the home, community, and the larger society (Stewart, 2014). It should not be an isolated part of the curriculum, but rather should be integrated into all aspects of it and the teaching process. Teachers' attitudes, behaviors, and ways of interacting with students must also promote a culture of peace, respect, and acceptance. Teaching peace education in a hostile and authoritative environment, where children are punished or shamed for their behavior, will not contribute to a more peaceful society. Instead, it will promulgate issues of marginalization, inequality, and injustice that often fuel violence.

Inherent in the peace-building process is the dialogical process between the teacher and student in which both work together to uncover problems and explore solutions. Peace education is not taught to children; it is taught with children. Engaging students in the peace-building process not only acknowledges their collective sense of agency but also nurtures the skills and characteristics that are necessary to recognize, reason, and ethically act against injustice (Crawford & Gil, 2013). Engaging youth in designing peace education programs, and providing them the leadership opportunities for implementing peace activities, forms the essential foundation for a sustainable program and a peaceful future. When students have ownership of a program, they are more likely to participate, engage in the learning, and ensure its long-term success.

Working in collaboration with a faculty member from the University of Juba and the consultant from EDUCARE, I interviewed secondary students from three schools in Juba who were actively engaged in peace-building activities. In addition, 10 student-teachers, who were enrolled in the pre-service teaching program at the University of Juba, were invited to attend a peace-building and counseling course. The next section provides a summary of how peace building was conceptualized and a brief explanation of the intersections between peace education and sustainability.

THEORETICAL FRAMEWORK: A BIOECOLOGICAL MODEL FOR PEACE BUILDING

The aim of this continuing research program in South Sudan is to identify the pre-service and in-service training needs of teachers and to use this knowledge to inform the content of future professional development workshops and university teacher preparation courses in the field of peace education. According to Galtung's (1969) the purpose of positive peace is to find practical strategies to address the needs of children who have been affected by war and violence.

Human rights education, social justice, and education for sustainable development are inextricably linked to the concepts of peace and peace education (Stewart, 2014). Yet Reardon (1988) posits that there is a difference between educating for peace and educating about peace; whereas the latter provides information about the importance of peace, the former provides concrete skills to *enact* peace. Concrete teaching strategies and practical activities that teach peace-building skills are required, and talking to teachers and students about their needs in relation to peace education and peace-building skills is essential. Paulson and Rappleye (2007) argue that theoretical and epistemological recommendations made by academics seldom address how to create practical programming that can be realistically implemented by practitioners. Moreover, ill-conceived training initiatives developed by outsiders, without the consultation of those who will ultimately implement the strategies, are doomed to fail. For education to play a critical role in the development of postconflict environments, there needs to be a comprehensive consultation process involving actors in multiple ecological systems: parents, students, teachers, district leaders, NGO staff, and ministry representatives.

Using Urie Bronfenbrenner's (2001) bioecological model, I developed a framework that included the various ecological systems that influence students' personal, social, and academic development. These ecological systems, ranging from the micro to the macro level, change over time. To Bronfenbrenner's model, I added the smaller "nano-system" (Stewart, 2011) or the systems that operate within the micro-system. The nano-system includes more "intimate systems" of relationships, which provide support for the individual. While micro-systems describe the context within which the individual lives and includes possible relations, the nano-system describes the patterns and groups of close relationships that exist within one's life. The inclusion of a nano-system perspective provides a closer examination into the people from the micro-system who connected most intimately with the students and who were instrumental in their lives. After the nano-system, the micro-system is the next closest system to the student with which he or she interacts; the meso-system embodies the various connections between the systems; the exo-system represents the distant systems that indirectly influence the student; the macro-system embodies the overarching ideologies or beliefs reflected in the culture that influence all systems; and the chrono-system represents the changes to the individual over time. The individual's biology will also affect his or her development, and thus this framework is more aptly called the "bioecological model." One of its key assumptions is that environment influences the individual and the environment can also be influenced by the individual (Bronfenbrenner, 2001).

By way of example, a child living in an internally displaced camp will be influenced by her physical condition (biology), as well as her family, cultural leaders, and community members. She may be influenced by the norms or roles established by the larger society that may limit her freedom or educational choices. Her family may be at higher risk for crime and violence, which may affect her overall development. An individual may emerge as most influential in her development, playing a key role in facilitating her long-term success, thus forming a nano-system of support.

This model and adaptations of it are widely used in studies examining human development and the role of ecological systems in the lives of children (Tudge, Mokrova, Hatfield, & Karnik, 2009). For the purposes of this study, the model provided a structure for determining who needed to be interviewed and what systems needed to be explored to better understand the educational issues affecting children and their teachers in a postconflict environment. Working collaboratively with the University of Juba faculty and the EDUCARE consultants helped me gain access to participants and to receive permission from the Ministry of Education, Science and Technology to invite teachers and students to the training.

METHODS

Despite political instability and difficulty traveling within the country that necessitated changes to the overall plan, the research program in South Sudan, which began in 2010, was able to expand its scope. Building on the theoretical underpinnings of the bioecological framework (Bronfenbrenner, 2001; Bronfenbrenner & Morris, 1999), the research program extended outside of the school and into the communities and organizations where people were actively engaged in helping children affected by conflict. Spanning over a period of four years, this research includes data from two pilot teacher training programs in 2012 (one in Juba involving 16 teachers and one in Aweil with 20 teachers); a week-long peace-building and counseling skills course with 45 participants in June 2014; and, semi-structured interviews with 22 primary and secondary teachers, 12 secondary-level students, 2 faculty members, and 6 representatives of NGOs between 2012 and 2014. The initial pilot teacher training projects in 2012 indicated a dire need for teacher training, infrastructure development, and personal support to cope with the effects of conflict, and the research program evolved to address these needs. Teachers requested a more in-depth exploration of how best to help children who were affected by war and training addressing anger management, peace education, guidance and counseling, and life skills, and this formed the curriculum for the peace-building and counseling skills course.

The Ministry of Education, Science and Technology (MoEST) of South Sudan granted permission to invite two to three teachers from specific schools in Juba to attend the week-long course. Written invitation letters were then sent to the Director General for Education, and the schools and their administrative staff selected the teachers. In total, the peace-building and counseling course consisted of 30 teachers, one female and one male, from 15 schools in Juba; 3 ministry representatives, 2 faculty members from the University of Juba; and 10 university students from the teacher training program at the University of Juba.

The 45 participants who took part in the peace-building and counseling skills course completed pre- and post-workshop questionnaires and took part in a series of focus group discussions held during the week of training. The course provided the opportunity for teachers, students, faculty members, and ministry officials to learn together and enabled the researchers to gain a deeper understanding of programming and training in a conflict-affected context.

To begin, the purpose of the course was discussed and participants were asked if they would provide consent for facilitators to collect data through questionnaires, field notes, and observations. A signed letter of consent was obtained from each participant. In the first session, participants were given a survey questionnaire about the needs and challenges for teachers in South Sudan. Then they rotated around the room in groups of four to five and discussed the six research questions; these small group discussions served to guide the large group discussion. The research questions related to the needs of children in South Sudan, the current strategies being used to support students, the training teachers have received, and what needs to be done to better support the students and teachers in South Sudan. These questionnaires and discussions helped determine how best to focus the rest of the workshop. Participants also volunteered to submit work samples and photos of the training to assist the researchers with collecting data. As the lead facilitator, I took field notes throughout the workshop. In addition, the senior consultant from EDUCARE, two faculty members from the University of Juba, and one EDUCARE youth worker took notes. At the end of each day, we five team members met to discuss observations and the key themes as they emerged from the participants. All field notes, questionnaires, and surveys were compiled and analyzed following the training.

After the course, at the suggestion of the participants, additional semi-structured interviews were conducted with 15 secondary-level students who were involved in school-based, extracurricular, life skills and peace-building clubs in three public schools in Juba. After MoEST sent a letter to the administrators of those three schools requesting the voluntary participation of the students, the faculty members guiding the clubs were contacted and informed about the research study. They asked the club members if they would consent to being interviewed for the purpose of sharing their stories and insights with researchers who were working to build additional peace education programs and teacher training programs in South Sudan. Permission from the head of each school was granted before the interviews began, and written consent was obtained from all students. Some of the students preferred to present their work in written form, which was permitted, and everyone participated anonymously.

Educational action research recognizes that there are no fixed goals to suit a desired outcome; rather, the role of the researcher or teacher is to work with participants to identify a focus, collect and analyze data, and then use new understandings to transform their practice. From our perspective as facilitators/researchers, our purpose was to understand the situation more fully by collaborating with participants to explore the constraints of the context and to identify the teachers' professional challenges. Although numerous main themes and subsidiary themes emerged, this chapter focuses on how children and teachers have been affected by war, how conflict influenced their current personal and professional life, and how peace education can contribute to a sustainable future. The following section includes examples and excerpts from the participants' comments to substantiate the findings and to support our conclusions and arguments.

It was the process of doing the activities in the peace-building and counseling skills course that enabled the group participants and the facilitators to gain a greater understanding and enhanced knowledge of the situation in South Sudan. Discussions revolved around personal and professional identity, the role of peace education in South Sudan, and the contextual implications and challenges of working in a postconflict situation. Dialogues on how to adapt lessons, how to reflect on content with students, and how to talk to students about difficult experiences provided the most insight into the current postconflict situation, the overall morale of the teachers, and the systemic issues affecting their teaching and learning. During the course, the facilitators involved participants in the exploration of theory in peace education and used experiential activities to generate a broader discussion on how theory could be adapted or linked to their current practice. Teachers learned practical lessons in peace education, gaining increased understanding of pedagogical methods that fostered student-centered learning. Together, the interviews, focus groups, and course also helped provide a composite picture of the future needs for training and development in this area. Collectively, we established a network of teachers, faculty, and students who are continuing to engage in research and development.

FINDINGS AND DISCUSSION

The people of South Sudan are experiencing what is best described as "collective trauma": No one is immune to the effects of conflict, and the population continues to be divided based on ethnicity, tribal affiliation, gender, and cultural beliefs. The research revealed tremendous disruption to daily living, feelings of loss and hopelessness, and overriding feelings of instability due to political tensions and the warring factions. Yet, participants most frequently discussed "how things were," as opposed to "how things are;" they talked about the conflict as having ended, and they referred to the present time as the start of peace and rebuilding. The overarching drive to rebuild the country and to build peace among the people seemed to motivate teachers, students, government officials, and NGOs to come together for reconciliation and healing. Conversations inevitably focused on what they wanted to do to create a better future. Most adults indicated that they had to put their efforts into helping what some referred to as a "lost generation of children." Even though teachers had their own trauma to deal with and were struggling to cope with their experiences, most felt an obligation to put aside their own feelings to help the children. Some even discussed having to hide how they were feeling and putting up a front to be strong for their students.

Throughout the teacher training course, it became clear that the style of teaching and learning we used was new to many of the participants. Some of the teachers said that they were aware of student-centered teaching, but had not yet practiced it. When the teachers engaged in many of the activities, we found that they were openly sharing their experiences of pain and uncertainty, using the group as a therapeutic or supportive mechanism for healing. As this sharing became more evident, the facilitators modified the course structure to include more opportunities for small group reflection and to give time for participants to discuss issues in an accepting environment. This model of counseling, teaching, and training provided a way of identifying conflict drivers and triggers, as well as unifying people and groups. With the representation of students, teachers, faculty, and government and NGO staff, the workshop laid the foundation for a multi-ecological examination of problems and the collaborative generation of solutions. Collective trauma calls for communities to come together and recognize a collective process of reconciliation and healing that will deepen connectedness and reduce divisive relationships.

DISRUPTION, LOSS, AND INSTABILITY

Having endured decades of conflict, South Sudan's independence was accompanied by hope for a more peaceful future and the expectation of more prosperity. Instead, political instability, corruption, and instability were quick to emerge in the newly formed country, bringing a resurgence of conflict and violence. Students and teachers discussed the recent conflict in December 2013, displaying overriding feelings of disappointment sadness, and hopelessness. They mentioned forced displacement, violence, and disruptions to daily living, as well as the loss of homes, family, and friends. Kadi, a 16-year-old student, commented, "Conflict brings loss of understanding, loss of culture, loss of land, loss of religion and loss of education." This sense of loss was coupled with both feelings of fear that more conflict would occur and sadness about the impact the conflict has had on the newly formed nation. Ester, a 16-year-old female student, acknowledged feelings of fear and she reflected on how the conflict affected students and the nation:

> On my part as a student, the conflict affected me internally and also in my studies . . . the schools were not opened on the set month of February . . . our teachers . . . some got injured till now are in hospitals and others died so suddenly and sad . . . people moved to other countries so our population is very low and who will take care of this three year old nation . . . I live in fear and sadness because anytime disagreements may occur and that really makes pain and sadness.

Disruptions in studies and loss of education due to instability can profoundly affect the long-term economic prospects of children (Machel, 2001). Lack of educational opportunities contributes to a sense of hopelessness about the future, leading to the recruitment of youth into armed groups, forced labor, drug trafficking, and prostitution (Davies, 2011). Wessells (2005) notes that youth join armed groups out of "disaffection with a political, social, and economic system that has failed them" (p. 365). As an 18-year-old male student stated, "If they can all get an education, they will not kill each other." Another male student, 17 years old, commented, "Society in general is not educated, so it can push you to participate in violence. . . . We need to construct more schools."

Without reconstruction and reform, schools might reinforce social and gender inequalities and further contribute to the alienation of students and the marginalization of women and girls. Yet, returning to school and resuming studies were dominant themes expressed by both teachers and students. Political tensions felt on both sides have limited movement within the country, and infrastructure and resources to support teaching and learning are lacking—two frequently mentioned causes of stress for teachers and frustration for the students.

The situation in South Sudan remains unsettled, and many displaced people have not returned to their communities. Those who have returned have found their property destroyed and their community infrastructure in ruins. One student commented, "Conflict interrupted my studies and there is loss of property during the conflict. People move from one place to another and while returning they find the property burned." A 14-year-old female student said, "We need school and school was destroyed by war. . . . I came here [the IDP camp] running from conflict and now I stay here with my sister."

Life in the camps is difficult. Participants discussed insecurity within the camps and their fear about leaving them, which caused some to miss school. Temporary schools in the camps were overcrowded and unable to accommodate the large numbers of school-age students. Students discussed their suffering in the camps caused by rain, disease, and the lack of medical care and education. Although the camps offered a level of security that was not felt outside, students indicated that there was ongoing conflict inside them as people struggled for resources and tried to deal with their troubles. Kuhari, age 18, stated,

> The reason people are fighting is because they are traumatized and their brothers and sisters were killed so they have traumatization. They came here and there is conflict in the camp. We don't have hope to go outside because yesterday my friend went out and he is gone—he never came back. I don't know the reason or if he was killed. I have no information. I have no hope of living.

Family separation, insecurity, and uncertainty about the future presented numerous challenges for people living both inside and outside of the camps. Fear of more violence and conflict also contributed to feelings of sadness, anger, and insecurity. Participants commented frequently about the overriding feeling of tension between groups, which they attributed to government inaction and corruption. Expressions of feelings of powerlessness and hopelessness were often followed by statements about how access to education would create a sense of normalcy and provide a solution to the resurgence of conflict. A teacher and mother of four children who was living in an IDP camp stated,

People are not happy. Children don't know where their fathers are. I don't know where my husband is. I worry about my children being abducted. I don't have hope. I worry because I don't know how long I will stay in the camp. I pray for a place to go and a home to go to so my children can go to school and not have to worry about the rain.

Teachers and students recounted the events of December 2013 and their fear that disagreements and violence could easily erupt at any time. Students and teachers discussed the need to resolve the conflicts and to return to their homes, schools, and communities. Most frequently discussed was the need to return to a "normal and peaceful" situation so that children and youth could return to school. Students discussed "needing to return back to a normal life and going home so they could study." A 16-year-old male student discussed the effects of conflict: "loss of life of people . . . we lost very many people . . . it is very painful to lose people because they are the leaders of tomorrow . . . it makes people live in fear . . . people feel that the conflict will come back." Similarly, a 20-year-old student reflected on the impact of conflict and on what he could do to bring peace to his country:

Conflicts can cause a person to feel anger, sadness, and even pain. . . . I came to realize that conflict affects my education. I lose my friends and saved myself while I was in the bush. I tried to ask myself, what can I do to bring peace?

The capacity of students to look at their own situation and to see how the conflict has affected their community and the nation is a demonstration of resilience. Despite the loss of family and community, students remained positive about the future as they discussed plans to build peace and to provide education to the leaders of tomorrow.

IMPACT ON TEACHERS

Teachers also had lived through the conflict and were coping with their own losses and displacement. Some were killed or targeted with violence, others fled the country or were internally displaced in temporary camps (World Bank, 2005). One teacher described her experiences and the need to provide support to both students and teachers:

> There were gunshots and people were running up and down; then you saw soldiers on the road with guns and you did not know where to hide yourself and you feel like your life is not secure. So we have witnessed people dying and we have witnessed people with a lot of fear. At night . . . I pretend not to show fear to my family, and really I feel that my life is not secure. I do not know who is my enemy. My students told me they have lost their friends and they have seen them die with their eyes. One student said he witnessed a student from our school shot dead. So it is really painful. . . . Teachers need to be prepared; they need skills in counseling and also for us because we have experienced pain . . . so we need it to help ourselves and our students.

Some teachers who returned to work have not been paid, and most lack adequate resources (Betancourt et al., 2008; Bretherton et al., 2005). They must also contend with overcrowded classrooms and the deterioration of school facilities (Sinclair, 2007). One student described this situation: "The teachers are not teaching . . . they are not teaching because they have not been paid . . . this is discouraging for us to come to come to school and sit doing nothing . . . this conflict has really affected our learning in school . . . our future is not ok." Teacher shortages and the lack of qualified teachers, combined with the large number of war-affected youth and demobilized soldiers who have not had a basic education, pose serious problems for the reconstruction of educational systems (Buckland, 2006). As already mentioned, teachers struggle with their own issues surrounding conflict and often assume the role of caregiver in a system that provides limited support and little, if any, resources. As Winthrop and Kirk (2005) note, the importance of teachers in children's lives is greatly increased in postconflict situations because children may have lost their parents or their parents may have difficulty supporting them.

Teacher education and the development of teachers are central to any process of educational change (Davies, 2002). Providing teachers with skills to help students cope with sensitive issues and giving them training on concrete strategies to deal with frustration, stress, and anger can help them support students when long-term or intensive therapy is unavailable (Betancourt, Agnew-Blais, Gilman, Williams, & Ellise, 2010). "The urgent task is to empower teachers (experienced or volunteers) from the affected community through supply of educational materials and in-service training" (Sinclair, 2007, p. 53). However, teachers in many conflict-affected countries are new to the profession, untrained, and lacking in confidence (Winthrop & Kirk, 2005). The effectiveness of training needs to be assessed, and as Davies (2011, p. 175) argues, "without supervision and follow-up after short-term training, the impact in most classrooms is likely to be minimal." Efforts to train teachers must therefore be aligned with a long-term strategy for monitoring and evaluating its impact on both student learning and teacher effectiveness. Unfortunately, there is little research on the effectiveness and sustainability of programs and services in postconflict environments (Tomlinson & Benefield, 2005). The overarching gap between theory and practice must be explored, and efforts to promote peace and community reconstruction need to be facilitated (Paulson & Rappleye, 2007).

Teachers and school personnel noted that a comprehensive curriculum that focused on peace education, conflict resolution, and guidance and counseling was essential to help rebuild communities and to teach children how to live together peacefully for a sustainable future. "Peace education" was a term that emerged from the participants and was used to encapsulate a variety of strategies to help children, including the following: dramatic arts, guidance and counseling, storytelling, peer support, advocacy, human rights awareness, conflict resolution, stress management, anger management, self-expression, community support, and environmental responsibility. Participants discussed the need to "build a peaceful country through the curriculum of peace education." One teacher noted, "The only way to heal this country is through the implementation of comprehensive peace education." In addition, teachers, support staff from NGOs, school leaders, and parents did not feel that they were provided with the necessary skills and training to adequately help the children who had suffered loss, trauma, displacement, and, in some cases, torture, violence, and abuse. Findings from this research demonstrate the need for a comprehensive countrywide peace education curriculum coupled with pre-service and in-service teacher training in peace education and education for sustainable development.

PEACE EDUCATION AND COUNSELING SKILLS FOR TEACHERS

When we asked participants in the training what they thought was needed to support students in South Sudan, the most frequent response was coordination with NGOs, government, and administration, followed by teacher training, guidance and counseling, and peace building/peace education. The provision of school materials and financial support was cited next. The majority of teachers said that they needed training in peace education, counseling skills, and general pedagogy. Through student-centered activities and group work, numerous instructional strategies, discussion sessions, and reflective activities were implemented in the training course, and then the group debriefed after each lesson to discuss how to use these strategies in their own teaching practice. All the lessons were taken from *Supporting Refugee Children: Strategies for Educators* (Stewart, 2011) and *The Anger Workout Book for Teens* (Stewart, 2002).

These lessons were adapted to fit the needs of the group. Because of limited resources and materials, the exercises and activities were modified to require few support materials. Activities were described using PowerPoint to limit the use of paper or art supplies. Minor adaptations were made to the lessons to adjust for cultural differences and pedagogical approaches. For example, when we presented a role-play scenario, we included a brief introduction and demonstration to discuss the use of drama as a tool for teaching and assessment. See table 13.1 for a brief outline of the five-day training course.

In the final evaluation activity in the training, participants were asked to trace their foot on both sides of a blank paper. On one side they were to write answers to the question, "Where have I been?" and on the other side they were to write answers to "Where am I going?" In addition to listing skills and concepts that participants learned throughout the week, many also noted that the workshop had an impact on both their personal and professional life. Comments on the "Where have I been?" side comprised three general themes: (1) new knowledge gained in the areas of peace education, guidance, and anger management; (2) personal change in terms of better communication or listening; and (3) changes to the way they will teach. The methodology used in the training was learner centered, and many participants noted that this was a new form of teaching and learning that they wanted to use more in their own practice. One participant wrote, "Personally I have completely changed. My ways of teaching and handling children will be different." Another participant wrote, "This workshop was a healing workshop and I got personal healing by

TABLE 13.1 Training Outline

DAY	TIME	THEME	DESCRIPTION
1	Morning	Self-management	Who are we as teachers? What issues have we come to the classroom with? How might these issues affect how we deal with children? How do we look after ourselves both inside and outside of the classroom? Dealing with our own issues. Working in the system and relating to the community. Problem solving and decision making.
	Afternoon	Student issues	What issues do our students come to the classroom with? What resources do we have? What challenges do we face in the classroom and in the community? What support do we have?
2	Morning	Peace building	What is peace? What is peace education? How do peace and sustainability connect? What are the strategies linked to peace education and sustainable development?
	Afternoon	Counseling skills, relating and responding, listening and communicating	How well do we listen and communicate effectively with students? How do we show we care for and support students and each other? What are the basic skills for communicating effectively and professionally? How do we create trusting relationships with students? How do we foster a climate of professionalism and care for students? What are the ethical issues involved in helping students? What are the qualities for fostering understanding, genuineness, and a positive regard for students? How do we relate and respond to students using basic counseling skills?
3	Morning	Storytelling as a path toward healing	How do stories influence us? How can stories assist with healing? How do we encourage healthy forms of storytelling to support children in the postconflict context?
	Afternoon	Stress reduction and wellness	Helping students cope with stress and loss. How can we help others while still looking after ourselves? How can we heal after loss and adversity?
4	Morning and afternoon	Anger management	Helping students who are angry or stressed and coping with our own emotions. How can we deal with our own issues and support the development of our students? How can we use anger to help and not hurt?
5	Morning	Focusing on hope, resilience, and peace	How we can remain positive and focus on our accomplishments? How do we promote a culture of peace and acceptance? What are our priorities for the future?
	Afternoon	Closing activities: Using what we learned and moving forward	Where have we been, and where are we going? What did we learn; what do we need to explore more? What are our challenges? What opportunities do we now have?

taking a look at what I have achieved in life. Now, my challenge is how can I help people who are undergoing the same phenomenon." And finally, one participant noted, "I have learned that as a teacher, I am an agent of peace."

Participants gave the following answers to the question of what they planned to do with the skills they learned: (1) start peace clubs in their schools; (2) use the lessons to help their students; (3) share the lessons with the college of education, school staff, and the community; (4) lobby the government and administration for resources for a peace education curriculum; and, (5) practice in their personal lives the anger management skills and stress reduction techniques that they had learned. A follow-up consultative workshop was held in June 2015 to learn about how teachers implemented the lessons and to gather additional data on strategies that help build peace.

Through the use of expressive arts activities such as drawing, role playing, drama, and storytelling, participants were actively engaged throughout the five days. The training provided an outlet for them to release their own traumatic experiences of living and surviving violence and conflict. Stories of violence and personal loss were recounted and shared during times of personal reflection and small group discussion. Although we did not solicit these stories, they naturally emerged as trust grew within the group. The tripartite process of training, researching, and counseling offered a new model of engaging with traumatized communities.

The findings from this study demonstrate a need for countrywide teacher training and capacity building in the areas of peace education, personal wellness, counseling, and mental health support. Educational policy at both the higher education and primary/secondary levels should address the need for comprehensive training for pre-service and in-service teachers; it should include specific training on child-centered learning and culturally responsive pedagogy. More importantly, teachers need support from the Ministry of Education (e.g., adequate remuneration, consistent policies and standards for practice) and strong leadership to help them better meet the needs of the students in South Sudan. A comprehensive analysis of the mental health issues for children in South Sudan should be conducted to fine-tune policy and practice and to develop protocols for assisting children with mental health concerns. Information about multidimensional levels of trauma should be incorporated into all teacher development programs, and teachers should be provided with general counseling skills to help them respond to children who are struggling with psychosocial issues. Because of the overarching feelings of insecurity and instability and because of the role education plays in providing a sense of

normalcy in postconflict societies, educational leaders and government officials need to prioritize education as a key development objective if they hope
to stabilize the country and provide hope for its citizens.

The findings revealed significant gaps in students' academic progress; some
students had not been able to attend school because of ongoing conflicts. Creative programming to help students catch up or to draw them back to school
is necessary so that this generation of children will have opportunities for
success. Vocational training (e.g., bicycle repair, crafting, word processing, carpentry, and metal work) and life skills development (e.g., anger management,
stress reduction, mediation) might help students who had not been able to
attend school or receive any formal education. Efforts must also be targeted to
address issues of gender inequality and the marginalization of girls and women.

The study also found that students had a tremendous sense of resilience
and were hopeful for a better future. Inclusion in the planning of programs
and in the implementation of policies is imperative to help empower these
youth toward building a sustainable and conflict-free country. Because South
Sudan is such a young country, its policies, regulations, administrative procedures, and protocols need to be developed and articulated to all teachers,
district leaders, and administrators. Without clear guidelines and procedures,
inconsistencies and discrepancies will continue to contribute to the lack of
stability and suspicions of corruption. This study also recommends the development and implementation of primary and secondary peace education
curricula as part of the regular school program and including peace-building
activities (e.g., peace clubs, community storytelling activities, stress reduction)
as adjunct programs through community groups or extracurricular school
programs. These interventions—across multiple ecological systems—would
benefit all students, community members and teachers who have been greatly
influenced by war and conflict. Unfortunately, resources to provide these
kinds of programs and services are severely limited, and collective efforts and
support from the community and local agencies, the government, NGOs, and
the international community will be required.

CONCLUSIONS

As the literature and research show, there is no one best practice or clear set of
policies on how best to support youth and their teachers in post-conflict contexts. However, Davies (2004), Gallagher (2005), and Sinclair (2007) present

compelling arguments for the need to incorporate peace-building activities into education in postconflict environments. Moreover, monitoring and evaluating programs are essential to determine the impact of interventions and to understand if strategies are actually influencing teaching and learning. Nationwide training and capacity-building efforts are required to build sustainable education systems and enable teachers to deliver peace education effectively. An integrated approach to teaching about sustainable environments and building a peaceful society is essential to understanding the interdependent relationship between the two fields (Stewart, 2014). Because the realities of a postconflict situation can often limit opportunities for proper follow-up and assessment, structured follow-up activities are essential to strengthen the capacity of teachers and educational systems.

The data gathered in South Sudan suggest that education is a top priority for students, teachers, parents, and the community—it represents hope and provides a sense of normalcy that conflict typically destroys. It is unrealistic to expect that the world's newest country will have the infrastructure and expertise to offer a full range of psychosocial and educational support to meet the needs of all students, and it is even more ambitious to expect that there will be qualified teachers who have the resources to provide all of these services. Expecting teachers to provide this kind of education without proper training and preparation will result in a system destined to fail both the teachers and students. As students reminded us, the children affected by conflict are the leaders of tomorrow and with them rests the hope for building a more peaceful society. Failing to provide peace-building activities and education to those who are desperate to receive it can put vulnerable children at more risk and be a catalyst for further conflict and marginalization. It is hoped that this research reinforces the need to actively engage with youth who are living in conflict-affected countries so that they have an active voice in the process of rebuilding and healing after war. These activities should also be helpful for refugee children who have been forcibly displaced and are now living in host countries such as Canada, Australia, and the United States. Considering the number of globally displaced people because of conflict, information about the impact of war on children and peace education should be incorporated into all teacher education programs throughout the world.

Although the short introductory training course described in this chapter just touched on the vast array of needs in this area, it was essential to providing follow-up to the data collection phase and responding to the identified needs of the participants. Subsequent training programs and university-level courses are currently being developed. In postconflict contexts where resources are limited and infrastructure is compromised, this methodological approach of interweaving training, research, and counseling is a model that can be replicated and adapted to fit the needs of teachers who are working in other conflict-affected countries.

The collaborative training model that was inclusive of students, teachers, ministry representatives, and faculty not only expanded an understanding of various ecological systems but also encouraged connections between systems and people. When students in the training stood up alongside their teachers to provide strategies for building peace, and when teachers worked with ministry representatives to develop solutions to increase teacher morale, we observed a collegial and respectful learning exchange that promoted peace and acknowledged the agency and capacity of all participants. As facilitators, we were also part of this collective, and rather than approaching the training as a top-down model of exchange from the facilitator to the student, we encouraged active and reciprocal learning that deepened our personal understanding of the situation and enhanced our knowledge of educational issues in South Sudan. Having found this methodological approach to be appropriate for this type of inquiry, we were able to explore issues from multiple and often simultaneous perspectives, thus contributing to richer data and more clarity on the multifaceted issues affecting people living in postconflict contexts. This approach to training should be helpful in other postconflict environments where issues are complex and all systems must be involved in developing solutions.

This study highlighted the importance of giving back to the communities and participants who contributed to the data in the early stages of the research, which should be a consideration for other researchers. Instead of a one-sided exchange of information in which the researchers come, take, and then leave, our study provides a model for fair exchange, reciprocal learning, and shared understandings. We responded to the needs identified by teachers by following up with training, which increased the level of trust in the group and the willingness to work together in subsequent phases of the research program. This method also allowed us to gain a deeper understanding of the complexities of the situation and the challenges for systemic change. As the research program continues, our connections and continuing conversations are integral to the success of the partnership and the quality of the research.

The complexity of the connection between education and conflict, coupled with the ambiguity and conflicting narratives surrounding peace education, creates tension and uncertainty about best practices and interventions to support children in postconflict environments. It is my hope that this study elicits further investigation and discussion about practices of providing peace education to children in postconflict settings and that some of the strategies discussed in this chapter are a catalyst for building peace together and finding peace within ourselves.

References

Barakat, S., Connolly, D., Hardman, F., & Sundaram, V. (2013). The role of basic education in post-conflict recovery. *Comparative Education*, 49(2), 124–142.

Betancourt, T. S., Agnew-Blais, J., Gilman, S. E., Williams, D. R., & Ellise, B. H. (2010). Past horrors, present struggles: The role of stigma in the association between war experiences and psychosocial adjustment among former child soldiers in Sierra Leone. *Social Science and Medicine*, 70(1), 17–26.

Betancourt, T. S., Simmons, S., Borisova, I., Brewer, S. E., Iweala, U., & De La Soudiere, M. (2008). High hopes, grim reality: Reintegration and the education of former child soldiers in Sierra Leone. *Comparative Education Review*, 52(4), 565–587.

Bretherton, D. Weston, J., & Zbar, V. (2005). School-based peace building in Sierra Leone. *Theory into Practice*, 44(4), 355–362.

Bronfenbrenner, U. (2001). The bioecological theory of human development. In N. J. Smelser & P. B. Baltes (Eds.), *International encyclopedia of the social and behavioral sciences* (Vol. 10; pp. 6963–6970). New York: Elsevier.

Bronfenbrenner, U., & Morris, P. (1999). The ecology of the developmental process. In W. Damon & R. Lerner (Eds.), *Handbook of child psychology* (5th ed., pp. 793–828). New York: Wiley.

Brown, G. (2012). *Education in South Sudan: Investing in a better future*. Retrieved from http://gordonandsarahbrown.com/wp-content/uploads/2012/03/Education-in-South-Sudan-investing-in-a-better-future.pdf.

Brown, G. K. (2011). The influence of education on violent conflict and peace inequality, opportunity and the management of diversity. *Prospects*, 41, 191–204.

Buckland, P. (2006). Post-conflict education: Time for a reality check? *Forced Migration Review Supplement*, 7–9. Retrieved from www.ineesite.org/uploads/files/resources/Buckland,_P.pdf.

Bush, K., & Salterelli, D. (Eds.) (2000). *The two faces of education in ethnic conflict*. Florence: UNICEF Research Center-Innocenti.

Cheney, K. E. (2005). Our children have only known war: Children's experiences and the uses of childhood in northern Uganda. *Children's Geographies*, 3(1), 23–45.

Crawford, K. S., & Gil, J. R. (2013). Empowering the children of ex-combatants through soccer and peace education in an after-school program in El Salvador. In I. Harris (Ed.), *Peace education from the grassroots* (pp. 65–78). Charlotte, NC: Information Age.

Davies, L. (2002). Possibilities and limits for democratization in education. *Comparative Education*, 38(3), 251–266.

Davies, L. (2004). *Education and conflict: Complexity and chaos.* New York: Routledge.

Davies, L. (2011). Learning for state-building: Capacity development, education and fragility. *Comparative Education*, 47(2), 157–180.

Denov, M. (2010). Coping with the trauma of war: Former child soldiers in post-conflict Sierra Leone. *International Social Work*, 53(6), 791–806.

Gallagher, T. (2005). Balancing difference and the common good: Lessons from a post-conflict society. *Compare*, 35(4), 429–442.

Galtung, J. (1969). Violence, peace and peace research. *Journal of Peace Research*, 6(3), 167–191.

Harris, I., & Morrison, M. L. (2013). *Peace education* (3rd ed.). Jefferson, NC: McFarland and Company.

Kirk, J. (2007). Education and fragile states. *Globalization, Societies and Education*, 5(2), 181–200.

Machel, G. (2001). *The impact of war on children.* London: Hurst & Company.

Mendenhall, M. A. (2014). Education sustainability in the relief-development transition: Challenges for international organizations working in countries affected by conflict. *International Journal of Educational Development*, 35, 67–77.

Ministry of General Education and Instruction. (2012). *General education strategic plan 2012–2017: Promoting learning for all.* Retrieved from http://planipolis.iiep .unesco.org/upload/South%20Sudan/South_Sudan_General_Education_Plan _2012_2017.pdf.

O'Brien, R. (1998). *An overview of the methodological approach of action research.* Retrieved from www.web.ca/robrien/papers/arfinal.html#_Toc26184653.

Paulson, J. (2011). *Education, conflict and development.* Oxford: Symposium Books.

Paulson, J., & Rappleye, J. (2007). Education and conflict: Essay review. *International Journal of Educational Development*, 27, 340–347.

Reardon, B. (1988). *Comprehensive peace education: Educating for global responsibility.* New York: Teachers College Press.

Republic of South Sudan (2010). *The Sudan Household Health Survey 2010.* Retrieved from www.southsudanembassydc.org/PDFs/others/SHHS%20II%20Report%20 Final.pdf.

Sinclair, M. (2007). Education in emergencies. *Commonwealth Education Partnerships*, 52–56. Retrieved from www.cedol.org/wp-content/uploads/2012/02/52-56 -2007.pdf.

Smith, A. (2011). *Education and peacebuilding: From "conflict analysis" to "conflict transformation"?* Retrieved from www.protectingeducation.org/sites/default/files /documents/education-and-peacebuilding-from-conflict-analysis-to-conflict -transformation.html.pdf.

Smith Ellison, C. (2014). The role of education in peacebuilding: An analysis of five change theories in Sierra Leone. *Compare*, 44(2), 186–207.

Stewart, J. (2002). *The anger workout book for teens.* Carson, CA: Jalmar Press.

Stewart, J. (2011). *Supporting refugee children: Strategies for educators.* Toronto: University of Toronto Press.

Stewart, J. (2014). Education for peace and sustainable development in conflict-affected countries. In F. Deer, T. Falkenberg, & B. McMillan (Eds.). *Sustainable well- being: Concepts, issues, and educational practices* (pp. 1–21). Winnipeg: ESWB Press.

Tomlinson, K., & Benefield, P. (2005). *Education and conflict research and research possibilities.* Slough, Berkshire: National Foundation for Educational Research (NFER). Retrieved from www.nfer.ac.uk/publications/ECO01/ECO01.pdf.

Tudge, J. R., Mokrova, I., Hatfield, B. E., & Karnik, R. B. (2009). Uses and misuses of Bronfenbrenner's bioecological theory of human development. *Journal of Family Theory & Review*, 1(4), 198–210.

UNHCR. (2014a). *Country operations profile–South Sudan.* Retrieved from www .unhcr.org/pages/4e43cb466.html.

UNHCR. (2014b). *US official wants more aid from refugees flowing to Ethiopia.* Retrieved from www.unhcr.org/53c3a25f6.html.

UNICEF. (2011). *As South Sudan looks to nationhood, education is pivotal* (Podcast #42). Retrieved from www.unicef.org/infobycountry/sudan_59092.html

UNICEF. (2014). *Basic education and gender equality.* Retrieved from www.unicef .org/southsudan/education.html.

Wessells, M. G. (2005). Child soldiers, peace education, and postconflict reconstruction for peace. *Theory into Practice*, 44(4), 363–369.

Winthrop, R., & Kirk, J. (2005). Teacher development and student well-being. *Forced Migration Review*, 22, 18–21.

World Bank. (2005). *Reshaping the future: Education and postconflict reconstruction.* Washington, DC: Author. Retrieved from http://reliefweb.int/sites/reliefweb.int /files/resources/B739C3B4CE9399E149256FF9001B6BBC-Reshaping_the _Future.pdf.

World Bank. (2013). *South Sudan overview.* Retrieved from www.worldbank.org/en /country/southsudan/overview.

CONCLUSION

Putting the Pieces Together: Future Directions in Research with Children Affected by Armed Conflict

Bree Akesson and Myriam Denov

WHETHER CROSSING AN INTERNATIONAL BORDER in the arms of a parent, playing with friends in a refugee camp, or holding a gun alongside militia groups, children tend to dominate the imagery of armed conflict. As one recent example, media attention around the Syrian conflict has produced several "heartbreaking" and "unforgettable" images intended to underscore the horrible conditions and potential for violence and death that these children experience, while also mobilizing political action on their behalf (Barnard & Saad, 2016; Walsh, 2015). It was the now-iconic image of 3-year-old Alan Kurdi's body washed up on a beach in Turkey in September 2015 that sparked public outcry and turned the world's attention to the forced migration crisis and the realities of war-affected children. Children's experiences of violence and victimization are real, devastating, and wholly unacceptable. However, this narrative of vulnerability and victimization, which is often used to mobilize financial and political support for humanitarian interventions, has sometimes led to bifurcated understandings of war-affected children as either victim or perpetrator, traumatized or resilient—thereby discouraging scholarship aimed at uncovering the diverse and complicated experiences of children. When examining the realities of war-affected children through these often opposing concepts, it is clear that each has provided important contributions to the literature. However, as discussed in the introduction, a danger exists of creating and promoting *conceptual binaries* through which war-affected children are analyzed, understood, and presented within mutually exclusive camps as either profoundly affected by traumatic events or "resilient" and able to overcome adversity. Thus far, efforts to bridge this divide have been few and far between.

This edited volume challenges dichotomies such as the trauma-resilience binary and bridges that divide by exploring the multiple elements that form children's experiences: age, gender, family, culture, trauma, discrimination, marginalization, resilience, agency, social supports, and physical environment, among others. When considered together, these elements provide a more nuanced understanding of the experiences of children affected by armed conflict. Tackling this complex puzzle, the chapters highlight how armed conflict may have an impact on children's lives in a varied range of ways that can be both direct *and* indirect, immediate *and* long term, individual *and* collective. The chapters underscore how, in addition to armed conflict, everyday postwar stresses—family violence, discrimination, stigma, sexual violence, substance use, teenage pregnancy, being out of school, heavy workloads, poverty, profound isolation, marginality, and neglect—are pressing challenges that can threaten longstanding "peace," reconciliation, and reintegration. Perhaps most importantly, the chapters challenge scholars and practitioners to consider new theories, methods, and practices that are appropriately aligned with the ways of knowing, doing, and actual needs of war-affected children, families, and communities.

Taken as a whole, these chapters highlight the complexity of armed conflict. This concluding chapter revisits some of their key findings, as organized by the volume's themes of theory, method, and practice. In reflecting on the chapters, the discussion is guided by three key questions: What lessons have we learned from these chapters that contribute to our knowledge base? What is still missing in our knowledge base? And what are some potential ways forward to address these gaps? We hope that by addressing what is missing we will enable even more diverse and holistic understandings of children's experiences that may ultimately contribute toward the amelioration of armed conflict's adverse effects.

THEORY

RETHINKING THE TRAUMA-RESILIENCE BINARY

Although the chapters in this volume provide evidence of an abundance of difficulties facing children in armed conflict, they also indicate children's capacity for resilience in the face of difficult and often tragic adversity. For example, in chapter 1, Chaudhry presents the narratives of children that convey an "unremitting sense of horror and loss" through their descriptions of "raising the dead." At the same time, the narratives also reveal how the children negotiated the violence around them, thereby challenging the conceptual binary of children as *either* traumatized *or* resilient. Similarly, in chapter 5, Lenz underscores the complicated nature of resilience, emphasizing that resilience was not only developed during the course of navigating adversity but also that it already existed in children—providing further evidence that resilience exists alongside trauma.

However, as suggested in the introduction, it is also important to consider whether, as a field, we are moving too far in the direction of resilience, over-emphasizing that concept while other mechanisms at play in children's lives remain underexplored. Moreover, do current conceptualizations of resilience rely too much on the examination of the individual child at the expense of compounded and collective forms of resilience? In future research, the growing emphasis on resilience would benefit from being critically interrogated, ensuring that multiple ways of knowing, inquiring about, and understanding war-affected children's lives are addressed, particularly those that are culturally and contextually relevant. Despite the potential for discomfort, it is important that researchers, scholars, and practitioners make efforts to work within the "gray zones" where the binaries and the concepts themselves—such as trauma and resilience—are challenged and thoughtfully bridged.

INCLUDING THE PHYSICAL ENVIRONMENT IN SOCIOECOLOGICAL APPROACHES

Aligned with the goals of this edited collection, many of the chapters use a socioecological lens to view the experiences of children affected by armed conflict. For example, Lenz in chapter 5 refers to the "broader ecological environment—the family, peers, adult relationships, and the wider social environment." Likewise, in chapter 13 Stewart develops a framework that includes the various socioecological systems that "influence the personal, social, and academic development of the student." These chapters underscore the importance of viewing the individual child within the context of the social systems that are such an integral part of his or her life.

Several chapters emphasize the role of the physical environment in their site selection and sampling strategies. For example, in chapter 1 Chaudhry includes children from a rural site, a small town, and a subregion that blends the suburban with the rural. Kostelny, Ondoro, and Wessells' research, presented in chapter 7, includes two of Somalia's three regions (Somaliland and Puntland), and within those regions, they study urban IDP camps, rural villages, and urban areas. Likewise, Veale, Worthen, and McKay's research in chapter 9 samples from communities in both rural (60%) and semi-urban (40%) settings, providing an opportunity for a comparison between different types of places and spaces.

Other chapters also use the physical environment in their analysis. Chapter 5 discusses how the experiences of girls in Sudan differ from those in northern Uganda. Girl soldiers who were taken to Sudan had increased responsibilities and more opportunities to develop and foster resilience than girls who remained in northern Uganda. Those living in Sudan had access to medical care, reliable sources of food, housing, and schools for their children, whereas these opportunities were not available to girls living in northern Uganda. Similarly, Landis and Stark in chapter 11 acknowledge the role of geography when discussing one of their study's limitations: Research was only carried out in the capital city of Monrovia, thereby excluding the experiences of girls who lived in rural settings. The authors note that in rural areas, police stations are often underfunded and understaffed, lacking the resources to investigate sexual assault that may be more readily available to girls in the urban Monrovia setting. Likewise, in chapter 12, Kachachi discusses the challenges of extending services to war-affected children in remote locations.

In addition to contributing to a geographically representative sample, the chapters in this volume suggest that understanding children's experiences within the context of armed conflict requires a close examination of their ever-shifting relationships with both the social *and* physical environment—both people *and* place. Yet, within the scholarship, there is still a tendency to emphasize the social environment over the physical environment (Akesson, Burns, & Hordyk, 2017). Future work with war-affected children would benefit from including both the social *and* physical, both people *and* place.

Future research may incorporate the concept of the physical environment by exploring the distinct intersections between children's engagement with physical space and the impact of this engagement on their experiences in the context of armed conflict. The field would also benefit from considering the different experiences of war-affected children based on geographical setting. For example, how do children tap into relational networks when these networks are located elsewhere? What do the concepts of trauma, resilience, reintegration, and agency look like for war-affected children in different spaces and places? How do opportunities for war-affected children vary in different geographical sites? As we explore new avenues of research to fill the gaps in our knowledge, the physical environment may be an effective and important lens through which to develop a theoretical framework, design methodology, and interrogate the data. Furthermore, such a lens may improve understandings of war-affected children's experience and shape subsequent interventions and policies.

CULTURE AND CONTEXT IN THEORY DEVELOPMENT

For the most part, theory development on children and families affected by armed conflict has emerged and been propagated within the context of the Global North. Academics and practitioners living in the Global North have developed concepts and theories that have then been applied to a multitude of children and families in contexts around the globe. This approach may not only silence existing local theories and concepts but also raises numerous ethical and contextual dilemmas regarding its appropriateness and overall practical effectiveness. In her discussion of *"cen,"* Akello in chapter 10 illuminates not only the importance of acknowledging local understandings of health, well-being and distress but also the need to support local mechanisms to address postwar suffering. Historically, Western domination of theories and ideas has been far reaching, often disrupting patterns of family life, culture, and religion; powering the expropriation of natural and human resources; and drawing boundaries for the convenience of the colonizers with little or no regard for local culture, understandings, and knowledge. The effects have been enduring and are replicated in newer forms of domination by the international economic order. Although the development of theories and ideas in the context of the Global North has been important and of value, it may wittingly or unwittingly create and perpetuate dominant paradigms and "ways of knowing" that may marginalize or silence local sources of knowledge and indigenous forms of practice.

A key future challenge for theory and practice in the realm of armed conflict is to address the "tension between establishing universal principles . . . through international collaboration in research and practice, while respecting indigenous uniqueness, distinct local traditions and cultural strength" (Link & Ramanathan, 2011, p. 10). It should be noted, however, that indigenous forms of knowledge, theory, and practice are not a panacea in and of themselves. Research and practice have highlighted that social injustice, inequality, and forms of exploitation and oppression may, at times, permeate indigenous practices and local interventions (Baingana, Fannon, & Thomas, 2005). None-theless, local knowledge, theories, and concepts must be carefully, rigorously, and respectfully included to ensure relevant and effective practice.

The theories and conceptual approaches drawn on in this volume, whether socioecological, postcolonial, social construction, social exclusion, or resilience, help frame and illuminate the multiple and complex realities of war-affected children. However, given the politics of theory and theory development, it is essential that we analyze existing theories with a critical eye, highlighting each one's strengths and limitations and illuminating any potential blind spots. When examining any theoretical perspective, it is vital to ask the fol-lowing questions: Are these theories "created" with multiple contexts and cultures in mind? In each theoretical perspective, who is speaking? Who is silent? What are the implications for practice? Such questioning will enable and facilitate ongoing reflection and analysis.

METHOD

BROADENING SAMPLING STRATEGIES TO INCLUDE YOUNG CHILDREN, GIRLS, AND ADULTS

In studying war-affected children, researchers often aim to obtain a sample that is as representative and unbiased as possible, while dealing with the chal-lenges of conducting research in precarious contexts. This often results in con-venience samples of school-age children, which exclude younger children and girls who are less likely to attend school in war-affected and postwar contexts (Akesson, 2014). The chapters in this collection suggest novel ways to broaden sampling strategies to include young children, girls, and adults to better learn about the diverse experiences of children affected by armed conflict.

There are several reasons why young children have not been prioritized as an important age group for research on war-affected populations (Akesson, 2011). Young children's abilities to communicate their experiences may be under-estimated, or research methods may not adequately address the skills that younger children may have. Young children may also not be included as often in research because of a reliance on certain methods, such as cross-sectional surveys, which may be easier to administer to older, school-age children in contexts of armed conflict. Therefore, several of the chapters in this collection are of critical importance in their contribution to research that includes young children. For example, in chapter 2 Hettitantri and Hadley present research that engaged young children between the ages of 3 and 7, using approaches that capture young children's natural ways of communicating through partici- patory methods, participant-led tours, and visual methods of drawings and photographs. Similarly, Kostelny, Ondoro, and Wessells's large sample in chapter 7 included children between the ages of 5 and 17 and used body mapping as a method appropriate to young children's unique ways of communicating. In chapter 6 Akesson and Denov also consider young children's role in socio- ecological research methods. They show that these methods can be developed and adapted to be used with families and to include all family members includ- ing young children. Yet, there are still too few research examples that engage with young children, representing a gap in our understanding of children affected by armed conflict. Future research may benefit from considering young children as an important cohort to enable a more nuanced understand- ing of the distinct experiences of children across different ages and stages.

Importantly, several of the chapters include and highlight the unique reali- ties of girls in armed conflict. For example, in chapter 1, half of the research participants were girls in a gendered context that tended to devalue girls' expe- riences. Likewise, in chapter 4 Ospina-Alvarado and colleagues purposively include a group of 20 female youth formerly associated with illegal armed groups who had returned to civilian life. Chapter 5 focuses on the roles that girls play in conflict, going beyond traditional gender roles. Because of the large number of girls not attending school in Somalia, chapter 7 underscores the importance of addressing discrimination, violence, and institutionalized inequities toward girls. Chapter 9 is based on interviews with girls and young women associated with fighting forces. It emphasizes the importance of focus- ing on girls, because armed conflict can have an especially grave impact on social systems' capacity to protect girls. In chapter 12 Kachachi addresses bar- riers to female participation. Finally, chapter 11 focuses on girl survivors of sexual violence in Liberia between the ages of 11–17.

We seem to have reached a turning point in the study of girls affected by armed conflict. Multiple studies, including those in this volume, have care- fully and thoughtfully documented girls' experiences, both during conflict and in its aftermath. We now have a much clearer understanding of girls' strengths and challenges and clear evidence of their overall systemic marginalization, both during wartime violence and in postconflict contexts. While being care- ful to avoid tokenism, research and practice agendas must continue to include, value, and prioritize the perspectives and experiences of girls.

What is now needed is the *implementation* of our learning to support girls in the aftermath of violence, particularly over the long term. Much more work is needed to develop and implement appropriate wartime and postwar programs that meet the unique needs of girls. The realities of young mothers and girls formerly associated with fighting forces illustrate in a striking way the ongoing gendered gaps—including the overall neglect of issues concerning reproductive health, infant health and development, child protection, and mother-and-child bonding—in postwar services and reintegration programs.

Finally, reflecting a socioecological perspective, future research with children affected by armed conflict could be further strengthened by including adults (e.g., parents, relatives, teachers, etc.) as partners, contributors, actors, and co-creators of children's experiences. Understanding the formative role of adults in the lives of children is important in understanding the experiences of children. As Reynolds (2004, p. 261) notes, "A consideration of the manner in which war affects children calls for analysis of the character of relationships between child and adult." Several chapters emphasize this dynamic relationship. For example, in addition to interviewing children, chapter 1 includes not only interviews with children but also focus group discussions with their family members and neighbors. Though adults are not explicitly included in the research sample in chapter 5, Lenz notes the importance to building the key capacities that lead to resilience of having at least one stable and committed relationship with a supportive adult, peer, or role model. Yet it is not just having a supportive relationship, but rather the "interconnectedness and capacities that grow from this relationship" that contribute to positive outcomes in the face of adversity. Similarly, in chapter 13 Stewart combines the voices of teachers, university students, secondary school students, NGO workers, and ministry officials in an exploration of teacher training and development in South Sudan. She acknowledges the importance of teachers in children's lives and considers how some teachers are also parents themselves. The inclusion of adults in research with children affected by armed conflict adds yet another piece to the puzzle of understanding the experiences of children and armed conflict as intrinsically connected to the experiences of adults.

Nevertheless, as some of the chapters explain, including adults in research with children may have the potential to reproduce unequal power dynamics. For example, in Chaudhry's research presented in chapter 1, children moved in and out of focus groups with adults, remaining mostly quiet. When children were interviewed in their homes and were given the option to have a parent present, most preferred to participate alone with the researchers. The Palestinian study described by Akesson and Denov in chapter 6 highlights how children's voices were sometimes obscured by the voices of their older family members during collaborative family interviews. Though challenging for the research process, these observations also contribute to an understanding of the child's role within the family system. These two examples highlight the importance of understanding the power differentials inherent within adult-child relationships and modifying research methodologies to ensure the inclusion of children's voices, while at the same time acknowledging the important role of adults in children's lives. Therefore, future research with children and armed conflict could be improved by the careful inclusion of adults' voices, while ensuring that children's voices are not eclipsed. This approach would ultimately challenge the dichotomy of *either* children *or* adults by considering children *and* adults.

VALUING CHILDREN'S VOICES: IS LISTENING ENOUGH?

Every chapter in this volume stresses the value of listening to the powerful narratives of children in their own words. Through the multiple methods described in the chapters, children eloquently convey their perceptions, beliefs, and attitudes regarding their lives and circumstances, thereby underscoring the importance of listening to children and their reflections on their diverse experiences in the context of armed conflict. Yet the chapters' unquestionable embrace of children's voices in research may override more critical discussions about children's voices. Indeed, some argue for the need to attend to the *limits* of children's voices as a means of developing a more critical and productive understanding of their experiences (Komulainen, 2007; Spyrou, 2011).

Spyrou (2016) notes that the critiques regarding the uncritical emphasis on children's voices have stemmed from the assumption that voice reflects "truth." Although "taking people's accounts of their experiences is a necessary element of knowledge of gendered lives and actual power relations," it is impossible to treat "experiential knowledge as simply true" (Ramazanoglu & Holland, 2002, p. 127). In other words, research needs to account for the ways in which narratives are constructed using children's voices. As Podder highlights in chapter 8, children's voices and narratives are influenced by many factors stemming from the sociopolitical and institutional contexts in which both researcher and participant are situated. Narratives are shaped and embedded in social interactions: "The notion of 'voice' is understood as a multidimensional social construction, which is subject to change" (Komulainen, 2007, p. 11). In essence, while enabling, and fostering, the voices of participants is important and potentially empowering, it certainly does not solve the ethical dilemmas inherent to the research process. Instead, listening to children's voices compels us as researchers and practitioners to reflect and act on the multiple ethical issues that are raised as a result.

Including and promoting the voices of children are only the first steps in providing them space to articulate their voices. Enabling "voice," in fact, raises new and vital ethical questions, because "once we re-conceive of children as autonomous and speaking subjects . . . , new ethical ground opens" (Meloni, Vanthuyne, & Rousseau, 2015, p. 107). Moreover, a vital question emerges: Is listening truly enough? Ricard-Guay and Denov (2016) have articulated the importance of moving beyond the inclusion of children's voices within research to explore the nonverbal component, silences, and undomesticated features of children's communication (Mazzei, 2009; Spyrou, 2016). Importantly, children's voices should not be an end result of research, but rather a starting point for strategic practice and policy approaches that can positively affect their lives. And as noted earlier, we should also seriously consider the inclusion of adult voices that have an impact on children's lives (e.g., parents, siblings, relatives, community leaders, teachers)—thereby ensuring that an emphasis on children's voices does not mean that other voices are silenced in the process.

RESEARCH AS A FORM OF INTERVENTION

The recent trend toward the use of participatory and arts-based methods with children affected by armed conflict, some of which are highlighted in this collection (see for example, chapters 2, 6, and 7), seeks to both empower and actively engage children in the research process by providing them with an opportunity to tell their stories. This approach may potentially promote recovery and increase well-being through the research, process, thereby serving as a form of intervention—whether direct or indirect (D'Amico, Denov, Khan, Linds, & Akesson, 2016). For example, in chapter 1 children's insistence on speaking their truth and articulating their traumas related to the armed conflict in Pakistan is framed as an assertion of agency and a manifestation of resilience. Another example comes from chapter 9, which presents the use of participatory action research (PAR) with war-affected young mothers. This participatory approach recognized the unique strengths of the participants, promoted self-efficacy and empowerment, and improved the young mothers' relationships with their families and the broader community. Likewise, in chapter 13 teachers were using the research process as a therapeutic or supportive mechanism for healing. Based on this finding, the research facilitators included more opportunities for small group reflection and discussion, thereby acknowledging both the collective trauma experienced by the teachers and the collective process of healing.

Many children in the research projects described in the chapters placed importance on having their stories officially recognized: That recognition was both a positive outcome of their involvement in the research and a form of intervention. For example, in chapter 1 participants in the research asked whether other people would hear their stories, as Chaudhry writes: "It seemed very important to them that I would carry their stories over the boundaries of Swat, Pakistan, so that those far away could listen to what happened to them." Relatedly, a 16-year-old participant in chapter 11 was eager to speak about her experience with sexual violence, seeing it as a means of helping other survivors: "The things that happen to me, I want to preach [about the issue of abuse]. I want to speak on it." In chapter 8 Podder notes that children's storytelling can be a powerful act of agency. Providing a space for children to talk about their experiences offered recognition of their everyday circumstances and comfort that someone was listening and thereby acknowledging their experience. These children may hope that through sharing their stories, their circumstances may change. Nevertheless, given this reality, those considering research as a form of intervention may want to consider the ethical implications when change cannot be guaranteed or is impossible to achieve (D'Amico et al., 2016). In this case, could research as a form of intervention be potentially damaging to children?

Ultimately, the methodologies used in these chapters helped capture children's complex understandings and responses to armed conflict. But they also represented a means of positively intervening in their lives by providing them an opportunity to participate in an alternative making of their experience within the context of armed conflict. Future research may want to consider how we can produce important data to advance our knowledge of children and armed conflict, while at the same time intervening positively in the lives of these children. Furthermore, we should continue to explore the practical, theoretical, and ethical issues that may arise when research also serves as a form of intervention (D'Amico et al., 2016).

PRACTICE

DEVELOPING INTERVENTIONS AND POLICIES THAT ARE RELEVANT TO THE EXPERIENCES OF CHILDREN

If the well-being of children affected by armed conflict is a priority for international actors, humanitarian agencies, and NGOs, then addressing the *actual* needs of children is crucial. Unfortunately, as some of the chapters show, practices to improve the well-being of children affected by armed conflict can be misguided, inappropriate, and thereby ineffective. For example, chapter 1 describes how children were dismissive of humanitarian-sponsored "safe space" programs, because they were not relevant to their daily lives where safety is an elusive concept. Likewise, in chapter 5, Lenz describes programs for former girl child soldiers that did not consider or tap into the unique skills that they learned during their time associated with the armed group. She explains that these skills could have been used to support their reintegration into their communities and to strengthen their sense of self and confidence. Yet, even when girls were vocal about their needs, current programs were not flexible enough to adapt to those changing needs and tended to overlook their skills, ultimately weakening their resilience. Similarly, in chapter 10, Akello emphasizes how interventions are often irrelevant to the experiences of children affected by armed conflict in northern Uganda. National school health programs in Uganda focused on deworming, oral hygiene, and vaccination, when the children stated the real need was for both material and psychological support. Furthermore, because the health programs were offered through the schools, many school-age children who were not attending school did not receive any services, representing yet another mismatch between policies, provision of services, and actual needs.

Ensuring that programs and policies address the true needs of children affected by armed conflict has been a consistent rallying cry for years. Yet, why are programs still developed and implemented that do not adequately address children's actual needs? Future research may benefit from exploring this question not only in contexts where children identify their needs but also at the program level where interventions are designed and implemented. Joining the expertise of researchers with program implementers would mean that programs for children affected by armed conflict could be adequately evaluated and subsequently improved, so that they can meet the actual needs of children in these contexts.

CONSIDERING THE ROLE OF FAMILY IN INTERVENTIONS

The children described in these chapters confront multiple challenges rang-ing from poverty to everyday violence, all of which are further influenced by armed conflict. Because these experiences do not occur in isolation from the experiences of their families, emphasis on family relationships is a critical aspect of programs and policies for children affected by armed conflict. Families are considered to be responsible for their children's health, living environ-ment, physical development, and protection from harm. And for children affected by armed conflict, the presence of a caring and competent adult is one of the most important factors promoting their protection and well-being. For example, chapter 1 finds that children who lived with family or friends after returning from armed conflict exhibited stronger psychosocial resilience than children living in refugee camps. This indicates that the well-being of children is strongly correlated with the well-being of their caregivers, who are typically responsible for their children's care and protection. Yet in contexts of instabil-ity, parents are often so preoccupied with basic tasks of survival or reestablish-ing their lives that they may find themselves unable to provide their children with the support necessary for healthy development (Akesson, 2015).

The chapters emphasize that programs for children affected by armed conflict should attempt to directly engage with all members of the child's household. For example, chapter 11 focuses on the importance of family in providing support to girls who have experienced sexual violence in Liberia. They recommend that interventions promote the family's active involvement in guiding and shaping programs for their children, so that they can be better integrated into their existing routines and therefore be more successful and sustainable. In many cultures, including the family is a sign of respect, giving them a sense of purpose during a time when they are overworked and over-burdened by unstable circumstances. Therefore, future work with children af-fected by armed conflict may also benefit from considering the family as a key element in research, practice, and policy.

Building on Ager's (2006) definition of family in the context of armed con-flict, research has found that the family may not always support a child's well-being. For example, in chapter 1, 14-year-old Jamal Khan stood up to his family and refused to participate in an armed battle against Taliban sympathizers, even though his family was pressuring him to do so. Some chapters also ad-dress instances of family violence, which again underscores that the most pressing form of adversity might not be armed conflict, but rather everyday forms of violence. For example, in chapter 11, Landis and Stark acknowledge that "family and friends hold the potential to provide the greatest level of support—or harm—for girls affected by sexual violence."

An overemphasis on the centrality of the family in children's lives may eclipse other socioecological structures in children's lives that may be equally or more important (Ager, 2006). For example, in chapter 3, Pepper criticizes aid distribution programs that "exclusively take the family as its target unit" as not adequately meeting the needs of individual children. Again, to challenge common conceptual dichotomies of family as *either* protective *or* harmful, future research would benefit from the consideration of the family as a dynamic element of children's lives—as yet another piece in the puzzle of children's lives.

ENSURING THAT RESEARCH INFORMS PRACTICE AND POLICY

The chapters in this volume make concrete suggestions for shaping and changing practice and policy. Some recommend that interventions be aligned with the actual needs of children affected by armed conflict, which the children must identify themselves. For example, Akello in chapter 10 challenges macro-system-level stakeholders to view these children as "a unique group with self-identified health needs" and suggests a redesign of national health policy in Uganda to consider the immediate health needs of children, including diseases and psychosocial trauma, as a result of armed conflict. The importance of children identifying their own needs and thereby influencing practice and policy is also stressed in chapter 7 by Kostelny, Ondoro, and Wessells, who note that when children have a voice in research, they are in a better position to contribute to efforts to strengthen systems that support their well-being. Similarly, Pepper in chapter 3 argues that the inclusion of agentic children is critical to the development and administration of effective interventions. And in chapter 12, Kachachi urges that the experiences and perspectives of children inform the planning, development, implementation, and evaluation of programs.

These chapters affirm the importance of research's impact on practice and policy. For example, to ensure that practice with children affected by armed conflict is aligned with their actual health needs, Akello's chapter 10 recommends that health care centers employ qualified health care workers who are also "vigorously" trained in mental health and who listen to these children. In the same way, some chapters emphasize the importance of considering the root causes of the challenges facing children affected by armed conflict. Most notably, chapter 11 by Landis and Stark stresses that practice and policy should focus on sexual violence within the home or community as opposed to the popular perception of violence at the hands of a stranger.

The chapters also highlight the role of already existing, culturally relevant, and local mechanisms that contribute to the well-being of children, urging that practice and policy uncover and use these resources. In Chapter 10, Akello emphasizes the importance of using existing local resources and mechanisms to treat children's health conditions and to provide psychosocial support for mental health issues that the children themselves identify. This recommendation is related to Chaudhry's suggestion in chapter 1 for culture-specific counseling services, as well as Landis and Stark's emphasis in chapter 11 on girls' social systems (e.g., family and friends) as having the potential to facilitate the care and rehabilitation of young female survivors of sexual violence.

Perhaps the only way to truly help children affected by armed conflict is through political action, because conventional humanitarian aid and postconflict development assistance cannot adequately address the ongoing violence, marginalization, and oppression often facing children living in these contexts (Hart & Lo Forte, 2010). However, given that this may not be a realistic focus of action, some chapters suggest broader, macro-level, systemic change as a means to positively affect the lives of children. At the end of chapter 1, Chaudhry asks, "How can policy makers at all levels work with the strengths of these remarkable children to facilitate better futures for *all* of them?" She goes on to explain how even though articulating and analyzing trauma have their place, systematic change is needed to make a positive impact on the daily lives of children. She suggests that it can be achieved through more open communication between citizens and government officials, who might ensure that citizens' voices are reflected in policies.

Echoing the introduction's call to draw from multidisciplinary perspectives, several chapters, such as that by Kachachi in chapter 12, argue that programs would benefit from a holistic approach to intervention, in which various actors can together address all the issues that children may encounter. Another example comes from Stewart who suggests in chapter 13 that the approach used in her research project—"interweaving training, research, and counseling"— is useful in other contexts affected by armed conflict. We should continue to strive to break out of our disciplinary silos. In other words, we would benefit from challenging the approach that one only works in *either* theory, research, practice, *or* policy. As do the chapters in this volume, we should continue to integrate theory, research, practice, and policy in an effort to bridge disciplinary divisions. Using a multidisciplinary approach, we will be in a better position to develop meaningful solutions to the realities and effects of armed conflict.

These suggestions for future directions are by no means exhaustive. In the spirit of improving the field of research, these ideas suggest possibilities to expand the conversation and bridge some of the divides that currently exist in the scholarship. And as a result, we hope these advances in knowledge will help to ameliorate the negative effects of armed conflict on children.

References

Ager, A. (2006). What is family? The nature and functions of family in times of conflict. In N. Boothby, A. Strang, & M. G. Wessells (Eds.), *A world turned upside down: Social ecological approaches to children in war zones* (pp. 39–62). Bloomfield, CT: Kumarian Press.

Akesson, B. (2011). Research with young children affected by family violence: Proposing a robust research agenda. *Early Childhood Matters, 116*, 22–25.

Akesson, B. (2014). Geographies of Palestinian children: A critical review of the research and a future research agenda. In K. Horschelmann & C. Harker (Eds.), *Conflict, violence, and peace* (Vol.11) of T. Skelton (Ed.), *Geographies of children and young people: Conflict, violence, and peace* (pp. 1–18). Singapore: Springer.

Akesson, B. (2015). Holding everything together: Experiences of Palestinian mothers under occupation. In T. Takseva & A. Sgoutas (Eds.), *Mothers under fire: Mothering in conflict areas* (pp. 40–56). Bradford, ON: Demeter Press.

Akesson, B., Burns, V., & Hordyk, S.-R. (2017). The place of place in social work: Rethinking the person-in-environment model in social work education and practice. *Journal of Social Work Education*.

Baingana, F., Fannon, I., & Thomas, R. (2005). *Mental health and conflicts: Conceptual framework and approach*. Washington, DC: World Bank.

Barnard, A., & Saad, H. (2016, August 21). One photo of a Syrian child caught the world's attention. These 7 went unnoticed. *New York Times*.

D'Amico, M., Denov, M., Khan, F., Linds, W., & Akesson, B. (2016) Research as intervention? Exploring the health and well-being of children and youth facing global adversity through participatory visual methods. *Global Public Health, 11*, 5–6.

Hart, J., & Lo Forte, C. (2010). *Protecting Palestinian children from political violence: The role of the international community* (Forced Migration Policy Briefing No. 5). Oxford: Refugee Studies Center, Oxford Department of International Development.

Komulainen, S. (2007). The ambiguity of the child's "voice" in social research. *Childhood*, 14(1), 11–28.

Link, R., & Ramanathan, C. (2011). *Human behavior in a just world: Reaching for a common ground*. Lanham, MD: Rowman & Littlefield.

Mazzei, L. A. (2009). An impossibly full voice. In A. Jackson & L. A. Mazzei (Eds.), *Voice in qualitative inquiry: Challenging conventional, interpretive, and critical conceptions in qualitative research* (pp. 45–62). London: Routledge.

Meloni, F., Vanthuyne, K., & Rousseau, C. (2015). Towards a relational ethics: Rethinking ethics, agency and dependency in research with children and youth. *Anthropological Theory*, 15(1), 106–123.

Ramazanoglu, C., & Holland, J. (2002). *Feminist methodology: Challenges and choices*. Thousand Oaks, CA: Sage.

Reynolds, P. (2004). "Where wings take dream": On children in the work of war and war of work. In J. Boyden & J. De Berry (Eds.), *Children and youth on the front line: Ethnography, armed conflict and displacement* (pp. 261–266). New York: Berghahn Books.

Ricard-Guay, A., & Denov, M. (2016). *Narratives of ambivalence: The ethics of vulnerability and agency in research on girls in the sex trade*. Unpublished manuscript.

Spyrou, S. (2011). The limits of children's voices: From authenticity to critical, reflexive representation. *Childhood*, 18(2), 151–165.

Spyrou, S. (2016). Researching children's silences: Exploring the fullness of voice in childhood research. *Childhood*, 23(1), 7–21.

Walsh, B. (2015, December 29). Alan Kurdi's story: Behind the most heartbreaking photo of 2015. *Time Magazine*.

CONTRIBUTORS

GRACE AKELLO is a senior lecturer and coordinator at a pioneering master of medical anthropology program at Gulu University, northern Uganda. Her training in medical anthropology was completed at the University of Amsterdam and Leiden University in the Netherlands, where she was a NUFFIC and WOTRO fellow, respectively. In 2012, she was appointed a research fellow at the African Studies Center in Leiden University. Her main research interests include how children and young people in complex emergencies and the context of HIV/AIDS identify, prioritize, and manage their health complaints. In this regard, Grace has published many articles and book chapters focusing on former child soldiers, forced motherhood in the context of war, and the silencing of distressed children in the context of war as a coping mechanism. Her book, *Wartime Children's Suffering and Quest for Therapy in Northern Uganda*, was awarded a PhD premium by the Amsterdam School for Social Science Research in the academic year 2008/2009.

BREE AKESSON is an assistant professor at Wilfrid Laurier University's Faculty of Social Work and the Social Justice and Community Engagement Graduate Program, as well as a research associate for the International Migration Research Center (IMRC) based at the Balsillie School of International Affairs. She is affiliated with research institutes at McGill University (the Center for Research on Children and Families) and Columbia University (the Child Psychiatric Epidemiology Group and the CPC Learning Network). With field experience in Africa, Asia, Europe, and the Middle East, she has worked with a range of international agencies including the International Rescue Committee, Save the Children, Terre des Hommes, UNICEF, and USAID. In recognition of her research, Bree has received several awards, including the Distinguished Dissertation Award from the Canadian Association of Graduate Studies (CAGS) and the Prix d'Excellence from the Association of Deans of Graduate Studies in Québec. She is presently conducting research with Syrian families living in Lebanon, exploring the experiences of pregnant women in contexts of forced migration, and using geographic information systems (GIS) technology to learn how families negotiate environments of displacement. She is also co-leading projects aimed at strengthening the child protection system in Ghana and the mental health system in Afghanistan.

SARA VICTORIA ALVARADO is the director of the Center for Advanced Studies on Childhood and Youth at Cinde-Universidad de Manizales and its doctoral program on Social Sciences,

Childhood, and Youth. She leads the "Political, Ethical and Moral Perspectives for Childhood and Youth" and "Political Socialization and Construction of Subjectivities" research groups. She is also the director of the Iberoamerican Network for Graduate Studies in Childhood and Youth. Sara has served as an OAS consultant on matters of indigenous and rural childhood, as well as a UNICEF consultant in knowledge on childhood management processes. She holds an MS in education and social development and a PhD in education from Nova University-Cinde. She earned a BS in psychology from Universidad Javeriana.

JAIME ALBERTO CARMONA is professor and academic coordinator of the doctoral program on Social Sciences, Childhood, and Youth at Cinde-Universidad de Manizales. He has been a visiting professor at Puerto Rican, Argentinian, and Costa Rican universities. He holds a PhD in social psychology from Universidad Complutense de Madrid. He graduated with two undergraduate majors and an MS in the social sciences from Universidad de Antioquia. Jaime earned the 2011 National Psychology Award of the Colombian Association of Psychologists in the "Innovation in Applied Psychology" category and was recognized by the mayor of Medellín for the "highest impact research in 2010."

LUBNA N. CHAUDHRY is an associate professor in the Department of Human Development at Binghamton University. She also has a joint title with the Women's Studies department and is an affiliated faculty member in the departments of Asian and Asian Diaspora Studies; Philosophy, Interpretation, and Culture; and Latin American and Caribbean Studies. After earning her PhD from the University of California, Davis, in the interdisciplinary field of sociocultural studies in education, she taught for three years at the University of Georgia, Athens, where she held a joint tenure-track position in Women's Studies and the Social Foundations of Education. After that, she was in Pakistan for five years where she primarily worked as a research fellow at the Sustainable Development Policy Institute in Islamabad. During this time, she also taught part time at the University of Punjab in Lahore, and for six months she directed the ASR Institute of Women's Studies. Lubna joined the faculty of Binghamton University in the fall of 2003 and subsequently has maintained a transnational existence between Pakistan and the United States. Her earlier scholarship, including her dissertation at UC Davis, focused on Muslim immigrants in the United States. She continues to address issues pertaining to immigrants, but her focus is on the structural violence and direct violence faced by disenfranchised communities in Pakistan. Presently, she is conducting fieldwork to understand the impact of armed conflict on children and youth in Swat Valley, Pakistan.

MYRIAM DENOV is a Full Professor of Social Work at McGill University and holds the Canada Research Chair in Youth, Gender and Armed Conflict. Her research and teaching interests lie in the areas of children and families affected by war, migration, and its intergenerational impact. She has worked with war-affected children and families in Africa, Asia, and the Americas. Dr. Denov has presented expert evidence in court on child soldiers and has advised government and nongovernmental organizations on children in armed conflict and girls in armed groups. She has authored or co-authored several books on the impact of war on children including *Child Soldiers: Sierra Leone's Revolutionary United Front* (Cambridge University Press) and *Children's Rights and International Development: Lessons and Challenges from the Field* (Palgrave). Her current research is exploring the intergenerational effects of wartime sexual violence and children born of wartime rape in Cambodia, northern Uganda, and Rwanda. Dr. Denov is a Trudeau Fellow and was recently inducted into the College of Royal Society of Canada.

FAY HADLEY is a senior lecturer at the Institute of Early Childhood at Macquarie University. She has extensive experience in the early childhood sector and has worked in early childhood settings—both in teaching and leadership roles—in the community and private sectors, as well as for nongovernmental organizations. Her dissertation focused on the connections between families and early childhood settings that serve to support families in their role as parents, and she was the recipient of the Early Childhood Australia Doctoral Thesis award. Fay's research and teaching interests include partnerships with families, international early childhood education and development, leadership in early childhood, professional learning, professional identity, and career pathways.

NANDITHA HETTITANTRI is a PhD candidate at the Institute of Early Childhood at Macquarie University, as well as a member of the International Advisory Group for the World Forum Foundation for Early Care and Education. She has extensive field experience in disaster and conflict-affected contexts in the Asia-Pacific region working in the capacity of a lecturer, resource person, country program director, and head of social research in academic, nongovernment, and private sector organizations. As a consultant, Nanditha has been affiliated with the Asia Pacific Regional Network for Early Care, the SAARC Disaster Management Center, the CPC Learning Network at the Columbia University, and a number of government and nongovernment organizations. Her research interests include young children in disaster and conflict-affected contexts and children's rights.

GHADA KACHACHI has served for more than 16 years in a number of roles with the United Nations Children's Fund (UNICEF) in Iraq, Sudan, Yemen, Burundi, and in UNICEF headquarters in New York. She held the position of chief of child protection in UNICEF Yemen and Sudan and was in charge of management of the Cluster of Children Affected by Armed Conflict in Sudan. Earlier, she coordinated the protection program within the UNICEF Special Emergency Operations in Darfur and managed the UNICEF protection and education programs in Iraq. She worked also in UNICEF headquarters providing global support for child protection in emergencies and acted recently as UNICEF deputy representative in short assignments in Burundi and Sudan. A specialist with practical field experience, Ghada has been engaged in providing technical and advisory support to governments, both national and international nongovernmental organizations, and civil society. She has also been involved in policy development, strategic planning, evaluation, advocacy, coordination, and partnerships to advance child protection efforts and maximize benefits for children.

KATHLEEN KOSTELNY is a researcher, evaluator, and program advisor in the fields of early childhood development, child protection, and children's psychosocial well-being. Her research includes an outcome study of the impact of child-centered spaces on young children's well-being in internally displaced person camps in northern Uganda, the impact of chronic community violence on children's well-being in Chicago, and an assessment of the impact of the Israeli military attacks and blockade on the education system in Gaza. She has helped develop community-based child protection programs and has conducted evaluations in emergency and postconflict contexts, including Afghanistan, Timor-Leste,

Sierra Leone, Uganda, Kenya, India, Aceh, and Sri Lanka. Kathleen was part of the UNICEF ethnographic study of community-based child protection mechanisms in Somaliland and Puntland and is currently the lead international researcher for interagency action research on strengthening community-based child protection mechanisms in Kenya.

DEBBIE LANDIS is a PhD candidate at Columbia University, with a strong background in child protection in emergencies and humanitarian affairs. Debbie has more than 10 years of program management and research experience with international humanitarian organizations, including Save the Children, the International Rescue Committee, World Vision, and Church World Service. She has conducted applied research on child protection in emergencies in a variety of contexts, including Haiti, sub-Saharan Africa, and Asia, as well as with recent projects in Ghana, Liberia, and the Democratic Republic of the Congo (DRC). She is a researcher with the Columbia Group for Children in Adversity and was previously a research associate with the CPC Learning Network. Debbie's current research focuses on the differential experiences with gender-based violence (GBV) among in-school and out-of-school girls in the DRC. She also currently serves as a technical advisor for Child Protection in Emergencies (CPIE) with Save the Children.

JESSICA A. LENZ is the senior program manager for protection at InterAction, where she leads on results-based protection and gender-based violence. She is also the founder and international child protection advisor at Creative Empowerment. Jessica has more than 17 years of experience working in child protection in emergencies in contexts such as northern Uganda, Sudan, Liberia, the Gambia, Indonesia, Sri Lanka, India, Cambodia, the Philippines, Egypt, Lebanon, and Colombia. As an independent expert for the majority of her career, Jessica has worked with countless NGOs, UN agencies, and donors focused on child protection. Her expertise relates to the prevention, response, and reintegration of children forced into armed groups. She brings a resilience perspective to her work and challenges actors to better understand and support locally driven protection mechanisms to foster empowerment and change. Jessica is the co-founder of the community-based organization, Empowering Hands—a female-led NGO in northern Uganda that supports the reintegration and psychosocial support of children affected by conflict. Jessica holds a BA from the American University of Paris and received a joint MSc magna cum laude through Oxford Brookes University and summa cum laude through the International Institute of Social Studies of Erasmus University, Rotterdam. Jessica is also an artist and certified birth doula.

SUSAN MCKAY is a distinguished emeritus professor in the College of Arts and Sciences at the University of Wyoming in the United States. For more than two decades, she has taught, researched, and published about women, girls, and armed conflict; women and peace building; and feminist issues in peace psychology. With Angela Veale, Michael Wessells, and Miranda Worthen, and in partnership with NGOs in Liberia, Sierra Leone, and northern Uganda, her team implemented participatory action research to study and improve the lives of young mothers and facilitate their reintegration into their communities (PARGirlMothers.com). Among her books are *Where Are the Girls? Girls in Fighting Forces in Northern Uganda, Sierra Leone, and Mozambique: Their Lives During and After War* and *The Courage Our Stories Tell: The Daily Lives and Maternal Child Health Care of Japanese-American Women at Heart Mountain, Wyoming*. Susan is a past president of the Division of Peace Psychology of the American Psychological Association, and her awards include the U.W. Presidential Faculty Achievement Award for Research and a fellowship in the American Psychological Association.

KEN JUSTUS ONDORO has a BA in sociology and economics from the University of Nairobi and an MA in social development and management from Maseno University, Kenya. He is a researcher and theory of change expert who has been extensively involved in research, monitoring, and evaluation in child protection. Ken has a great deal of experience in qualitative and quantitative methods of data collection and analyses, health information management systems, project management and field coordination, supervision, and financial management. He has been involved in child protection research in Somalia (Somaliland and Puntland), Sierra Leone, and Kenya.

HECTOR FABIO OSPINA is an emeritus professor and researcher in the doctoral program on Social Sciences, Childhood and Youth at Cinde-Universidad de Manizales. He is the director and editor of the *Latin American Journal on Social Sciences and Youth*. He is the director of the "Education and Pedagogy: Knowledge, Imaginaries, and Intersubjectivities" research group. Hector holds an MS in education and social development and a PhD in education form Nova University-Cinde. He earned a BS in philosophy from Universidad Javeriana.

MARÍA CAMILA OSPINA-ALVARADO is a professor at Cinde-Universidad de Manizales, Universidad Pedagógica Nacional, and CLACSO (Latin American Council of Social Sciences). She leads the "Peace Building Processes in Educational Environments Towards Citizenship and Coexistence" research group. She also participates in the "Political, Ethical and Moral Perspectives for Childhood and Youth" research group, studying the social construction of children in the context of armed conflict in Colombia. She is a PhD candidate in the social sciences program at Tilburg University/TAOS Institute. María holds an MS in clinical psychology from Pontificia Universidad Javeriana in Colombia, where she earned top academic honors. She has a BS in psychology from Universidad de los Andes in Colombia.

MOLLIE PEPPER is a PhD candidate in the Department of Sociology and Anthropology at Northeastern University. She also holds an MA in law and diplomacy from the Fletcher School of Law and Diplomacy at Tufts University. Her work builds on her experience as an aid worker with Burmese refugees in Thailand and in development aid in Bolivia. Mollie has worked with a number of agencies, including the International Rescue Committee, the American Refugee Committee, and Pro Mujer. Her doctoral dissertation examines ethnic minority women's political participation in Myanmar's ongoing economic and political transition.

SUKANYA PODDER is a lecturer at the Center for International Security and Resilience at Cranfield University. Her research, advisory, and consulting work is focused on issues of postconflict reconstruction, state building, nonstate armed groups, security sector reform, and youth involvement in conflict and peace building. She is co-editor of *Child Soldiers: From Recruitment to Reintegration* (2011) and co-author of *Youth in Conflict and Peace Building: Mobilization, Reintegration and Reconciliation* (2015). Sukanya's recent work has been published in *Third World Quarterly, Peacebuilding, Civil Wars, International Peacekeeping, Contemporary Security Policy, Journal of Intervention and Statebuilding, Conflict, Security and Development*, and *Politics, Religion and Ideology*.

LINDSAY STARK is an associate professor of population and family health at Columbia University's Mailman School of Public Health. She serves as director of research of the Program on Forced Migration and Health and as executive director of the CPC Learning Network, a consortium of agencies and academic institutions that work together on global learning associated with children in disaster and war settings. Lindsay has more than a decade of experience leading applied research on the protection of women and children in humanitarian settings in Africa, Asia, and the Middle East. Her particular area of expertise is measuring sensitive and difficult-to-measure social phenomenon. She is the author of many publications on the rehabilitation and resiliency of former child soldiers and survivors of sexual violence.

JAN STEWART is a full professor and the coordinator of Advanced Studies in Education in the Faculty of Education at the University of Winnipeg. She was the director of the Institute for Children Affected by War at the Global College from 2006–2011. Jan is the lead investigator of a three-year national research program funded by the Social Sciences and Humanities Research Council, the Canadian Education and Research Institute for Counselling, and Mitacs Canada to study educational strategies and career development programs to support refugee and immigrant youth in Canada. She has been the project lead for international research and teacher development programs in Zimbabwe, South Sudan, and Uganda. Jan has conducted numerous seminars at national and international conferences on the needs and challenges of children who have been affected by conflict, violence, abuse, mental health issues, neglect, and human rights violations. She is the author of *The STARS Program, The Tough Stuff Series, The Anger Workout Book for Teens*, and her most recent book, *Supporting Refugee Children: Strategies for Educators*, was published by the University of Toronto Press.

ANGELA VEALE is a lecturer in applied psychology at the University College Cork and a child and adolescent psychotherapist. Her major research interests include postconflict social reintegration of children and families; children, globalization, and "new migrations;" and psychosocial interventions. Her writing takes a sociocultural, politically situated understanding of the psychological well-being of children and families. Angela was partner to the NORFACE- funded Transnational Child-Raising Between Europe and Africa project and co-director of the Provictimus/Oak Foundation-funded project on the social reintegration of young mothers formerly associated with armed groups in Sierra Leone, Liberia, and northern Uganda. She is a former Fulbright Scholar.

MICHAEL G. WESSELLS is a professor at Columbia University in the Program on Forced Migration and Health. A long-time psychosocial and child protection practitioner, he is former co-chair of the IASC Task Force on Mental Health and Psychosocial Support in Emergency Settings. He has conducted extensive research on the holistic impacts of war and political violence on children, and he is the author of *Child Soldiers: From Violence to Protection* (Harvard University Press, 2006). Currently, he is lead researcher on an interagency, multicountry research study of community-driven interventions for strengthening linkages of community-based child protection mechanisms with government-led aspects of national child protection systems. Michael regularly advises UN agencies, governments, and donors on issues of child protection and psychosocial support, including in communities and schools. Throughout Africa and Asia he helps develop community-based, culturally grounded programs that assist people affected by armed conflict and natural disasters.

MIRANDA WORTHEN is an assistant professor in the Department of Health Science and Recreation at San Jose State University in California, where she teaches undergraduate and graduate classes in epidemiology and global health and directs the undergraduate program in health science. Her research is multidisciplinary and has primarily been in conflict or postconflict settings in West Africa, Nepal, and Ireland. Miranda's most recent work has been on the experiences of military service members and veterans in the United States, particularly examining gender differences in the experience of anger and posttraumatic stress. She holds an MPhil in International Development from Oxford University and a PhD in epidemiology from University of California, Berkeley.

INDEX

Abuja II accord (Liberia, 1996), 186
abuse of children, 176–177, 180
Acholi culture (Uganda), 123, 248–249,
    251n1
adolescents, 12
adults: family members, 331–332;
    included in research samples, 326–327;
    included in socioecological approach,
    151–153; in supportive relationships,
    115; in trusting relationships with
    Ugandan girls, 122–123
African Union Peace Keeping Mission,
    293n3
age, in Somali study, 176–177
agency, 25; of Burmese Muslim children
    in Thailand, 66–67, 84; in children's
    participation in war, 199–200; of girls
    in Colombia, 90, 101; of Liberian
    children, 186–190; relational, 138;
    social constructionist theory on, 94
Ager, A., 331
Akello, Grace, 7, 229–230, 323, 330, 332,
    333
Akesson, Bree, 137
alcohol abuse, 173–174
Al-Shabaab (Somalia), 164
Alvarado, Sara Victoria, 20
Antonsich, M., 44
appreciation, sense of, 124–125

approval, sense of, 124–125
Arabs, in Darfur, 280
armed conflicts: definitions of, 12; girls
    in, 112–113; global, history of, 91–92;
    relationship between education and,
    296–297; state of current research
    on impact on children of, 140–141;
    See also wars
arts-based and visual methods, 155–156
atika plant, 241–246, 250
Aung San Suu Kyi, 80, 86n2
Ayala, J., 5

beating of children: in Liberia, 193; in
    Somalia, 176–177, 180
belonging, sense of, 44–45; in Sri Lanka,
    58–59, 61
Belsky, J., 234
bioecological model for peace building,
    299–301
birth control, 220
Bolton, P., 236
Boothby, N., 141, 143
Boyden, J., 8, 9
boys: Liberian war story of, 192–195, 198;
    masculine war stories of, 189; Muslim,
    in Thailand, 76; Somali girls raped
    by, 174–175; in Sri Lanka, 54–55; in
    Swat, 36–37